AF716253

THE ONE MIND

The One Mind: C. G. Jung and the future of literary criticism explores the implications of C. G. Jung's *unus mundus* by applying his writings on the metaphysical, the paranormal, and the quantum to literature. As Jung knew, everything is connected because of its participation in universal consciousness, which encompasses all that is, including the collective unconscious. Matthew A. Fike argues that this principle of unity enables an approach in which psychic functioning is both a subject and a means of discovery—psi phenomena evoke the connections among the physical world, the psyche, and the spiritual realm.

Applying the tools of Jungian literary criticism in new ways by expanding their scope and methodology, Fike discusses the works of Hawthorne, Milton, Shakespeare, Wordsworth, and lesser-known writers in terms of issues from psychology, parapsychology, and physics. Topics include the case for monism over materialism, altered states of consciousness, types of psychic functioning, UFOs, synchronicity, and space-time relativity. *The One Mind* examines Goodman Brown's dream, Adam's vision in *Paradise Lost,* the dream sequence in "The Wanderer," the role of metaphor in Robert A. Monroe's metaphysical trilogy, Orfeo Angelucci's work on UFOs, and the stolen boat episode in Wordsworth's *The Prelude*. The book concludes with case studies on Robert Jordan and William Blake. Considered together, these readings bring us a significant step closer to a unity of psychology, science, and spirituality.

The One Mind illustrates how Jung's writings contain the seeds of the future of literary criticism. Reaching beyond archetypal criticism and postmodern theoretical approaches to Jung, Fike proposes a new school of Jungian literary criticism based on the unitary world that underpins the collective unconscious. This book will appeal to scholars of C. G. Jung as well as students and readers with an interest in psychoanalysis, literature, literary theory, and the history of ideas.

Matthew A. Fike is a Professor of English at Winthrop University in Rock Hill, South Carolina, where he teaches courses in the human experience, critical thinking, Shakespeare, and Renaissance literature.

THE ONE MIND

C. G. Jung and the future of literary criticism

Matthew A. Fike

Routledge
Taylor & Francis Group
LONDON AND NEW YORK

First published 2014
by Routledge
2 Park Square, Milton Park, Abingdon, Oxfordshire OX14 4RN

and by Routledge
711 Third Avenue, New York, NY 10017

First issued in paperback 2016

Routledge is an imprint of the Taylor & Francis Group, an informa business

© 2014 Matthew A. Fike

The right of Matthew A. Fike to be identified as author of this work has been asserted by him in accordance with sections 77 and 78 of the Copyright, Designs and Patents Act 1988.

All rights reserved. No part of this book may be reprinted or reproduced or utilised in any form or by any electronic, mechanical, or other means, now known or hereafter invented, including photocopying and recording, or in any information storage or retrieval system, without permission in writing from the publishers.

Trademark notice: Product or corporate names may be trademarks or registered trademarks, and are used only for identification and explanation without intent to infringe.

British Library Cataloguing in Publication Data
A catalogue record for this book is available from the British Library

Library of Congress Cataloging in Publication Data
Fike, Matthew.
The one mind : C. G. Jung and the future of literary criticism/Matthew A. Fike.
pages cm
Includes bibliographical references and index.
1. Literature—Psychology. 2. Jung, C. G. (Carl Gustav), 1875–1961. 3. Psychology and literature. 4. Jungian psychology. I. Title.
PN56.P93F55 2014
809'.93353—dc23

2013012664

ISBN 13: 978-0-415-71188-3 (pbk)
ISBN 13: 978-0-415-81974-9 (hbk)

Typeset in Times New Roman
by RefineCatch Limited, Bungay, Sufolk

FOR KINDNESS

Portions of some chapters of *The One Mind: C. G. Jung and the Future of Literary Criticism* draw from the following previously published materials.

- Chapter 1: "We Are One Psyche: A Jungian Approach to Hawthorne's 'Young Goodman Brown,'" *Postscript* 27, no. 9 (2012): 1–20, www.pachome.org; and "The Literary Matrix of Loren Eiseley's 'The Secret of Life,'" *The CEA Critic* 72, no. 3 (2009): 17–36.
- Chapter 2: Review of Thomas Campbell's *My Big TOE: A Trilogy Unifying Philosophy, Physics, and Metaphysics*, *TMI Focus* 31, no. 3–4 (Summer/Fall 2009): 1–14.
- Chapter 3: "'The Wanderer' and the Psychology of Sailing," in *Reading the Sea: New Essays on Sea Literature*, ed. Kevin Alexander Boon (New York: Fort Schuyler, 1999), 77–99.
- Chapter 4: "Thinking Metaphysically: The Challenge to Fundamentalism in the Works of Robert A. Monroe," *Peer English: The Journal of New Critical Thinking* 3 (2008): 91–104.
- Chapter 6: "*Light at Midnight* and the Art of Synchronicity," *Conversations in the Field* 1, no. 7 (2010): 1–8, www.thejungiansociety.org.

The editors/publishers of the pieces listed above have provided permission to include and adapt my earlier work as part of this book. In addition, Tor/Forge granted permission to quote from Robert Jordan's *New Spring* and *The Wheel of Time* series, volumes 1–13, in chapter 8.

CONTENTS

ACKNOWLEDGMENTS

I wish to thank the Jungian Society for Scholarly Studies for many opportunities to present my work and Winthrop University for financial support that enabled me to travel to the JSSS and other conferences. I deeply appreciate the support of my family members, Francis Fike and Deborah Brower; the encouragement of my department chair, Gregg Hecimovich; and the guidance of Peter Schakel. Great thanks also go to the staff of the Dacus Library at Winthrop University, especially Bob Gorman and Nancy White. Finally, I am grateful to Kirsten Buchanan, my editorial consultant at Routledge, who worked with me throughout the publication process.

IN-TEXT CITATIONS

References to *The Collected Works of C. G. Jung* are to volume and paragraph/page numbers. For example, a reference to paragraph 460 on page 272 of volume 6 appears as follows: (*CW* 6, 460/272). The abbreviation E refers to David V. Erdman's *The Complete Poetry and Prose of William Blake*, rev. ed. (1982); *MDR* to Jung's *Memories, Dreams, Reflections*; and *OED* to *The Oxford English Dictionary*, 2nd ed. Shakespeare quotations are taken from David Bevington's *The Complete Works of Shakespeare*, 4th ed. Citations to all of these works and to the primary literary text(s) under consideration in a given chapter appear parenthetically.

INTRODUCTION

In *Religio Medici* Sir Thomas Browne writes:

> We carry with us the wonders we seek without us: there is all Africa and her prodigies in us; we are that bold and adventurous piece of nature, which he that studies wisely learns in a compendium what others labor at in a divided piece and endless volume.

According to Laurens van der Post, who shared the quotation with C. G. Jung, the Browne quotation elicited the following reaction: "He was deeply moved, wrote it down, and exclaimed, 'That was and is just it!'"Although "just it" refers to the theory of the collective unconscious, Browne's statement can also mean that each human being participates in an even greater field of consciousness, an idea that is present in Jung's works but that has received little attention. Following Erwin Schrödinger, I call it the One Mind.[1]

There is only One Mind in the universe, and its implications for literary criticism are my subject. In particular, this book proposes a "metaphysical criticism" partly based on the overarching unity of time, space, matter, and thought. (Here "metaphysical" refers to "that [which] is above or goes beyond the laws of nature; belonging to an operation or agency which is more than or other than physical or natural; supernatural.")[2] More broadly, the study considers phenomena that arise from or relate to connections via the One Mind, the unifying energy that flows through all things, including nonphysical realms. Jung's works provide a reference point; however, he did not espouse a position that is tailor-made for every subject considered here, largely because he did not see himself as a metaphysician, as his statements in two footnotes reveal.[3]

> There are people who, oddly enough, think it a weakness in me that I refrain from metaphysical judgments. A scientist's conscience does not permit him to assert things he cannot prove or at least show to be probable. No assertion has ever yet brought anything corresponding to it into existence. "What he says, is" is a prerogative exclusive to God.
>
> (*CW* 9ii, 304/195, n. 32)

Yet Jung is undeniably a scientist who likes to think in conventional ways about unconventional subjects—for example, by applying his theory of the collective unconscious to altered states—which leads him into the borderland between science and metaphysics, where he receives criticism from both camps. He complains about their "misunderstanding" of his point of view:

> It is a common and totally unjustified misunderstanding on the part of scientifically trained people to say that I regard the psychic background as something "metaphysical," while on the other hand the theologians accuse me of "psychologizing" metaphysics. Both are wide of the mark: I am an empiricist, who keeps within the boundaries set for him by the theory of knowledge.
>
> (*CW* 10, 623/328, n. 12)

It is precisely because Jung imbricates science and metaphysics that he provides appropriate benchmarks for the present study, which seeks to expand the subject matter and methodology of literary criticism. Jungian psychological criticism appropriately provides a foundation, starting point, touchstone, and bridge between science and metaphysics. In short, my goal is to complement and upgrade that traditional psychological approach by highlighting literary connections to the One Mind. The readings that emerge below are thus "post-Jungian" insofar as they go beyond traditional archetypal criticism, apply Jung's writings to literature in heretofore untried ways, and sometimes take issue with Jung's conclusions and limitations. As a result of this shifted paradigm, the "Self" (Jung's term for the archetype of wholeness or the integrated psyche) expands to include a comprehensive unity of persons, places, events, and things, whether physical or nonphysical, past or present.[4]

This is not a science book, though it draws various assumptions and concepts from developments in physics and parapsychology that post-date Jung's death in 1961. Nor is it an apology for psychic functioning (psi), whose existence from an informed perspective is a foundational assumption rather than a hypothesis in need of demonstration.[5] The question at issue is rather as follows: within a framework that recognizes separation as illusion, what critical tools and literary interpretations arise in connection with Jung's works? In suggesting answers, *The One Mind: C. G. Jung and the Future of Literary Criticism* seeks to anticipate trends that will gain favor as the gap between science and spirituality continues to narrow.

Jungian literary criticism

Jung himself advances a theory of literary art in two essays that provide a relevant starting point (*CW* 15, 65/97–105/162).[6] "On the Relation of Analytical Psychology to Poetry" (1922) distinguishes between "introverted" or conscious invention and an "extroverted" process whereby art arises from the collective unconscious whose archetypes manifest as literary images. "Psychology and Literature" (1930) frames the same contrast in different terms, the "psychological" and the "visionary." Regarding the extroverted/visionary, because material that arises "from the hinterland of man's mind" (*CW* 15, 141/90) is mysterious and does not convey its entire meaning all at once, human development enables each generation of readers to find new insights as the meaning of a literary text continues to unfold (*CW* 15, 153/98). This process of incremental discovery characterizes the reception of Jung's own work and is precisely the spirit of the chapters that follow. As we shall see, Jungian psychology provides an appropriate theoretical grounding because it anticipates scientific discoveries that have only recently begun to influence literary study. In a sense, the future of literary criticism is enfolded in his writings.

Like Jung's two essays, Jungian literary criticism applies concepts of his analytical psychology to both artists and literary texts. Naturally such an approach to literature reflects the two principal ways in which Jungian psychology deviates from Freudian. First, libido, for Freud, is sexual energy, whereas Jung considers it a more general psychic energy that includes sexuality. In his essay "On Psychic Energy," however, he stops short of considering libido to mean life force energy (*CW* 8, 32/17).[7] Second, for Freud, the unconscious is completely personal, whereas Jung acknowledges the personal dimension of the unconscious but sees beneath it a collective unconscious that transcends individuality as well as space-time—a sort of repository of racial memory. The collective unconscious is the seat of the archetypes, a term used here to mean the *potential* for representation in human culture but especially in literary texts and mythology, for archetypes are not "inherited *ideas* . . . but inherited *possibilities* of ideas" (*CW* 9i, 136/66; emphasis in the original). In other words, invention is the process of activating an archetype, which leads to images in literature, religion, or mythology. Jung sometimes refers to archetypes as images, but it is more helpful to say that images are culture's response to the archetypes. As Daryl Sharp observes, "Archetypes are irrepresentable in themselves but their effects are discernible in archetypal images and motifs."[8] In turn, archetypal criticism considers these images, especially images related to shadow, anima/animus, hero, trickster, and the Self; and explores a spectrum of psyche that ranges from an individual person's consciousness to the most collective dimension of the unconscious. Simply put, a Jungian critic examines the role of archetypes and their associated literary images in the individuation process, which involves making the unconscious conscious as one moves toward psychic wholeness.

Richard P. Sugg's anthology, *Jungian Literary Criticism* (1992), contains a fine array of essays on the history and application of the concepts just summarized; and Susan Rowland's *C. G. Jung and Literary Theory: The Challenge from Fiction* (1999) provides an important upgrade by engaging with poststructuralist thought in order to bring what her introduction calls "Traditional Jungian Literary Criticism" into the mainstream. The most up-to-date survey of Jungian literary studies is Terence Dawson's essay, "Literary Criticism and Analytical Psychology," in the second edition of *The Cambridge Companion to Jung* (2009).[9] Dawson's section on the future, however, overlooks the possibility of incorporating insights from the new science into literary interpretation. Indeed, poststructuralism and the new science can come together, as Ian Marshall and Danah Zohar point out: "The postmodern developments in the humanities were paralleled by corresponding developments in science" such as "multiple frames of reference," "complementary but equally valid pairs of opposites," the importance of context, as well as "holism, acausality, observer participation (contra dualism), and nonlinearity (discontinuity)."[10] As this list suggests, the new science is not merely a parallel development; some of its characteristics are in themselves relevant to literary study and can help take Jungian criticism beyond the archetypal and the postmodern into the quantum and the metaphysical.

The choice of Jung as a starting point is a natural one for me because of my experience with the traditional Jungian approach in my previous book, *A Jungian Study of Shakespeare: The Visionary Mode*. Like earlier Jungian analyses, mine examines selected plays in terms of concepts and archetypes: the collective unconscious, myth, syzygy, the trickster, the primitive, the shadow, and the anima. Despite such homage to tradition, the book arose from a desire to do what I once called "parapsychological criticism," the analysis of psychic functioning in literature, which is a subset of what I am now calling "metaphysical criticism." Knowing that such an approach was unlikely to elicit support from traditionalists, I turned to Jung for a theoretical grounding. Although *A Jungian Study of Shakespeare* was not about Shakespeare and psi, the first chapter, "The Collective Unconscious and Beyond in *A Midsummer Night's Dream*," explores possibilities that tend in that general direction. I examine the play's depiction of three ways of gaining access to the unconscious—dream, imagination, and vision. The section on vision explores Bottom's experiences with Titania, the Fairy Queen, as an allegory of a paranormal event related to the other-worldly experiences that Paul, to whom Bottom alludes, reports in his letters to the Corinthians.[11] Do Bottom and Paul merely explore the collective unconscious, or do their respective voyages into the unknown take them further out into the spirit world? Whereas the former possibility represents the visionary mode of production, the latter is also worthy of consideration, especially since the play attributes ontological status to spirits. Shakespeare's reference to ghosts in *A Midsummer Night's Dream* (3.2.382–87) and his depiction of the ghost in *Hamlet* suggest a belief in the continuity of consciousness beyond physical death, whereas Jung prefers to believe that ghosts may be psychic projections or ambulant archetypes (*CW* 8, 598/316). Here, I believe, Jung falls victim to the success of his own theory; for his terminology limits his consideration of alternatives. My chapter concludes as follows:

> It is beyond doubt that Shakespeare is depicting the visionary mode in the play; that dream, imagination, and vision are means of accessing the unconscious, whether it is personal or collective; and that vision may reach beyond the psychological realm into the spirit world.[12]

Having made that suggestion, however, I draw back and devote the rest of the book to a discussion of the plays in terms of archetypes and other Jungian concepts.

The One Mind and the New Cosmology

The One Mind attempts to capitalize on the potential for further inquiry in my work on *A Midsummer Night's Dream*, and in doing so it taps a vein of *The Collected Works of C. G. Jung* that has been overlooked by literary critics. Like the shift from the personal to the collective unconscious, the shift from the psychological to the metaphysical, or from the collective unconscious to the One Mind, gives new meaning to phenomena previously considered merely psychological or even illusory. Like the collective unconscious, the One Mind is a connector; but whereas the former connects all human minds, the latter unites all things, including the human mind. Psi exists, as Jung acknowledges; but considering it a function of the collective unconscious is unnecessarily reductive. A more likely possibility is that the underlying unity of all that is, in which the collective unconscious plays a role, accounts for the plethora of psi phenomena that have been studied since the days of J. B. Rhine's work at Duke University, which so fascinated Jung in *Synchronicity: An Acausal Connecting Principle* (*CW* 8, 833/432–840/435 and 975/523–980/524).

In defining the One Mind, however, I diverge from Jung's definition in "Psychological Commentary on *The Tibetan Book of the Great Liberation*" (1939). A bit of summary is necessary before the key point can emerge. Jung contrasts the Eastern "introverted tendency" with the Western "extraverted tendency," which is basically the difference between inner and outer (*CW* 11, 786/493). In the East, "mind" connotes something metaphysical, something deep and pervasive that is available to one who looks within, whereas we in the West "do not assume that the mind is a metaphysical entity or that there is any connection between an individual mind and a hypothetical Universal Mind" (*CW* 11, 759/475–76). He adds that Westerners do not consider the anima to be a "spark of the *Anima Mundi*, the World Soul" (*CW* 11, 759/476). Yet in keeping with the theory of the archetypes, "the Eastern assertion that the Universal Mind is without form . . . yet is the source of all forms, seems to be psychologically justified" (*CW* 11, 782/490). Turning to the concept of oneness, he offers this characterization of the East: "By means of the transcendent function we not only gain access to the 'One Mind' but also come to understand why the East believes in the possibility of self-liberation" (*CW* 11, 784/491).[13] Seeming even-handed, he then notes that the East "underrates the world of consciousness," whereas the West undervalues the One Mind. "The result is that, in their extremism, both lose one half of the universe; their life is shut off from total reality, and is apt to become artificial and inhuman" (*CW* 11, 786/493). In describing the "Universal Mind" or "One Mind," then, Jung seems to hint at something that antedates and undergirds the collective unconscious whose archetypes *are* forms; but he is actually equating the Universal Mind with the unconscious, both personal and collective (*CW* 11, 782/490, 793/496, and 820/505), which is correct only so far as it goes. Here Jung and I part ways. The unconscious surely participates in the One Mind, but so does everything else.

Jung's term *unus mundus* appears be synonymous with my redefinition of the One Mind as an overarching unity of matter, mind, and spirit. As Rowland writes, "*Unus mundus*, as the term suggests, reflects Jung's belief in the fundamental unity of the cosmos, of matter with soul and spirit."[14] This inclusive definition is permissible because Jung's own definition is paradoxical. He speaks of the "*unus mundus* (unitary world)" or "one world" (*CW* 10, 778/409; 14, 760/534), which he takes to be the "background of our empirical world" (*CW* 14, 769/538) and more specifically "the original, non-differentiated unity of the world or Being . . . the primordial unconsciousness" (*CW* 14, 660/462). "Our world has shrunk," Jung writes, "and it is dawning on us that humanity is *one*, with *one* psyche" and that "all reality would be grounded on an as yet unknown substrate possessing material and at the same time psychic qualities," which brings us "closer to the idea of the *unus mundus*" (*CW* 10, 779–80/410–11; emphasis in the original). On the one hand, he characterizes that substratum as "primordial unconsciousness" or spirit; on the other, it is both material and psychic. So Jung attributes both psychic and physical aspects to the archetypes but describes the *unus mundus* as a larger category that encompasses matter, mind, and spirit. In other words, Jung's cosmology, much like contemporary "theories of everything," attempts to account for all reality by describing a continuum that encompasses low-grade primordial consciousness, physical matter, and even human consciousness. Let us now explore the many divisions on this continuum.

The physical world. To begin with, there is the physical world where separation masquerades as reality. Physicist David Bohm uses the term the "explicate order" (meaning the unfolded order) to describe the everyday world of separation and the "implicate order" (meaning the enfolded order) to describe the deeper unity from which the physical world emerges. The difference is between what is separate and local (explicate) and what is unified and nonlocal/acausal (implicate). He states that "what 'carries' an implicate order is the *holomovement*, which is an unbroken and undivided totality." Reality is holographic in that the part "enfolds the whole and is therefore intrinsically related to the totality from which it has been abstracted."[15] Moreover, the totality includes consciousness, which is why authors like physicist and computer scientist Maureen Caudill mention the connectedness of the implicate order to explain the existence of psi.[16]

Jung in his visionary text *Seven Sermons to the Dead* (1916) anticipates Bohm's conclusions by discussing two terms, "pleroma" and "creatura." According to Robert A. Segal, pleroma is "the godhead" or primordial, undifferentiated (un) consciousness, from which emerges the creatura or "the first god." Segal writes, "Just as the pleroma stands for incipient unconsciousness, so creatura and the created beings stand for the ego. The development of created beings from or through creatura signifies the gradual development of the ego." The difference is between "the undifferentiated totality" and degrees of individuation.[17] Since Jung defines the *unus mundus* as "undifferentiated consciousness," *unus mundus* and pleroma appear to be synonyms.

Whereas Segal focuses on the relationship between pleroma/creatura and the psyche, I am more interested in the fact that Jung's terms reflect the distinction between the implicate and the explicate orders. As F. David Peat points out in *Synchronicity: The Bridge Between Matter and Mind*, published five years before Segal's anthology *The Gnostic Jung*, pleroma is "a ground or 'godhead' out of which all reality is born"; it is "at once both empty and perfectly full, and as in Bohm's implicate order, a universe is enfolded within each of its points, for 'Even in the smallest point is the PLEROMA endless.'"[18] Creatura and pleroma are Jung's subject in a key paragraph in Sermon 1:

> CREATURA is not in the pleroma, but in itself. The pleroma is both beginning and end of created beings. It pervadeth them, as the light of the sun everywhere pervadeth the air. Although the pleroma pervadeth altogether, yet hath created being no share thereof, just as a wholly transparent body becometh neither light nor dark through the light which pervadeth it. We are, however, the pleroma itself, for we are a part of the eternal and infinite. But we have no share thereof, as we are from the pleroma infinitely removed; not spiritually or temporally, but essentially, since we are distinguished from the pleroma in our essence as creatura, which is confined within time and space.[19]

Jung's statement exemplifies the inclusive, both/and nature of subtle reality. We are made of pleroma (it "pervadeth" us; we are the pleroma itself), yet differentiation removes us from it to an infinite degree. Moreover, pleroma is "both beginning and end" (that is, beyond time), whereas we who participate in it are "confined within time and space" yet are somehow "not spiritually or temporally" removed from the pleroma, which suggests the potential of the human mind to transcend space-time. The both/and nature of pleroma crystallizes a few paragraphs later when Jung states that

> created being is the very quality of the pleroma, as much as non-creation which is the eternal death. In all times and places is creation, in all times and places is death. The pleroma hath all, distinctiveness and non-distinctiveness.[20]

He goes so far as to list pairs of opposites that balance each other (the effective and the ineffective, fullness and emptiness, and many others). In the pleroma (implicate order), opposites can coexist; or as Jung says, "each balanceth each";[21] but the creatura (explicate order) is the realm of duality and mutual exclusivity.

Reality, then, is a spectrum that begins with nothingness ("I begin with nothingness," says Sermon 1);[22] there emerges pleroma, undifferentiated consciousness; differentiation begins with creatura or the beginning of organized consciousness; then creation leads to physical matter and culminates in the human psyche, which is distantly removed from (different in "essence") yet intimately connected to its primordial beginnings (alike in time and spirit). In this fashion, Jung's cosmology portrays the origin of the physical world in nothingness, with some sort of mental realm in between whose gradations are as yet unknown. Dead center in such a system is the basement dimension of physical reality. As Marshall and Zohar observe, "The ground state of energy in the universe, the lowest possible level, is known as the quantum vacuum. It is called a vacuum because it cannot be perceived or measured directly; it is empty of 'things.'" After comparing the quantum vacuum to "the Buddhist Void or the concept of Sunyata," which means emptiness, they note that it is not empty but rather "replete with potentiality."[23] Therefore, the quantum vacuum is somewhat akin to the archetypes, which contain the potential to create images but are not images themselves. Beyond this vacuum or void lies the spirit world.

Not surprisingly, psyche's perception on both sides of that great divide is subject to heavy distortion because of mental traps such as those Dean Radin points out in *The Conscious Universe*. These limiting views include believing that "the universe is composed of material objects" (materialism) and assuming "that physical objects and systems could be understood in terms of their parts" (reductionism).[24] More precisely, reductionism claims that the whole is equal merely to the sum of its parts. Together these models of understanding reality promote the illusion that existence is limited to what humans can observe through their senses or through scientific method. Michael Talbot contributes this excellent—and humbling—statement in *The Holographic Universe* about the difficulty of accurate perception:

> For the first time I realized that the eye/brain is not a faithful camera, but tinkers with the world before it gives it to us. . . . Some studies suggest that less than 50 percent of what we "see" is actually based on information entering our eyes. The remaining 50 percent plus is pieced together out of our expectations of what the world should look like (and perhaps out of other sources such as reality fields). The eyes may be visual organs, but it is the brain that sees. . . . The brain artfully fills in the gaps like a skilled tailor reweaving a hole in a piece of fabric. What is all the more remarkable is that it reweaves the tapestry of our visual reality so masterfully we aren't even aware that it is doing so.[25]

For Radin, another dimension of perception's subjectivity is that when humans are presented with alternatives to their current beliefs, cognitive dissonance leads to "retrocognitive memory distortion (revisionist history)." Charles T. Tart develops such cognitive traps at greater length, calling them "pathologies of knowing and learning"; and his "Law of Universal Retrospective Rationalization" is synonymous with Radin's "revisionist history."[26]

The quantum. Our diurnal world, filled with perceptual distortion, closely aligns with the personal unconscious (PU) whose job is to process, compensate for, and sometimes repress our experiences in the illusory medium of space-time. The PU's manifestations—dream, imagination, and vision—are gateways in turn to the collective unconscious (CU). We now move down the ladder of materiality to the quantum and the CU, which are like opposite sides of the same coin. For example, Jung and physicist Wolfgang Pauli collaborated on a volume that paired Pauli's *The Interpretation of Nature and the Psyche* with Jung's *Synchronicity: An Acausal Connecting Principle*.[27] Both men knew "that living matter has a psychic aspect, and the psyche a physical aspect" (*CW* 10, 780/411). The quantum is where matter and mind meet and where the laws of classical physics yield to nonlocal/acausal phenomena. This is the realm of "field theory," which describes the way in which the One Mind connects all things.

Three examples will suffice to illustrate the operation of field theory.[28] First, Rupert Sheldrake's "morphogenetic fields" account for "the characteristic form and organization of systems at all levels of complexity, not only in the realm of biology, but also in the realms of chemistry and physics." Sheldrake "is concerned with the *repetition* of forms and patterns of organization." He says that if a rat learns a particular task, the easier it becomes for other rats to learn it.[29] In our own lives, we see this principle at work when, as more and more people solve the crossword puzzle in the newspaper, it becomes easier to solve as the day wears on. Jung anticipates Sheldrake in stating that

> the law of the duplication of cases is known to all doctors engaged in clinical work. An old professor of psychiatry at Würzburg always used to say of a particularly rare clinical case: "Gentlemen, this case is absolutely unique—tomorrow we shall have another just like it." I myself often observed the same thing during my eight years' practice in an insane asylum. On one occasion a person was committed for a very rare twilight state of conscious—the first case of this kind I had ever seen. Within two days we had a similar case. . . .
>
> (*CW* 10, 121/59)

Second, Ervin Laszlo speaks of the physical, the biological, and the transpersonal, the last of which is of greatest interest in my own study of the One Mind. For example, in a section on transpersonal coherence, Laszlo identifies what makes psi possible, "a physically real information-transmitting field accessed by the supersensitive quantum brain."[30] And third, Radin, in speaking of "field consciousness" or "a continuum of nonlocal intelligence, permeating space and time," follows J. E. Lovelock in suggesting that the billions of individual psyches on Earth function much like the billions of neurons in the brain, making human beings "something like a 'global' mind."[31] Quantum field theory thus points to the concept of holism, which opposes atomism in that one cannot account for a part without considering its relationship to the whole. It also reflects the concept of entanglement, Schrödinger's term, which explains Albert Einstein's "spooky actions at a distance" or nonlocality/acausality.[32] As Marshall and Zohar write in their section on quantum physics, "In the quantum universe—and this is the *whole* universe—every 'part' is subtly linked to every other, and the very identity—the beings, qualities, and characteristics—of constituents depends upon their relation to others."[33]

Jung, who writes of Einstein, "He was often in my house, and I pumped him about his relativity theory" (*CW* 18, 140/68), anticipates the theory of entanglement in believing that the archetype straddles the realms of matter and psyche. By "psychoid" Jung means the archetype's dual nature, a connection that gives rise to "synchronicity" or "meaningful coincidence." As Peat writes,

> Synchronicities give us a glimpse beyond our conventional notions of time and causality into the immense patterns of nature, the underlying dance which connects all things and the mirror which is suspended between inner and outer universes.[34]

Relying on Jung and Peat, Michael Conforti explains synchronicity as a manifestation in the concrete world of the alignment of two energy fields, that of the psychological complex and that of the archetype.[35] But regardless of the terminology one uses to describe the complementary relationship between matter and mind (the quantum and the CU), the subatomic is a realm in which, as hologram theory suggests, every part or "fractal" contains a pattern of the whole. To illustrate this point, Talbot rightly quotes William's Blake's "Auguries of Innocence":

> To see a World in a Grain of Sand
> And a Heaven in a Wild Flower,
> Hold Infinity in the palm of your hand
> And Eternity in an hour.
>
> (E 490)

Talbot attributes the same idea to Gottfried Leibniz who "proposed that the universe is constituted out of fundamental entities he called 'monads,' each of which contains a reflection of the whole universe." The favorable references to Leibniz in *The Collected Works* suggest that Jung was intrigued by a forerunner of hologram theory.[36]

All of these authors would agree that, in the realm of subtle energy, space-time does not behave in complete accordance with physical laws. Jung states that

> the psyche's attachment to the brain, i.e., its space-time limitation, is no longer as self-evident and incontrovertible as we have hitherto been led to believe. . . . It is not only permissible to doubt the absolute validity of space-time perception; it is, in view of the available facts, even imperative to do so.
>
> (*CW* 8, 813/413–814/414)

Whether one speaks of time, space, matter, or thought, the fundamental characteristics of this middle quantum realm of reality are unity and connectedness rather than division and separation. Rowland's summation is worth quoting here: "Einstein's relativity challenged reductionism by showing that reality was far more like an inter-dependent fabric than discrete and atomistic. Everything really is connected to everything else!"[37] But Bohm's distinction between relativity theory and quantum theory suggests a more precise formulation. The former, he says, "requires continuity, strict causality (or determinism) and locality," whereas "quantum theory requires non-continuity, non-causality and non-locality."[38] Thus the quantum world, or the realm of tiny particles, is characterized by less differentiation; greater holism, which means connectedness and the idea that the whole is greater than the sum of its parts; nonlocality, the absence of causation; and inclusivity, the both/and as opposed to either/or nature of reality.

Pure spirit. As the PU is a gateway to the CU, so the latter opens up into the third part of the continuum, which I am calling "the realm of *pure* spirit" to underscore its nonphysicality. Here natural laws, even those of quantum physics, do not apply; and thought is action, plain and simple. Our world of time, space, and matter is a refinement, manifestation, or emanation of the potential inherent in pure spirit, much like the relationship between the archetype and the archetypal image. Psychics can experience this spiritual realm firsthand, and some claim that they have charted that ethereal territory and understood its gradations; but physicists, parapsychologists, and transpersonal psychologists study merely its manifestations as psi phenomena, not pure spirit itself, because science has not evolved instruments to study what lies beyond the quantum vacuum. (That said, however, we are at the dawn of "instrumental transcommunication" or ITC, a subject that I discuss in this book's final pages.)

The conclusion that emerges is that the CU encompasses space-time and individuality by means of its participation in the One Mind, which unites *everything*: matter, mind, and spirit; past, present, and future; consciousness and the unconscious, both personal and collective; all levels of life ranging from the vegetative to the rational; worlds both physical and nonphysical; and the human as well as the extraterrestrial. The CU has connective properties because it participates in a greater, more pervasive unifying field. But whereas the CU is anthropocentric, the One Mind (analogously, Jung's *unus mundus*) includes but transcends the human unconscious.

The paranormal and the metaphysical

Although Jung reduces the One Mind to the PU and the CU, he is clearly fascinated by the psyche's outer limits. At the beginning of his career, he wrote his medical school dissertation, *On the Psychology and Pathology of So-Called Occult Phenomena* (1902), about his cousin Helly Preiswerk's channeling of different voices during séances. In the dissertation, Jung refers to her as S. W., a choice that Ronald Hayman's biography illuminates: "The initials he used—S. W.—may have been taken maliciously from Krafft-Ebing's *Textbook of Insanity*, where S. W. is a seamstress whose delusions of grandeur were aggravated by eroticism and coquetry."[39] Although the teenager at first seemed to be a gifted psychic, Jung's dissertation finds grave fault with her. She had "at least considerable talent as an actress"; he "often tried to give her some critical explanation" to counter her belief in the visions' reality; after he caught her cheating, she soon abandoned the séances; and he sums up her experiences as "a case of somnambulism belonging to the purely pathological" (*CW* 1, 40/19, 43/23, 71/43, and 150/88). In his reaction to his cousin's apparently fraudulent and pathological spiritualism, we find two principles that characterize much of Jung's later work: first, the idea that there are distinct voices within each of us, which no doubt later contributed to the theory of the archetypes; and second, a tendency to reduce psi to merely psychological processes.

Volume 11 of *The Collected Works* contains various texts that further illustrate Jung's guarded interest in the paranormal. Besides his commentary on *The Tibetan Book of the Great Liberation*, we find a commentary on *The Tibetan Book of the Dead*, "Yoga and the West," "The Psychology of Eastern Meditation," and "Foreword to the *I Ching*." The volume defines *abaissement du niveau mental* as that "which abolishes the normal checks imposed by the conscious mind and thus gives unlimited scope to the play of the unconscious 'dominants" (*CW* 11, 848/520). It is this *abaissement*, or lowering, that characterizes meditative experience, altered states, and conscious access to the unconscious. His observation, "The manner in which the *I Ching* tends to look upon reality seems to disfavor our causal procedures" (*CW* 11, 969/591), anticipates his later work, *Synchronicity: An Acausal Connecting Principle* in *CW* 8. In addition, volume 18 contains Jung's statement in "On Occultism" that he is open to substantial evidence for psi if it becomes available in the future; but for the time being, he chides spiritualists for their exaggerated claims. Similarly, in "Psychology and Spiritualism," he displays his usual tendency to psychologize potentially spiritual phenomena, claiming, for example, that "ghost stories and spiritualistic phenomena practically never prove what they seem to" (*CW* 18, 761/319).

Jung's attitude mingles openness and enthusiasm for psi, if it is examined from a scientific point of view, with skepticism and doubt as regards anecdote and parlor tricks. Jungian literary critics have overlooked his qualified interest in the paranormal, and this omission leads to important questions. Given the three realms within the *unus mundus* or the One Mind (the physical/PU, the quantum/CU, and pure spirit), what principles arise that may take Jungian literary criticism beyond the archetypal and the poststructural into the metaphysical? What key concepts animate metaphysical criticism? If entanglement characterizes the strange connections between matter and mind in all of their forms, does something similar obtain in the relationship between matter, mind, and spirit?

Some preliminary answers may be ventured at this point. To begin with, all things, whether quantum or physical, implicate or explicate, matter or spirit, are emanations of the One Mind. What seems to characterize the physical world—the separation of space, time, matter, and thought—is an illusion. Reality's true nature is an overarching connectedness, with every part, as in a hologram, containing a pattern of the whole. The quantum void is a crossing point between physical matter and pure spirit, with entanglement characterizing the physical side of the divide and the overarching unity of mind or consciousness tying together the physical and the nonphysical/spiritual. Given the presence of entanglement and the reality of spirit, materialism and reductionism are false concepts; and via altered states the human mind can reach beyond physical matter to engage with the quantum/CU and the realm of pure spirit, all of which make up the One Mind. In other words, psi is real; and critics will attribute heightened verisimilitude to examples of it in literary works because it points toward a greater-than-physical reality. A related assumption is that human consciousness survives physical death because we *are* ghosts in machines. Nor are humans alone in the universe. As Marshall and Zohar note, "The Cosmological Principle holds that the universe is much the same everywhere. What we see from our vantage point is a fair sampling of the whole."[40] The implication is that extraterrestrial intelligence is a reality, not merely a human projection, as Jung argues in *Flying Saucers: A Modern Myth of Things Seen in the Skies* (*CW* 10, 589/311–824/433). Synchronicity—a meaningful bridge between the implicate and the explicate orders—is also a worthy object of study. The term may expand so that an episode previously related only to the PU now becomes a quantum moment; a manifestation of the CU; an example of field consciousness; or a case study, as Werner Heisenberg would argue, of the impact of perspective on observation. In order to solve literary conundrums, researchers will be able to reach out across space-time to gather information previously thought unavailable through conventional means. As Radin states,

> We might imagine a future "Clairvoyant Space Corps" tasked with exploring distant galaxies. Likewise, we normally think of precognition and retrocognition as seeing across vast gulfs of time, and may envision teams of Indiana Jones-like "time historians" who explore ancient and future civilizations.[41]

Critics will also work to understand the role of the unconscious in the writing process—the mysterious ways in which, as Shakespeare says, the poet "gives to airy nothing / A local habitation and a name" (*Dream*, 5.1.16–17). Part of this inquiry into invention will include the study of art created by those in the afterlife and brought into physical manifestation by talented psychics, much as Jung apparently channeled *Seven Sermons*. Meanwhile, a new theory will argue that fantasy literature appeals to readers because, in shearing away the psi uncertainty principle, it dramatizes psi phenomena that illustrate the abilities latent in all of us because of the unity of the One Mind. Finally, critics will study psychic authors *as* psychics. As a result, a text's portrayal of concepts like the simultaneity of time, nonlocality/acausality, unity, and the One Mind will emerge more clearly.

The points just adumbrated correspond to the organization of material in *The One Mind*, and all chapters engage to one degree or another with Jung's thinking in *The Collected Works*. The argument incorporates some of my previous publications. These articles have been reduced to eliminate nonessential material and revised to include connections to Jung (in effect, they are new products), but the notes and bibliography will guide readers who desire greater detail to full text. That said, chapter 1 illustrates two preliminary matters: the traditional approach to Jungian literary criticism and the problems that arise from materialism and reductionism. Nathaniel Hawthorne's "Young Goodman Brown" enables an example of the archetypal approach, but even here the analysis begins to advance the book's thesis by showing elements in the narrative that point toward unity via the collective unconscious, as well as the holographic relationship between one psyche and all others. The chapter then describes how Loren Eiseley's "The Secret of Life" elegantly enacts the problems that arise from materialism and reductionism, problems that metaphysical criticism must counteract. Jung's nature writings inform the plight of Brown and the situation of Eiseley. Chapter 2 considers John Milton's scale of being in *Paradise Lost*, book 5, as a counterpoint to Eiseley's troubled essay. Similarities emerge between Milton's cosmology and Jung's, as well as physicist Thomas Campbell's "theory of everything." In short, the first part of the book models traditional Jungian criticism, discusses the problem of materialism, and explores a cosmological model more in keeping with the One Mind.

The middle portion concerns the implications and consequences of the One Mind. Chapter 3 considers altered states, particularly dream and hallucination. In connection with Jung's comments on altered states and the ocean as a metaphor for the CU, I reinterpret the "dream sequence" in the Old English consolation "The Wanderer" (a sea poem, I assert) in order to upgrade dream and vision to thematically relevant components in the traveler's journey toward faith and wholeness. Chapter 4 explores a similar altered state, the out-of-body experience, by relating Jung's near-death experience in 1944 and his essay "The Soul and Death" to Robert A. Monroe's trilogy on astral projection. Monroe is especially relevant because he strongly affirms the One Mind thesis in his comment on the "(M) Field," defined as the "nonphysical energy field that permeates space-time including our Earth Life System, but is not a part of current human scientific knowledge or study."[42] Of greatest interest to literary critics is Monroe's use of metaphor to describe the realm of pure spirit. A brief discussion of Frederick Henry's near-death experience in Ernest Hemingway's *A Farewell to Arms* anchors the discussion in canonical literature. Chapter 5 analyzes Jung's *Flying Saucers: A Modern Myth of Things Seen in the Skies* and takes issue with his dismissive reading of the work of Orfeo M. Angelucci, a UFO experiencer. I assert that Angelucci's account is more credible than Jung believes because of its parallels to the work of Steven M. Greer, M.D., a prominent contemporary UFO researcher.[43] UFOs are not mere projections of unconscious material, as Jung would have us believe.

The next two chapters bring together three ways of gaining information in unconventional ways, all of which have a basis in Jung's writings and in the unity that springs from the One Mind: synchronicity, remote viewing, and channeling. In chapter 6, the underpinnings of synchronicity theory complement a Jungian reading of the stolen boat episode in Wordsworth's *The Prelude* in order to suggest that the young William's terror lies not only in the PU but also in connectedness that transcends the individual psyche. Chapter 7 shows how Jung's statements on space-time relativity for psychics gave rise to an experiment in which a professional remote viewer (a clairvoyant operating within a double-blind format) was tasked with gathering information on the identity of the Dark Lady in Shakespeare's Sonnets. As well, Jung's position on the role of the unconscious in writing and problem solving leads to consideration of four sonnets channeled, apparently, from Edward de Vere, the Earl of Oxford, through an intermediary spirit and a professional psychic. The poems appear in Percy Allen's all but forgotten book, *Talks with Elizabethans*, which engages with the perennial authorship debate swirling around Shakespeare's plays by arguing for collaboration among Oxford, Shakespeare, and Bacon.

The last two chapters shift from works that illustrate specific implications and consequences of the One Mind to case studies of texts that encompass multiple manifestations. Chapter 8 examines the plethora of psychic phenomena in Robert Jordan's *The Wheel of Time* series, including its latest volumes, which were ghost written following his death by Jordan Sanderson. Jungians will take particular interest in Jordan's terminology in relation to Jung's—the One Power, *saidin*, and *saidar* versus pleroma, animus, and anima. I propose a theory in which fantasy literature is appealing because it dramatizes the potential for psi in everyone by amplifying or exaggerating its effects. Jung's concept of "quaternity"—God the Father, Son, Holy Spirit, and Satan—structures the discussion of Jordan's material (material that rivals in length *The Collected Works*). Chapter 9 serves as a capstone by considering Blake's *Milton* as a psychic author's poem about psychic experience of connections via the One Mind. Finally, the conclusion reflects on the insights developed in the preceding chapters and makes predictions about literary criticism in the distant future.

As Radin notes, however, radical developments have to go through a process of incorporation into mainstream consciousness.[44] In stage one, when skeptics will declare an idea or phenomenon to be impossible, their view will prevail. There is a strong connection between stage one and "misoneism, fear of the new and unknown" (*CW* 18, 439/194). In stage two, those skeptics concede that the idea may in fact be possible. In stage three, as the public realizes the idea's importance, it gains acceptance. In stage four, the idea's former critics become believers. Eventually, *not* believing the idea becomes the heretical position. This process of incorporation is arduous. On the one hand, I believe that the approaches implemented in *The One Mind* are the wave of the future; but I am under no illusions about their immediate acceptance. On the other, this book takes literary criticism a significant step closer to a unity of science and spirituality than any previous study, Jungian or otherwise. Its purpose is to open a new vein, and the following chapters will not be the last ore ever extracted on the subject. Some may dismiss metaphysical criticism and view me as a "true believer" or a crank, but eventually opinion will swing in the direction that I am proposing and that Jung anticipated over a half century ago. What may seem like fantasy today should prove to be common sense in the future. Individuation may accompany and drive this further revelation, for as Jung says in *On the Nature of the Psyche*,

> The more unconscious a man is, the more he will conform to the general canon of psychic behaviour. But the more conscious he becomes of his individuality, the more pronounced will be the difference from other subjects and the less he will come up to common expectations.
>
> (*CW* 8, 344/160–61)

Notes

1 Sir Thomas Browne, *Religio Medici*, in *The Broadview Anthology of Seventeenth-Century Verse & Prose*, ed. Alan Rudman et al. (Peterborough, Canada: Broadview, 2000), 474; and Laurens van der Post, *Jung and the Story of Our Time* (New York: Vintage, 1975), 51. For Erwin Schrödinger, see *Mind and Matter* (Cambridge, UK: Cambridge University Press, 1959), 62.

2 *OED*, s/v "metaphysical," def. A.II.4.c.

3 For a contrasting view, see Aniela Jaffé, *Was C. G. Jung a Mystic? and Other Essays* (Einsiedeln, Switzerland: Daimon Verlag, 1989); and Gary Lachman, *Jung the Mystic: The Esoteric Dimensions of Carl Jung's Life and Teachings* (New York: Penguin, 2010). For a critique of Jung's relationship to the New Age movement, see David Tacey, *Jung and the New Age* (Philadelphia, PA: Brunner-Routledge, 2001).

4 Jung does not capitalize the word "Self," but upper case is used here to distinguish the archetype of wholeness from "self," the individual person.

5 Helpful support for this position comes from Dean Radin's two books, *The Conscious Universe: The Scientific Truth of Psychic Phenomena* (New York: HarperEdge, 1997) and *Entangled Minds: Extrasensory Experiences in a Quantum Reality* (New York: Paraview Pocket, 2006), as well as from Charles T. Tart's *The End of Materialism: How Evidence of the Paranormal is Bringing Science and Spirit Together* (Oakland, CA: New Harbinger, 2009).

6 I explore these two texts at greater length in the introduction to *A Jungian Study of Shakespeare: The Visionary Mode* (New York: Palgrave Macmillan, 2009), 2–6. See also Susan Rowland, *Jung as Writer* (New York: Routledge: 2005), 1–23.

7 I comment on this oversight in "Reiki and Jung: An Introduction," *Conversations in the Field* 1, no. 2 (2010): 1–10, http://thejungiansociety.org. One interpretation of Reiki, or universal life force energy, is that it is the primordial undifferentiated consciousness out of which all things, physical and nonphysical, are made. If this assumption is correct, then Reiki is analogous to what Jung calls "pleroma" in Sermon 1 of his *Seven Sermons to the Dead*, in *The Gnostic Jung*, ed. Robert A. Segal (Princeton, NJ: Princeton University Press, 1992), 181–93. Pleroma is discussed below.

8 Daryl Sharp, *C. G. Jung Lexicon: A Primer of Terms & Concepts* (Toronto, Canada: Inner City, 1991), 27.

9 Richard P. Sugg, ed., *Jungian Literary Criticism* (Evanston, IL: Northwestern University Press, 1992); Susan Rowland, *C. G. Jung and Literary Theory: The Challenge from Fiction* (New York: St. Martin's, 1999); and Terrence Dawson,

"Literary Criticism and Analytical Psychology," in *The Cambridge Companion to Jung*, ed. Polly Young-Eisendrath and Terrence Dawson, 2nd ed. (New York: Cambridge University Press, 2008), 269–98.

10 Ian Marshall and Danah Zohar, *Who's Afraid of Schrödinger's Cat? All the New Science Ideas You Need to Keep Up with the New Thinking* (New York: William Morrow, 1997), 16 and xxviii. Jung favors a holistic approach to psychology: "A fundamental change of attitude (*metanoia*) is required, a real recognition of the whole man" (*CW* 10, 719/379). He means, however, a unity of consciousness and the unconscious or primitive part of the psyche, not a holism that encompasses all that is.

11 For Paul, see 1 Corinthians 2:9 and 2 Corinthians 12:2–4. For Bottom's allusion to Paul, see *A Midsummer Night's Dream*, 4.1.209–12.

12 Fike, *A Jungian Study*, 39.

13 Sharp defines transcendent function as "a psychic function that arises from the tension between consciousness and the unconscious and supports their union." He adds that "the Transcendent function is essentially an aspect of the self-regulation of the psyche. It typically manifests symbolically and is experienced as a new attitude toward oneself and life" (*Jung Lexicon*, 135–36). See also "The Transcendent Function" in *CW* 8, 131/69–193/91.

14 Rowland, *C. G. Jung and Literary Theory*, 12.

15 David Bohm, *Wholeness and the Implicate Order* (New York: Routledge, 1980), 191 and 218.

16 Maureen Caudill, *Suddenly Psychic: A Skeptic's Journey* (Charlottesville, VA: Hampton Roads, 2006), 102.

17 Robert A. Segal, introduction to *The Gnostic Jung*, ed. Robert A. Segal (Princeton, NJ: Princeton University Press, 1992), 39–40.

18 F. David Peat, *Synchronicity: The Bridge Between Matter and Mind* (New York: Bantam, 1987), 196–97.

19 Jung, *Seven Sermons*, 182.

20 Ibid., 183.

21 Ibid., 184.

22 Ibid., 181.

23 Marshall and Zohar, *Who's Afraid*, 303–4.

24 Radin, *Conscious Universe*, 252.

25 Michael Talbot, *The Holographic Universe* (New York: HarperCollins, 1991), 163.

26 Radin, *Conscious Universe*, 230–1; and Tart, *The End of Materialism*, 47 and 141.

27 C. G. Jung and Wolfgang Pauli, *The Interpretation of Nature and the Psyche. Synchronicity: An Acausal Connecting Principle* (New York: Pantheon, 1955). Jung's treatise is reprinted in *CW* 8, 816/419–968/519.

28 For a literary application of field theory, see N. Katherine Hayles, *The Cosmic Web: Scientific Field Models and Literary Strategies in the Twentieth Century* (Ithaca, NY: Cornell University Press, 1984). Using the metaphor of the "cosmic web," she stresses the interconnectedness of all things and the resulting self-referentiality. That is, because everything is connected, "the autonomy assigned to individual events by language is illusory" (10). Other principles include the observer as a participant, holism, acausality, and the role of perspective. Hayles's application of field theory to literature deals with paradoxes like the following: can a whole simultaneously contain and be contained by the part, and can linear words represent a holistic field? Chapter 3 on D. H. Lawrence deals with the unconscious, but *The Cosmic Web* differs from my study in two major respects: it is not Jungian, and it does not consider the One Mind. Two further studies also deserve mention. For metaphor and the unreliability of language in physics, see Liliane Papin, "This Is Not a Universe: Metaphor, Language, and Representation," *PMLA* 107, no. 5 (1992): 1253–65. For a treatment of physics and visual art, see Leonard Schlain, *Art & Physics: Parallel Visions in Space, Time &*

Light (New York: HarperCollins, 1991). Schlain's chapter 20, pages 290–304, deals with literature and physics; and he mentions various topics that are relevant to *The One Mind*: Jung on synchronicity (24), the collective unconscious (413), Blake (93–96), and "*universal mind*" (387).

29 Rupert Sheldrake, *A New Science of Life: The Hypothesis of Formative Causation* (Los Angeles, CA: Tarcher, 1981), 13–14.

30 Ervin Laszlo, *The Connectivity Hypothesis: Foundations of an Integral Science of Quantum, Cosmos, Life, and Consciousness* (Albany: State University of New York Press, 2003), 47.

31 Radin, *Conscious Universe*, 159 and 157. See also Peter Russell, *The Global Brain: Speculations on the Evolutionary Leap to Planetary Consciousness* (Los Angeles, CA: Tarcher, 1982).

32 Radin, *Entangled Minds*, 226. Radin quotes Einstein's letter to Max Born: "'I cannot seriously believe in [the quantum theory] because it cannot be reconciled with the idea that physics should represent a reality in time and space, free from spooky actions at a distance.'"

33 Mashall and Zohar, *Who's Afraid*, 298.

34 Peat, *Synchronicity*, 2.

35 Michael Conforti, *Field, Form, and Fate: Patterns in Mind, Nature, and Psyche*, rev. ed. (New Orleans, LA: Spring Journal, 2003), 24.

36 Talbot, *Holographic*, 50 and 291. For Jung's commentary on Leibniz, see, for example, *Synchronicity: An Acausal Connecting Principle* (*CW* 8, 937/498–939/501).

37 Susan Rowland, *C. G. Jung in the Humanities: Taking the Soul's Path* (New Orleans, LA: Spring Journal, 2010), 106.

38 Bohm, *Wholeness*, 223.

39 Ronald Hayman, *A Life of Jung* (New York: Norton, 1999), 61.

40 Marshall and Zohar, *Who's Afraid*, 118.

41 Radin, *Conscious Universe*, 292.

42 Robert A. Monroe, *Ultimate Journey* (New York: Doubleday, 1994), 274.

43 Today it is widely believed, but not officially acknowledged, that ETs are visiting the Earth. See Steven M. Greer, "The Disclosure Project," 2010, http://www.disclosure project.org. My review of two of Greer's books appears in *TMI Focus* 32, no. 3–4 (Summer/Fall 2010): 10–13, http://www.monroeinstitute.org/resources/book-reviews/hidden-truth-forbidden-knowledge.

44 Radin, *Conscious Universe*, 1.

1

A TRADITIONAL APPROACH TO HAWTHORNE AND THE PROBLEM OF MATERIALISM IN EISELEY

A statement that Jung makes in his *Zarathustra Seminar* resonates meaningfully with the plight of Hawthorne's Goodman Brown:

> You know, to the late Christian you can convey the idea that one ought to be interested in oneself in the way, say, of a schoolmaster or a doctor. They understand that one needs some education of the soul, some loving care of one's own spiritual welfare, provided that the body is excluded. The thing people are most afraid of is not so much the soul, which to them is practically non-existent, but the body. That is what they don't want to see, the animal or the evil spirit that is waiting to say something to them when they are alone. That is exceedingly disagreeable. So even if they agree that one could be a bit more careful with oneself, it is only with the guarantee that the body is excluded and has nothing to do with it. The body is the darkness, and very dangerous things could be called up. It is better to play the piano in order not to hear what the body says.[1]

At its core, "Young Goodman Brown" is a story that enacts the psychological and spiritual consequences of failure to acknowledge the physical body. As Jung understood, "Nature *must not* win the game, but she *cannot* lose" (*CW* 13, 229/184; emphasis in the original).

Although much has been written about Nathaniel Hawthorne's "Young Goodman Brown" from a Jungian perspective, even some about the role of the body, I was able to discuss numerous unnoticed connections in my article on the story. Some of its highlights, as well as my newer insights, appear below to illustrate the standard Jungian approach to literary criticism. Whereas shadow and anima engage with Goodman Brown's personal unconscious, elements of his "dream journey," especially the presence of a Jungian quaternity, point toward greater unity via the collective unconscious: one psyche is a microcosm of all others, and there is no "Other." In contrast to a Jungian analysis of "Young Goodman Brown," Loren Eiseley's "The Secret of Life," my subject in another article, displays a disturbing materialism, which does not accord with an archetypal or metaphysical approach. But as we shall see, Jung's comments on nature inform both Hawthorne's story and Eiseley's essay in important ways.[2]

"Young Goodman Brown"

Previous criticism. The remarks of other psychological critics, many of them Jungian, provide an appropriate beginning. Richard P. Adams notes that a male must encounter the shadow, the anima, and the wise old man in this order; and he emphasizes sexuality's role in "the transformation from childishness or adolescence to maturity." Reginald Cook stresses that the forest represents the unconscious, both personal and collective; and he believes that the title character enacts a failed version of what Joseph Campbell calls the hero's journey—descent, encounter, and return. Richard Predmore stresses "the elements excluded from the Puritan consciousness," which emerge as compensatory projections of the shadow and anima. For Michael Tritt, the two parts of the projection process—locating evil in others and believing oneself to be without fault—explain the isolation that Brown suffers for the rest of his life. Edward Jayne, noting that the Browns' marriage is unconsummated, proposes that the story's initial images—the "threshold" and Faith's "pretty head"—anticipate Brown's sexually-charged encounter in the forest. Finally, D. J. Moores advances a reading of Brown's shadow in terms of the Puritans' hostility to nature, natural impulses, and the body.[3]

Shadow and anima. Since the shadow is not evil but merely inferior, the goal is to acknowledge and integrate it, to defang its negatives and incorporate its strengths (*CW* 11, 134/78). But Brown's encounter with the shadow, rather than propelling him toward wholeness, constitutes an *enantiodromia,* which Daryl Sharp defines as "the emergence of the unconscious opposite in the course of time."[4] In the opening sentence, "Young Goodman Brown came forth at sunset into a street of Salem village; but put his head back, after crossing the threshold to exchange a parting kiss with his young wife" (65).[5] The threshold image anticipates Jung's ominous statement in *Psychology and Religion* that the encounter with the shadow involves crossing "the *threshold* of the unconscious and [taking] cognizance of those impersonal forces which make you the unconscious instrument of the wholesale murderer in man" (*CW* 11, 86/49; my emphasis). Jung views Protestantism as a particularly insufficient barricade against unconscious content because of its loss of sacred images and rituals (*CW* 11, 75/43). His emphasis in *Psychology and Religion* on Protestantism's disintegration as a church (*CW* 11, 85/48) anticipates Michael J. Colacurcio's comment on Brown's status as a third-generation Puritan, which signals an erosion of the standards required for full church membership.[6] It is bad enough psychologically that Brown is a Protestant, worse that he is a third-generation Puritan, and ominous that he intentionally casts off such outer restraints as the Puritan church still provides in order to encounter his shadow alone at night in the "unconverted wilderness" (73). In other words, Brown casts off the one-sided Puritan persona of the "good man" in order to swing to the opposite in pursuit of "his present evil purpose" (66).

Along with anticipating Brown's imminent confrontation with his shadow, the opening resonates powerfully with another part of his unconscious that he has failed to integrate—the anima. Leaving his wife behind means not only that he abandons his protective religious faith but also that he *sets aside* his anima. On the one hand, there is perhaps some logic in Brown's departure from his wife, as Jung observes: "It is normal for a man to resist his anima, because she represents . . . the unconscious and all those tendencies and contents hitherto excluded from conscious life" (*CW* 11, 129/75). On the other, setting out on his own is a critical mistake because "the anima plays the role of the mediatrix between the unconscious and the conscious" (*CW* 10, 715/378). Allegorically, Faith represents the anima, which he needs to integrate; literally, she is a helpmate in the individuation process. Without her, he sets out in ways that are both strange and precarious to encounter the unconscious on his own.

Within the linkage of the anima and the unconscious, Jung also asserts a wider, more mercurial nature for the anima in the following statement:

> Like the "supraordinate personality," the anima is bipolar and can therefore appear positive one moment and negative the next; now young, now old; now mother, now maiden; now a good fairy, now a witch; now a saint, now a whore.
>
> (*CW* 9i, 356/199)

It is hard to imagine a more appropriate summary of the role of anima in "Young Goodman Brown," for the feminine archetype manifests in nearly all of these ways. She is both young like Faith and old like the matrons whose spectral representations Brown encounters in the woods. The narrator explains,

> At least there were high dames well known to her "the lady of the governor," and wives of honored husbands, and widows, a great multitude, and ancient maidens, all of excellent repute, and fair young girls, who trembled lest their mothers should espy them.
>
> (72)

The anima is both a maiden like Faith and the mother whose spectral form Brown sees just before the dream ends. There is no hint of the anima-as-fairy in the story, but Hawthorne mentions such supposed witches as "the Quaker woman" lashed "so smartly through the streets of Salem" (67) and Goody Cloyse who "was accused as a witch and was in prison awaiting sentence in 1692 when the witchcraft persecutions ended."[7] Faith's spectral presence marks her as guilty by association; that and her pink ribbon make her, in Brown's estimation, a whore.

At the beginning of his journey, Brown calls Faith "'a blessed angel on earth'" and after this one night will "'cling to her skirts and follow her to heaven'" (65). Several of Jung's statements support Frederick Crews's belief that Brown views Faith "more as an idealized mother than as a wife."[8] First, "The odour of sanctity may be far reaching, but to live with a saint might cause an inferiority complex or even a wild outburst of immorality in individuals less morally gifted" (*CW* 11, 130/76). What is Faith if not a saint? What is Brown's journey into the forest if not "a wild outburst of immorality"? A second statement that illuminates Brown's inner reflection appears in Jung's discussion of initiation rituals in primitive cultures: "Because the mother is the first bearer of the soul-image, separation from her is a delicate and important matter of the greatest educational significance" (*CW* 7, 314/197). Jung seems to share with Freud the notion that a young male needs to separate from the mother and align with the father, but here that separation is shifted from young childhood to the bridge from adolescence to adulthood. A bit later, Jung describes the consequences of failing to undergo a ritual transformation:

> The modern civilized man has to forgo this primitive but nonetheless admirable system of education. The consequence is that the anima, in the form of the mother-imago, is transferred to the wife; and the man, as soon as he marries, becomes childish, sentimental, dependent, and subservient, or else truculent, tyrannical, hypersensitive, always thinking about the prestige of his superior masculinity.
>
> (*CW* 7, 316/197)

The passage informs the changing psychological landscape in which Brown sees himself as a man who intends to cling to his wife's skirts after his night of decadence in the forest. Although he has made the physical transition from mother to wife, he has merely transferred his dependence onto his mate. Failure to integrate the maternal anima results in dependence, and dependence eventually results in resentment. The journey into the woods transforms his initial goal of subservient piety into a hypersensitive psychological tyranny that blights the rest of his life. He swings from Puritan morality to a confrontation with evil but never makes it all the way back.

Jung's third statement that bears meaningfully upon the spousal relationship portrayed at the story's opening relates to the order in which a man must do his inner work. In the individuation process, the difference between shadow and anima is quite pronounced. Jung writes, "If the encounter with the shadow is the 'apprentice-piece' in the individual's development, then that with the anima is the 'master-piece'" (*CW* 9i, 61/29). Specifically, a male must make his shadow conscious before he can have a successful contra-sexual relationship precisely because shadow and anima are largely distinct. "Primitive" initiation rituals provide a support system for dealing with shadow integration before one marries; but in a more "civilized" culture like Puritan New England or our own modern culture, the lack of a clear demarcation means that shadow work and anima work—the "apprentice-piece" and the "master-piece"—occur simultaneously. Or in Brown's case, he has attempted anima work in marriage before confronting his shadow in the woods.

The "dream" portion of the story bears out this tangled web of shadow and anima, particularly in details related to those whom the Puritans have harmed. Shadow is projected onto the Native Americans and the anima onto the supposed witches. As a result, Brown's *enantiodromia*, his blasphemous swing to the opposite of his everyday morality, does not yield to *coniunctio*, "the union of opposites and the birth of new possibilities,"[9] or what Jung himself in "Psychotherapists or the Clergy" calls a "reunion of the warring halves of the personality" (*CW* 11, 526/342). Brown descends to encounter the opposite of his Puritan persona; but in fixating on the sin in others and never affirming his own shadow, he thwarts the potential for individuation that his reunion with Faith represents. The black mass—one of Marie-Louise von Franz's illustrations of the collective shadow[10]—is a compensatory stage where Brown interacts with projections of his personal unconscious. But regarding projection, he misses a key point. The devil says:

> By the sympathy of your human hearts for sin ye shall scent out all the places—whether in church, bed chamber, street, field, or forest—where crime has been committed, and shall exult to behold the whole earth one stain of guilt, one mighty blood spot.
>
> (74)

Ironically, the remark contains the seed of its own undoing: the perception of others' sin, says the devil, arises from the existence of sin in one's own heart. The devil is peddling projection by calling attention to that very psychological mechanism, and Brown misses the full significance of this revelation by focusing instead on the planetary blood stain.

Quaternity. Until my work was published, no one had forged a connection between the black mass and Jung's concept of the quaternity—the Father, Son, and Holy Spirit, plus "the fourth aspect which represents the reprehensible part of the Christian cosmos" or "the evil principle" (*CW* 11, 105/61 and 103/59). Elsewhere Jung calls "the fourth function . . . the undifferentiated or inferior function which characterizes the shadow side of the personality" (*CW* 10, 775/408). As an illustration of the compensatory nature of the unconscious, the fourth person corresponds to the unconscious and balances the Trinity. For example, the devil's snake-like staff represents the shadow, as Jung states in the first English version of *The Integration of Personality*: "Taking it in its deepest sense, the shadow is the invisible saurian tail that man still drags behind him. Carefully amputated, it becomes the healing serpent of the mysteries. Only monkeys parade with it."[11] Jung also asserts "how great an importance was attributed to the quaternity by the American Indians" (*CW* 11, 99/57). Such persons—"the Indian priests, or powwows," as the narrator calls them (72)—are of course present at the black mass. The forest realm of the Native Americans, then, sets the stage for the main encounter with "the fourth aspect," the natural, sexual, instinctual, and demonic contents of the dream. In particular, the imagery at the black mass anticipates the quaternity symbol that Jung recognizes in a patient's dream: "This is the peculiar arrangement of burning candles in four pyramid-like points" (*CW* 11, 90/51). Similarly, Hawthorne's narrator describes "four blazing pines, their tops aflame, their stems untouched, like candles at an evening meeting" (72). There is also a connection between quaternity and the four elements present in the story. Here is Jung in *Psychology and Religion*:

> The natural philosophers of antiquity represented the Trinity . . . as . . . water, air, and fire. The fourth constituent, on the other hand, was . . . the earth or the body. They symbolized the latter by the Virgin. In this way they added the feminine element to their physical Trinity, thereby producing the quaternity. . . . The natural philosophers of the Middle Ages undoubtedly meant earth and woman by the fourth element.
>
> (*CW* 11, 107/62–63)

Besides the burning pines, we have air ("a roar of the wind" [74]), water ("a hanging twig, that . . . besprinkled his cheek with the coldest dew" [74]), and of course the forest itself and all the sexual suggestiveness of the black mass.

After the publication of my article, I realized the relevance of another patient's dream to "Young Goodman Brown." Jung considers it twice in *The Collected Works*, with extended commentary in *Psychology and Alchemy* (*CW* 12, 307–14/203–8) and with lesser commentary in *Psychology and Religion* (*CW* 11, 111/65–66). The dream is of a "world clock," which Jung considers a mandala and therefore a symbol of quaternity, harmony, and the Self. He writes, "We shall hardly be mistaken if we assume that our mandala aspires to the most complete union of opposites that is possible, including that of the masculine trinity and the feminine quaternity" (*CW* 12, 311/205; 11, 13/66). The clock's link to quaternity suggests a connection between the imagery of the four elements in the forest and the devil's statement earlier in the story: "'You are late, Goodman Brown,' said he. 'The clock of the Old South was striking as I came through Boston; and that is full fifteen minutes gone'" (66).[12] Brown is departing from a life in which religion claims wholeness to be achievable in *chronos*, clock time, so that he can encounter the repressed element in his psyche in the woods: namely, his sexuality, his body life, the fourth "person" of the quaternity. If Brown had properly integrated this aspect within his psyche, he would have returned home to achieve *kairos*, time characterized by the art of living well. Although he does experience procreative sexuality, his remaining time on Earth is marked not by quality but merely by quantity:

> And when he had lived long, and was borne to his grave, a hoary corpse, followed by Faith, an aged woman, and children and grandchildren, a goodly procession, besides neighbors not a few, they carved no hopeful verse upon his tombstone; for his dying hour was gloom.
>
> (75)

The collective unconscious. Although Hawthorne is clearly exploring the dynamics of Brown's personal unconscious, details of the black mass hint that there is a connection to the collective unconscious or to some greater overarching unity. Here "Young Goodman Brown" engages directly with the thesis of this book—the idea that the One Mind, in which the collective unconscious participates, connects all that is. For example, there is a curious detail in the narrator's description of those in attendance at the black mass: "Some affirm that the lady of the governor was there" (72). If the night journey in the forest is Brown's dream, or if it is real and he never breathes a word of it to anyone for the rest of his days, how can "Some affirm" anything about the attendees at the black mass? The detail makes no sense unless one of two things is the case: either Hawthorne nodded; or the black mass, perhaps as well as the entire journey, somehow participates in a level of awareness that includes but transcends the personal unconscious. Whereas much of the foregoing analysis rests on the assumption that Brown's journey is intrapsychic and arises from his personal unconscious, the strange detail about "the lady of the governor" implies that his inner experience has somehow become part of the treasure house of human beings' shared experience, the collective unconscious.

The black mass confirms this point by including another detail that suggests the relationship between the personal and collective aspects of the unconscious. As in a hologram, the other attendees have coalesced in Brown's vision and are simultaneously *apart from* yet *a part of* his individual psyche.

> But, irreverently consorting with these grave, reputable, and pious people, these elders of the church, these chaste dames and dewy virgins, there were men of dissolute lives and women of spotted fame, wretches given over to all mean and filthy vice, and suspected even of horrid crimes. It was strange to see that the good shrank not from the wicked, nor were the sinners abashed by the saints. Scattered also among their palefaced enemies were the Indian priests, or powwows, who had often scared their native forest with more hideous incantations than any known to English witchcraft.
>
> (72)

Everyone is here: the good, the wicked, men, women, whites, natives. Here they all are, united for a common purpose, which is apparently to affirm the fourth aspect of the quaternity, the one that Brown, in his Puritan morality and possible sexual ambiguity, has repressed. Like Brown himself, other Jungian critics have not recognized that, if "the good shrank not from the wicked," then the assembled crowd fulfills "his present evil purpose" (66), represents the individuation on which his future life depends, and anticipates Jung's statement that "the smallest part of the end of the work of Creation [Brown's psyche], contains the whole [all psyches]" (*CW* 8, 926/490). In other words, the gathering is an image of the Self, "the archetype of wholeness and the regulating center of the psyche."[13] Although the black mass provides a visual representation of how shadow, anima, and primitive could harmonize in his psyche, Brown misses the forest for the trees by fixating on the immorality implied by the presence of familiar persons along with wretches and criminals. That is, he violates the principle of holism by failing to see the greater whole that arises from the sum of the parts. One can scarcely find a better critique of his reaction than Jung offers:

> Christ espoused the sinner and did not condemn him. The true follower of Christ will do the same, and, since one should do unto others as one would do unto oneself, one will also take the part of the sinner who is oneself. And as little as we would accuse Christ of fraternizing with evil, so little should we reproach ourselves that to love the sinner who is oneself is to make a pact with the devil. Love makes a man better, hate makes him worse—even when that man is oneself.
>
> (*CW* 12, 37/32)

A passage in "Psychotherapists or the Clergy" amplifies the point:

> But what if I should discover that the least amongst them all, the poorest of all beggars, the most impudent of all offenders, yea the very fiend himself—that these are within me, and that I myself stand in need of the alms of my own kindness, that I myself am the enemy who must be loved—what then?
>
> (*CW* 11, 520/339)

Brown's vision of the black mass constitutes an image of his own psychic contents working together in a display of integration. He sees what he needs, and what he needs he eschews—all because his Puritan programming dooms him to see the Other when he is really seeing himself.

Goodman Brown's journey into the night woods, especially his exposure to a vision of his male ancestors, is a failed version of a young man's initiation rite. It fails for many reasons, not least the presence of females, including a spectral representation of his mother. It fails because of his Puritan programming, his projection, and his consequent failure at individuation. And it fails because he gives his visions more credence than he assigns to the sunlit world in which he has grown up. The consequence of his failure is summed up in Jung's belief that "it is highly moral people, unaware of their other side, who develop peculiarly hellish moods which make them insupportable to their relatives" (*CW* 11, 130/76). This sentence—"A stern, a sad, a darkly meditative, a distrustful, if not a desperate, man did he become from the night of that fearful dream" (75)—indicates that Brown suffers inflation and dissociation, which Jung believes are "typical of people who cannot project the divine image any longer" (*CW* 11, 156/95). Consequently, Brown is subject to judgment: "Who are forgiven their many sins? Those who have loved much. But as to those who love little, their few sins are held against them" (*CW* 11, 537/347).

Ultimately, Brown's psychological failings in the woods become his sad destiny because he never tells anyone about his night journey. His plight therefore resembles that of the murderess who confessed to Jung about the consequences of concealing the truth—her life had soured in the same way that Brown's does (*MDR*, 123). As Laurens van der Post comments, "though one could keep such things secret in oneself, one could not prevent life from knowing it from the consequences of the murder one had done to oneself in the process."[14] This is Brown's situation precisely. If telling one's story promotes a kind of healing that Brown denies himself, then there is no corollary in his future life to the function that Hawthorne's story achieves in the Puritan community, a public revelation of the inner processes that lead to dysfunction. As a result, whatever hints "Young Goodman Brown" may provide of a transpersonal realm that unites all psyches, it is ultimately the dysfunction within the personal unconscious that seals his fate.

Archaic man. "Young Goodman Brown" is not an allegory or enactment of the primordial consciousness that underlies the collective unconscious—Jung's pleroma or *unus mundus*, which I am calling the One Mind. Nor does the story reflect the realm of pure spirit. But Brown's personal tragedy does dramatize the importance of achieving unity with nature—both the external woods through which he travels and his own sexuality. Although he beholds an image of the Self at the black mass, the Puritan structure of his belief system tricks him into seeing both nature and body as the Other, with the result being that he blights the rest of his life.

Because of that separation from nature, Brown is far from being the sort of "archaic man" whose intimate connection with nature Jung describes. The psyche of that "original" man is characterized by instinct rather than consciousness, and his view of nature is subjective or "primitive" insofar as it involves the projection of psychic contents onto the external world, a process that Jung, following Lévy-Bruhl, calls *participation mystique* (mystical participation). In this respect, archaic man has a magical mentality that leads to Lévy-Bruhl's "collective representations," which are the myths humans tell themselves about a power greater than the natural order—"widely current ideas whose truth is held to be self-evident from the start, such as the primitive ideas concerning spirits, witchcraft, the power of medicines, and so forth" (*CW* 10, 106/51). Just as a primitive has great reverence for spirits in nature, which bear his projections, he also pays great attention to his dreams. For archaic man, then, there is such a close connection between external nature and the collective unconscious that reality is a combination of psyche and the objective world, a view that reflects the psychoid nature of the archetype. As a result, our ancient ancestors nourished their souls through a sense of unity and harmony with nature and harbored misoneism (fear of change) with regard to alternative ways of being. Jung expresses his own close relationship with nature as follows:

> At times I feel as if I am spread out over the landscape and inside things, and am myself living in every tree, in the plashing of the waves, in the clouds and the animals that come and go, in the procession of the seasons.

The passage illustrates what he describes later on as "a feeling of kinship with all things" (*MDR*, 225–26 and 359).[15]

Goodman Brown is clearly a world apart from the archaic state of mind just described, but neither is he a perfect fit with Jung's analysis of the modern psyche. Modern man's embrace of consciousness, intellect, reason, language, and writing makes it difficult to achieve the kind of unity consciousness that Jung describes in his autobiography. An objective, technological, and scientific viewpoint makes nature the Other, a thing to be analyzed and used. By emphasizing mechanical causation and materialism, scientific inquiry rejects anything that cannot be measured. Reality is objective—sans psyche. As a result, human beings become dissociated from the natural world, sever communication with the collective unconscious, repress their instincts, suffer neuroses, and compensate through violence. With nature shorn of all spirit, technology becomes the bearer of nature spirits, leading to misuse (especially the atom bomb). As Jung puts it,

> We have stripped all things of their mystery and numinosity; nothing is holy any longer. . . . The word "matter" remains a dry, inhuman, and purely intellectual concept, without any psychic significance for us.[16]

He also notes that "life has grown desiccated and cramped, crying out for the rediscovery of the fountainhead" (*CW* 12, 74/60). This is a powerfully negative diagnosis by a psychologist who believes that physical reality and psyche intertwine.

Eiseley's scientific materialism

"Dessicated" is part of Loren Eiseley's description of external nature in "The Secret of Life," the thirteenth and final essay in his first book, *The Immense Journey*.[17] Other key words such as "analysis," "dissection," and "materialism" signal that Eiseley matches Jung's diagnosis. If Goodman Brown's problem is a lack of connection with inner and outer nature, Eiseley's problem is that he is too firmly rooted in an objective, scientific, technological, and materialist view of nature. Although Brown has a negative reaction to the numinous, he at least encounters it, perhaps via a dream, which Jung would consider a positive sign: his unconscious is talking to him. Eiseley's psychic life is dry because he is unable to affirm, much less experience, anything beyond measurable reality. Yet there is hope for Eiseley in precisely the terms that Jung articulates. If nature imbricates psyche and if Eiseley is exploring nature, then landscape becomes inscape and must be read for its psychological significance. Mind and matter are not totally separate, and Eiseley's purpose is to put the connection in an evolutionary context. In *The Immense Journey*, he reflects on the main events in the history of evolution, the objective trail of evidence left to be discovered in external nature; but being unable to connect with the archaic man within himself, he can only intellectualize about the possibility of the numinous, which he longs to experience.

In contemplating early man, Eiseley may be aware of a primordial wellspring of human existence but cannot put his finger on it, much less make it part of his own individuation. Jung sums up the disconnection between the rational, conscious part of the modern psyche and the two-million-year-old man within as follows:

> Primitive man was much more governed by his instincts than are his "rational" modern descendants, who have learned to "control" themselves. In this civilizing process, we have increasingly divided our consciousness from the deeper instinctive strata of the human psyche, and even ultimately from the somatic basis of psychic phenomena. Fortunately, we have not lost these basic instinctive strata; they remain part of the unconscious, even though they may express themselves only in the form of dream images.
>
> Modern man does not understand how much his "rationalism" (which has destroyed his capacity to respond to numinous symbols and ideas) has put him at the mercy of the psychic "underworld." He has freed himself from "superstition" (or so he believes), but in the process he has lost his spiritual values to a positively dangerous degree. His moral and spiritual tradition has disintegrated, and he is now paying the price for this break-up in worldwide disorientation and dissociation.[18]

"Disorientation and dissociation" are apt descriptions of Eiseley's depression, loneliness, and severed relationship to instinct and the numinous. "The Secret of Life" is not a dialogue between Eiseley-as-scientist and the archaic man who slumbers within him, and musing about a creator God does not spark a mystical union with nature or unlock the collective unconscious. Eiseley uses the tools of materialist science—observation, dissection, careful analysis—to look for the secret of life (the process that sparked the transition from inert matter to living matter), an event that may not be purely physical. When he engages his imagination, however, he considers ways of thinking that arise from a magical mentality and result in collective representations. In this respect, he moves in the direction that Jung prescribes: "What is needed is to call a halt to the fatal dissociation that exists between our so-called higher and lower being; instead, we must unite conscious man with primitive man."[19] But *moves in the direction* does not mean that Eiseley does as Jung advises. Despite engaging his imagination, Eiseley remains deaf to the archaic man within him, largely because, through it all, he remains anchored to consciousness, language, and science. Even as he muses, he does so in words; even as he considers the numinous, he remains a materialist.

Unlike Brown, one must acknowledge that affirming nature is essential if one is to move toward the wholeness of the Self. Eiseley, to his credit, makes some progress away from a purely materialistic vision of nature, though he achieves neither the mystical sense of unity that Jung describes in *Memories, Dreams, Reflections* nor a definitive conclusion about God's role in creation. But, as a writer and observer, he does fulfill Jung's sense "that man is indispensable for the completion of creation; that, in fact, he himself is the second creator of the world, who alone has given to the world its objective existence . . ." (*MDR*, 256). Paradoxically, then, although Eiseley fails to achieve the goal that Jung would favor—enhancing the benefits of consciousness with connections to the collective unconscious—"The Secret of Life" does enact the collaboration between mind and nature that produces something greater than either and makes the artist a co-creator with God.

After concluding that both science and imagination do not reveal the secret of life, Eiseley turns to religious explanations, invoking James McCosh, who asserts a complementary relationship between divine causation and natural evolution. Yet Eiseley remains aloof, referring to McCosh as the "Scotch theologue" (152) rather than by name. The essay's concluding sentence is even more evasive, though quite a beautiful allusion to Thomas Hardy:

> Rather, I would say that if "dead" matter has reared up this curious landscape of fiddling crickets, song sparrows, and wondering men, it must be plain even to the most devoted materialist that the matter of which he speaks contains amazing, if not dreadful powers, and may not impossibly be, as Hardy has suggested, "but one mask of many worn by the Great Face behind."
>
> (210)

The allusion is to Hardy's "The Last Chrysanthemum," appropriately set in autumn "when leaves like corpses fall / And saps all retrocede." The poem concludes with these lines:

> I talk as if the thing were born
> With sense to work its mind;
> Yet it is but one mask of many worn
> By the Great Face Behind.[20]

The ur-source for both Hardy and Eiseley may be the famous statement in *Moby Dick*, chapter 36:

> All visible objects, man, are but as pasteboard masks. But in each event—in the living act, the undoubted deed—there, some unknown but still reasoning thing put forth the mouldings of its features from behind the unreasoning mask. If man will strike, strike through the mask![21]

Evidently Melville, Hardy, and Eiseley share the belief that nature hints at something beyond itself. Eiseley's later notion of a mere "procreative void" that lies "behind visible nature" now seems cold in light of the theological emphasis in the literary background of "The Secret of Life."[22] Whatever lies beyond the mask is not a Nothing but a Something. However, Eiseley's technique in the essay's final sentence, like the earlier reference to McCosh, qualifies the theological speculation. The technique is called "litotes," which means stating the negative of the opposite of what one wants to say. When Eiseley wants to suggest that nature has a supernatural element, he says that "'nature is not as natural as it looks'" and further distances himself from the notion by attributing the claim to the unnamed McCosh. When Eiseley wants to say that nature may possibly be one of the masks of some Great Face behind it, he says that nature may "not impossibly be" such a mask. The effect in each case is to create a sense that the theological conclusion is tenuous; and it is made more tenuous still by the substitution of "Great Face" for Creator, Deity, Designer, God, First Cause, Lord, or Prime Mover. Once more, the text acts out the tentative nature of its author's claims by invoking possibilities to which it does not commit.

In that final sentence, Eiseley reaches the end of his contemplative journey and remains a scientist to the core, but the inability to find the secret of life on his autumn walk has made him suspect that there is more to nature than science's "pipettes" and "blue-steel microtomes" can dissect (206 and 202). He finally arrives at the possibility, despite his earlier denial of "supernatural explanations" (200), of a possible role for God in the creation of life. He just cannot bring himself to say it that directly: his scientific paradigm makes it difficult for him to acknowledge this possibility with anything more than a literary flourish. Toward the end of his life, however, he does make a direct statement about the tension between his scientific frame of mind and the possibility of something extra-natural. The comment comes in the context of his ruminations on the giant wasps:

> I am an evolutionist. I believe my great backyard Sphexes evolved like other creatures. But watching them in the October light as one circles my head in curiosity, I can only repeat my dictum softly: in the world there is nothing to explain the world. Nothing to explain the necessity of life, nothing to explain the hunger of the elements to become life, nothing to explain why the stolid realm of rock and soil and mineral should diversify itself into beauty, terror, and uncertainty.

He continues: "I was seeking an undiscoverable place, glimpsed long ago by the poet Shelley 'built beyond mortal thought / far in the unapparent.'"[23] The line is from *Adonais*, Shelley's elegy for John Keats who is now "Far in the Unapparent," a realm that human perception normally cannot penetrate.[24] Although Eiseley strongly suspects that there is something beyond nature, he has no idea what it might be. Nearly two decades after the publication of *The Immense Journey*, he is still puzzling over ultimate origins.

Lines that frame Eiseley's autobiography provide a final perspective on "The Secret of Life": "Before nothing / behind nothing / worship it the zero."[25] In the context of evolution, "nothing" may be the unknowable void of which Eiseley writes, while the "zero" may be the moment when evolution began, the crossing point of life when inert matter came alive, and time, in a sense, began. "'And this is where the kind of time that bewitched you began,'" the Player (Fate?) says to him in an imaginary dialogue. "'Remember? *Behind nothing, before nothing*. This is the country of vertical time. I will leave you to add the zeros. The gods always carried them here'" (emphasis in the original).[26] The strange phrase "vertical time" implies that space and time are not really separate things and that the aging Eiseley is beginning to contemplate space-time and the metaphysical. Here perhaps the zero represents the present moment, which "The Secret of Life" celebrates and enacts, with evolution stretching back to time immemorial and ahead to an unknown future when God and/or nature might improve on human beings. Of course, the zero is also an "O" shape that symbolizes the unity that Eiseley sees between personal experience and scientific inquiry, art, and some unknowable force that may lie beyond nature. If he had a personal faith, however, it was a Wordsworthian "natural piety" upgraded to include the possibility of supernatural agency.[27] As Eiseley might put it, it is *not inadvisable* to remember that he also wrote, "For many of us the Biblical bush still burns, and there is a deep mystery in the heart of a simple seed."[28]

To this idealistic declaration, Jung might well reply, "Oh, the poor fellow is as disconnected from nature as he is from psyche; and the one disconnection leads on to the other." He would probably then note that the "O" shape of the zero is also a circle, a symbol of the Self, which the three-line poem empties out as though wholeness must forever remain elusive. Although Eiseley may believe in wholeness as a theoretical construct, the poem implies that he himself cannot achieve it. Jung would blame Eiseley's materialism for this failure to individuate. While it is true that he is not a *diehard* materialist who considers nothing beyond what science can observe and measure, his materialism keeps him not only from wholly affirming divine agency in the secret of life but also from developing a personal relationship with a creator God. The essay does celebrate the human mind as the apex of creation, yet that achievement is heavy with irony. What enables Eiseley's ability to analyze the evolutionary process in *The Immense Journey* is human consciousness, whose evolutionary rise requires the dissolution of the very bond with nature that consciousness now registers in the form of loneliness and depression. As the sad poem in his autobiography implies, he seems unable to enhance, as Jung would advise, the fruits of intellection with the riches of nature and the unconscious. Nature provides plenty of material for scientific and personal reflection; but despite the quality of Eiseley's literary achievement in *The Immense Journey* and his success in the field of anthropology, at the end of his life he contemplates nothingness. He should have realized what Jung asserts:

> We delude ourselves with the thought that we know much more about matter than about a "metaphysical" mind or spirit, and so we overestimate material causation and believe that it alone affords us a true explanation of life. But matter is just as inscrutable as mind.
>
> (*CW* 8, 657/342)

Notes

1 C. G. Jung, *Zarathustra Seminar*, ed. James Jarrett (Princeton, NJ: Princeton University Press, 1988), 800. The passage is helpfully reproduced in *C. G. Jung on Nature, Technology & Modern Life*, ed. Meredith Sabini (Berkeley, CA: North Atlantic, 2008), 169.

2 My articles are as follows: "We Are One Psyche: A Jungian Approach to Hawthorne's 'Young Goodman Brown,'" *Postscript* 27, no. 9 (2012): 1–20, www.pachome.org; and "The Literary Matrix of Loren Eiseley's 'The Secret of Life,'" *The CEA Critic* 72, no. 3 (2009): 17–36.

3 Richard P. Adams, "Hawthorne's *Provincial Tales*," *The New England Quarterly* 30, no. 1 (1957): 39–57; Reginald Cook, "The Forest of Goodman Brown's Night: A Reading of 'Young Goodman Brown,'" *The New England Quarterly* 43, no. 3 (1970): 473–81; Richard Predmore, "'Young Goodman Brown': Night Journey into the Forest," *Journal of Analytical Psychology* 22, no. 3 (1977): 250–57; Michael Tritt, "'Young Goodman Brown' and the Psychology of Projection," *Studies in Short Fiction* 23, no. 1 (1986): 113–17; Edward Jayne, "Pray Tarry With Me Young Goodman Brown," *Literature and Psychology* 29 (1979): 100–13; and D. J. Moores, "Young Goodman Brown's 'Evil Purpose': Hawthorne and the Jungian *Shadow*," *Journal of Evolutionary Psychology* 27, no. 3–4 (2005): 4–16. I discuss the previous criticism in greater detail in my article.

4 Daryl Sharp, *C. G. Jung Lexicon: A Primer of Terms & Concepts* (Toronto, Canada: Inner City, 1991), 50.

5 Quotations from the story are taken from *Nathaniel Hawthorne's Tales*, ed. James McIntosh (New York: Norton, 1987), 389–404.

6 Michael J. Colacurcio, "Visible Sanctity and Specter Evidence: The Moral World of Hawthorne's 'Young Goodman Brown," in McIntosh, *Nathaniel Hawthorne's Tales*, 389–404.

7 McIntosh makes the point about 1692 in *Nathaniel Hawthorne's Tales*, 68, n. 3.

8 Frederick Crews, *The Sins of the Fathers: Hawthorne's Psychological Themes* (New York: Oxford University Press, 1966), 105 and 103.

9 Sharp, *Jung Lexicon*, 42.

10 Marie-Louise von Franz, *Shadow and Evil in Fairy Tales*, rev. ed. (Boston, MA: Shambhala, 1995), 7–9.

11 Jung's remark is quoted in Jolande Jacobi and R. F. C. Hull, *C. G. Jung: Psychological Reflections; A New Anthology of His Writings 1905–1961*, Bollingen Series 31 (Princeton, NJ: Princeton University Press, 1970), 243. Jung uses the word "saurian" to convey the fact that each of us contains the evolutionary history of our species. He states, "I always say that our psychology has a long saurian's tail behind it, namely the whole history of our family, of our nation, of Europe, and of the world in general" (*CW* 18, 169/81).

12 The devil has traveled (flown?) at a speed slightly in excess of sixty miles per hour. McIntosh notes that "Salem village was sixteen or more miles from colonial Boston" (*Nathaniel Hawthorne's Tales*, 66, n. 2).

13 Sharp, *Jung Lexicon*, 199.

14 Laurens van der Post, *Jung and the Story of Our Time* (New York: Vintage, 1975), 117.

15 Many of the conclusions in this paragraph arise from Jung's essay "Archaic Man" (*CW* 10, 104/50–147/73).

16 C. G. Jung, "Approaching the Unconscious," in *Man and His Symbols*, ed. C. G. Jung et al. (New York: Doubleday, 1964), 94.

17 Loren Eiseley, "The Secret of Life," in *The Immense Journey* (New York: Random House, 1957), 195–210.

18 Jung, "Approaching the Unconscious," 52 and 94.

19 C. G. Jung, *C. G. Jung Speaking: Interviews and Encounters*, ed. William McGuire and R. F. C. Hull, Bollingen Series 97 (Princeton, NJ: Princeton University Press, 1997), 397.
20 Thomas Hardy, "The Last Chrysanthemum," in *The Complete Poems of Thomas Hardy*, ed. James Gibson (New York: Macmillan, 1976), 149.
21 Herman Melville, *Moby Dick or the White Whale* (New York: Signet, 1961), 167.
22 Loren Eiseley, *The Unexpected Universe* (New York: Harcourt, 1964), 31.
23 Loren Eiseley, *All the Strange Hours: The Excavation of a Life* (New York: Scribner's, 1975), 249 and 254.
24 Eiseley also borrowed the phrase "the firmament of time" from Percy Bysshe Shelley, "Adonais: An Elegy on the Death of John Keats," stanza 44. The poem appears in *English Romantic Writers*, ed. David Perkins (Fort Worth, TX: Harcourt, 1995), 1106–14.
25 Eiseley, *Hours*, 12 and 270–71.
26 Ibid., 270.
27 William Wordworth, "My Heart Leaps Up When I Behold," in Perkins, *English Romantic Writers*, 330.
28 Loren Eiseley, *The Firmament of Time* (New York: Atheneum, 1960), 8.

2

PRIMORDIAL CONSCIOUSNESS

Transcendental monism in Milton's *Paradise Lost*

So far, we have observed two aspects of human beings' separation from nature—Goodman Brown's disconnection from the body and Loren Eiseley's materialist assumption that only what can be measured by science exists, though he seems to yearn for a higher alternative. Both positions are heavy with psychological implications that stymie individuation and spiritual life. We turn now to *Paradise Lost* where John Milton's monist "Scale of Being" offers a vastly different perspective on materialism.[1] As Dean Radin explains, there are two relevant types of monism. "*Materialistic monism* says that matter causes mind, that the mind is essentially a function of the activity of matter in the brain. The basic stuff of the universe is matter and energy." "*Transcendental monism* says that the mind is primary, and in some sense causes matter. The ultimate stuff of the universe is consciousness" (emphases in the original).[2] Milton's monism is materialistic insofar as everything proceeds from "one first *matter*" (5.472; my emphasis),[3] but he applies that concept not only to Adam, Eve, and Eden but also to the nonphysical world of angels and spirits. The primordial source of all things has "substance" (5.474); but for the purposes of this chapter, it is understood as consciousness.

The notion that consciousness has substance is a difficult paradox, but Jung's pleroma and the new physics offer a helpful analogy. As the introduction describes, he anticipated insights in physics that would be achieved a half century later. F. David Peat, for example, identifies Jung's pleroma as "a ground of 'godhead' out of which all reality is born." Similarly, Peat's comment on the combination of mind and matter nicely informs Milton's description: "If mind and matter can be understood as emerging out of a common order, then it will no longer be helpful to think of them both as distinct substances but rather as inseparable manifestations of the one undivided whole."[4] If the "one first matter" out of which everything has been made is analogous to Jung's pleroma, then Milton posits a transcendental monism in which primordial consciousness has a material aspect. If everything proceeds from "one first matter" and if that matter is really consciousness, then the implication is the *unus mundus*, the unitary world or the One Mind—a pervasive consciousness that unites all things, which, though they are distantly removed in time from pleroma, are not really separate. In the same way, though we post-date the Big Bang by nearly fourteen billion years, the matter that makes up our bodies was present in that primordial cataclysm.

Milton tracks physical creation back to its origin in primordial consciousness in the same way that physicists attempt to create theories of everything. This chapter singles out one such theory by nuclear physicist Thomas Campbell to demonstrate striking parallels to Milton's Scale of Being, to suggest a connection between that key passage and Adam's vision, and thus to demonstrate how metaphysical criticism can merge insights from the new physics and the New Age.[5] Jung, physicists, and New Age thinkers all agree that reality is characterized not by the dualistic separation that even a materialist like Eiseley rejects but by connectedness, which arises from primordial consciousness and implies the human mind's capacity to perceive beyond the boundaries of waking consciousness. There are connections to be made, then, between the Scale of Being and the visionary experiences in books 11 and 12, which fall into two categories. With Michael's help, Adam's consciousness is cleansed and heightened so that he can see the future while awake. Meanwhile, Eve has a profound dream, which illustrates Jung's *abaissement du niveau mental*, or a lowering of consciousness.

As the *Scale* of Being, Raphael's description participates in a nexus of images that includes various bridges and bridge-like structures elsewhere in the poem. The most prominent bridge in *Paradise Lost*, of course, is the "Bridge" that Sin and Death forge in between Hell and Earth (2.1028; 10.301 and 371), later called a "Causey" or causeway (10.415) and, punningly, a "Pontiface" (10.348). The narrator also refers to two bridge-like structures: Zeus's "golden Chain" (2.1005) and "The Stairs . . . whereon *Jacob* saw / Angels ascending and descending" (3.510–11). In the words of Sir Thomas Browne, Raphael's description in book 5 is of "a stair, or manifest scale of creatures, rising not disorderly, or in confusion, but with a comely method and proportion."[6] Stephen M. Fallon calls it an "ontological ladder" or "up escalator" (186), Barbara Kiefer Lewalski "a chain of being" (476), and most scholars the "scale of nature."[7] My own discussion of the passage rests on a bridge between the monism in Milton's statement and Campbell's conclusions. In proposing a scale of creation, both authors advance theories about humans' ultimate origin in primordial substance, degrees of development or evolution from that original material, and the continuity between the physical and the nonphysical. This parallelism qualifies the conclusions of Howard and Joy Schultz hold that man must accept his mental "finitude" and that things higher on the scale contain the lower.[8] In a revisionist spirit, then, chapter 2 uses the tension between what the epic *claims* about human potential in Raphael's speech and what it *enacts* in Adam's visionary experience to explore transcendental monism's optimistic implication for humans' spiritual advancement in the fallen world.

The scale of being and creation *ex Deo*

Milton's conception of God lays the basis for his monism, which holds that all of creation proceeds from one original substance that Raphael calls "one first matter."

As D. Bentley Hart states, "the oneness of the primary matter underlying the diversity of all its secondary manifestations constitutes also a continuity of substance between things and God, such that all substances are contained by the divine substance." Hart insists that Milton's is a material monism or "panhylism," yet Michael's remarks seem more in character with the position that the critic denies, metaphysical monism, "the belief that the hierarchy of Being is a system of divine emanation and return, or at least that the creation is ontologically continuous with the divine." In other words, Hart denies exactly what Milton has Raphael express. My purpose here is to explore the implications of the "divine emanation and return" that arise from what Hart properly calls a "metaphysical unity of God and creation."[9] For Milton, then, creation is not *ex nihilo* but rather *ex Deo*, as he states in *Christian Doctrine*: "God produced all things not out of nothing but out of himself," and "all things come not only from God but out of God."[10] Jung would agree. Milton quotes support for his position from the letters of Paul. For example, in 1 Corinthians 8:6, "*there is one God, the Father, from whom all things are and in whom we are, and one Lord Jesus Christ, through whom all things are and through whom we are*"; and in Romans 11:36 "it is the Father *by whom* and *from whom* and *through whom* and *in whom all things are.*"[11] God's exact nature, of course, is obscured from mortal view, which is why Milton notes that "God, as he really is, is far beyond man's imagination, let alone his understanding" and why he then quotes 1 Timothy 6:16 where God is said to be "*dwelling in unapproachable light.*"[12] The passage is the likely origin of the poet's claim in *Paradise Lost* that "God is light," "Bright effluence of bright essence increate," the "Fountain of Light," and "glorious brightness" (3.3, 6, and 375–76). Harris Francis Fletcher believes that "the 'essence increate' . . . was the essence of God, itself uncreated and eternal"; and Catherine Gimelli Martin, explicating the same line, sees Milton's "God only as a source of energy inevitably *prior* to light, and light itself as a theoretical vanishing point," which explains why the heavenly choir notes that "Dark with excessive bright thy [God's] Skirts appeer" (3.380). Being infinite, eternal, and omnipresent, God as "Omnipotent Intelligence" constitutes both the efficient and the primary cause.[13]

Thus we have the theological foundation for Raphael's monist description of the scale of nature. Everything on it is made of the "one first matter," which is God; and the higher contains the lower, much as the lower participates in, but is not equal to, the higher. In *Christian Doctrine* Milton writes,

> Moreover spirit, being the more excellent substance, virtually, as they say, and eminently *contains* within itself what is clearly the inferior substance; in the same way as the spiritual and rational faculty *contains* the corporeal, that is, the sentient and vegetative faculty.
>
> (my emphasis)[14]

Milton's critics staunchly affirm the idea that the greater contains the lesser.[15] The containment metaphor also appears earlier in book 5 where the "Intelligential" and "Rational" substances

> "both *contain* / Within them every lower facultie / Of sense, whereby they hear, see, smell, touch, taste, / Tasting concoct, digest, assimilate, / And corporeal to incorporeal turn." (5.409–13; my emphasis)

Given the central assumption that the greater contains the lesser, difference on the scale of nature is of degree, not kind, and relates to the type of form that is applied. Indeed, form itself is corporeal in Milton's ontology—forms "are themselves material."[16] As Walter Clyde Curry articulates,

> Milton's conception [is] that the bodies of angels and the bodies of men and all other created things are formed out of the *same*, originally homogeneous matter, and that the composition of matter and material form is found not only in the material world but also in all spiritual substances.[17]

Further elaboration appears in *A Fuller Institution of the Arte of Logic*, where Milton states that "*Matter is the cause out of which a thing is*" but that "*The form is the cause through which a thing is what it is*."[18] In any case, the higher one looks on the Scale of Being, the "more refin'd, more spiritous, and pure" the object becomes (5.475). From roots to stalks to flowers and their odors, plants provide an analogy for what Fallon calls "atherealization" or movement up the scale; and the critic rightly views "digestion as an analogy for and example of the ascent along the hierarchy of being."[19] Similarly, the human digestive process transforms, or sublimes, "flours and thir fruit" into "vital Spirits" (5.482–83), which are "The animating or vital principle in man (and animals); that which gives life to the physical organism," and correspond to the vegetative soul.[20] These spirits in turn form the basis for the sensible or "animal" soul and for the rational or "intellectual" soul (5.484–85); and Milton sums up the vegetative, the sensible, and the rational by noting life, sense, fancy, understanding, and reason, with reason as both discursive (linear, processual) and intuitive (instantaneous).[21] As this list implies, even the faculties within the human soul are in a dynamic scale. Therefore, one's location on that scale is less important than the direction in which one is headed. Through obedience, Adam and Eve may ascend; through disobedience, Satan has descended, which is why he sits at the very bottom of a depiction of the Great Chain of Being in Didacus Valades's *Rhetorica Christiana* (1579).[22]

Previous critics, however, have left unexplored the structure of the key passage. Raphael's speech, which is a giant chiasmus, or ABBA pattern, describes the movement from that "one first matter" to physical form, reviews the cognitive states that humans experience, and finally raises the possibility that the physical body may become spirit in a transformation out of nature if man remains obedient.[23] Insofar as Raphael's explanation moves from spirit to body, then from body to spirit, with faculties of mind as the hinge in the chiasmus, Milton underscores the importance of reason in the return that the passage partially enacts. Here is the passage in full, with my emphases in boldface.

To whom the winged Hierarch repli'd.
O *Adam*, one Almightie is, from whom
All things proceed, and up to him return,
If not deprav'd from good, created all
Such to perfection, one first matter all,
Indu'd with various forms, various degrees
Of substance, and in things that live, of life;
But more refin'd, more spiritous, and pure,
As neerer to him plac't or neerer tending
Each in thir several active Sphears assignd,
Till body up to spirit work, in bounds
Proportiond to each kind. So from the root
Springs lighter the green stalk, from thence the leaves
More aerie, last the bright consummate floure
Spirits odorous breathes: flours and thir fruit
Mans nourishment, by gradual scale sublim'd
To vital Spirits aspire, to animal,
To intellectual, give both life and sense,
Fansie and understanding, whence the Soule
Reason receives, and reason is her being,
Discursive, or Intuitive; discourse
Is oftest yours, the latter most is ours,
Differing but in degree, of kind the same.
Wonder not then, what God for you saw good
If I refuse not, but convert, as you,
To proper substance; **time may come when men**
With Angels may participate, and find
No inconvenient Diet, nor too light Fare:
And **from these corporal nutriments perhaps**
Your bodies may at last turn all to Spirit
Improv'd by tract of time, and wingd ascend
Ethereal, as wee, or may at choice
Here or in Heav'nly Paradises dwell;
If ye be found obedient, and retain
Unalterably firm his love entire
Whose progenie you are. Mean while enjoy
Your fill what happiness this happie state
Can comprehend, incapable of more.

(5.468–505)

Clear verbal echoes reinforce the chiastic movement and the sense of potential progress up the scale. For example, the passage begins, "All things proceed, and up to him return / If not deprav'd from good," and ends, "Your bodies may at last turn all to Spirit . . . If ye be found obedient, and retain / Unalterably firm his love entire / Whose progenie you are" (5.470–71, 497, and 501–2). The statements are virtually the same but for the addition of love in the second position. Upward movement requires Christ-like obedience, the virtues encompassed by the "paradise within" (12.587), and the retention of love—both God's love of man and, by implication, man's love of his fellows. These lines, of course, anticipate Raphael's caveat:

> In loving thou dost well, in passion not,
> Wherein true Love consists not; love refines
> The thoughts, and heart enlarges, hath his seat
> In Reason, and is judicious, is the scale
> By which to heav'nly Love thou maist ascend,
> Not sunk in carnal pleasure.
> (8.588–92)

A similar chiasmus appears early in the passage with "Till body up to spirit work" (5.478), but later the benefit of the ascent is made clear: "time may come when men / With Angels may participate" (5.493–94). Here is yet another example of chiasmus in Raphael's speech: "Mans nourishment, by gradual scale sublim'd / To vital Spirits aspire" (5.483–84), whereas later "from these corporal nutriments perhaps / Your bodies may at last turn all to Spirit" (5.497–98). "Spirits," again, are the vital principle of biological existence, whereas "Spirit," which refers to "incorporeal or immaterial being, as opposed to *body* or *matter*" or simply to the soul,[24] implies a transcendence of the animal and the intellectual, as well as a transition out of nature—corporeality becoming ethereality. In other words, these examples indicate that the passage has the chiastic ABBA structure, with progress being made around the central core of references to the human mind—fancy, reason, understanding, and intuition. Though man has fallen, Milton engages these faculties to explore how that return to Spirit might work and, poetically, to enact a version of it.

Campbell's "Absolute Unbounded Oneness" and Jung's "pleroma"

Charting the Scale of Being is essentially Campbell's project as well.[25] The substance of his theory of everything begins with two important assumptions: consciousness and evolution. He does not know where consciousness or the One Source or Absolute Unbounded Oneness (AUO) came from (much as the poet's "one first matter" and Jung's pleroma are of unknown origin), but he awkwardly states that it is "the fundamental [digital] energy that is the media of reality."[26] In other words, Campbell opens with a Milton-like affirmation that all things participate in an original source; however, as Jung would agree, that substance is not God as Omnipotent Intelligence but rather a low-grade primordial consciousness that has yet to differentiate. Evolution, the "Fundamental Process" of trial and error or what Campbell more colloquially calls "bootstrapping," moves toward greater "profitability" by increasing consciousness and decreasing entropy, which sounds much like moving up Milton's Scale of Being.[27]

When Absolute Unbounded Oneness realizes that it can change itself in the direction of greater awareness, evolution takes over and produces a series of fractals. A fractal is "a geometric pattern that is repeated at ever smaller scales" or "a mathematically conceived curve such that any small part of it, enlarged, has the same statistical character as the original."[28] So, as in a hologram, a part contains a pattern of the whole. Campbell is thinking along the same lines as Peat who states, "Indeed within each moment of a person's life, or a speck of dust on the ground, is enfolded the whole universe, which is, itself, the manifestation of an unimaginable and unnamable creativity."[29] The similarity is striking, though the influence cannot be clearly established. In any case, this Absolute Unbounded Oneness evolves Absolute Unbounded Manifold (AUM), which is "aware, active, purposeful" and constitutes a "brilliant love-consciousness."[30] From here, evolution leads to the Even Bigger Computer, The Big Computer, multiple nonphysical-matter realities, Our System, physical-matter reality (where space-time exists with its various rules such as the speed of light), the Earth, human beings, computers, and (probably someday) computers designed and created by computers.

Campbell's statements about the relationship between AUO and AUM are not unlike the relationship in *Paradise Lost* and in *Christian Doctrine* between God and the Son. God clearly states, "This day I have begot whom I declare / My onely Son," who is to be "great Vice-gerent" (5.603–4 and 609) rather than an equal partner. Later, Adam recalls another of God's statements, which underscores Milton's Arian vision of the Trinity:

> What thinkst thou then of mee, and this my State,
> Seem I to thee sufficiently possest
> Of Happiness, or not? Who am alone
> From all Eternitie, *for none I know*
> *Second to me or like, equal much less.*
> (8.403–7; my emphasis)

Milton articulates this theological position in *Christian Doctrine*, stating that the Father created the Son out "of his own substance," which means that the Son is of a lesser degree or "essence" rather than "co-essential"; even more bluntly, God and the Son are "not equal to each other."[31]

But to return to Campbell: The purpose of evolution in the fractal system we inhabit is the development of consciousness. Absolute Unbounded Manifold evolved us to enhance the quality of its consciousness, and we come to Physical Matter Reality to evolve our own. To that end, we must engage our free will to move away from lower-energy consciousness states like ignorance, fear, and ego toward higher-energy consciousness states like knowledge, wisdom, and love. As Milton would say, obedience and virtue enable progress up the Scale of Being. In addition, the digital nature of consciousness enables our minds to travel between dimensions, investigate alternative pasts and futures in The Big Computer, communicate instantaneously on the Reality Wide Web, and manifest a variety of other psi phenomena—formulations just as figurative as the metaphors of bridge, ladder, and scale in *Paradise Lost*. For neither Milton nor Campbell is the Great Chain of Being a static system because mental faculties enable us to reach beyond and above the human station. J. H. Adamson's summary of Milton's debt to Plotinus nicely sums up Campbell's conclusion as well:

> the Uncreated Essence overflowed with life which penetrated down into all levels of being. Having reached the lowest level, it turned again and, yearning for its source, traveled back through the levels of being until it once more reached the Divine.[32]

In short, both writers use cognitive faculties to track physical matter back to its original source in what Jung calls pleroma.

Of course, compared with the beauty and economy of Raphael's speech to Adam, Campbell's *My Big TOE* is almost intolerable. He is not a reliable wordsmith, much less a great poet, but merely a smart man with a word processor and a love of pseudo-scientific jargon. Nevertheless, his monistic understanding of creation as an emanation from Absolute Unbounded Oneness, which shares striking similarities with Raphael's description of the Scale of Being, may illuminate Milton's depiction of Adam's vision in books 11 and 12. Whereas Campbell's general purpose is to develop a single coherent system that encompasses the major branches of learning, his particular purpose is to account for psychic functioning. Indeed, he has some important things to teach his readers about evolving their consciousness to the point where psi phenomena begin to occur. Given our connection through mind to nonphysical matter reality, the key task is to begin to shift from intellectual awareness that comes, say, from reading *My Big TOE*, to personal experience through meditation. A related assumption is the TOE's fundamental difference from Milton's reductive monism, in which the whole contains the part, and the part may be considered a synecdoche for the whole. More correctly, Campbell understands the part to be a fractal that contains a pattern of the whole, a point on which he unknowingly echoes the theory of correspondences, a philosophical doctrine that Jung surveys in *Synchronicity: An Acausal Connecting Principle* (1952).

For Jung, as in fractal theory, thinkers including the ancient Chinese, classical philosophers, and medieval natural philosophers hold that "the great principle or beginning, heaven, is infused into man the microcosm, who reflects the star-like natures and thus, as the smallest part and end of the work of Creation, contains the whole" (*CW* 8, 926/490). More specifically, he summarizes the philosophy of Leibinz:

> He conceived each monad to be a "little world" or "active indivisible mirror." Not only is man a microcosm enclosing the whole in himself,

> but every entelechy or monad is in effect such a microcosm. Each "simple substance" has connections "which express all the others." It is "a perpetual living mirror of the universe." He calls the monads of living organisms "souls":. . . . This clearly expresses the idea that man is a microcosm. "Souls in general," says Leibniz, "are the living mirrors or images of the universe of created things."
>
> (*CW* 8, 937/499)[33]

The idea of man as a microcosm implies the *unus mundus* or unitary world, which Jung addresses in *Mysterium Coniunctionis* (1944):

> Everything divided and different belongs to one and the same world, which is not the world of sense but a postulate whose probability is vouched for by the fact that until now no one has been able to discover a world in which the known laws of nature are invalid. That even the psychic world, which is so extraordinarily different from the physical world, does not have its roots outside the one cosmos is evident from the undeniable fact that causal connections exist between the psyche and the body which point to their underlying unitary nature.
>
> (*CW* 14, 767/538)

Whereas the pleroma is the primordial conscious out of which everything is made, the *unus mundus* describes the resulting unity in the present day. As in Raphael's speech, there is continuity between the physical and nonphysical universes, which are part of the same whole. Peat makes the point this way: "If mind and matter can be understood as emerging out of a common order, then it will no longer be helpful to think of them both as distinct substances but rather as inseparable manifestations of the one undivided whole." To experience what is greater than ourselves, then, we do not have to go Out There because the universe—in fact, all of creation or at least a pattern of it—exists within each of us. As Peat explains, "the nature of this reality can therefore be touched both by reaching outward into the explicate forms . . . or inward to the implicate order itself."[34] Or as William Blake declares more poetically in *The Marriage of Heaven and Hell*, the senses can discover "the infinite in every thing," for "if the doors of perception were cleansed every thing would appear to man as it is: infinite" (E 38–39).

Adam's vision

This sort of cleansing, which Milton describes in connection with Adam's vision, deconstructs the poet's emphasis on the whole as containing the part. The narrator states:

> but to nobler sights
> *Michael* from *Adams* eyes the Filme remov'd

> Which that false Fruit that promis'd clearer sight
> Had bred; then purg'd with Euphrasie and Rue
> The visual Nerve, for he had much to see;
> And from the Well of Life three drops instill'd.
> So deep the power of these Ingredients pierc'd,
> Eevn to the inmost seat of mental sight
> That *Adam* now enforc't to close his eyes,
> Sunk down and all his Spirits became intranst.
> But him the gentle Angel by the hand
> Soon rais'd, and his attention thus recall'd.
> (11.411–22)

William Kerrigan rightly notes the autobiographical undertone—euphrasy and rue were thought to have healing effects on the eye—and states that "Michael renovates that intuitive power manifest in visionary dreams and unmeditated songs."[35] But one must press on a bit further. The word "instranst," of course, echoes Adam's perception of Eve's creation: when "Mine eyes [God] clos'd, but op'n left the Cell / Of Fancie my internal sight, by which / Abstract as in a *transe*," he observes Eve's creation from his rib (8.460–62; my emphasis). The reference to "internal sight" suggests that Adam's vision of Eve's creation, like his vision of the future, arises from "the inmost seat of mental sight." Contrary to Roy Flannagan's suggestion regarding the former,[36] neither vision is an "ecstasy," in which, as Augustine says, "the attention of the mind is completely carried off and turned away from the senses of the body."[37] According to Campbell's inclusive physics-based monism, though Milton describes the vision in book 11 as a phenomenon external to Adam, it originates within him because human consciousness is a fractal of the trans-temporal divine essence. Though now fallen, Adam no longer sees through a glass darkly, an exception to Jung's idea that the unconscious recedes in direct proportion to human beings' separation from the natural world (a point lost upon Goodman Brown). Michael cleanses and renews Adam's perception while he is in a trance so that, upon returning to awareness, he is capable of visionary perception in an altered state of consciousness. The aid that the angel provides is to remove the filters that block the higher perception of which Adam is already capable.

The resulting vision diverges sharply from the false and purely intrapsychic perturbations that arise from melancholy in Robert Burton's *The Anatomy of Melancholy*. His point is that sources of agitation—the imagination, *enthusiasmus* (enthusiasm, creative energy), the body, bad diet, and melancholy—produce inner vision of a negative sort. Burton, who lumps "meditation" in with "preposterous zeal," is evidently not a *Big TOE* kind of fellow.[38] But while Adam's vision is not the purely subjective experience that Burton describes, neither is it purely objective. The vision, though *described* as extrapsychic so that it conveys the force and objectivity of divine Providence to Adam and to the reader, is a function of inner attunement. In a highly focused state, he is able to transcend time because Adam-as-fractal already contains all that is and will be, though the Fall has rendered it inaccessible without angelic mediation and impossible in book 12 where mere verbal narration supersedes inner vision because Adam's psyche is exhausted. Michael's reference to the failure of Adam's "mortal sight" and "human sense" of "objects divine" (12.9–10) is metaphorical, transcends mere eyesight (a synecdoche for greater vision), and includes a higher state of percipience. As Margaret Miles says of Augustine's theory, "spiritual vision ultimately includes seeing with the eyes of the body,"[39] a point akin to Jung's sense that experiencing the natural world facilitates a reconnection with the unconscious. As Martin Jay writes of vision in general, "the so-called third eye of the soul is invoked to compensate for the imperfections of the two physical eyes."[40] Therefore, Milton's description of the vision as coming in through the physical senses does not obviate inner vision: Adam sees both *with* and *through* his physical eyes, and exhaustion implies the engagement of something more than physical eyesight. Insofar as humans participate in the "one first matter" and have infinity within them, they are a fractal of the universe. The key difference, then, is not of kind (body versus spirit), for that would be dualism. As monism implies, the difference is rather in degree of access to that infinite source, access that the Fall may diminish and obstruct but cannot destroy. As Tennyson aptly states in a different context, "Though much is taken, much abides."[41]

This optimistic reading of the vision is in the spirit of Prolusion 7, where Milton states

> that the great Creator of the world . . . infused into man . . . a certain divine spirit, a part of Himself . . . which is immortal, imperishable, and exempt from death and extinction. . . . This eternal life [in heaven] . . . is to be found in contemplation alone, by which the mind is uplifted, without the aid of the body, and gathered within itself so that it attains, to its inexpressible joy, a life akin to that of the immortal gods.[42]

Perhaps the word "contemplation" echoes the hermit Contemplation in book 1, canto 10 of Edmund Spenser's *The Faerie Queene*. The settings also suggest the relevance of the Redcrosse knight's experience to Adam's: Redcrosse's vision of the Celestial Jerusalem takes place on "an hill,"[43] and Adam's is set on "This hill" (11.367), much as *Paradise Lost* opens with references to Oreb, Sinai, and "th' Aonian Mount" (1.7 and 15). Since the knight's healing at the House of Holiness involves extensive regeneration on physical, psychological, and spiritual levels, the episode involves a more extended and religiously conventional rejuvenation than Adam's purgation "with Euphrasie and Rue." In each case, however, inner work precedes and enables trans-temporal vision.

Of course, by saying that God infuses human beings with "a certain divine spirit, a part of Himself," Milton is not stating that we *are* God or that we *contain* the whole of God. In *Christian Doctrine*, he even appears to contradict his earlier view by stating

> that when God breathed that breath of life into man, he did not make him a sharer in anything divine, any part of the divine essence, as it were. He imparted to him onely something human which was proportionate to divine virtue.

Further on, Milton widens the ontological gap by stating that "all form—and the human soul is a kind of form—is produced by the power of matter."[44] In other words, God created matter, and the soul is what results when form is imposed on matter. As Curry puts it, "Matter *per se* is completely passive and has no power within itself to produce anything until it is prepared for the reception of forms by the efficient cause, who is God."[45] This statement's reference to "forms" resonates meaningfully with Jung's sense in *Answer to Job* that "nothing can happen without a pre-existing pattern, not even creation *ex nihilo*, which must always resort to the treasure-house of eternal images in the fabulous mind of the 'master workman'" (*CW* 11, 641/405). Although it sounds as if Milton dissociates the soul from the "divine spirit" mentioned in the Prolusion, evidence from *Paradise Lost* suggests an alternative reading. If the soul is matter plus form, and if both participate in the "one first matter" that is God, then surely the soul—especially if inseparable from the physical body, as Milton believes—contains within it something of the divine. If Milton's God can say, "Boundless the Deep, because I am who fill / Infinitude, nor vacuous the space" (7.168–69), from what part of creation is he absent?[46] As Milton implies in his Prolusion, perhaps human consciousness, as in Campbell's *TOE*, not only constitutes a synecdoche for the divine whole but also contains a pattern of that whole. If so, then the human psyche not only *sums up* all the rungs on the scale of nature below the human station but also *participates in* all those above, including God's ability to behold "past, present, [and] future" (3.77–78). These possibilities, implicit in Milton's early thought, illuminate the mechanics of Adam's vision. His trance, "a more or less prolonged suspension of consciousness and inertness to stimulus,"[47] is a necessary precondition of Adam's vision because looking outward in time or space requires turning inward in meditation.

Adam's fractal, a pattern of the whole that links him to all that is, endures the Fall, though perception becomes less intuitive and more discursive (5.488)—a glass darkly. In Jungian terms, higher perception recedes into the unconscious. Yet in spite of foreknowing the Fall, God acknowledges that men will be "by degrees of merit rais'd" through "long obedience" (7.155–61). Flannagan calls this "the ultimate optimism of humankind's potential to work its way back up to Heaven"; and he adds that

> before (or even after) the Fall, humankind will be able to raise itself by degrees of merit, proving its obedience over a long period of time, to the

> point where the distinction between Heaven and Earth will no longer be necessary.[48]

Although the Fall corrupts physical matter, the link between human and divine is not completely severed because everything, through participation in "one first matter," is different in degree but not in substance and connected via the One Mind. As a result, it is possible for humans to enhance their intuitive reason and to transcend spatial and temporal limitations, though the Fall, along with the exigencies that becloud waking consciousness, makes such psychic functioning difficult. For Adam and Eve, the objective in the fallen world is to gain access, while still fully incarnate, to the timeless spiritual realm via inner means like dream and intuition, which survive the Fall, much as Campbell urges meditation as a conduit to spiritual enhancement. For example, Eve, who experiences some of the content of Adam's vision in a different type of altered state of consciousness, notes that "God is also in sleep, and Dreams advise, / Which he hath sent propitious" (12.611–12). "Eve acknowledges the fact that her dream is a vision of the future," says Flannagan.[49] In other words, the couple's visionary experiences are not only examples of the type of perception toward which humans may evolve but also a poignant reminder of what, if not lost, has been seriously impeded.

Yet the presence of the Scale of Being in book 5, along with the other bridges and bridge-like structures throughout the poem, underscores the dynamism of the human situation. One can work toward intuitive reason in hopes that one will "turn all to Spirit." One can descend to hell on Satan's causeway or ascend toward heaven on Jacob's ladder. It is this free will to choose that is ultimately expressed in the final lines of *Paradise Lost* when the narrator notes that Adam and Eve in the fallen world may "choose / Thir place of rest, and Providence thir guide" (12.646–47). The syntax allows dual readings that privilege the couple's free will: they will make choices with Providence as their guide, but they may also choose whether or not Providence will *be* their guide. They now head out into a landscape that is really an inscape of their own mortal condition, a fallen world where they will have to choose directionality on the Scale of Being—upward toward God or downward toward Satan. Contrary to a reductive monism, however, because the lower contains the higher, "finitude" is a function of point of view rather than an ironclad conclusion. As God acknowledges, Adam and Eve may make their way up the Scale of Being in spite of the Fall; for as with physics, so with a revisionist view of Milton's monism: to look within is to discover the whole universe because every part contains a pattern of the whole.

Notes

1 I use the term "Scale of Being" because Milton's ladder of reality includes the realm of angels. Jung's scale of creation includes only the natural world, and he revises the

hierarchy in the Great Chain of Being. Man is not at the top of the scale in Jung's estimation, a conclusion that arises from his observations in Africa: They [primitives] say that the wisest of all animals, the most powerful and divine of all beings, is the elephant, and then comes the python or the lion, and only then comes man. Man is by no means on top of creation: the elephant is much greater, not only on account of his physical size and force but for his peculiar quality of divinity. And really the look of wisdom in a big elephant is tremendously impressive. See Jung's *Zarathustra Seminar*, ed. James Jarrett (Princeton, NJ: Princeton University Press, 1988), 1393–94.

2 Dean Radin, *The Conscious Universe: The Scientific Truth of Psychic Phenomena* (New York: HarperEdge, 1997), 255.

3 John Milton, *Paradise Lost*, in *The Riverside Milton*, ed. Roy Flannagan (Boston, MA: Houghton, 1998). All references to the poem appear in the text.

4 F. David Peat, *Synchronicity: The Bridge Between Matter and Mind* (New York: Bantam, 1987), 196 and 154.

5 Thomas Campbell, *My Big TOE: A Trilogy Unifying Philosophy, Physics, and Metaphysics*, 3 vols. (United States: Lightning Strike, 2003).

6 Sir Thomas Browne, *Religio Medici*, in *The Broadview Anthology of Seventeenth-Century Verse & Prose*, ed. Alan Rudrum et al. (Peterborough, Canada: Broadview, 2000), 480.

7 Stephen M. Fallon, *Milton among the Philosophers: Poetry and Materialism in Seventeenth-Century England* (Ithaca, NY: Cornell UP, 1991), 186; and Barbara Kiefer Lewalski, *The Life of John Milton: A Critical Biography*, rev. ed. (Malden, MA: Blackwell, 2000), 476. I also considered commentary on Raphael's statement by the following critics: J. H. Adamson, "The Creation," in *Bright Essence: Studies in Milton's Theology*, ed. William Bridges Hunter et al. (Salt Lake City: University of Utah Press, 1971), 81–102; Walter Clyde Curry, *Milton's Ontology, Cosmology, and Physics* (Lexington: University of Kentucky Press, 1957) and "Milton's Scale of Nature," *Stanford Studies in Language and Literature*, ed. Hardin Craig (Stanford, CA: Stanford University Press, 1941): 173–92; Phillip J. Donnelly, "'Matter' versus Body: The Character of Milton's Monism," *Milton Quarterly* 33, no. 3 (1999): 79–85; D. Bentley Hart, "Matter, Monism, and Narrative: An Essay on the Metaphysics of *Paradise Lost*," *Milton Quarterly* 31, no. 1 (1996): 16–27; William B. Hunter, *The Descent of Urania: Studies in Milton, 1946–1988* (Lewisburg, PA: Bucknell University Press); Maurice Kelly, *This Great Argument: A Study of Milton's* De Doctrina Christiana *as a Gloss upon* Paradise Lost (Princeton, NJ: Princeton University Press, 1941); William Kerrigan, *The Sacred Complex: On the Psychogenesis of* Paradise Lost (Cambridge, MA: Harvard University Press, 1983); Michael Lieb, "Milton and the Metaphysics of Form," *Studies in Philology* 71 (1974): 206–24; Marjorie H. Nicolson, "The Spirit World of Milton and More," *Studies in Philology* 22, no. 4 (1925): 433–52; Denis Saurat, *Milton: Man and Thinker* (New York: Dial, 1925); and A. S. P. Woodhouse, "Notes on Milton's Views on Creation: The Initial Phases," *Philological Quarterly* 28, no. 1 (1949): 211–36.

8 Howard Schultz and Joy Schultz, "Metaphysics," in *A Milton Encyclopedia*, ed. William B. Hunter, Jr. et al., vol. 5 (Lewisburg, PA: Bucknell University Press, 1979), 116 and 119.

9 Hart, "Matter," 22 and 16.

10 John Milton, *Christian Doctrine*, in *Complete Prose Works of John Milton*, ed. Don M. Wolfe (New Haven, CT: Yale University Press, 1953–1982), 6:310, bk. 1, ch. 7.

11 Ibid., 6:216–17, bk. 1, ch. 5.

12 Ibid., 6:133, bk. 1, ch. 2.

13 Harris Francis Fletcher, *The Intellectual Development of John Milton* (Urbana: University of Illinois Press, 1961), 191; Catherine Gimelli Martin, "'Boundless the

Deep': Milton, Pascal, and the Theology of Relative Space," *English Literary History* 63, no. 1 (1996): 67; and Curry, *Milton's Ontology*, 45, 27, and 33.

14 Milton, *Christian Doctrine*, 6:309, bk. 1, ch. 7.

15 See Curry, *Milton's Ontology*, 40; Fallon, *Milton among the Philosophers*, 243; Hart, "Matter," 20; Kerrigan, *The Sacred Complex*, 163; and Saurat, *Milton*, 138.

16 Milton, *Christian Doctrine*, 6:308, bk. 1, ch. 7.

17 Curry, "Milton's Scale," 174.

18 Milton, *A Fuller Institution of the Arte of Logic*, in *Complete Prose Works of John Milton*, 8:230 and 232, bk. 1, ch. 7.

19 Fallon, *Milton among the Philosophers*, 119 and 121.

20 See Theodore E. B. Wood, *The Word "Sublime" and Its Context 1650–1760* (The Hague: Mouton, 1972); Sandy Feinstein, "Milton's Devilish Sublime," *Ben Jonson Journal: Literary Contexts in the Age of Elizabeth, James and Charles* 5 (1998): 149–66; and *OED*, s.v. "Spirits," def. I.1.a.

21 Sir Thomas Browne is aware of this distinction when he states that "it is but attending a little longer, and we shall enjoy that by instinct and infusion [intuitive reason] which we endeavour at here by labour and inquisition [discursive reason]." Browne is extolling the value of quiet contemplation versus a stressful striving for insight. See *Religio Medici*, in Rudman et al., *The Broadview Anthology*, 486.

22 The image is reproduced in Anthony Fletcher, *Gender, Sex, & Subordination in England, 1500–1800* (New Haven, CT: Yale University Press, 1995), n.p.

23 For a general study of this technique, see Max Nänny, "Chiasmus in Literature: Ornament or Function?" *Word & Image* 4 (1988): 51–59. Nänny mentions Milton on 52–54 and 56, citing at one point Brian Vickers, *Classical Rhetoric in English Poetry* (London: Macmillan, 1970), 153. My reading of Raphael's speech is in sync with Nänny's conclusion that "chiasmus is not just an ornament but . . . [also] an important structural device which fuses word and image" (58).

24 *OED*, s.v. "Spirit," def. I.1.d and 2.a–b.

25 The summary of Campbell's work is a slightly abridged excerpt from my review in *TMI Focus* 31, no. 3–4 (Summer/Fall 2009): 11–14, http://www.monroeinstitute.org/resources/book-reviews/my-big-toe.

26 Campbell, *TOE*, 1:181.

27 Because Campbell's three volumes cite no sources whatsoever, they tempt the unwary reader to believe that his thinking is original. Given the common ground with Milton's monism, the TOE is clearly not wholly original. The derivative nature of Campbell's thinking is also clear from the following quotation: "In wide-ranging speculation [William A.] Tiller even suggests that the universe itself started as a subtle energy field and gradually became dense and material through a similar ratchet effect." And "if this is true, it suggests that the human body is holographic in another way, for each of us truly would be a universe in miniature" (Michael Talbot, *The Holographic Universe* [New York: HarperCollins, 1991], 189). Talbot's source is William A. Tiller, "Consciousness, Radiation, and the Developing Sensory System," as quoted in *The Psychic Frontiers of Medicine*, ed. Bill Schul (New York: Ballantine, 1977), 95.

28 *Dictionary.com*, s.v. "Fractal"; and *OED*, s.v. "Fractal."

29 Peat, *Synchronicity*, 189.

30 Campbell, *TOE*, 2:140.

31 Milton, *Christian Doctrine*, 6:209, 211, and 219, bk. 1, ch. 5.

32 Adamson, "The Creation," 83.

33 As stated more emphatically in Sufi tradition, "'Thinkest thyself a puny form when within thee the universe is folded?'" quoted in Steven M. Greer, *Hidden Truth—Forbidden Knowledge* (Crozet, VA: Crossing Point, 2006, 25–26). For more on Greer, see chapter 5.

34 Peat, *Synchronicity*, 154 and 176.
35 Kerrigan, *The Sacred Complex*, 253.
36 Flannagan, *The Riverside Milton*, 575, n. 135.
37 Augustine, St., *The Literal Meaning of Genesis*, trans. John Hammond Taylor, vol. 2, in *Ancient Christian Writers*, ed. Johannes Quasten et al., no. 42 (New York: Newman, 1982), 194.
38 Robert Burton, *The Anatomy of Melancholy* (New York: Dutton, 1932), 1:254, 401, 423, 426; 3:344 and 372.
39 Margaret Miles, "Vision: The Eye of the Body and the Eye of the Mind in Saint Augustine's *De trinitate* and *Confessions*," *The Journal of Religion* 63, no. 2 (1983): 139.
40 Martin Jay, *Downcast Eyes: The Denigration of Vision in Twentieth-Century French Thought* (Berkeley, CA: University of California Press, 1993), 12.
41 Alfred Tennyson, "Ulysses," in *Victorian Poetry and Prose*, ed. Lionell Trilling and Harold Bloom (New York: Oxford University Press, 1973), 416–18, line 65.
42 Milton, Prolusion 7, in *Complete Prose Works*, 1:291.
43 Edmund Spenser, *The Faerie Queene*, in *Edmund Spenser's Poetry*, ed. Hugh Maclean and Anne Lake Prescott, 3rd ed. (New York: Norton, 1993), 131, I.x.46.
44 Milton, *Christian Doctrine*, 6:317 and 322; bk. 1, ch. 7.
45 Curry, "Milton's Scale," 189.
46 "For the Spirit of the Lord filleth the world . . . " (Solomon 1:7). See "Apocryphal or Deuterocanonical Books," *Christian Classics Ethereal Library*, http://www.ccel.org/
47 *OED*, s.v. "Trance," def. 2. The *OED* uses the passage on Adam's trance at 11.419–20 as an illustration of definition 1, "To throw into a trance," and also cites 1.301 where Satan and his legions "lay intrans't" in a more negative sense.
48 Flannagan, *The Riverside Milton*, 542, n. 56.
49 Ibid., 709, n. 187.

3

ALTERED STATES

"The Wanderer" and the psychology of sailing

As shown in chapter 2, Adam and Eve experience two of the possible types of psychic experience—vision and dream. Adam's vision takes place in a state of expanded awareness once the filters that attend waking consciousness are removed; and the vision, though it is described as externally enabled, arises from within him as a function of the fractal-like way in which a human being—or anything—contains the greater whole. The universe is "enfolded" within each of us (much like David Bohm's notion of the "implicate order"), and Adam's vision suggests that one can have access to all times and places if the "doors of perception are cleansed." Or as Maureen Caudill writes, "Perhaps entering an altered state is merely a way of accessing the other dimensions of our own selves."[1] Whereas Adam's vision exhausts him, Eve's dream takes place in the refreshing medium of sleep. In a sense, his experience depicts the conscious/masculine/active, whereas hers illustrates the unconscious/feminine/passive. But both vision and dream suggest that Adam and Eve carry with them an inner connection to the One Mind as they journey in the fallen world.

The present chapter on the Anglo-Saxon consolation "The Wanderer" bears various similarities to what has come before. Like Eve, the wanderer has a significant dream; and though it is not true in his case that "God is also in sleep," it is certainly true that "dreams advise." Like Eiseley, the wanderer experiences the limitations of physical nature and longs for spiritual fulfillment; but unlike Eiseley, he ultimately embraces faith in a creator God. The wanderer's experience, like Goodman Brown's, takes place in a setting that represents the unconscious. Instead of Hawthorne's forest, we now have the sea, which would resonate with Jung, who was himself a sailor. Indeed, the sea is a primary metaphor in his works, for it "always signifies a collecting-place where all psychic life originates, i.e., the collective unconscious" (*CW* 16, 15/12–13). He develops the relationship *between* the collective unconscious and consciousness in metaphorical terms as well.

> By virtue of its indefinite extension the unconscious might be compared to the sea, while consciousness is like an island rising out of its midst. This comparison, however, must not be pushed too far; for the relation of conscious to unconscious is essentially different from that of an island to

> the sea. It is not in any sense a stable relationship, but a ceaseless welling-up, a constant shifting of content; for, like the conscious, the unconscious is never at rest, never stagnant. It lives and works in a state of perpetual interaction with the conscious. Conscious contents that have lost their intensity, or their actuality, sink into the unconscious, and this we call forgetting. Conversely, out of the unconscious, there rise up new ideas and tendencies which, as they emerge into consciousness, are known to us as fantasies and impulses. The unconscious is the matrix out of which consciousness grows; for consciousness does not enter the world as a finished product, but is the end-result of small beginnings.
>
> (*CW* 17, 102/51)

Jung proposes that the unconscious is to consciousness as the sea is to an island; but he immediately recognizes the homology's inaccuracy—consciousness is not, in Shakespeare's words, "an ever-fixèd mark / That looks on tempests and is never shaken" (Sonnet 116). A better metaphor is needed to describe consciousness, and Jung finds it in seafaring. "The ship is the vehicle that bears the dreamer over the sea and the depths of the unconscious" (*CW* 12, 305/202). He also states that "despite our individual consciousness it ['the collective quality of the psyche'] unquestionably continues to exist as the collective unconscious—the sea upon which the ego rides like a ship" (*CW* 10, 285/138). Though the passage amounts to a mixed metaphor because he returns to island imagery, the right homology emerges: the unconscious, whether personal, collective, or both, is to the sea as consciousness is to a boat; those who wish to make psychological progress must dip their oars into the unknown.

The point for the wanderer, then, is that messages from the depths filter up to consciousness because solitude on the sea is conducive to psychic phenomena. In addition, projection paves the way for revelation:

> The darkness and depths of the sea symbolize the unconscious state of an invisible content that is projected. Inasmuch as such a content belongs to the total personality and is only apparently severed from its context by projection, there is always an attraction between conscious mind and projected content.
>
> (*CW* 12, 436/329)

The wanderer's experience illustrates this projection process: his solitary voyage on the sea removes barriers between the conscious mind and the unconscious so that the former registers the content of the latter. More precisely, it is the content of the personal unconscious that comes up to meet him in the "dream sequence," which is the term critics use for the passage that describes memory, dream, and hallucination. These phenomena signal inner work that enables the wanderer to shift toward the wholeness of the Self by moving from pagan heroism to classical wisdom and finally to Christian faith.

Before beginning our journey through the poem, it is worth quoting a longer passage from *Psychology and Alchemy* that includes many points relevant to the wanderer's situation:

> The sea is the symbol of the collective unconscious, because unfathomed depths lie concealed beneath its reflecting surface. Those who stand behind, the shadowy personifications of the unconscious, have burst into the *terra firma* of consciousness like a flood. Such invasions have something uncanny about them because they are irrational and incomprehensible to the person concerned. They bring about a momentous alteration of his personality since they immediately constitute a painful personal secret which alienates and isolates him from his surroundings. It is something that we cannot tell anybody. We are afraid of being accused of mental abnormality—not without reason, for much the same thing happens to lunatics. . . . [Isolation] causes an activation of the unconscious, and this produces something similar to the illusions and hallucinations that beset lonely wanderers in the desert, seafarers, and saints. The mechanism of these phenomena can best be explained in terms of energy. Our normal relations to objects in the world at large are maintained by a certain expenditure of energy. If the relation to the object is cut off there is a "retention" of energy, which then creates an equivalent substitute. For instance, just as persecution mania comes from a relationship poisoned by mistrust, so, as a substitute for the normal animation of the environment, an illusory reality rises up in which weird ghostly shadows flit about in place of people. That is why primitive man has always believed that lonely and desolate places are haunted by "devils" and suchlike apparitions.
>
> (*CW* 12, 57/48–49)

The passage is very true to the spirit of the wanderer's experience in the poem. He is unable to tell anyone about his inner pain because that degree of self-revelation is not part of the Anglo-Saxon warrior's heroic ethic. Repression is the rule, but spending time alone on the sea "causes an activation of the unconscious," which enables the repressed material to surface as hallucinations. These are "shadowy personifications of the unconscious" and "weird ghostly shadows [that] flit about in place of people," but their appearance means that the wanderer is moving toward "momentous alteration of his personality." In particular, "The Wanderer" is a poem about a man's transition from pagan life to Christian faith. Since the psychic phenomena in the dream sequence all relate to the wanderer's past experiences, the poem illustrates the movement within his personal unconscious toward greater wholeness and well-being. This movement—from a pagan past to greater spiritual life, via a hallucination of psychic content during a difficult and lonely voyage on the sea—is essentially the three-part pattern of the hero's journey in Joseph Campbell's *The Hero with a Thousand Faces*.[2] The journey is an archetype, and the wanderer's journey in the poem is an archetypal image that arises from culture and constitutes myth. In this way, the personal and the collective commingle in the poem.

So far, Jungian psychology fits "The Wanderer" with great precision; but whether there is more to be said remains to be seen. It may be that the wanderer's hallucination is not just the product of a brain that is dreaming while he is awake but also the reappearance of the spirits of his fallen comrades. Of course, as I stressed in the introduction, Jung is skeptical regarding psi in the absence of supporting data and tends to psychologize phenomena that may be paranormal. In the absence of evidence, he does not want to take a firm stand, as in this passage about the existence of a "Universal Mind":

> Psychology accordingly treats all metaphysical claims and assertions as mental phenomena, and regards them as statements from certain unconscious dispositions. It does not consider them to be absolutely valid or even capable of establishing a metaphysical truth. We have no intellectual means of ascertaining whether this attitude is right or wrong. We only know that there is no evidence for, and no possibility of proving, the validity of a metaphysical postulate such as "Universal Mind."
>
> (*CW* 11, 760/476)

Maybe there is, and maybe there is not, such a thing as Universal Mind. But the metaphysical criticism that is the subject of this book recognizes the need to look at a phenomenon like the wanderer's hallucination of his old friends not just as a psychological curiosity but also as a visitation by the spirits of his old friends. Along the way, there will be opportunities to bring in related material about the strange experiences of lone voyagers.

Previous Criticism. Source-based criticism of "The Wanderer" has focused almost entirely on works that predate the poem such as the Bible, Latin literature, and the Church Fathers, or on contemporaneous works such as Anglo-Saxon homilies.[3] A smaller number of scholars read the poem from the vantage point of theory or literature that postdates the poem itself. For example, D. S. Brewer, noting a parallel passage in Melville's "John Marr," suggests "a remarkably close similarity between them [the two poems] in their connection with the sea, their sense of loss, their bitter-sweet memory of past comradeship." Melville's use of the word "float" to describe the "shadowy fellowship" of the old seaman's past companions enables Brewer to offer a sensible gloss on the words *swimman* and *fleotan*. Thus,

> if it can be shown that the poetic meaning normally given to the passage arises spontaneously in another poem written in English by a sailor, on a similar subject, then we have some evidence that the meaning itself may be natural and unforced.[4]

This reading strategy suggests that "The Wanderer" as sea literature—and the dream sequence in particular—can benefit from an openness to insights sparked by later sailing writers who may not have been familiar with the poem. Adopting Brewer's retrospective method, the present chapter demonstrates a heightened sense of verisimilitude and thematic unity within the poem by offering a positive reading of the dream sequence in light of a body of material that has been overlooked by all previous critics. The actual accounts of singlehanded sailors since the 1890s, in combination with recent psychological and paranormal research, reveal the positive potential of dreaming at sea.

The critical consensus has been that waking from a dream of his former life drives home the enormity of the wanderer's loss and emphasizes the need to change from a gold-driven *comitatus* relationship with his lord, which he still seeks, to wisdom and faith. But the "dream sequence" itself is viewed with overwhelming negativity. Antonia Harbus believes that the wanderer has two dreams (not a dream, then a hallucination) and that they oppose his spiritual progress. Constance B. Hieatt notes that in medieval dream theory (Macrobius) dreams can be either true or false. Similarly, Andrew Galloway and his source Peter Clemoes see nothing in dream theory (Ambrose) to suggest that the wanderer's dream is true. Even G. V. Smithers, who suggests that "The Wanderer" depicts the soul setting out on the path taken by the dead, fails to affirm anything positive in the dream sequence. Roy F. Leslie, however, correctly understands

> the psychological phenomena which overtake the solitary are when mind and spirit are taxed by sorrow. His experience is clearly of three kinds, each involving the resurrection of the past in a different form, each more intense and less subject to his control than the one which precedes it: memory, dream, and hallucination.[5]

But the wanderer's sorrow over his lost companions only partly accounts for his dream and hallucination. Equally important is the effect of being on the sea in a small craft. *Eardstapa* (translated as "wanderer" but literally as "earth-stepper") suggests terrestrial wandering, but modern critics have held that at least part of the wanderer's experience involves travel on the sea. There the wanderer is not likely to see men's faces on another ship, as W. J. B. Owen and Suzie I. Tucker maintain.[6] Robert Hasenfratz offers this excellent summary of views on the wanderer's hallucination:

> These phrases have been variously interpreted as the hovering ghosts of the Wanderer's dead friends, who "swim" or melt away; a boat load of warriors in a neighboring ship; a ship or fleet which floats away, the abstract embodiment of his memories, and, finally, as dream-images of his dead companions which suddenly turn out to be seabirds as he wakes from his dream.

Nor, in an offshore setting, is the hallucination attributable only to seagulls, as Graham Midgley holds.[7] Instead, the motion, isolation, and sleepless fatigue of a sea voyage are conducive to altered states of consciousness—frequent vivid dreams, which yield to hallucination. My approach also invalidates an issue that has been debated since B. Huppé published his work on the poem's theme and structure in 1943: namely, whether the poet recounts his own seafaring or creates an imaginary voyager.[8] At our distant remove from the 10th century, to argue one way or the other is to commit the intentional fallacy. The key point is that the dream sequence, whether actual or fictitious, is described in highly verisimilar terms. Like Melville in "John Marr," the Anglo-Saxon poet created the same psychological phenomena that lone voyagers have written about in our own age. Whereas the prevailing premise has been that the dream is false, the remainder of this chapter, using the experiences of singlehanded sailors, reinterprets the dream sequence by showing the positive potential of dreaming at sea.

The wanderer's boat and its psychological effects

The wanderer's psychological duress will come into clearer focus if we first consider a crucial element of the setting: his boat. Modern singlehanded sailors have crossed the Atlantic in monohulls ranging from the from the 5'4" *Father's Day* to the 236-foot *Club Mediterranée*.[9] But the most typical craft for lone sailing—for reasons of economy and ease of handling—range from 25 to 40 feet, a size highly conducive to the fatigue that produces altered states of consciousness. The wanderer's boat, made either of skin sewn over a wooden framework or of lapstrake planking, cannot exceed 20 feet—large enough to travel on the open sea but small enough to be handled by one person.[10]

If the wanderer's boat was a small oar-powered craft, modern seafaring provides an important analogue. John Ridgway and Chay Blyth rowed across the Atlantic in the late 1960s and lived to tell the story of their adventure in their appropriately-titled book, *A Fighting Chance*. Their dory, *English Rose III*, was 20-feet in length, but it had been specially designed for ease of rowing, seaworthiness, load-carrying ability, and shelter.[11] In addition, Blyth and Ridgway were British Army paratroopers in top physical condition (at the time, Blyth had left the military, but Ridgway was still active). Our wanderer, by contrast, suffers "what the Anglo-Saxon culture took to be the ultimate in hardships: destitution, and enforced separation from one's kindred or clan."[12] The total loss of his former life and the attendant sorrow make it highly unlikely that he would have been able to summon the physical strength to row or sail for days on the open sea. In order for such a man to make headway under oar power, the craft would have had to be small indeed—probably equivalent in size to an east coast rowing dory, or 10–14 feet in length.

The wanderer's boat is crucial to an understanding of his psychological vulnerability. Being alone on a wintry sea in a small open boat, not as a sportsman in summer like Ridgway and Blyth but as a castaway, signals the same extreme vulnerability to altered states of consciousness experienced by modern singlehanded sailors. Whereas a modern sailor is virtually certain of arriving safely at the destination in all weather even in a micro-cruiser, calamity was an ever-present possibility in Anglo-Saxon times. For example, Green quotes Sidonius, "a fifth-century nobleman of Roman Gaul," in connection with the crews of craft from which Viking ships descended: "'to these men [rowers] a shipwreck is capital practice rather than an object of terror. The dangers of the deep are to them, not casual acquaintances, but intimate friends.'" Green continues: "Historians have sometimes suggested that Sidonius exaggerated, but a study of these boats confirms that the risks of shipwreck must have been great."[13] If the risks were great for a crew of able-bodied men on a vessel of 50 feet or more, one can easily imagine the wanderer's vulnerability alone in his open boat. And if his psychological vulnerability is even greater than that of modern singlehanders, then their experiences of dream and hallucination are all the more relevant to the poem.

Fully apart from the sorrow the wanderer feels, the conditions of a small boat voyage on the open sea—constant rhythmic movement, monotonous sound, and isolation, acting together as a nautical analogue to the sensory-deprivation chamber—make the content of the unconscious extraordinarily available to conscious perception. As Henderson notes, for example, "rhythmic motions produced by wave action can contribute to a tendency to hallucinate."[14] Such phenomena have a clinical designation—Restricted Environmental Stimulation Therapy or Technique (REST), which has been the subject of over one thousand articles over the last forty years (some of them on sailors and Antarctic explorers). For our purposes Peter Suedfeld's summary of its effects will suffice to set the scene for the dream sequence in "The Wanderer." When the mind is deprived of external stimuli, or when external stimuli are monotonous, the mind compensates by shifting its focus inward toward dream, hallucination, and other perceptual phenomena that occur at the borderline between sleep and wakefulness. The shift is accompanied and enabled by enhanced performance of the right hemisphere (intuition) and a diminution of left hemispheric functions (analysis, language, and logic). Suedfeld states:

> The hypothesis that REST is an environmental way to achieve the temporary dominance of right hemisphere functioning is certainly an intriguing one, and is compatible with the view that the situation is an externally structured analogue of meditation and similar states.[15]

EEG results confirm that stimulus deprivation causes a slowing of alpha waves and an increase in the theta wave activity that characterizes sleep. Further results of REST include facilitated problem solving, increased persuasibility, and eventual attitude destabilization.

Elements of REST parallel the findings of The Monroe Institute® in Virginia, founded by Robert A. Monroe whose work is the subject of the next chapter.

TMI uses an audio technology called Hemi-Sync® to synchronize the brain's left and right hemispheres and to shift brain-wave activity into the theta range. In combination with a state of deep relaxation, Hemi-Sync enables conscious access to altered states, including levels on which departed souls exist. A recent description of the sound technology by Joseph M. Felser suggests that it works, somewhat like Adam's trance, by stripping away conscious distractions. Hemi-Sync

> is essentially what I would call a blinder-removal tool, an anti-technology technology, or a cultural deprogramming device. Properly speaking, Hemi-Sync isn't a vehicle that takes you to some other place; it just helps you remove the narrow limits on your natural, wider perception. Then you can see what is—and that you are, in fact, already—There. Which is, of course, right Here.[16]

REST and TMI's research have prompted some authors to claim that dreaming and the hypnogogic state are portals to highly relevant information, even communication with other realms. If so, the unconscious mind can provide authentic transport, not just false imagery. Sounding remarkably like Jung, Joseph McMoneagle asserts that "the subconscious is the gateway to the great unknown. That is the fertile ground from which the psychic information comes; it has access to all knowledge, all realities, and all possibilities."[17] As in Adam's vision, one may view distant times and places in an altered state of consciousness. McMoneagle ought to know: he is a world-class remote viewer and former psychic spy for the U.S. Army. In light of the factual authenticity of present-day psychic functioning, the notion that the wanderer's dream and the paranormal experiences of modern sailors may be something other than false imagery begins to take on a measure of credibility. This sense is confirmed by numerous modern singlehanded sailors, whose unusual experiences directly parallel the wanderer's.

Singlehanded sailing and altered states

Dreams, which the wanderer *oft* experiences, are a clear extension of memories of his former life with his lord and fellow thanes.

> "Even in slumber his sorrow assaileth,
> And, dreaming he claspeth his dear lord again,
> Head on knee, hand on knee, loyally laying,
> Pledging his liege as in days long past.
> Then from slumber he starts lonely-hearted.
> Beholding gray stretches of tossing sea,
> Sea-birds bathing, with wings outspread,
> While hailstorms darken, and driving snow.

> Bitter then is the bane of his wretchedness,
> The longing for loved one: his grief is renewed."
> (lines 35–44)

I take the poem's shift at this point from first to third person to be the speaker's stylized way of chronicling his own experience, rather than a sign that he is talking about someone else. The shift suggests that his wanderings participate in a larger pattern of human experience; but it also suggests that he has transcended his earlier pagan life and now, as he speaks the poem, enjoys present enlightenment. The reader should note that the original poem was untitled, lacked quotation marks and was ambiguous in both narrative and syntax. If any interpretation necessarily involves an act of completion, viewing the wanderer himself as speaker despite the shift to third person is a valid approach. (A modern example of this person-shift technique suggesting transcendence of past experience appears at the end of Milton's "Lycidas.")

Harbus and other critics of the wanderer's dream have overlooked the fact that the transition from dreaming about what one desires to awakening into a setting that cannot support it is highly characteristic of singlehanded sailors' experiences, as circumnavigator Tania Aebi comically illustrates in *Maiden Voyage*: "Often, I'd awaken, calling out to somebody or reaching up to grab for a roast chicken, an ice cream cone or a fresh salad." Later she offers an excellent account of the phenomenon of dreams at sea:

> I began to have whoppers of dreams that were so vivid I had trouble differentiating them from reality. . . . Friends turned up in the oddest places and we would have long conversations. . . . I . . . watched as the dreams overflowed into my days, triggering a vast variety of memories and solutions to problems worked out during the night.[18]

The frequency and vividness of Aebi's dreams at sea relate to sensory deprivation, and dreaming of old friends clearly parallels "The Wanderer"; but her final statement is more suggestive for our study of the poem because it transcends dreams' startling clarity. The isolation and sensory deprivation of a singlehanded passage unlock the portal to the unconscious mind. When Aebi's waking mind was troubled by a problem, her unconscious mind, in sleep, found a solution, which she remembered and implemented after waking up. This instance of problem solving suggests that dreams can be a vehicle through which complementary parts of the psyche work together to promote one's well-being.

Whereas Aebi regards her dreams only as a curiosity worth noting, Robin Knox-Johnston, the first person to sail around the world nonstop, speculated on the significance of his dreams at sea:

> I wondered at the capacity of the subconscious mind to store vast quantities of information which we are unable to unlock. So often when

> one awakes and can vividly recall a dream it appears to be nonsensical, but the experience of recalling forgotten people made me wonder whether these other dreams should not be taken more seriously.[19]

Knox-Johnston's comment on the "subconscious mind" takes on special significance in light of McMoneagle's statement about the subconscious as the gateway "to all knowledge, all realities, and all possibilities." Perhaps Aebi and Knox-Johnston were in some way present with their old friends when they dreamed about them; and perhaps the wanderer enjoys something more likely from a present-day point of view—a brief reunion with his fallen comrades who have awakened into the realm of pure spirit. Psychic explorer Bruce A. Moen supports the theory that dreams enable such communication between the living and the dead:

> The levels of consciousness in which dreams occur include the same levels in which people in the Afterlife exist. So, the easiest way for you to communicate from the Afterlife with a physically living person [or the reverse] is during their dreaming.[20]

Given this possibility, the seascape's inability to sustain the content of the wanderer's dream does not obviate his genuine comfort among old friends, which it provides through psychic transport to the pagan afterlife. In dreams, spirits find a bridge between their world and the psyche of living persons. The dream does not have to be false and unsustainable in the waking world for the wanderer to be misguided in his search for another lord. In fact, a true dream at this point would heighten the poem's dramatic logic: upon awakening, the wanderer feels the enormity of his loss to a greater degree if his dream is true, though he is not yet ready to search for an alternative to his previous life.

In the annals of sailing non-fiction, the most famous dream experience, recorded by Captain Joshua Slocum in his account of the first solo circumnavigation in the 1890s, supports the sense of other-worldly possibility in the wanderer's dream.[21] Delirious with cramps, Slocum passed out on the cabin sole and later awoke to find a man dressed in the rig "of a foreign sailor" at the helm of the *Spray*. Said the man,

> I have come to do you no harm. I have sailed free . . . but was never worse than a *contrabandista*. I am one of Columbus's crew . . . I am the pilot of the *Pinta* come to aid you. Lie quiet, señor captain . . . and I will guide your ship to-night.

The part of Slocum's story most significant for the wanderer's dream occurs the next night. "Then who should visit me again but my old friend of the night before, this time, of course, in a dream. 'You did well last night to take my advice,' said he, 'and if you would, I should like to be with you often on the voyage, for the love of adventure alone.'" Slocum concludes: "I awoke much refreshed, and with the feeling that I had been in the presence of a friend and a seaman of vast experience."

Either Slocum's hallucination and subsequent dream were mere projections of his own mind and therefore false (though a great yarn), or the pilot of the *Pinta*, who had "sailed free" of his physical body, was actually present, in which case extreme physical discomfort broke down the barrier separating Slocum's conscious mind from the afterlife. As Moen observes, "A state which thins the boundary between the physical and nonphysical worlds such as great physical or emotional distress [the wanderer experiences both, of course] can make it possible" to communicate with a living person. Similarly, Ken Eagle Feather recalls that "the extreme fatigue served a purpose in allowing me to briefly touch another level of myself" and that "fatigue took me beyond my everyday concerns to a deeper level of myself." The Native American vision quest provides yet another example. Through fasting, self-mortification or mutilation, a brave receives a spiritual manifestation in the form of a trance, vivid dream or advice from a spirit or the Great Spirit.[22] Jung supports this point in stating,

> A great many ritualistic performances are carried out for the sole purpose of producing at will the effect of the *numinosum* by means of certain devices of a magical nature, such as invocations, incantations, sacrifice, meditation and other yoga practices, self-inflicted torture of various descriptions, and so forth.
>
> (*CW* 11, 7/7)

In light of the enhanced well-being brought by the experience of the *numinosum*, it is especially interesting that Slocum's account (hallucination, *then* dream) reverses the order of these phenomena in the poem. His dream is the sign of recovered psychological balance, and the promise of the pilot's continuing presence must have given him pleasure and security.

It is possible, of course, to have negative and debilitating psi experiences while at sea, the prime example being *The Strange Last Voyage of Donald Crowhurst*.[23] While competing in the same round-the-world race as Knox-Johnston, Crowhurst suffered from the kind of fatal psychological distress from which the wanderer draws back. Without ever leaving the south Atlantic, Crowhurst falsified his log book to make it look as if he had made eastward progress so that he could later head north and pretend to finish, but not win, the race. When it became clear that so many competitors had dropped out that he might actually win if he finished, he succumbed to a sense of guilt and jumped overboard. His boat *Teignmouth Electron*, a 40-foot Arthur Piver trimaran, which was unsuited for sailing in great southern ocean, was found abandoned. In other words, his psyche unraveled along with his scheme. As the months wore on, his perception expanded. Though believing that he was decoding the meaning of the universe, it was more likely that he was experiencing delusions of prophetic brilliance. In addition, he found himself "hallucinating beasts of the Sargasso Sea" but evidently had genuine psychic experiences as well. In his journal he maintains "that he has the power to free his mind from his 'physical existence'—that is to say, his body—whenever he wishes. To float away from *Teignmouth Electron* as a disembodied soul!"[24] The authors seem unconvinced, but astral projection is one of the expanded states of consciousness that can be produced by extended isolation. Other sailors have experienced the same phenomenon—seeing a ship while out of body and, hours later, actually encountering it in the physical waking state. A description aptly appears in the Anglo-Saxon poem "The Seafarer": "Yet still, even now, my desire outreaches, / My spirit soars over tracts of sea, / O'er the home of the whale, and the world's expanse."[25]

The wanderer's dream may be correspondingly positive (that is, a reunion with old friends); but it is situated between a memory of his comrades and a hallucination of them, the latter reflecting an even higher order of distress. Henderson's common-sense explanation of the transition from dream to hallucination is a helpful gloss on the dream sequence in "The Wanderer": "If we are denied dreams through lack of sleep, we are subject to an alternative in the form of hallucinations, which are very near relatives of dreams." When a mariner dreams, his conscious mind is either asleep or awake, depending mainly on the wind and waves. Borrowing terms from stimulus deprivation researcher John C. Lilly, Henderson then identifies two types of hallucinations: a "'fatigue' type caused by exhaustion and lack of sleep," and a "'surplus-energy' type, caused primarily by monotony. In reference to the latter type, psychiatrists may use the term 'stimulus deprivation.'"[26]

In illustrating the fatigue type, however, Henderson overlooks the verifiable truth of some paranormal experiences at sea, a point that is relevant to the wanderer's predicament. The following story, originally told by Frank Robb, is especially remarkable because it occurred before the days of depth sounders in small craft.[27] Fatigued after four days of heavy weather in the Caribbean, a sailor reportedly found a busy protected harbor, anchored in eight fathoms and fell asleep. The next morning he awoke to find his boat indeed anchored but with no land in sight. Henderson stresses the illusion of the harbor and disregards the truth of the sounding: the sailor's unconscious mind accurately identified a 48-foot anchorage in the middle of a vast expanse of open water. The hallucination of the harbor provided justification for the conscious mind to accept the truth about the water depth so that the man could get some sleep. Robb's story is important because it identifies an element of objectively verifiable truth in a sailor's hallucination and demonstrates the possibility of authentic psychic experience on board a small craft. Of course, hallucinations at sea may be completely illusory, as were Robert Manry's on board the 13-foot *Tinkerbelle* in the middle of the Atlantic. Manry's hallucinations are highly relevant to our poem because his boat was approximately the same length as the wanderer's. He experienced hallucinations that lasted for hours; for example, one imaginary person motivated him to sail around in circles in search of an island. Manry offers this explanation:

> The lack of sleep and the drug I took to keep myself alert no doubt accelerated the appearance of the hallucinations, but the visions themselves were largely the result of my mind's efforts to cope with the solitude and danger. My mind invented people, both friends and enemies, so that I wouldn't be alone or without help in facing the hazards of the vast, empty ocean.[28]

A common parallel is that many lone sailors have experienced an undeniable inner order to wake up when their boats have been in danger, usually from an approaching ship—a phenomenon Henderson dismisses as "*déjà vu*, the illusion of having already experienced something actually experienced for the first time."[29] As in Robb's story, such an order indicates that the isolation and sensory deprivation of lone voyaging enable, exactly as Jung recognized, greater communication between the conscious mind and the unconscious. Here again is ostensibly objective evidence that an unconscious process responds to an actual physical condition. It is not just, as McMoneagle states, that the unconscious is the portal to all knowledge but also that some higher part of oneself—an aspect of oneself normally hidden from consciousness—has an investment in the physical body and does not want it to be crushed by the hull of a passing ship.

The notion of the "higher self" calls to mind strange phenomena that Charles Lindbergh experienced during his Atlantic crossing. Jung is aware that "such a situation [pilots' isolation above the earth] provides the ideal conditions for spontaneous psychic phenomena, as everyone knows who has lived sufficiently long in the solitude, silence, and emptiness of deserts, seas, mountains, or in primeval forests" (*CW* 10, 648/341). Reflecting directly on Lindbergh's experience, Reinhold Niebuhr suggests that the higher self or soul transcends body and mind:

> In Charles Lindbergh's account of his memorable flight across the Atlantic two decades ago, he gives an admirable account of the unity and the difference between the self and its body and mind. The statement occurs in his description of his effort to master physical fatigue after thirty hours of flying across the Atlantic. He writes: "For immeasurable periods I seemed divorced from my body as though I were an awareness, spreading through space, over the earth and into the heavens, unhampered by time and substance, free from the gravitation that binds men to heavy human problems of the world."[30]

The experience of expanded awareness is similar in nature to Crowhurst's, but Lindbergh's much more positive outcome is apparently due to its short duration. Whereas Crowhurst languished at sea for months, Lindbergh's Atlantic crossing took only 33.5 hours; and the wanderer's sea travel may be even shorter, for he otherwise would be unlikely to survive the poor conditions.

The true object of sailors' psychological experiences (a proper anchorage, a need to wake up) supports the veracity of the dream sequence in "The Wanderer." His hallucination finds a further positive parallel in the literature of singlehanded sailing.

> "The forms of his kinsmen take shape in the silence;
> In rapture he greets them; in gladness he scans
> Old comrades remembered. But they melt into air
> With no word of greeting to gladden his heart.
> Then again surges his sorrow upon him;
> And grimly he spurs his weary soul
> Once more to the toil of the tossing sea."
> (lines 46–51)

Peter Heaton summarizes a modern-day analogue, in which the reference to sleep suggests that the account is another example of a fatigue hallucination. While crossing the Atlantic, Peter Woolass "found himself below decks conversing with his brother and his daughter, who had been on board shortly before he set sail. He even found himself making tea for three!" Woolass fell asleep and, upon waking, wept to find them no longer there.[31] In each case, the "forms" are either true or not. In the wanderer's case the fleetingness of the images reinforces his need to make a transition to a life not based on "'seeking a gold-lord,'" as he puts it earlier in the poem (line 23). In order to worship God, one must abandon hope of further service to Mammon and self-glorification through acquiring the things of this world. I differ from critics like Harbus, however, in finding something positive: the dream sequence in "The Wanderer" reflects not only a stage of material attachment that the lone wanderer must overcome on his way to wisdom and faith but also a transitional phase between old pagan ways and the secular wisdom of the wise man. When physical extremity opens the portal to the unconscious, a lone sailor can improve his life, given the heightened persuasibility experienced in REST. If the wanderer's higher self is actively guiding his personal growth, the dream sequence is a hinge between having a lord and realizing that all earthly things pass away, rather than a static state that the wanderer must overcome—false imagery yields to the truth of Christ.

The wanderer's friends comfort him while he is still receptive to their positive presence, but they take their leave at the moment of his greatest fatigue when physical and mental extremity have opened him to the development of wisdom. I do not think that the wanderer experiences a vision at this point; however, my reading of the hallucination does suggest that it shares a common element with vision: the image of his comrades may reflect their genuine presence. Moreover, if we give credence to Smithers's view that a sea journey represents a journey to the land of the dead, then a further possibility emerges: the wanderer's fallen companions have come to help him leave his physical body, but they return to the world of pure spirit when he decides to stay in this world. Either way, the psychology of sailing supports the position that the dream sequence is dynamic. Elizabeth A. Hait's sense that the wanderer is "pulled in two directions at once, back toward the hall-joys of the past and forward toward the heavenly kingdom" is only the surface truth. A more fundamental conclusion is that of D. G. Calder, who states that "the visions have taught him [the wanderer] that his own exile and his own loss were but types of the whole pattern of loss and mutability in the world."[32] In other words, the wanderer's journey on the sea enacts an archetypal pattern, but his waking contact with his unconscious mind helps him transcend his old heroic values and embrace wisdom and Christian faith.

Notes

1 Maureen Caudill, *Suddenly Psychic: A Skeptic's Journey* (Charlottesville, VA: Hampton Roads, 2006), 168–69.

2 Joseph Campbell, *The Hero with a Thousand Faces* (Princeton, NJ: Princeton University Press, 1985).

3 Cross considers the book of Job; Galloway and Clemoes, Ambrose's *Hexaemeron*; Harbus, Anglo-Saxon poetry and medieval dream lore; Hasenfratz, a parallel to Virgil's *Aeneid*; Lumiansky, Boethius's *The Consolation of Philosophy*; and Smithers, Anglo-Saxon homilies and Latin ecclesiastical writings. See J. E. Cross, "On the Genre of *The Wanderer*," *Neophilologus* 45 (1961): 63–75; Andrew Galloway, "Dream-Theory in *The Dream of the Rood* and *The Wanderer*," *The Review of English Studies* 45, no. 180 (1994): 475–85; Peter Clemoes, "*Mens absentia cogitans* in *The Seafarer* and *The Wanderer*," in *Medieval Literature and Civilization: Studies in Memory of G. N. Garmonsway*, ed. D. A. Pearsall and R. A. Waldron (London: Athlone, 1969), 62–77; Antonia Harbus, "Deceptive Dreams in *The Wanderer*," *Studies in Philology* 93, no. 2 (1996): 164–79; Robert Hasenfratz, "*Wanderer*, lines 45–57 and the Birds of Diomede," *Journal of English and Germanic Philology* 92, no. 3 (1993): 309–24; R. M. Lumiansky, "The Dramatic Structure of the Old English *Wanderer*," *Neophilologus* 34 (1950): 104–12; and G. V. Smithers, "The Meaning of *The Seafarer* and *The Wanderer*," *Medium Ævum* 26, no. 3 (1957): 137–53.

4 D. S. Brewer, "*Wanderer*, Lines 50–57," *Modern Language Notes* 67, no. 6 (1952): 389–99. Despite the parallel to Melville's character who stands on land, I maintain below that our wanderer is at sea. All Old English quotations are taken from Roy F. Leslie's edition of *The Wanderer* (Manchester, UK: University of Manchester Press, 1966). Quotations in modern English translation, including "The Seafarer," are from Charles W. Kennedy, trans., *An Anthology of Old English Poetry* (New York: Oxford University Press, 1960). References to "The Wanderer" are cited in the text.

5 For past opinion of the dream sequence, see Harbus, "Deceptive Dreams"; Constance B. Hieatt, *The Realism of Dream Visions: The Poetic Exploitation of the Dream-Experience in Chaucer and His Contemporaries* (The Hague: Mouton, 1967), 23–33; Clemoes, "*Mens absentia*"; Galloway, "Dream-Theory," 481; Smithers, "The Meaning," 138–39; and Leslie, introduction to *The Wanderer*, 8. See also Hasenfratz, "*Wanderer*"; Galloway, "Dream-Theory"; Mary Rohrberger, "A Psychoanalytic Reading of 'The Wanderer,'" *Cimarron Review* 1, no. 2 (1967): 70–74; Steven F. Kruger, *Dreaming in the Middle Ages*, Cambridge Studies in Medieval Literature, no. 14 (New York: Cambridge University Press, 1992); Hieatt, *The Realism of Dream Visions*, 23–33; "Dreams," in *Harper's Encyclopedia of Mystical & Paranormal*

Experience, ed. Rosemary Guiley (New York: HarperCollins, 1991), 158; and Macrobius, *Commentary on the Dream of Scipio*, trans. William Harris Stahl, Records of Civilization, Sources and Studies, no. 48 (New York: Columbia University Press, 1952), 87–90. For a more detailed discussion of the criticism on the poem, see my essay, "'The Wanderer' and the Psychology of Sailing," in *Reading the Sea: New Essays on Sea Literature*, ed. Kevin Alexander Boon (New York: Fort Schuyler, 1999), 77–99.

6 W. J. B. Owen, "*Wanderer*, Lines 50–57," *Modern Language Notes* 65, no. 3 (1950): 163; and Susie I. Tucker, "Return to *The Wanderer*," *Essays in Criticism* 8, no. 3 (1958): 234.

7 Hasenfratz, "*Wanderer*, lines 45–57," 310. For interpretations of *swimman* and *fleotan*, see Graham Midgley, "*The Wanderer*, Lines 49–55," *Review of English Studies* n.s. 10, no. 37 (1959): 53–54; and Owen, "*Wanderer*, Lines 50–57."

8 B. Huppé, "The *Wanderer*: Theme and Structure," *Journal of English and Germanic Philology* 42 (1943): 516–38. Elliott, Gordon, Lumiansky, and Tucker believe that "The Wanderer" describes a real experience. Greenfield and Rumble hold that the experience is imaginary. See Ralph W. V. Elliott, "The Wanderer's Conscience," *English Studies* 39, no. 5 (1958): 193–200; I. L. Gordon, "Traditional Themes in *The Wanderer* and *The Seafarer*," *The Review of English Studies*, n.s. 5, no. 17 (1954): 1–13; Lumiansky, "The Dramatic Structure"; Tucker, "Return"; S. B. Greenfield, "*The Wanderer*: A Reconsideration of Theme and Structure," *Journal of English and Germanic Philology* 50 (1951): 451–65; and Thomas C. Rumble, "From *Eardstapa* to *Snottor on Mode*: The Structural Principle of 'The Wanderer,'" *Modern Language Quarterly* 19, no. 3 (1958): 225–30.

9 In 1968, the record was set by the 6-foot *April Fool*. For this boat and *Club Med*, see Richard Henderson, *Singlehanded Sailing: The Experiences and Techniques of the Lone Voyagers*, 2nd ed. (Camden, ME: International Marine, 1988), 46 and 32. For information on *Father's Day*'s record-breaking 1993 passage, see David G. Bolduc, "Famous Small Boats," 2009, http://www.microcruising.com/famoussmallboats.htm (accessed July 30, 2012).

10 The history of ancient watercraft supports this point. See Percy Blanford, *An Illustrated History of Small Boats: A History of Oared, Poled and Paddled Craft* (Buckinghamshire, UK: Spurbooks, 1974), 22 and 29; Tim Severin, *The Brendan Voyage* (New York: Avon, 1978); and Charles Green, *Sutton Hoo: The Excavation of a Royal Burial-Ship* (London, UK: Merlin, 1963), 63. For an inquiry into how a Viking-type ship would have sailed, see Edwin and Joyce Gifford, "The sailing characteristics of Saxon ships as derived from half-scale working models with special references to the Sutton Hoo ship," *The International Journal of Nautical Archaeology* 24, no. 2 (1995): 121–31.

11 John Ridgway and Chay Blyth, *A Fighting Chance* (Philadelphia: Lippincott, 1967); and "Atlantic Rowing History," *The Atlantic Rowing Race*, http://challengebus.co.uk/race/tarr/history/htm.

12 Leonard H. Frey, "Exile and Elegy in Anglo-Saxon Christian Epic Poetry," *Journal of English and Germanic Philology* 62, no. 2 (1963): 294.

13 Green, *Sutton Hoo*, 49.

14 Henderson, *Singlehanded Sailing*, 72–73.

15 Peter Suedfeld, *Restricted Environmental Stimulation: Research and Clinical Applications* (New York: Wiley, 1980), 44. See also Peter Suedfeld and Jean L. Kristeller, "Stimulus Reduction as a Technique in Health Psychology," *Health Psychology* 1, no. 4 (1982): 337–57.

16 Joseph M. Felser, *The Myth of the Great Ending: Why We've Been Longing for the End of Days Since the Beginning of Time* (Charlottesville, VA: Hampton Roads, 2011), 185.

17 Joseph McMoneagle, *Mind Trek: Exploring Consciousness, Time, and Space Through Remote Viewing*, 2nd ed. (Charlottesville: Hampton Roads, 1997), 188. For more on McMoneagle, see chapter 7.
18 Tania Aebi with Bernadette Brennan, *Maiden Voyage* (New York: Simon and Schuster, 1989), 55 and 95.
19 Robin Knox-Johnston, *A World of My Own* (New York: Pocket, 1971), 128.
20 Bruce A. Moen, "Answers to Frequently Asked questions," *Afterlife Knowledge*, http://www.afterlife-knowledge.com/answers.html (accessed July 30, 2012). See also Moen's four-volume *Exploring the Afterlife Series* (Charlottesville, VA: Hampton Roads, 1997–2001).
21 Joshua Slocum, *Sailing Alone Around the World* (1900; repr. New York: Dover, 1956), 39–42.
22 Moen, "Answers"; Ken Eagle Feather, *Travelling with Power: The Exploration and Development of Perception* (Charlottesville, VA: Hampton Roads, 1992), 30 and 47; and "Vision quest," in Guiley, *Harper's Encyclopedia*, 634.
23 Nicholas Tomalin and Ron Hall, *The Strange Last Voyage of Donald Crowhurst* (New York: Stein and Day, 1970).
24 Ibid., 236 and 239.
25 "The Seafarer," in Kennedy, *An Anthology of Old English Poetry*, 20.
26 Henderson, *Singlehanded Sailing*, 72. See also the excellent examples in the section on "Hallucinations and Voices" in Andrew Evans, *Thoughts, Tips, Techniques & Tactics For Singlehanded Sailing*, The Singlehanded Sailing Society, www.sfbaysss.org/tipsbook, section 2.4 (accessed July 30, 2012).
27 Henderson, *Singlehanded Sailing*, 73.
28 Robert Manry, *Tinkerbelle* (New York: Harper, 1966), 233.
29 Henderson, *Singlehanded Sailing*, 72.
30 Reinhold Niebuhr, *The Self and the Dramas of History* (New York: Scribner's, 1955), 26. See also Charles Lindbergh, *The Spirit of St. Louis* (New York: Scribner's, 1953).
31 Peter Heaton, *The Singlehanders* (London, UK: Hastings House, 1976), 171.
32 Elizabeth A. Hait, "The Wanderer's Lingering Regret: A Study of Patterns of Imagery," *Neophilologus* 68, no. 2 (1984): 287; and D. G. Calder, "Setting and Mode in *The Seafarer* and *The Wanderer*," *Neuphilologische Mitteilungen* 72, no. 2 (1971): 272. See also Galloway, "Dream-Theory," 483.

4

OUT-OF-BODY EXPERIENCE

Metaphor in Monroe's metaphysical trilogy

There is a metaphysical dimension to the wanderer's experience—specifically, his hallucination is an extrapsychic event in which his dead friends come to help him make a transition, and they withdraw when he decides to stay in the world and embrace classical wisdom and Christian faith. Jung would find this interpretation hard to swallow, as he signals in his essay "The Soul and Death" (1934). He writes, "I shall certainly not assert now that one must believe death to be a second birth leading to survival beyond the grave," though he acknowledges that all the great religions do so (*CW* 8, 804/408). Earlier, in "The Psychological Foundations of Belief in Spirits" (1920), he reduces souls to autonomous complexes from the personal unconscious and spirits to complexes from the collective unconscious (*CW* 8, 591/312), so that spiritual manifestation is simply a matter of projection. Though acknowledging "universal reports of . . . post-mortem phenomena in the form of ghosts and haunting," he is convinced that "ghosts and suchlike have to do with *psychic* facts of which our academic wisdom refuses to take cognizance, although they appear clearly enough in our dreams" (*CW* 8, 598/316; my emphasis).

Over a decade later, in "The Ascent of the Soul" (1946), Jung takes a much different position, though it comes with a contextual qualifier. In commenting on the "Rosarium Philosophorum," he states that "as in real death, the soul departs from the body and returns to its heavenly source" (*CW* 16, 475/267).[1] It could be that this statement is merely a theoretical view rather than a personal position; but perhaps, in subtle ways, his point of view shifts so that he gravitates in his work to a series of illustrations that provide an opportunity to acknowledge the soul as a continuous essence. Whereas the earlier reluctance to affirm life after death reflects the scientist in Jung who desires to discuss death in terms of energy, teleology, telepathy, and psyche (he does not actually say anything about the soul), the greater acceptance of an afterlife in his later remark may reflect his own near-death experience (NDE) in 1944, following a heart attack at the age of sixty-eight. His experience—described in *Memories, Dreams, Reflections*, chapter 10, and in a letter that he wrote to Kristine Mann in 1945—is a classic NDE.[2]

In the vision, Jung's consciousness is a thousand miles out in space, over the Middle East and the Mediterranean Sea. "The sight of the earth from this height was the most glorious thing I had ever seen." Floating in space, he sees a stone temple where a black Hindu sits in the lotus position. As he approaches the temple, his Earth life is "sloughed away," leaving only his experiences and accomplishments. As he prepares to enter the temple, his doctor appears in the vision and calls him back to Earth. He writes, "Dr. H. had been delegated by the earth to deliver a message to me, to tell me that there was a protest against my going away. I had no right to leave the earth and must return." The vision abruptly ceases. Following the experience, Jung suffered weeks of depression and had to relearn the will to live. Apparently, the NDE connects him to his psychic potential. During those weeks, he would awaken in the middle of the night in a state of ecstasy—"as though I were floating in space . . . in a state of purest bliss, 'thronged round with images of all creation.'" As his health improves, however, the visions grow "fainter" and disappear altogether within three weeks. He caps off the account by stating,

> Although my belief in the world returned to me, I have never since entirely freed myself of the impression that this life is a segment of existence which is enacted in a three-dimensional boxlike universe especially set up for it.[3]

He embraces the world but forever perceives its limitations.

Six pages into the story of the NDE, Jung asserts that "the visions and experiences were utterly real; there was nothing subjective about them; they all had a quality of absolute objectivity." That is, the visions actually took place; but a question remains. "I had reached the outermost limit, and do not know whether I was in a dream or an ecstasy" (*MDR*, 289). Here is the scientist's dilemma of not knowing whether his visions—real though they were to him—are intrapsychic ("a dream") or extrapsychic ("an ecstasy"). Was his experience one of the "subjectively experienced levitations in moments of extreme derangement" that he notices in his patients, or was it akin to "the parapsychic levitations reported of many saints" (*CW* 16, 477/268; 15, 149/95)? This standard dilemma is best expressed in 2 Corinthians 12:2–4, where Paul refers to himself in the third person:

> I know a man in Christ who fourteen years ago was caught up to the third heaven—whether in the body or out of the body I do not know, God knows. And I know that this man was caught up into Paradise—whether in the body or out of the body I do not know, God knows—and he heard things that cannot be told, which man may not utter.[4]

Whereas Jung had an NDE at an advanced age when he had an understanding of myth and psyche that helped him process it, Robert A. Monroe (1915–1995), a secular businessman, first experienced the out-of-body state in 1958 at the age of forty-two but had no prior knowledge of occult lore, mysticism, or spirituality. And whereas Jung had only one such experience, Monroe's out-of-body experiences (OBEs) continued for over thirty years, nearly until his death in 1995 at the age of seventy-nine. While out-of-body, he explored the physical world and the astral plane, eventually turning over his OBEs to his higher self. At first, Monroe's OBEs involved a conscious separation from the physical body—a bilocation, ecstasy, or standing apart that made him wonder if he was dying or going crazy. Over the course of many years, he developed the ability to phase shift into other realms without having to float out of his body. In other words, Monroe's OBEs were eventually neither In Here nor Out There but both. Therefore, Jung's uncertainty about his NDE—dream or ecstasy?—is the wrong question because there really is no difference. What Jung experienced was both intrapsychic *and* extrapsychic because, as in a hologram, the part (a single mind) is a copy of the whole (the One Mind). The drop is not just a part of the sea but a whole ocean unto itself. Monroe's achievement thus resolves the mystic's dilemma in a way that is compatible with the principle of unity that is this book's premise.

Both Jung and Monroe use poetry to address the issue of separation and duality versus the true unified nature of reality—a state of oneness in which earthly opposites are reconciled. Jung's poem in *Seven Sermons to the Dead* highlights a series of opposites: effective and ineffective, fullness and emptiness, living and dead, difference and sameness, light and darkness, hot and cold, force and matter, time and space, good and evil, beauty and ugliness, one and many. His point regarding these dualities is that "in the pleroma they are balanced and void; in us not," for "the pleroma hath no qualities."[5] We perceive our "three-dimensional boxlike universe" in terms of opposites that disappear if we shift our attention to the basement level of reality. Similarly, Monroe's poem expresses both the presence of opposites and their reconciliation in unity, and it does so more fully and eloquently. Whereas Jung in *Seven Sermons* is apparently responding to questions from nonphysical persons, a nonphysical source provides Monroe with insight in a form he calls a "ROTE" (Related Organized Thought Energy), for which "thought ball" and "gestalt" are reasonable synonyms. The poem is Monroe's linear articulation of that ROTE in the medium of language. It emphasizes a series of qualities over duality: change (not beginning or end), remembering (not teacher or student), expression (not good or evil), oneness (not union or sharing), love (not joy or sadness), balance (not greater or lesser), motion (not stasis or entropy), being (not wakefulness or sleep), and plan (not limit or chance).[6] The poem thus emphasizes the contrast between separation via duality and the unity of all things via the One Mind. Jung's comment in "On Life after Death," the chapter that follows his NDE, is helpful here. He states, "One, as the first numeral, is unity. But it is also '*the* unity,' the One, All-Oneness, individuality and non-duality—not a numeral but a philosophical concept, an archetype and attribute of God, the monad."[7]

Monroe's poem appears toward the end of his final book, *Ultimate Journey*, the volume in which his vision of reality culminates; he was already an old man when he published it in 1994. In contrast, Jung was in his early forties when he composed *Seven Sermons to the Dead* in 1916. It was not a work that he was proud of; in fact, it so embarrassed him that he kept it out of *The Collected Works*.[8] Although Jung backed away from his channeled text, Monroe would have approved of its insights. The most one can say is that Jung's NDE possibly made him *less skeptical* about the existence of an afterlife in some nonphysical dimension. He writes:

> Although there is no way to marshal valid proof of continuance of the soul after death, there are nevertheless experiences which make us thoughtful. I take them as hints, and do not presume to ascribe to them the significance of insights.[9]

The statement refers primarily to dreams, and only a hard-headed scientific point of view accounts for a statement about "valid proof of continuance" when one has had as profound an NDE as Jung's. At this point, Monroe, though he would still be patient with Jung, would remind the great psychologist that some dreams, *as* OBEs, should be taken literally and that rather than applying the theory of the unconscious to the afterlife, Jung should attempt to turn "beliefs" into "knowns" by finding out for himself through meditation.

That sort of exploration is what Monroe's three books are all about. *Journeys Out of the Body* (*JOOB*) is Monroe's attempt to overcome doubt and fear and to establish objective evidence that his consciousness is traveling outside his physical body. The middle volume, *Far Journeys* (*FJ*), shows him growing in confidence, doing experiments, and adding categories of experience to his resume. *Ultimate Journey* (*UJ*) is a remarkably successful attempt to use language to record experiences that lie *beyond* language but about which he has no doubts. It may be said that Jung mapped the psyche or the soul, but Monroe's three books map his own past lifetimes and establish a cosmology of the Earth Learning System that includes not only our "three-dimensional boxlike universe" but also a series of gradations of energy that surround the planet. Although metaphysicians and parapsychologists have taken note of Monroe's achievements, the English profession has not yet applied the tools of literary criticism to his works. But just as mainstream culture is catching up with Monroe, I hope that my discussion of his texts will bring them closer to canonical status as visionary works of American literature. The goal of this chapter, then, is to consider the metaphorical cosmology that Monroe maps out in his three volumes.[10]

Monroe's three texts deal with the cutting edge of consciousness exploration in ways that demonstrate, beyond a reasonable doubt, the objective reality of his experiences. He blends the anecdotal approach that characterizes metaphysical literature with some degree of the scientific rigor that characterizes laboratory-based parapsychology. But he is also an iconoclast, using his OBEs as the basis for making provocative statements about prayer, heaven, hell, God, and reality in *Journeys Out of the Body*, chapter 8, entitled "'Cause the Bible Tells Me So"—statements that he intends to explode religiously and scientifically conservative paradigms. Monroe's remarks in *Far Journeys* and *Ultimate Journey* inform the earlier experiences on which he reflects in that provocative chapter. Of particular relevance is a series of "rings" that center on the earth; they are not actual places but what Monroe's biographer, Ronald Russell, calls "metaphors for states or phases of consciousness."[11] Monroe later called them "focus" levels, but that terminology is not part of the nomenclature of *Journeys Out of the Body*.[12] Here in the rings and in other locales that Monroe visits nonphysically, two truths emerge as paramount: thoughts are things, and like attracts like.

Monroe's metaphorical cosmology

Monroe discovers, in the nonphysical world, that "thoughts are things" and "like attracts like" are organizing principles. Specifically, around the physical earth are a series of "recycling rings" or "human energy rings" or "semitransparent radiant globes" (*FJ* 94 and 101; *UJ* 32). He means that these concentric spheres are where souls go before they recycle back into the physical plane, each ring containing a collection of souls who share the same "frequencies" or thought patterns (*FJ* 64). His metaphor for this ring system is the "Interstate" because he perceives it to be "a major highway into the Unknown" (*UJ* 110). The "entry ramps" are physical death (*UJ* 228); there are "exit ramps" for the various soul states (*UJ* 126 and 202–3); there are "highways and byways" (*UJ* 14); and he eventually discovers "a bridge or bypass over . . . [the dangerous] areas—with Caution signs posted along the way" (*UJ* 124). More properly, the Interstate of Consciousness is a "conceit," or extended metaphor. "Death is an entry ramp" (a metaphor) participates in "the Interstate of Consciousness" (a conceit made up of multiple related metaphors). The difference is like that between a politician who, like a sniper, "takes out" his opponent and a whole political campaign, with lots of secondary metaphors—weapons, allies, battlegrounds, skirmishes, Pyrrhic victories, etc. But it is difficult to stay within the confines of a single conceit: politics is also a boxing match, a geological event, a horse race, and more. It is so with Monroe as well. Helpful as the "Interstate" conceit may be, it does not suffice. Other metaphors are needed, and none of them completely suffices to describe a realm that is beyond language. The Afterlife is a ring system, except when it is an interstate, except when it is something else; and in any case, the language is not the thing itself.[13]

Monroe understands these rings to have a coherent pattern. Halfway out is what he calls the "null point" (*FJ* 199), a sort of dividing line between souls for whom the space-time illusion is foremost and souls for whom nonphysical reality is the primary construct. The closer to the Earth a ring appears, the more spatial-temporal its inhabitants will be, and the sooner they will reincarnate; the farther beyond the null point, the more *non*spatial-temporal the inhabitants will be, and the longer they remain before reincarnation. The individual rings, though not infinite, expand to accommodate different types of human experience. Again, thoughts are things: as new thoughts arise, they are accommodated in the afterlife.

A few examples will illustrate the organization just sketched. The innermost ring is for souls who fail to realize that they are no longer physically alive.

They therefore attempt to participate in physical life without success; they are "totally and compulsively bonded to time-space materiality," with "extreme distortions of the original survival imprint" (*FJ* 239–40). One may rightly assume that such souls are sometimes perceived as ghosts. Closely akin to these sad souls are those who know that they are dead but who remain addicted to the physical world and are unaware of other possibilities; this area includes those whom Monroe calls "Wild Ones," souls who assume that, because they are dead, their bad behavior no longer matters (*FJ* 240). The best example, analogous to the second circle of Dante's Inferno, is called the Flesh Pile, a "huge mass of ex-physical humans, [who are] writhing and struggling in an endless [futile] attempt to have sex with one another" (*UJ* 128). They are so addicted to sex that they are undeterred by lack of copulative success and "unaware of any other existence" (*FJ* 89). Monroe cannot even get their attention.

Out from there, Monroe found the largest ring, which contains what he calls the Belief System Territories. I want to pause on that concept and provide some examples relevant to his chapter because this is where "heaven" and "hell" are located in the Monroe cosmology (*FJ* 245).[14] The Belief System Territories are an area with as many "exit ramps" as there are addictive human beliefs. The area is for those who know that they are dead but who are unable to transcend particular thought patterns. Remember: thoughts are things, and like attracts like. Monroe writes of the inhabitants, "*Their belief system is all they have to go on. So they go where they think there is some kind of security*" (*UJ* 175; Monroe's emphasis here and below). Judgment means going where one belongs. For example, a belief system territory is where one goes to be with those who share the same dogmatic religious beliefs, a potentially offensive notion to fundamentalists. In such a region, a female soul calls the astrally projected Monroe "*spawn of the devil*" (*FJ* 195); and another female remarks, "*Our minister says there is no such person as a visitor here*" (*FJ* 199). He also encounters a male soul who is slightly more self-aware and who has the opposite view of earthly religion: "'Nobody told me it was going to be like this! Those bastards yelling and screaming about gates of heaven, hellfire and damnation—they didn't know what they were talking about!'" (*UJ* 121). Nonetheless, it is probably here in the Belief System Territories that Monroe encounters something that reminds him of common preconceptions of heaven: an experience of "indescribable joy" so intense that his guide has to shield him from it (*FJ* 179).

There are three rings beyond the Belief System Territories. The next one is for "*Fantasy Land*" or "The Park" (*FJ* 196 and *UJ* 237), an area that other authors sometimes call "Summerland." Jung mentions the park in *Synchronicity: An Acausal Connecting Principle* as "a glorious, park-like landscape shining in the brightest colours, and in particular an emerald green meadow with short grass, which sloped gently upwards beyond a wrought-iron gate leading into the park" (*CW* 8, 950/508). This description appears in a section of the treatise where Jung is discussing NDEs. Monroe writes, "It was a place to calm down in after the trauma of physical death—a way station, for relaxation and decision as to what to do next" (*UJ* 237). As in the Belief System Territories, thoughts are things: the Park is a "human creation" (*UJ* 238). Here souls may do whatever they want, provided that they do not violate anyone else's free will. Beyond the Park is a ring for "Last-Timers" who await their final incarnation. And beyond that are the "I-There" clusters—soul groups "containing all [of one's] previous and present lifetimes" (*UJ* 139), which await the return of their individual parts. Eventually Monroe discovers that he is a probe or scout sent from his soul cluster to play a crucial role in its development.

Earlier I referred to the Flesh Pile—the greatest hell in Monroe's works—as Dantesque; but that is only partly correct. In the rings as in the Inferno, thoughts are things; but in Monroe's cosmology progress is possible because thoughts can be dynamic. As souls become "*hooked*" (*FJ* 142) on the earth experience, they drop to a lower ring with each incarnation; but there is also upward progress even in the afterlife. A terrific example comes not from Monroe but from a student of his system of meditation named Bruce Moen whose book *Voyage Beyond Doubt* contains a chapter entitled "Max's Hell." In life, Max was "a mean-spirited, gifted, emotional sadist," who now inhabits "a Hell made to order for him. Everyone living there with him, every man, woman, and child, had the same emotionally sadistic nature he did!" Like attracts like. He is now trapped in "a vicious circle of sadism," which he both inflicts and suffers. But thoughts are things: "If he ever begins to question his choice of beliefs," writes Moen, "it will be the beginning of leaving his Hell. . . . He'll be pushed out of his Hell by a repulsive force."[15]

The I-There cluster's short-term goal is to recover errant probes like Max, but its long-term objective is to achieve "escape velocity" (*FJ* 246)—that is, to acquire enough experience and love energy to escape the addictive gravity of the Human Compressed Learning System. (The metaphor has shifted from geometry to driving to rocketry, complete with "lift-off points" [*FJ* 261]). Then souls just disappear, which may be what Monroe observes in "'Cause the Bible Tells Me So":

> At the Signal ["almost like heraldic trumpets"], each living thing lies down—my impression is on their backs, bodies arched to expose the abdomen . . . with head turned to one side so that one does not see Him as He passes by. The purpose seems to be to form a living road over which He can travel. I have gleaned the idea that occasionally He will select someone from this living bridge, and that person is never seen or heard from again. . . . As He passes, there is a roaring musical sound and a feeling of radiant, irresistible living force of ultimate power that peaks overhead and fades in the distance. . . . Is this God? Or God's son? Or His representative?
>
> (*JOOB* 122–23)

Because Monroe marvels at this powerful entity but does not answer any of his own questions, the passage invites discussion. What actually happens here, and is there a role for thoughts in a soul's disappearance? It may be that thoughts have sufficiently matured to prepare a soul for another lifetime on Earth, incarnation in another planet's learning system, the departure of the I-There cluster, a higher realm of spiritual experience, or surrender of individual consciousness in union with thc Godhead.

The final metaphorical pieces of Monroe's cosmology—metaphorical because language can only indirectly capture the essence of ineffable experience in the nonphysical world[16]—lie beyond the I-There clusters: an "Aperture," though which one enters and exits the Earth Learning System; and an "Emitter," the energy source that creates the hologram or dream in which we live (*UJ* 215–16 and 219). The Creator, whose existence Monroe affirms, lies beyond Aperture and Emitter (*UJ* 224) but is not the God of Sunday school lessons, much less Jesus the Christ.

The realm of pure spirit that we have just charted, from earth to infinity, includes one of the states that Monroe mentions in "'Cause the Bible Tells Me So": the terror of demons or demon-like beings that try to gnaw at him. Just as the Flesh Pile is a perversion of the survival instinct, the gnawing demons are perversions of the predatory instinct; indeed he proposes a "predator theory" of earthly life.[17] Howard Storm's near-death experience provides a helpful gloss on Monroe's text. Storm writes:

> Now I was being forced by a mob of unfeeling people toward some unknown destination in the encroaching darkness. They began shouting and hurling insults at me, demanding that I hurry along. The more miserable I became, the more enjoyment they derived from my distress. . . . The hopelessness of my situation overwhelmed me. I told them I would go no further, to leave me alone, and that they were liars. I could feel their breath on me as they shouted and snarled insults. They began to push and shove me about. I began to fight back. A wild frenzy of taunting, screaming, and hitting ensued. . . . These creatures were once human beings. The best way I can describe them is to think of the worst imaginable person stripped of every impulse of compassion.[18]

Storm encounters Monroe's "nibbling and tormenting beings" (*JOOB* 120) in an area of the Interstate that Monroe eventually learns to pass through unimpeded and quickly as if on the previously mentioned "bridge." Again, thoughts are things, and like attracts like: Storm experiences such negativity because he lived a life of bottled-up anger, "devoid of love, hope, and faith" and centered on self-interest. He writes, "It dawned on me that I was not unlike these miserable creatures that had tormented me."[19]

Unlike the gnawing hell, Monroe's experience includes a place that corresponds to stereotypical notions of heaven, where he encounters "pure peace"; exquisite emotions, particularly love and joy; warm clouds; and pleasing colors, music, and shapes. He has the sense that this is "Home."

> Each of the three times I went There, I did not return voluntarily. I came back sadly, reluctantly. Someone helped me return. Each time after I returned, I suffered intense nostalgia and loneliness for days. I felt as an alien might among strangers in a land where things were not "right," where everything and everyone was so different and so "wrong" when compared with where you belonged. Acute loneliness, nostalgia, and something akin to homesickness. So great was it that I have not tried to go There again. Was this heaven?
>
> (*JOOB* 123–25)

Later he realizes that "Home" is not in the nonphysical part of the Earth Learning System at all; it is rather his extraterrestrial—and nonphysical—point of origin, which he arbitrarily calls KT-95. Apparently his spiritual essence is *nonhuman*. When he later returns to Home he discovers why he left in the first place: the clouds, the music, the colors—everything is on "a repeating loop" (*UJ* 26). He left Home prior to his many physical Earth incarnations because of curiosity to experience something new. He now realizes that he does not belong there because there is "no growth, nothing new to learn or experience" (*UJ* 30). Home is "a blind alley" (*UJ* 209). To sum up, Monroe's experiences of gnawing beings and of Home in "'Cause the Bible Tells Me So" seem to take place outside the Belief System Territories, where he later came to locate heaven and hell: the gnawing beings are close to the Earth, and Home is extraterrestrial. Only the heaven-like place of "indescribable joy" may be part of a belief system.

Monroe concludes his chapter with the admission that he misremembers "as a child swimming in a pool that had underwater deep-hued colored lights set in the wall." He tries to recreate the effect in his "country home" but later discovers, upon visiting "the site of my childhood[,] that the pool had no colored lights under water." The chapter's last word is "Reality, Reality!" (*JOOB* 126). Thus a segment critical of prayer and heavily laden with eschatological speculation ends not with more of the same but on a lighthearted note that suggests an important question. If thoughts are things and reality is malleable, may even an incorrect memory be true in some sense? Apparently, the observer has influence even if the object of perception is one's own memories.

Conclusions

Jung would appreciate Monroe's emphasis on the role of psyche—thought—in determining one's destiny in the afterlife. They are alike in valuing individuation, the process of making the unconscious conscious; but it would be easy to overestimate the similarities between the two thinkers. Psychotherapy and OBE, though they both effect a similar movement toward psychic wholeness, are vastly different endeavors. Since Monroe's first book was published in 1971, there was no chance that Jung, who died in 1961, could have heard about him. But Monroe had probably heard of Jung. Although there are no direct references to him anywhere in Monroe's three books, the chapter that follows "'Cause the Bible Tells Me So" does nod in Jung's direction. It is called "Angels and Archetypes," and it concerns the assistance Monroe received from nonphysical guides during various OBEs. The title is a misnomer because there is neither any reason to believe that these helpers are angels nor any mention of what Jung defined as archetypes. Jung would find the imprecise use of his term a bit annoying and would probably read Monroe's experiences on the astral plane as exercises in active imagination, in keeping with his tendency to view the metaphysical through a psychological lens.

Here, though, is just one of many examples from *Journeys Out of the Body* that suggest the literal reality of Monroe's astral travels. The story unfolds in chapter 3, "On the Evidence." On a Saturday between 3:00 and 4:00 p.m., he decides to visit a female business associate, R.W., who knows of his abilities but has not been apprised of his present intention to project himself to her location at the New Jersey shore and communicate with her. He finds her in a kitchen, sitting in a chair and conversing with two teenage girls (a blond and a brunette). The three of them are consuming beverages. Monroe is unable to attract the girls' attention, but when he asks if R.W. knows that he is there, she replies in the affirmative. Monroe suspects that her "*superconscious*" is communicating with him because her conscious mind is still engaged in a conversation with the girls. When he asks if she will remember his visit, she states that she is certain that she will. Just to make sure, though, Monroe "pinche[s] her in the side, just above the hips and below the rib cage," which she finds so physically painful that she cries out, "'*Ow*'" (*JOOB* 56). Always seeking confirmation of his nonphysical experiences, Monroe asks her the next Tuesday about his visit.

> *Here is what she reported today: On Saturday between three and four was the only time there was not a crowd of people in the beach cottage where she was staying. For the first time, she was alone with her niece (dark-haired about eighteen) and the niece's friend (about the same age, blond). They were in the kitchen-dining area of the cottage from about three-fifteen to four, and she was having a drink, and the girls were having cokes. They were doing nothing but sitting and talking.*

R.W. remembers nothing else until Monroe asks her if she remembers the pinch.

> *A look of complete astonishment crossed her face.*
>
> *"Was that you?" She stared at me for a moment, then went into the privacy of my office, turned, and lifted (just slightly!) the edge of her sweater where it joined her skirt on the left side. There were two brown and blue marks at exactly the spot where I had pinched her.*
>
> *"I was sitting there, talking to the girls," R.W. said, "when all of a sudden I felt this terrible pinch. I must have jumped a foot. I thought my*

> *brother-in-law had come back and sneaked up behind me. I turned around, but there was no one there. I never had any idea it was you! It hurt!"*
>
> (*JOOB* 57)

Monroe goes on to list six things that confirm the reality of the experience: location, number of persons, description of the girls, the actions of those present, acknowledgement of the pinch, and a resulting physical mark. The account is anecdotal, but some of Monroe's other verifiable experiences take place in a laboratory setting. If objective evidence supports his journeys out of the body to points in the physical world, then those in the nonphysical world deserve careful consideration as states of awareness that anyone can achieve. OBEs may have an "archetypal" or intrapsychic element, but Monroe's experiences point to the realm of the extrapsychic.

What this means for literary study is simple. A portrayal of an OBE should be understood as a genuine metaphysical event. Consider, for example, what happens to Frederick Henry near the beginning of *A Farewell to Arms* when he is hit by a mortar blast:

> I felt myself rush bodily out of myself and out and out and out and all the time bodily in the wind. I went out swiftly, all of myself, and I knew I was dead and that it had all been a mistake to think you just died. Then I floated, and instead of going on I felt myself slide back. I breathed and I was back.[20]

The experience is akin to Jung's description in *Synchronicity: An Acausal Connecting Principle* (published in 1952, eight years after his NDE) of the "very distinct and impressive sensation of hallucination of levitation" that persons with "a severe head injury" sometimes experience (*CW* 8, 948/506). The passage is particularly relevant to Hemingway's account because both describe an NDE caused by severe injury. From a psychological point of view, hallucination is a logical conclusion, which aligns with Jung's tendency to psychologize an event by shearing away its spiritual dimension. In a metaphysical reading of Jung's remark, the injured man's soul lifts out of his body in much the same way that Henry describes. Unlike Jung, he does not travel a thousand miles out into space or have profound visions; unlike Monroe, he does not connect with guides, chart the Interstate, or pinch a female colleague. Henry does not range far from his physical body and is soon back in it; but his NDE is clearly a metaphysical moment, not a mere hallucination, because he realizes that "it had all been a mistake to think you just died." In keeping with Monroe's dictum that we *are* more than our physical bodies, Henry realizes that death is not the terminal point that he, in his atheism and materialism, previously assumed. Frederick Henry's tragedy, then, is that he fails to integrate the realization that consciousness survives physical death into a belief system that acknowledges the afterlife.

Consequently, when his lover Catherine Barkley dies in childbirth, there is no spiritual consolation available to him like the wanderer's Christian faith. Rather than making a connection between her transition to the realm of pure spirit and his own brief NDE, Henry is limited to such consolation as the world around him provides, which is none at all. Catherine becomes a statue, and he walks back to their hotel in the rain.

Notes

1 I quote and discuss the relevance of Jung's comments to Shakespeare's *A Midsummer Night's Dream* in *A Jungian Study of Shakespeare: The Visionary Mode* (New York: Palgrave Macmillan, 2009), 34–35.
2 *MDR*, 289–98; and *C. G. Jung: Letters*, ed. Gerhard Adler and Aniela Jaffé, trans. R. F. C. Hull, Bollingen Series 95, vol. 1 (Princeton, NJ: Princeton University Press, 1973), 357–58. See also Barbara Hannah, *Jung: His Life and Work—A Biographical Memoir* (New York: Putnam's, 1976), 276–84; and Ronald Hayman, *A Life of Jung* (New York: Norton, 1999), 379–80.
3 *MDR*, 295.
4 *Harper Study Bible*, ed. Harold Lindsell (Grand Rapids, MI: Zondervan, 1971), Revised Standard Version.
5 C. G. Jung, *Seven Sermons to the Dead*, in *The Gnostic Jung*, ed. Robert A. Segal (Princeton, NJ: Princeton University Press, 1992), 183–85.
6 Robert A. Monroe, *Ultimate Journey* (New York: Doubleday, 1994), 217. Monroe's other books are *Journeys Out of the Body*, updated ed. (1971; New York: Doubleday, 1977) and *Far Journeys* (New York: Doubleday, 1982).
7 *MDR*, 310.
8 Segal, introduction to *The Gnostic Jung*, 36.
9 *MDR*, 312.
10 In my article on Monroe's work, I devote significant attention to his precarious critique of mainstream religion in chapter 8 of *JOOB*, "'Cause the Bible Tells Me So." See "Thinking Metaphysically: The Challenge to Fundamentalism in the Works of Robert A. Monroe," *Peer English: The Journal of New Critical Thinking* 3 (2008): 91–104.
11 Ronald Russell, *The Journey of Robert Monroe: From Out-of-Body Explorer to Consciousness Pioneer* (Charlottesville, VA: Hampton Roads, 2007), 320.
12 In Monroe's system, Focus 10 is the state of "mind awake and body asleep"; Focus 12, expanded awareness; Focus 15, the state of "no time"; Focus 18, heart energy; and Focus 21, the bridge between the physical world and the nonphysical world. Focus 22 is the zone of those in comas, on drugs, or under anesthesia. In Focus 23 souls are strongly attached to the physical plane and may not know that they are dead. Focus levels 24–26 are the Belief System Territories. Focus 27 is the Garden or Park inhabited by souls who are not subject to restricting belief systems. Focus 35 is the "Gathering" of extraterrestrials who are observing the Earth changes. Focus levels 42 and 49 are the realm of the I-There Clusters (soul groups).
13 Patricia Leva furthers the Interstate metaphor in her volume *Traveling the Interstate of Consciousness, a Driver's Instruction Manual: Using Hemi-Sync To Access States of Non-Ordinary Reality* (Longmont, CO: Q Central, 1997).
14 Russell, *The Journey of Robert Monroe*, 312.
15 Bruce Moen, *Exploring the Afterlife Series*, vol. 2 (Charlottesville, VA: Hampton Roads, 1998), 87–91.
16 David Bohm and F. David Peat deal with the connection between poetic and scientific metaphors in *Science, Order, and Creativity* (1987; New York: Routledge, 2000),

32–38, 40–5, and 72–5. The difference between metaphor and conceit, or extended metaphor, would have strengthened their discussion.

17 Russell, *The Journey of Robert Monroe*, 287.

18 Howard Storm, *My Descent into Death and the Message of Love Which Brought Me Back* (Great Barrington, MA: Clairview, 2000), 19–20.

19 Ibid., 26.

20 Ernest Hemingway, *A Farewell to Arms* (1929; New York: Scribner's, 1957), 54.

5

UFOs

Dr. Jung versus Dr. Greer and the case of Orfeo M. Angelucci

One of the strange phenomena that Robert A. Monroe reports in *Ultimate Journey* is the following encounter near the moon, which responds to his request to "be shown one nonphysical, nonhuman intelligence which I could talk with easily." He writes:

> I was astonished. Just twenty feet above me and stretching for what seemed to be miles was a huge, circular, saucer-shaped object, a typical "flying saucer" as so often described, but a thousand times larger. Much too big to credit—but as I had that thought, it shrank instantly to some two hundred feet in diameter.

At this point, a door opens in the bottom of the craft, and out walks an extraterrestrial who presents himself as the spitting image of W. C. Fields and who identifies himself as an "'exporter'" of human humor, jokes, and fun (commodities in which ETs are evidently in short supply). Nor is this his only mention of extraworldly visitation to the Earth Learning System. In *Far Journeys*, Monroe devotes a chapter to "The Gathering" where ET species wait and watch the development of the human species.[1]

> We were out in space somewhere between the earth and the moon, indeterminate distance, fifty thousand miles plus from the surface of earth. It was very clear and detailed, not as it was before. I turned to look at the moon and blanked [failed to understand]. No more than a thousand feet away, or so it seemed, was an immense, solid-appearing object gray in color, long and slender, conical shaped with a hemispheric dome at the widest end—the other end was somewhere in the distance, at least several miles. It appeared motionless, but I had the definite percept [perception, insight, intuition] of M Band [*sic*] radiation from it. A spaceship, a physical spaceship?

His nonphysical companion replies:

> *In your terms, that is correct. It is not a human construct. There are many of such* [*sic*] *around the physical earth at this point. Their origins are of your physical universe but not necessarily of your time reference.*[2]

Monroe explains that the "(M) Field" is a "nonphysical energy field that permeates time-space including our Earth Life System, but is not a part of current human scientific knowledge or study."[3] However, according to Monroe's biographer, Ronald Russell, the (M) Field

> is part of the energy spectrum surrounding the Earth that is commonly used for thought. It is not electronic, electric, magnetic, nucleonic, or anything else. M Band noise is caused by uncontrolled thought. Monroe perceived this as a sort of chaotic cacophony and learned to hurry through it as fast as he could.

Russell later forges a connection between the (M) Band and the Zero Point Field, quoting Lynne McTaggart's description of the latter as "'a field of energy connected to every other living thing in the world,'" which makes the (M) Band sound much like the collective unconscious, a subset of the One Mind or the *unus mundus*.[4]

Monroe's two accounts are relevant to the present chapter's consideration of Jung's work on UFOs for at least two reasons. First, the shapes of the supposed space craft that Monroe observes resonate meaningfully with the shapes that Jung discusses. Second, Monroe touches on the two main alternatives under consideration here: UFOs are real extraterrestrial vehicles, or they are psychological phenomena—mere projections of the human mind ("*a human construct*"). But there may also be a middle ground between nonhuman intelligence and psychic projection, as Michael Talbot suggests in *The Holographic Universe*. UFOs may be both physical *and* psychological:

> They are indeed a product of the collective human psyche, *but they are also quite real*. Put another way, they are something the human race has not yet learned to comprehend properly, a phenomenon that is neither subjective nor objective but "omnijective" [or "imaginal"].

As such, then like near-death experiences and shamanism, they constitute "further evidence that reality is a multilayered and mind-generated hologram." That is, "the imaginal is not confined to the afterlife realm, but has spilled over into the seeming solidity of our sticks-and-stones world." As for his own view, Talbot "believe[s] that probably no single explanation can account for all the varied aspects of the UFO phenomenon"; but he concludes with an extension of hologram theory that is relevant to the One Mind thesis of this book. Citing physicist John

Wheeler, he notes that when we create subatomic particles, they may also be creating us. Talbot writes, "Seen in this light, UFO entities may very well be archetypes from the collective unconscious of the human race, but we may also be archetypes of their collective unconscious."[5] The statement sounds remarkably similar to Jung's comment about his dream of a yogi:

> When I looked at him more closely, I realized that he had my face. I started in profound fright, and awoke with the thought: "Aha, so he is the one who is meditating me. He has a dream, and I am it." I knew that when he awakened, I would no longer be.
>
> (*MDR*, 323)[6]

Talbot's holographic middle way between two opposite views—UFOs as more physical than psychological and UFOs as more psychological than physical—is a fascinating possibility, one that Jung does consider but not in any well-developed way. Lacking (in his view) sufficient information for actual ET visitation of Earth, he considers primarily these extremes and discusses UFO sightings as myths based on human projection. Jung's comments on the UFO phenomenon appear in two places in *The Collected Works*. The first is a six-page, twenty-paragraph collection of letters and statements from the 1950s assembled in volume 18 under the title "On Flying Saucers." Here Jung engages with the news media such as United Press International, several journals dealing with UFOs, and a major in the United States Air Force. These short statements span the years 1954–1958.

Holding fast to a purely psychological reading requires some legerdemain in light of the information presented by the aforementioned Air Force officer. His name is Major Donald E. Keyhoe; and his book, *Flying Saucers from Outer Space* (*CW* 18, p. 627, n. 4), uses information released by the United States Air Force to argue convincingly that UFOs are interplanetary, interstellar, or both; however, he does not know why extraterrestrials are visiting the Earth. Perhaps Keyhoe has the likes of Jung in mind when he writes, "Radio stations were putting psychiatrists on the air to debunk the saucers as figments of imagination."[7] Jung's 1958 letter to him blends outrage and disbelief:

> If it is true that the AAF or the Government withholds telltale facts, then one can only say that this is the most unpsychological and stupid policy one could invent. Nothing helps rumours and panics more than ignorance. It is self-evident that the public ought to be told the truth, because ultimately it will nevertheless come to the light of day.

Then, echoing one of Keyhoe's points, Jung states, "There can be hardly any greater shock than the H-bomb and yet everyone knows of it without fainting." Jung's conclusion, that he is "still far from certain about the Ufos' physical reality," is remarkably short-sighted in light of the strong case that Keyhoe builds (*CW* 18, 1449/633 and 1450/633).

Jung's second contribution, a 124-page book entitled *Flying Saucers: A Modern Myth of Things Seen in the Skies*, was first published in 1958; the 1959 translation by R. F. C. Hull is reproduced in volume 10. After considering UFOs in several contexts (rumors, dreams, and modern paintings), Jung presents the previous history of the phenomenon (delving as far back as the twelfth century) and finally, though half-heartedly, considers UFOs in a nonpsychological light. Although he does not reach a definitive conclusion on the nature of UFOs, he strongly favors a psychological reading in which flying saucers, as projections of the human mind, constitute symbols of the Self and thus a "modern myth" of individuation.

Naturally, the epilogue, where Jung summarizes and comments on several books published after he finished the main sections of his manuscript, continues the psychological approach. The first to be discussed is the main subject of this chapter: *The Secret of the Saucers* (1955) by Orfeo M. Angelucci, who at the time of his experiences in 1952–1953—the same period that Keyhoe discusses—was an employee of the Lockheed Aircraft Corporation. The present chapter analyzes and evaluates both Angelucci's book and Jung's conclusions about it in order to argue that the reported experiences are not necessarily, as Jung claims, merely the "mystic experience associated with a Ufo vision" or "Orfeo's fantasies" (*CW* 10, 802/423 and 809/425). That is, Angelucci is not writing about a purely psychological phenomenon; there are good reasons to believe that he actually experienced something from another world. *The Secret of the Saucers* is more Jungian than even Jung imagines, and the book's many parallels to the work of the foremost UFO researcher/experiencer of our time, Steven M. Greer, M.D., suggest that the intrapsychic significance of an ET encounter does not obviate but rather enhances the extrapsychic nature of Angelucci's account. In other words, the reported encounters are both real *and* psychologically significant.

Jung on UFOs

Since Jung cannot say whether UFOs are genuinely extraterrestrial—"The conclusion is: *something is seen, but one doesn't know what*" (*CW* 10, 591/312; emphasis in the original)—his purpose in *Flying Saucers* is to examine their psychological significance. Chapter 1 (on rumor) mentions but discounts evidence from radar traces and eyewitnesses, including accounts of Foo fighters in World War II and the flight patterns of UFOs, whose sharp turns defy the law of gravity. These objects in the sky may be physical, but Jung's purpose is to discuss "their undoubted psychic aspect" (*CW* 10, 594/313). They result when archetype leads to vision; and "collective visions" may generate a "*living myth*," "*visionary rumour*," or "mass rumour" (*CW* 616/324, 614/322, and 597/314). Although fears related to the Soviets, nuclear bombs, World War III, and scarce resources result in projections of "extraterrestrial invasion" (*CW* 10, 600/315), a more positive possibility emerges. As analogies to the mandala or "symbol of totality," flying disks represent the archetype of the Self, "the totality composed of the conscious *and* the unconscious," which "has always expressed order, deliverance, salvation, and wholeness" (*CW* 10, 619/325, 621/326–27, and 624/328).

In chapters 2 through 4, Jung uses the "amplificatory method" (*CW* 10, 771/406)—the same technique that he uses in *Symbols of Transformation* (*CW* 5) to approach Miss Frank Miller's psychic experiences (some would say fantasies)—to analyze UFOs in dreams, paintings, and other visual images. In essence, he applies the theory of UFOs propounded in chapter 1 to specific cases in order to shore up his conclusions. Now the twin images of saucers and cigar-shaped flying craft lead to a distinction between feminine and masculine: the saucers suggest that "the anima is the quintessence of the Ufo"; and Jung reminds us that "the anima plays the role of the mediatrix between the unconscious and the conscious" (*CW* 10, 715/378), whereas the phallic-shaped craft signify something procreative (*CW* 10, 638/337). Like the cross, the two images signify "a union of opposites" and "bid each of us remember his own soul and his own wholeness, because this is the answer the West should give to the danger of mass-mindedness" (*CW* 10, 762/402 and 723/382). Most important in these chapters, however, is the following statement about the psychological origins of the UFO phenomenon:

> The plurality of Ufos, then, is a projection of a number of psychic images of wholeness which appear in the sky because on the one hand they represent archetypes charged with energy and on the other hand are not recognized as psychic factors. . . . When, therefore, the archetype receives from the conditions of the time and from the general psychic situation an additional charge of energy, it cannot, for the reasons I have described, be integrated directly into consciousness, but is forced to manifest itself indirectly in the form of spontaneous projections. The projected image then appears as an ostensibly physical fact independent of the individual psyche and its nature. In other words, the rounded wholeness of the mandala becomes a space ship controlled by an intelligent being.
>
> (*CW* 10, 635/335)

More simply stated, when historical conditions activate the archetype of the Self, the inability to integrate psychic content results in the projection of a disk or symbol of wholeness in the sky, which, in turn, through the coloring of myth, becomes a space ship under intelligent control.

In chapter 5 Jung acknowledges that UFOs have been seen, tracked on radar, and photographed; but this information does not convince him of their reality because not all things that are seen appear on radar and vice versa. Thus he settles on two alternatives: "It boils down to nothing less than this: that either psychic projections throw back a radar echo, or else the appearance of real objects affords an opportunity for mythological projections" (*CW* 10, 782/413). He adds that "even if the Ufos are physically real, the corresponding psychic projections are not actually caused, but are only occasioned, by them" (*CW* 10, 783/413)—that is, unidentified things seen in the skies are synchronistic.[8] As well, UFOs compensate for the waning of Christianity: the idea of "a mediator and god who became man" is yielding to "a saviour myth" in which extraterrestrials possess "numinous and mythical powers" (*CW* 10, 783–84/414–15). But because Jung affirms the ontological status of the UFO phenomenon yet is uncertain of the saucers' true nature, he concludes by adumbrating three alternatives that, he hopes, may serve as the basis for future research: UFOs are weightless, which would account for their gravity-defying behavior; they are "a materialized psychism," which means "something psychic that is endowed with certain physical properties" (*CW* 10, 788/416); or they are actual physical craft from outer space.

Jung styles the epilogue as an update on UFO literature published after the completion of the five chapters, and it is devoted to three texts, one of which, John Wyndham's novel *The Midwich Cuckoos* (1957) about a UFO's effect on a rural English village, is considered so insignificant as to merit only four paragraphs of summary and discussion in a concluding "*Supplement*."[9] In Wyndham's novel, persons in the village of Midwich experience a UFO-induced "dayoff," their term for a loss of consciousness that lasts for twenty-four hours. During this artificial sleep, sixty-one women are impregnated and soon give birth to golden-eyed extraterrestrial children—changelings or cuckoos—who bear no genetic relation to their host mothers. The boys have a collective consciousness, as do the girls; and all of them have the power to compel humans. Similar children among the Africans, Eskimos, and Siberians are dispatched at an early age by various means; but the children in Midwich are allowed to grow and learn for nine years, at which point they look sixteen and have the reasoning capacity of highly educated adults. The children kill six humans and injure many others when they feel threatened, but more ominous is their apparent intention to achieve global domination. As the novel ends, their teacher, Mr. Zellaby, on the pretext of providing the children with a movie night at their residence, The Grange, ends their lives and his own with a bomb. *The Midwich Cuckoos* is thus a novel about the fear of confronting a superior extraterrestrial race and finding ourselves in the subaltern position. Jung considers the children to be "divine progeny" and the humans to be analogous to Neanderthals who enforce the status quo by genocidal means. The children, he writes, "represent an unexpected capacity for a wider and higher consciousness, superseding a backward and inferior mental state," but not the moral advancement necessary to use it wisely (*CW* 10, 823–24/432–33).

The previous twenty-nine paragraphs of Jung's *Flying Saucers* address Angelucci's *The Secret of the Saucers* and Fred Hoyle's novel *The Black Cloud* (1957). Jung's strategy is first to summarize each work and then to explain how its contents confirm the psychological interpretation that he has advanced in the preceding chapters. Angelucci and Hoyle receive major attention because they portray, Jung believes, the same psychological process, despite the vast differences between books and men: whereas Angelucci, an uneducated laborer and dabbler in scientific theory, presents his experience as true, Hoyle, "a well-known authority on astrophysics" (*CW* 10, 810/426), considers his own work "a 'frolic,' a jest" in a tiny preface (*CW* 10, 810/426).[10] Jung's elitism surfaces in the following passage:

> If we compare this tale [Hoyle's] with the naïvetés of Angelucci, we get a valuable picture of the difference between the uneducated and the scientifically educated attitude. Both shift the problem on to a concrete plane, the one [Angelucci] in order to make us believe in a saving action from heaven, the other [Hoyle] in order to transform this secret yet somewhat sinister expectation into an entertaining literary joke. Both, poles apart though they are, are activated by the same unconscious factor and make use of essentially the same symbolism in order to express the unconscious straits we are in.
>
> (*CW* 10, 820/431)

Jung believes, for example, that the intelligent black cloud that blocks the sun's light and causes natural disasters on the Earth represents the nigredo of the conscious mind's encounter with the collective unconscious. The book "illustrates a characteristic aspect of the psychological problem which arises when the light of day—consciousness—is directly confronted with night, the collective unconscious" (*CW* 10, 814/428). In this respect, the Earth's encounter with the cloud parallels the free world's past struggle with socialism and its current experience of "the Communist inundation, where an archaic social order threatens our freedom with tyranny and slavery" (*CW* 10, 818/430).

Jung's summary of *The Secrets of the Saucers* is reasonably fair-minded, though it omits the crucial concluding material. Only a brief account of Angelucci's story is necessary as a prelude to Jung's conclusions. On various occasions Angelucci encounters a traveler from another world, a male figure whom he refers to as Neptune. The author journeys on a flying saucer into outer space where he sees a cigar-shaped mother ship. He spends seven days dwelling within Neptune's body on another planet, where he encounters the beautiful Lyra and other extraterrestrials, while Neptune guides Orfeo's body through its daily routine in California.[11] The final vision of Christ, who comes down off the cross and speaks to the author in deeply meaningful ways, is not present in the summary.

Jung argues in the epilogue that these purported experiences illustrate intrapsychic processes rather than an actual ET encounter. First of all, they arise from an *abaissement du niveau mental*, an altered or lowered state of consciousness. He then writes:

> Without having the faintest inkling of psychology, Angelucci has described in the greatest detail the mystic experience associated with a Ufo vision. A detailed commentary by me is hardly necessary. The story is so naïve and clear that a reader interested in psychology can see at once how far it confirms my previous conclusions.

> Orfeo's book is an essentially naïve production which for that very reason reveals all the more clearly the unconscious background of the Ufo phenomenon and therefore comes like a gift to the psychologist. The individuation process, the central problem of modern psychology, is plainly depicted in it in an unconscious, symbolical form, which bears out previous reflections, although the author with his somewhat primitive mentality has taken it quite literally as a concrete happening.
>
> (*CW* 10, 803/423 and 809/426)

Angelucci's story is merely a projection of psychic content, and it receives the ultimate downgrade in the phrase "his somewhat primitive mentality." Jung means that the subject mistakes his own psychic content for a separate object and then attributes numinous significance to it. At the end of chapter 1 of *Flying Saucers*, he makes a comment that anticipates this criticism of Angelucci and that reminds the contemporary reader of the film *The Gods Must Be Crazy*: "For primitive man any object, for instance an old tin that has been thrown away, can suddenly assume the importance of a fetish. This effect is obviously not inherent in the tin, but is a psychic product" (*CW* 10, 625/329).[12] In other words, Jung's reduction of Angelucci's experiences to a myth of individuation is much in the spirit of his point in *Symbols of Transformation* that "the scientific approach disregards metaphysics" (*CW* 5, 95/62). His analysis allows mysticism but not metaphysics, the intrapsychic but not the extrapsychic, the psychological but not the extraterrestrial. If there is nothing numinous in such a naïve account, just projected psychic content, then the hydrogen atom that is burned into Angelucci's flesh is merely "the symbol of the self, of absolute wholeness or, in religious language, God" (*CW* 10, 806/424).

Jung also makes less predictable comments on Angelucci's use of names, noting, first, that "his cosmic friends bear the names of stars." Jung's summary, however, includes an inaccuracy that involves naming. He states that during Angelucci's seven-day soul exchange "he discovered that his heavenly friend was not called Neptune but Orion, and that 'Neptune' had been his own name while he was still dwelling in this heavenly world" (*CW* 10, 801/423). Orion is someone else (94), and the being whom Angelucci calls Neptune is actually named Astra (95). Jung correctly notes that the extraterrestrials tell Angelucci that he was named Neptune in a past lifetime—the exact sort of metaphysical point that Jung resists. Then he makes the following extended comment on the names used in *The Secret of the Saucers*:

> The author certainly lives up to his name, for just as his wife, *neé* Borgianini, is in his opinion a descendant of the Borgias of unhappy memory, so he, an earthly copy of the "angels" and a messenger bringing Eleusinian tidings of immortality, must style himself a new Orpheus, divinely appointed to initiate us into the mystery of the Ufo. Not even the Orphean strains are lacking. If the name is a deliberately chosen

> pseudonym, we can only say *è ben trovato* [it is well invented]. But if it appears in his birth certificate, then the matter becomes more problematical.
> (*CW* 10, 809/425–26)

Birth certificates in New Jersey are not available to nonfamily members; however, a website entitled Archives (www.archives.com) lists Orfeo as Angelucci's name on his birth and death records. The only indication I have been able to find online that Jung may be on the right track is Wikipedia's doubtful mention in parentheses that Orfeo is really *Orville* Angelucci.[13] Strangely, Jung overlooks the very clear discussion of naming that appears in the text. During the vision of Christ, the author reveals that his middle initial stands for Matthew.

> And then I heard him say: "But Matthew was a publican. And were you not as a publican [an unbeliever in UFOs] before May 23, 1952? . . . Do not be ashamed, Orfeo. Don't you remember I always chose the publicans and harlots over self-righteous hypocrites?"

In an unequivocal example of the kind of metaphysical statement that Jung resists, Angelucci then writes, "Veils were dropping from my eyes and I was remembering details of a life lived many lives ago back in Time" (137). He does not claim to be the reincarnation of the Apostle Matthew, but the implication is there for the reader to ponder.

A psychological reading

Jung overlooks many things in *The Secrets of the Saucers* that would have strengthened his argument that Angelucci's account represents a psychological process rather than an encounter with actual extraterrestrials. To begin with, Jung affirms the *unus mundus* (*CW* 10, 780/411), the one world or what I am calling the One Mind, which, in connecting all things and all persons, is even more fundamental than the collective unconscious. Angelucci calls it "the infinite mind" (135). The moral of the story is "the great essential basic truth that *we are one and an integral part of God* " (112). Unity through God the Father is the natural state of spiritual intelligences throughout the universe (115). And Neptune states that our "'great world of tomorrow [is] a world of brotherly love and fellowship when Man is for Man and bound in unity through the love of the Father'" (124). Throughout the text Angelucci refers to this ideal state of affairs as "unity of being," a concept that means release "from the bonds of individuality" or the erasure of "boundaries of self" (56 and 108). As Orion tells him, "'individualized aspects such as you know upon Earth are non-existent'" (95). Whereas Hoyle's black cloud may represent the conscious mind's encounter with the collective unconscious, Angelucci aims beyond achieving individuation by engaging with the unitary as a way to overcome the separation that characterizes the human condition.

Unity of being is difficult to achieve because of the illusion of separation that bedevils modern persons in particular, a fact that Angelucci frankly acknowledges: "It was as though each person lived in a world apart; encased in a tomb of separation and living death" (114). The Cold War setting of *The Secret of the Saucers* throws that problem into bold relief through a powerful fear of the Communist Other. As Angelucci says to Neptune, "'There is the ever-constant fear of the H-bomb and of other horribly destructive weapons being developed in the laboratories. Also there is the creeping menace of Communism that is threatening the world, and so many other things'" (45). Communism, in fact, is the ultimate example of the collective shadow, but for Angelucci it has such personal significance that those who try to expose him as a fraud at UFO conventions appear to be Communist sympathizers: "Like little demons they parroted elementary physics and could see practical, intelligent action only behind the Iron Curtain" (80). On a tour of the East, Angelucci, who refuses to be converted to Communism, is asked, "'Well then, just what do you think is wrong with Communism?'" He replies:

> Absolutely everything is wrong with it! There is not one iota of right in it. Its only possible good is its ability to awaken to action the positive forces of good which are often sleeping. Communism is the negation of all that is honest and good in the world and in humanity. [Communists] would enslave the human mind.
>
> (129–30)

Given such disorder on Earth, humans project their separation and bellicosity onto peaceful extraterrestrials: "We, by our own standards, expected them to have predatory ideas of conquest and enslavement of mankind. As a result the flood of horror films of monstrous extraterrestrial invaders has not yet ceased" (162). In other words, whereas Angelucci seeks to erase the illusion of separation by promoting the truth of humanity's fundamental unity through the One Mind, Communists, like the ETs of science fiction, would use violence to violate people's free will by enforcing a soul-deadening sameness-in-conformity.

The ideal unity that Angelucci espouses is distantly removed, of course, from modern humanity's psychic state; but individuation provides an important step in that right direction. *The Secret of the Saucers* enacts this process in ways that Jung overlooks. There is, as Jung mentions, the frank acknowledgement that the Earth is "a purgatorial world" (24; *CW* 10, 796/421). But Angelucci drives the point home in a plethora of further references. Earth is "the plane of darkness" (26) and "the kingdom of death" (32). As Neptune tells him, "'Earth is regarded as 'the accursed planet', the 'home of the reprobate, fallen ones'. Others call your Earth 'the home of sorrows'. For Earth's evolution is evolution through pain, sorrow, sin, suffering and the illusion of physical death'" (43). It is "a prison-world of materiality called Earth" (92), "'the dark planet of sorrows'" (100), "'the Dark World'" (103), "an underworld of illusion where we mistake false shadows for reality and dream selfish dreams of separateness from our brothers" (103–4), "a strange shadowed region called Earth" (107), a "world of shadows" (112), "a prison world where each man is a bondsman locked in a prison cell" (115), "the valley of sorrows that is Earth" (138), and simply "Hell" (153). Since overarching shadow is the Earth's characteristic state, our material/physical plane is an appropriate setting for the work of individuation; and acknowledging the darkness is a first step in that positive direction. Flying disks, Orion tells Angelucci, "'are in your space-time frame as harbingers of mankind's coming resurrection from the living death'" (103). As the symbols of wholeness that Jung believes them to be, they point the way toward individuation.

Angelluci's encounters with extraterrestrials strengthen the sense that Earth is a purgatorial dimension by adding a myth about human origins, something that Jung omits from his commentary on *The Secret of the Saucers*. The account takes place in chapter 8, "My Awakening on Another Planet," in the author's conversations with Orion. Between the orbits of Mars and Jupiter, there was once a planet called Lucifer, whose great prince went by the same name. Through pride and a desire to rule the universe (to overcome God), many of the Luciferians "'"fell" into embodiments in one of the most dense material evolutions, which is the animalistic evolution of Earth'" (99). Angelucci was one of them, though he is informed that he had been one of the most reluctant members of the resistance. Referring to the time prior to the planet Lucifer's destruction, Angelucci notes, in what appears to be an example of projection, that "in their world, I was, or had once been, Neptune!" (95). Those who did *not* fall were the distant ancestors of those extraterrestrials who have contacted him. In a moment of crystal clear anagnoresis, Angelucci realizes that he is of the devil and (one might add) a counterpart to the rebel angels in *Paradise Lost*: by not only having a shadow but also being descended from the ur-personifications of evil, he is guilty of the ultimate separation from God the Father. Angelucci realizes as well his separation from God the Son in chapter 11, "I Have a Vision." As he remembers a previous lifetime, perhaps as the Apostle Matthew, he remarks, "I hid my face from His sight and tears of shame and remorse blinded my sight" (137). The author's journey, then, enacts the function of the confessional, whose purpose is to make the believer more aware of his participation in the Fall because, in psychological terms, the conscious acknowledgement of the shadow is the first step in the individuation process.

Angelucci's statements about time and space help amplify and refine the point that he is making about shadow recognition. He writes, "What we call Time exists only in the physical worlds and is an illusion of the senses. Also, I know now that our concept of space is entirely erroneous" (37). Jung does not say that space-time is completely illusory; but he inclines in that direction when he states, "For the psyche has yet another property which most of us would rather not admit, namely, that peculiar factor which relativizes space and time, and is now the object of intensive parapsychological research" (*CW* 10, 655/346). Time, whether wholly illusory or merely relative to the perceiving subject, has implications for

Angelucci's vision of Christ. "Slowly the sword was transfigured into a cross and upon it I saw the figure of a Man in death" (136). Christ then comes down off the cross and engages Angelucci in a conversation whose point is not just an unveiling of his past life and the recognition of his shadow but also the establishment of the crucifixion as an ongoing event. Humans crucify Christ every day. Similarly, the movement from projecting guilt onto the crucified Jesus to befriending the Christ whom the cross does *not* kill may also be a daily occurrence. In psychological terms, individuation is not something that can ever be fully completed; as a process that is ever-present in each moment, it constitutes the work of a lifetime.

Chapter 4 of Jung's UFO book comments on the cross image in terms of *coniunctio*: "Here the cross signifies a union of opposites (vertical and horizontal), a 'crossing'; as a plus sign, it is also a joining together, an addition" (*CW* 10, 762/402). *Coniunctio* is indeed the right concept to describe the inner process that plays out allegorically in Angelucci's encounters with extraterrestrials and in his marital life. In his first encounter with Neptune, he is given a cup of nectar that calms his nerves and alters his awareness (not an *abaissement du niveau mental* but an *elevated* state of consciousness) so that he can perceive subtle energy more clearly. The beverage has the same cleansing effect as the "Euphrasie and Rue" have on Adam's vision in *Paradise Lost*. And then:

> Within the luminous screen [inside the ET craft] there appeared images of the heads and shoulders of two persons, as though in a cinema close-up. One was the image of a man and the other of a woman. I say man and woman only because their outlines and features were generally similar to men and women. But those two figures struck me as being the ultimate of perfection.
>
> (7)

Just as unity of being, the state of unity via the One Mind, provides a goal for humanity, this image of ideal harmony between animus and anima functions as a goal for Angelucci in his personal journey through the book.

That harmony, however, proves elusive because of another aspect of the individuation process, *enantiodromia*, which he experiences multiple times during the book. First, during his trip into outer space on a flying saucer, "The Reasoner" that he has become yields to tears for the first time since early childhood (24). He achieves an emotional response, but then he swings back when the Reasoner reasserts itself in Angelucci's dogged determination to tell the world about his experiences, much to the exasperation and shame of his loyal wife Mabel. The Reasoner is on hand when Angelucci awakens in Astra's body on the alien home world, and it is fully engaged in the discussion of our Luciferian origins. With that formal lesson concluded, Angelucci has another swing to the opposite when he looks at Lyra: "Suddenly, I was fully aware for the first time of all her exquisite feminine beauty and loveliness. Involuntarily, a wave of desire for her swept over me." All conversation stops abruptly because his hosts see what he himself views in the mirror, "an ugly mottled red and black cloud enveloping my head and shoulders." The incident gives him "the strong telepathic impression that sexual desire is merely another of the erroneous manifestations of materiality" (105). Eventually, he and Lyra become "as one being, enfolded in an embrace of the spirit untouched by sensuality or carnality" (107), much like the astral sex that Monroe recounts in *Journeys Out of the Body*.[14] This dualism of body and spirit continues in the conclusion that "only selfless love and not the carnality which is often mistaken here on Earth for love" is worthy of pursuit (140).

There is still not a proper earthly *coniunctio* of love and passion until very near the end of the book, where Mabel supersedes Lyra in Angelucci's affections. "Within her I beheld all the mystery and wonder of womanhood: she was like a reflection of Lyra, the highest potential of feminine evolution" (142). When he kisses her ("more tenderly than I had in months") he achieves, unlike Goodman Brown in Hawthorne's story, not only the proper balance of reason, sexual passion, and love but also the human equivalent of the ideal unity of masculine and feminine shown to him on the screen during his space flight. It is as if his experience of the archetype of femininity (Lyra) prepares him for fully embracing a relationship with its earthly manifestation (Mabel). Although he has not achieved the unity of being—the transcendence of individuality—that may be humanity's ultimate goal, he *has* achieved a greater measure of individuation than he possessed at the beginning of his experiences, as well as an understanding of the true nature of the human experience. Angelucci hopefully mentions the goal toward which he believes humanity should strive:

> When we have learned the meaning of true brotherly love [namely, the unity of all via the One Mind]; when we have overcome to a greater degree the evil inherent in our selfish hearts [that is, have integrated the shadow], then perhaps we will be worthy to meet the infinitely wiser and gentler brothers of your world.
>
> (50–51)

Unity of being and individuation are prerequisites for extraterrestrial contact on a larger scale (the psychological leads to the metaphysical), and the sort of inner work that Angelucci has done may have global and cosmic implications if enough people follow his example.

Angelucci and Jung are alike in affirming overarching unity-consciousness, the collective shadow of communism, the role of shadow in the individuation process, the problem of *enantiodromia*, and the proper *coniunctio* of male and female within a man's psyche. Since *The Secret of the Saucers* is thus more Jungian than Jung himself acknowledges, the preceding analysis strengthens his argument that Angelucci's book may be a purely psychological document. That conclusion would have been even stronger if Jung had been able to incorporate comments on Angelucci's second book, *Son of the Sun* (1959), which is very clearly a novel rather than an attempt to report the author's own experiences, though Angelucci makes himself a character. (It is possible that Jung eventually read the novel because he uses the phrase "a son of the sun" in his autobiography.)[15] Why is the story an obvious fiction? The Alpha Centaurians speak perfect English, and Angelucci-as-narrator writes in a novelistic style that embellishes on what Adam has supposedly told him.[16] The science that is recited in chapter 8, "Nature of Infinite Entities," and in chapter 9, "Adam's Moment of Illumination," echoes Angelucci's twenty-page treatise, *Nature of Infinite Entities*, whose main insight is that "atoms, and all known entities are, then, vacuums, vertices, or bubbles in the ETHER."[17] Adam knows the contents of *The Secret of the Saucers* as well because the Alpha Centaurian children have managed to download it prior to its terrestrial publication. In addition, *Son of the Sun* uses a frame tale: the main character, Adam, tells Angelucci his story; and Angelucci tells it to the reader in embellished form. Their interaction, like that between Roger Walton and Victor Frankenstein, creates verisimilitude, though in this case the story sets a successful individuation process in the wondrous world of flying saucers and on Andromeda, an artificial world ten miles in diameter that hovers in the atmosphere of Venus.

Adam, a thirty-eight-year-old medical doctor who never had time for a wife and who expects to die of cancer within seven months, meets Angelucci in Tiny's Café in Twentynine Palms, California. Over the course of several days, with the aid of the aforementioned nectar, Angelucci absorbs Adam's story. The plot is Aristotelian in its tripartite structure, with each part emphasizing Adam's attraction to an extraterrestrial female. On the outbound voyage, Adam falls in love with Vega (beginning); on Andromeda, he loves Launie, his alien guide, who, because she is one of the slowest among the Alpha Centaurians, can communicate more easily with him (middle); and in the book's climax, Adam and Aleva, Eve for short, fly into the sun on the finest of space ships in a spiritual rite of passage (ending). Adam is a son of the sun because of his status as an Earth man, but his fiery plunge into the sun makes him truly deserving of that moniker. At the book's close, Adam departs for the Pacific northwest where his earthly love, Dora, awaits him, leaving Angelucci with the task of writing down what he has heard. As with Angelucci's encounter with Lyra in *The Secret of the Saucers*, Adam's encounters with extraterrestrial women who approximate the perfection of the feminine archetype enable him to embrace a healthy relationship with an earthly partner. One cathexis follows another—"'In the presence of all goodness, seen and unseen, I am yours'" (84); "he loved her in a vastness far beyond his control" (195)—until anima possession yields to anima integration. Jung, had he commented on the novel, would have fixed on a single statement by Adam that encapsulates the role of anima integration in the individuation process: "'So, I am to learn first the meaning of woman in the consciousness of man'" (90).

A metaphysical reading

It should be clear from my own analysis of Angelucci's two works, *The Secret of the Saucers* and *Son of the Sun*, that Jung's psychological interpretation constitutes a valuable approach. In attributing Angelucci's metaphysical claims regarding actual alien encounters to naïveté, Jung arrogates to himself the role of adjudicator of someone else's paranormal experience. One wonders, though, how Jung would have responded if others had debunked as naïve his own claims about seeing the Earth from hundreds of miles out in space during his near-death experience. In any case, Angelucci has a ready-made reply for such skeptical criticism: "I saw then that the human mind does not want to believe anything it cannot understand; it will rationalize to any extent rather than face the unknown" (67). A bit later he adds, "For I have seen other persons actually see a saucer and refuse to believe the evidence of their own sight" (72). Others "who have seen spectacular displays of UFOs . . . go their way skeptical and unimpressed" (153). "Presented with the true, simple explanation of the flying saucers, some people find it harder than ever to accept" (158). At one point, Angelucci even directly addresses a skeptical Jung-figure, "Good, old Mr. White, the weatherman," who reduces extraterrestrial lights in the night sky to a meteor shower. "Now, Mr. White," Angelucci writes, "these people, dozen[s] of them, are either falsefiers [*sic*], or else they saw something out of this world which cannot be neatly explained away by your pat little explanation" (128). In a sense, Angelucci, Jung, and White are of fallacy-thinking all compact, for each one sees the phenomenon only through the lens of his own intellectual training and/or personal experience. The weatherman thinks that he sees a meteorological event. The famous psychologist zeroes in on the psychological content of one man's account and ignores his frequent mentions of multiple eyewitnesses' accounts. And the UFO experiencer insists on the literal truth of the events that he reports but shears away much of their psychological content. In denying UFOs extraterrestrial status, Jung and White are guilty of the mechanism noted in the introduction, Charles T. Tart's Law of Universal Retrospective Rationalization, by which humans protect themselves from the impact of events and ideas that are incompatible with their existing belief systems. Tart notes that "we clever humans can always find a seemingly plausible reason why things happened the way they did; we're very, very smart pattern makers."[18] In contrast, Angelucci was once a skeptic himself; and his breaking out of a rigid pattern calls for a more inclusive reading than psychological analysis allows. Jung has had his say. It is time to defend *The Secret of the Saucers* on its own terms.

Of course, it is true that the believability of Angelucci's account wanes when it is set against the historical aftermath of his experiences in 1952–1953. Neptune tells him of a future event known as "'The Great Accident,'" which is foretold to occur in 1986 and receives other dire names: "'the hour of tragedy,'" "'the bloody holocaust of Armageddon,'" "'the War of Desolation,'" and "'the War of the End of an Age'" (46, 110, and 123–24). But at approximately the time dark forces should have been marching to the final battle, communism in the Soviet Union and elsewhere in Eastern Europe was on the wane. Perhaps the prediction of doomsday in 1986 was part of the nigredo of a new world order. Or not: "In reality," Angelucci admits, "this age of discord and stark materialism is already in the past and we have entered into the New Age" (143). Nevertheless, to reduce the book to an inaccurate prediction of doomsday or a mere expression of psychological content would be to commit the fallacy of mistaking the part for the whole. It does not follow that Angelucci's claims about extraterrestrial visitors are false just because their prediction is incorrect. Since the future is not fixed, what Neptune shows Angelucci may be merely one of Earth's *possible* futures.[19]

Nor does Angelucci do himself a favor when he contradicts himself on the matter of factual proof. On the one hand, he states that "ideas preponderantly spiritual cannot now and have never been capable of proof by material methods. Hence no material proof of the reality of my experiences may be given to satisfy skeptics" (164). On the next page he remarks, "In the space being's [*sic*] contacts with me there has actually been some factual evidence—almost enough to serve as proof, even to materialists. But not quite enough!" (165). Perhaps he is referring to multiple sightings of UFOs by groups of fair-minded persons or to the welt that spontaneously developed on his finger as an exact replica of the hydrogen atom that was burned into his side during his space flight (36 and 54). Naturally, Jung considers Angelucci's "sign of the hydrogen atom" as "the symbol of the self, of absolute wholeness or, in religious language, God" (*CW* 10, 806/424). However, Jung incorrectly states that, "on going to bed, he noticed a burning sensation on the left side of his chest" (*CW* 10, 799/422). He feels that sensation during his space flight; only upon inspecting his chest at bedtime does he realize that he has been branded (36). In any case, "no material proof" versus "some factual evidence" is a direct contradiction that illustrates not only an uneducated man's inept attempt to convince a skeptical public but also a psychic's struggle with self-doubt and his need to ascertain the ontological status of his personal experiences.

Despite the text's limitations, the reader can be reasonably certain that something unusual did happen to Orfeo M. Angelucci. At the very least, his account spurs us to consider the possibility that intelligent life could exist in dimensions—"the higher octaves of light," as he calls them in a nice example of synesthesia (133)—that we are unable to perceive with our limited senses. Let us pause for a moment to consider the author's interesting phrase, "the higher octaves of light," for its intertextual significance. Angelucci's *The Secrets of the Saucers* was published in 1955, two years after Desmond Leslie and George Adamski's *Flying Saucers Have Landed*, which Jung references in (*CW* 18, p. 627, n. 2). In the first twenty chapters (book 1), Leslie discusses wide-ranging evidence in support of flying saucers. One wonders if he may have inspired Angelucci's use of the word "octaves." Leslie writes:

> Most of the objects seen in the sky come from our two neighbours, Mars and Venus—particularly Venus. Dr. [Meade] Layne and his fellow scientists dwell at some length on the probability that life on Venus takes place in a higher octave of matter than on Earth; in other words, at a higher vibrationary rate, and that by reducing this vibration to the rate of that of earthy gasses, liquids and solids, the Venusians are able to appear here in solid or semi-solid forms, as they will.[20]

In book two, Adamski, a "philosopher, student, teacher, saucer researcher" and amateur astronomer,[21] describes his own telescopic observations, presents a number of his own excellent photographs of saucer- and cigar-shaped craft, and describes an encounter with a male from Venus, which unfolds in a number of ways that resemble Angelucci's encounters with Neptune. Both men's contacts take place in an expanded state of awareness, involve telepathic communication, make the Earthlings feel like children, and have an effect that lasts longer than the visitation itself. "This feeling of being in two worlds," writes Adamski, "at the same time continued with me for a couple of weeks, and even now when a strong memory of the experience overtakes me, this feeling returns."[22]

On the one hand, it is strange that the ever-critical Jung did not seize upon the possible influence of Leslie and Adamski's book on Angelucci's in order to propose influence and imply the latter's lack of originality and credibility. On the other, the exact opposite could also be argued: similarity adds credibility. Perhaps Jung's omission is due to the presence of photographs in plate 13 of the affidavits signed by the six persons who witnessed Adamski's alien encounter from a distance. By not engaging with Adamski's account, Jung sidesteps the difficulty of dealing with such powerful pieces of documentary evidence. Moreover, since Adamski's encounter took place in November (Angelucci's in May) of 1952, "a particular case" Adamski asks the alien about on page 203 may be that of Angelucci. Given that Angelucci published portions of his book in other venues, some of the material that eventually became *The Secrets of the Saucers* may have influenced Adamski's work rather than the reverse. Yet Adamski does receive mention in Keyhoe's *Flying Saucers from Outer Space*. In reading Adamski's account skeptically, Keyhoe unfairly omits the documentary evidence and affidavits presented in *Flying Saucers Have Landed*, much as Jung overlooks the evidentiary material in Angelucci's work.[23] These two experts—the military officer and the famous psychologist—are not above reproach, for both attempt to diminish what does not fit their respective paradigms.

Angelucci offers an interpretation of UFOs that contrasts with Jung's sense that they are a synchronous meeting of archetype and projected content. Says Angelucci, "It was further explained that the Etheric entities in reality had no need of space-craft of any type and when they were employed by them it was only for the purposes of material manifestation to men" (10–11). Instead of being projections of the human mind, perhaps UFOs are projections that extraterrestrial consciousness has designed to get the attention of our limited sensory apparatus and to nudge us toward individuation and beyond. If so, what kind of argument might further our progress on that evolutionary path by adding credibility to his account? The remaining pages of this chapter pose an analogical argument that may open the way. In making it, I hope to avoid the fallacy of false dichotomy present in Jung's UFO book, the belief that a phenomenon is psychological but not metaphysical, a manifestation of a single mind rather than of the One Mind.

I begin with a preliminary analogy to psychic functioning. As Rhine, Radin, Tart, Jung himself, and many others have amply shown in both scientific studies and accounts of personal experiences, there is no longer any doubt from a statistical perspective that psi is real. The key issue now is what we can *do* with the human ability to perceive psychically, which arises from connections via the One Mind. Regarding extraterrestrials' visitation of the Earth, a similar situation obtains. The issue is no longer whether they are here but instead how we should proceed to interact with them. Of course, Angelucci's single account is not an open-and-shut case; but the work of Steven M. Greer, M.D. offers solid justification for believing that we are not alone in the universe or even on our own planet. Verifiability hinges on three components, and Greer has all three, Angelucci merely two.

The first is the subjective, unverifiable accounts of ET experiencers (for example, Angelucci and Greer ride into outer space on ET craft). The second is sightings of UFOs by these experiencers while they are part of groups of people, sometimes including skeptics, who can corroborate the information. The news media also play a role in extablishing the existence of lights in the night sky that make right angle turns, fly in formation, or wink out, and in arguing that they are something other than meteors. *Hamlet* provides a relevant analogy: one person's ghost sighting may be a delusion; but when several persons see the same spirit, the entity's existence and presence are no longer in doubt, though its intentions and morality remain uncertain. In just this way, Angelucci and Greer both witness UFOs in groups of people; and both of them make statements about others who are present—statements, in Angelucci's case, that Jung omits from his analysis because they compromise his purely psychological interpretation. For example, Angelucci states:

> Every one of the men saw the red disk hanging overhead in the sky. . . . Every man told precisely the same story. . . . Every one of these men will affirm the details of this sighting. . . . All of them believed they had seen a flying saucer.
>
> (69–70)

Angelucci is referring to UFOs seen in the middle of the night by the very hard-headed Lockheed production workers who had mocked his earlier claims. Greer's experiences, especially those reported by multiple UFO investigators in his 2009 book, *Contact: Countdown to Transformation—The CSETI Experience 1992–2009*, add photographic and video evidence to the equation. On this basis, there is simply no doubt that not all unidentified things seen in the skies are the product of modern myth.[24]

The third component of verification is the testimony of expert witnesses such as members of Congress, military personnel, pilots, astronauts, governmental employees, and former members of covert projects. Angelucci pursues this avenue only obliquely, but it is Greer's stock in trade. The purpose of his organization, The Disclosure Project, has been to gather information from hundreds of witnesses, to publish this material in *Extraterrestrial Contact: The Evidence and*

Implications (1999) and *Disclosure: Military and Government Witnesses Reveal the Greatest Secrets in Modern History* (2001), to release it in forums such as a major press conference at the National Press Club in 2001, and to maintain a continuous presence on the Internet (especially on youtube.com). Jung might see paranoia in Greer's autobiography, *Hidden Truth—Forbidden Knowledge* (2006), when he claims that a secret government is covering up information on, and technology from, alien spacecraft and using it for military advantage but otherwise sequestering it until catastrophe is imminent.[25] But the claim is in the spirit of Neptune's remarks to Angelucci: "'The aggressive men of Earth want our scientific advancements. For these they would shoot our crafts from the skies—if they could'" (31); and "'the governments of the world could say much more to the people about the saucer situation, but they will not until the zero hour is at hand'" (123). Like Greer, Angelucci is so convinced of the sort of massive paper trail that Greer has made public that he makes statements not only about "hundreds of news reports of saucer activity" in 1953 but also about a claim by Wilbert B. Smith, head of Canada's Project Magnet ("a UFO detection station"), of "95% probability that UFOs do exist" based on "the massive files of data on well-authenticated sightings on hand" (128–29). This preponderance of evidence is precisely the thrust of The Disclosure Project today.[26]

Having the solid, objective, on-record testimony of hundreds of reliable eyewitnesses, along with government documents, radar traces, and other pieces of objective evidence makes Greer's claims about his own subjective, unverifiable experiences more credible. It is one thing for Jung to cherry pick and psychologize Angelucci's account in order to put it all down to the naïveté of an uneducated man—and quite another to extend that criticism to a fellow medical doctor in possession of a CIA memo that attributes the death of Marilyn Monroe to her intention to hold a press conference on UFO secrets that President Kennedy had revealed to her.[27] The purpose of dwelling on such hard evidence is to establish the basis for an analogical argument that runs as follows. UFOs are here, and we know from the sort of evidence that Greer has assembled that they are alien spacecraft. Since they are here, Greer's claims about his interaction with the ETs, including those not witnessed by others, take on greater credibility. Thus, to the extent that Angelucci's experiences align with Greer's, they too take on a measure of objective truth and would seem to be more than the naïve projections of an uneducated man. I will argue, then, that *The Secret of the Saucers* has not only psychological content, as Jung agrees, but also metaphysical significance as the record of the author's genuine paranormal and extrapsychic experiences. Of course, we do not have to believe as literal truth the myth about the planet Lucifer or the claim that Christ is a sun spirit to acknowledge that something out of the ordinary happened to Angelucci. Nor do we have to believe Greer's more extravagant claims in order to believe the central truth about ETs' presence. But if humans are genuinely interacting with extraterrestrials, then it would make sense for multiple persons to have similar encounters; and such similarities, like the sightings of King Hamlet's ghost by various persons, lend credibility to an individual person's claims about ET contact.

A fundamental assumption. Since extraterrestrials who are capable of interstellar travel have the capacity to transcend the limits of time and space (that is, dwell in more than the dimensions that human beings generally regard as absolute limits), communicating with such beings often takes place telepathically via the unconscious and the One Mind. It helps, therefore, to acknowledge, as Angelucci and Greer both do, that these assumed limits are illusions and that the part and the whole are as one. Angelucci affirms "the infinite mind" as the link between all conscious beings (135) and maintains that "one becomes a universe within himself" (138). Or more boldly, "The universe is you—and you are the universe" (144). Likewise, Greer frequently repeats a point from Sufi tradition: "'Thinkest thyself a puny form when within thee the universe is folded?'" Also, "the unbounded Divine Mind is always folded within us," and "nothing exists separate from mind." Here is a more expanded statement (by Greer) that supports what I have said in the introduction about hologram theory:

> Seeing then, in perfection the creation, the Creator and the Infinite Mind, we are now aware that it is true that every created thing is a doorway to the Infinite, and that the unbounded and infinite Being is truly omnipresent, omniscient, ever-abiding at every point in space and time and at every level of creation. And that indeed folded within us and within all things, is a perfect quantum hologram of all that there is.[28]

The statement is a helpful gloss on Blake's famous pronouncement quoted in chapter 3: "If the doors of perception were cleansed every thing would appear to man as it is: infinite" (E 39). They will appear to be infinite, if we follow Greer's way of thinking, because the one is everywhere and the whole universe is present in the one. As if to echo Blake, Greer states, "Thus, every created thing is a doorway to the Creator."[29] It follows that there is no Other either on the Earth or in outer space because we are all in each other, connected via the One Mind.

A common awakening. What does this fundamental assumption about the One Mind mean for extraterrestrial contact? It means that being attuned to subtle energies and capable of psychic functioning makes it easier to communicate with visitors from other worlds. In fact, psychic communication is what Greer calls the Rosetta stone of ET contact. He has been psychic since his boyhood, capable of out-of-body travel among many other things, including remote viewing, precognition, lucid dreams, clairvoyance, and levitation. His telepathic experiences with extraterrestrials are only a subset of a more general psychic awakening, and the same holds for Angelucci: "Hundreds of volumes could never put into words all that has transpired in my life and states of consciousness within the last two years" (133). The more noteworthy parallel is that each man developed the capacity for expanded awareness because of physical illness—both had medical problems that increased their sensitivity to subtle energy. In Greer's case, one suspects that growing up in a troubled family may have led to dissociation, which in turn blossomed into astral projection. But Greer's sepsis-related near-death experience at the age of seventeen connected him with the One Mind in an experience of cosmic consciousness and thus augmented his pre-existing sensitivity to subtle energy. A more pervasive physical debility, however, appears to have been the precondition for Angelucci's psychic awakening. In Neptune's words, "'It is only because your physical body is weakened and your spiritual perceptions thereby keener that we have been able to contact you'" (27). The particular sensitivity of his nervous system enables him to discern regular aircraft lights from saucer lights (59) and to feel a saucer's presence through a tingling in his skin (145). For Jung, this "inherent constitutional inadequacy in the extreme degree" contributes to the overall lack of credibility (Angelucci, x–xi; *CW* 10, 796/421); but it is quite parallel to Greer's more authoritative account of near death leading to cosmic consciousness and to Jung's expanded awareness following his heart attack. In Angelucci's awkward formulation, "I seemed to be projected beyond Time and Space and was conscious only of light, Light, LIGHT!" (34). The difference is that transcendent experience opens the way for Greer to communicate with ETs, whereas ET communication opens the way for Angelucci to achieve high states of consciousness. But in each case physical infirmity precedes and serves as a fundamental seedbed for psychic contact with alien visitors.

Further autobiographical parallels are also worth mentioning. Angelucci and Greer both witnessed extraterrestrial spacecraft when they were boys, as if the visitors were laying the foundation for more direct contact later in life. Both are scientifically oriented. Though not college educated, Angelucci loved to read textbooks on science and to speculate on the fabric of the universe, as he does in *Nature of Infinite Entities*. He later helped manufacture metal and plastic aircraft parts for Lockheed. Before becoming a UFO researcher, Greer was an emergency room physician in Boone, North Carolina. Each considers himself to be the salt of the earth. Angelucci is "a humble aircraft worker—a nobody" (8); and Neptune emphasizes the importance of humility in stating that "we singled out three individuals . . . simple, humble and presently unknown persons" for contact (9). Similarly Greer repeatedly calls himself just a country doctor. But these self-descriptions come with heavy qualifications. Angelucci confesses to taking pride in his rationality (24) and says of his coworkers, "They are both simple, humble men, average workers like myself, yet *potential gods*!" (112). Further acknowledgement of pride comes in the myth of the planet Lucifer, when Angelucci realizes that he has fallen to Earth because of excessive pride. Jung might diagnose *enantiodromia*, a swing between positive and negative inflation—nimble Reasoner and fallen angel versus humble aircraft worker. Greer too is proud of his rational powers, courage, fortitude, integrity, and perseverance; and Jung might note that at times in *Contact* Greer sounds more like a messianic figure than a guy who fixes broken bones.

Similar conclusions. Both Angelucci and Greer do much more than report their respective experiences with extraterrestrials; they also lay out a cosmology that attempts to convey truths about life in the physical universe. This is especially the case with Greer, who devotes the concluding chapters of *Hidden Truth* to expounding on spiritual truth as he sees it. Parallels between the two authors branch out into similar observations about the extraterrestrials themselves and about matters that straddle the line between the anagogical and the metaphysical. First, they both discuss the ETs themselves. "We, by our own standards, expected them to have predatory ideas of conquest and enslavement of mankind," states Angelucci (162). But both authors are also adamant that "All [ETs who are visiting the Earth] are of kindly intent and none will harm man" (12). Greer explains the reasoning behind that point in a scattered way, but the essence of it is as Angelucci states: we can rest assured that ETs are peaceful "because only the highest degree of harmony and the finest perception can survive space navigation" (155). Both authors also call attention to a terrestrial development that may have attracted the attention of extraterrestrial species: namely, the detonation of nuclear weapons in the atmosphere. Since everything is connected, such explosions on Earth may have a deleterious impact on alien worlds despite the light years that lie in between.

Second, as regards the anagogical and the metaphysical, the authors also come to very similar conclusions about death, deity, and evil. Having died at the age of seventeen, Greer is unafraid of death and occasionally calls the bluff of his opponents in the shadow government by bluntly stating that they are welcome to take him out if they wish. Angelucci expresses a similar confidence in the continuity of consciousness when he states, "I know now there is no death other than that which men upon Earth call life" (141). Naturally, both confidently believe in the existence of God. Angelucci asserts, "I knew God as a tangible, immutable Force that reaches to the furthest depths of Time and Eternity" (25). Both also claim special status for Jesus. As Jung notes (*CW* 10, 797/421), Neptune asserts that Jesus is "'Lord of the Flame—an infinite entity of the sun'" (32), while for Greer Jesus is an avatar, a higher order of spiritual entity than human souls. Whereas God and Jesus are sources of profound goodness, the authors stress a karma-like principle that obtains in matters of evil. When Greer is attacked with a sophisticated electronic weapon in chapter 18 of *Hidden Truth*, he tracks the beam back to a laboratory and sees the technician who is operating it. Apparently, the tech sees Greer seeing him, feels ashamed of himself, and ceases the assault. Greer notes, however, that often such persons are themselves struck down by the harm that they would project onto others. Whereas he is referring to individual persons, Angelucci applies the point to the macrocosm: "For one of the immutable laws of the cosmos is that evil projected to its limits is self-destroyed; hence too great a preponderance of evil invariably results in self-destruction and a new beginning in greater densities of matter" (165). The passage relates to my earlier observation that the crucifixion is an ongoing process for humans; now it seems that neither is the Fall a one-time descent from a higher to a lower state of being but instead an adjustment process that may occur at multiple points in history if lessons—especially lessons about environmental stewardship—are not learned.

Similar claims about ET technology and science. Having a scientific bent, both Angelucci and Greer make statements about the nature of extraterrestrial technology. They agree, for example, that UFOs are created in the realm of thought and that they emerge whole into the physical world. As Angelucci puts it, "Among the etheric beings . . . it is possible to create a saucer of any degree of materiality merely from a projected thought form which attracts material substance to it" (156–57). Alien spacecraft employ highly sophisticated means of generating energy (magnetism in Angelucci's view, anti-gravity and zero-point technology in Greer's). Being inter-dimensional, these spacecraft can vanish from sight, that is, leave the physical plane, though sometimes saucers "were invisible to Earthly eyes and could only be detected by radar," a point that obviates Jung's objection to the validity of radar traces (11). Moreover, having figured out the physics of nonlocality, extraterrestrial people are able to transcend space-time in order to travel either near the speed of light (Angelucci) or faster than the speed of light (Greer). Specifically, Greer believes that our extraterrestrial visitors have mastered the science of "nonlocality" so that their spacecraft can transit vast distances in the physical universe by entering what might be variously termed the ether, the astral plane, or hyperspace.[30] ETs also have highly advanced devices that facilitate communication with humans across the language barrier and with the home world despite vast distances, and Greer clarifies this point by stating that they have technology-assisted consciousness and consciousness-assisted technology. As a result of being exposed to alien spacecraft and communication devices, Angelucci and Greer both conclude that time, space, and separation are illusions. Both authors add that the military is highly interested in acquiring and reverse engineering ET technology.

Similar attitudes toward media and public opinion. Angelucci and Greer are alike in criticizing the government for not promulgating what is known about extraterrestrial visitation, the media for sanitizing news of UFO sightings, and science fiction writers for projecting the human shadow onto persons from other star systems (for example, Greer cites *Independence Day*). Angelucci takes the argument regarding fictional accounts in a slightly different direction by commenting on a lull in the projection process:

> As I looked about that busy room [at the science fiction convention] I thought that it was small wonder that the concoctors of science-fiction horror diets had declared the saucers "taboo". Far too much beautiful reality was on the side of the saucers. Harmony and beauty are much too tame for the horror boys. They have joined forces with the materialists, subversives and egoists to fight the "flying saucer sensationalists" down at every turn.
>
> (83)

This lack of interest has a fortunate result: "During the welcome lull the actual flying saucer phenomena and the extraterrestrials were left to the inexperienced but honest handling of rank amateurs" such as himself. "Had the professional spinners of horror-fiction stuck to the theme of flying saucers, the true contacts should never have been able to perform their missions" (83).

Angelucci and Greer both feel great responsibility for disseminating information about ET visitation. As Neptune says, "'For the present you are our emissary, Orfeo, and you must act! Even though people of Earth laugh derisively and mock you as a lunatic, tell them about us!'" (30). Angelucci recalls, "My insistence upon the absolute truth of my experiences finally appeared to be definitely alienating my friends and even my family" (39). "'Don't you understand,'" he says to his wife, "'these things really happened to me! It is my duty to tell what I know!'" (58). But in the final chapter, he states, "Although my story is given in good faith, some are bound to doubt me" (164). Jung's reductive psychological reading is certainly an apt example of the latter, but his snide remarks about "America [as] the land of superlatives and of science fiction" (*CW* 10, 595/314) and about "California, the classic Saucer country, so to speak" (*CW* 10, 704/372) are tame compared with the ridicule that Angelucci suffered at Lockheed and in the media for his assertions about the veracity of his experiences.[31] Fortunately, the humble plastics worker eventually received some positive recognition for his writing and became a featured speaker on the UFO circuit, which Jung reduces to "his career as an evangelist" for UFO activity (*CW* 10, 800/422). Greer too feels the ETs' imperative to go public, and he has suffered far more than the derision that Angelucci mentions. Because Greer has publicized not only word of aliens' visitation but also evidence of a global cover up of the greatest news story in the history of our planet, he has endured everything from attempts to subvert him and his organization to attempted murder by high-tech means.

Futurist predictions. Finally, Angelucci and Greer both anticipate a difficult transitional period in human history—a nigredo—that will be followed by a period of peace. As previously noted, Neptune calls the latter "'the shining reality of your great world of tomorrow—a world of brotherly love and fellowship when Man is for Man and bound in unity through the love of the Father'" (124). In more secular terms, our present divisiveness and separation will yield to unity and harmony through realization of connections via the One Mind. In fact, both Angelucci and Greer claim that, despite present turbulence, humanity has already begun a positive new age. "In reality this age of discord and stark materialism is already in the past and we have entered into the New Age," states Angelucci (143). Greer refers to it as a 500,000-year period of peace whose birthing pains we are now enduring. And both men agree, in Angelucci's words, that "the coming of the saucers will ultimately prove one of the most tremendous struggles of the ages in the evolving consciousness of mankind" (161), with profound consequences for every aspect of life on Earth.

Conclusion

The evidence that Greer has assembled, especially in print and on the Internet, suggests that his more subjective experiences are real events. In turn, all of the similarities between *The Secret of the Saucers* and *Hidden Truth—Forbidden Knowledge* lend credibility to Angelucci's claims about extraterrestrials; his book is not just a good-faith attempt to convey profound experiences to a lay audience but also an accurate account of actual ET contact. It may be that the more doubtful aspects of his account—Jesus as Lord of the Flame, Lucifer as a destroyed planet in our own solar system—are attempts to render extra-dimensional experience in an earthly language that cannot adequately capture nonverbal content. They may be mythical in the Jungian sense—not factually accurate but helpful in conveying truth about the human experience. If so, it is wrong to downgrade the whole of Angelucci's story as a naïve effusion, as Jung does. Of course, none of this *proves* that Angelucci's story is real; and my own readers are free to believe what they will. But the striking parallels between the two UFO authors do suggest that there are more things in the heavens and on Earth than are dreamed of in Jungian psychology and that the gulf between reality and Jung's interpretation of it might diminish if UFOs were understood to be an implication of the One Mind. There will no doubt be consequences of attempting to assert an interpretation that is at once literal and metaphysical, of arguing that accounts of extra-dimensional experience with visitors to our world are true—though fortunately not consequences like Angelucci's difficulty in finding a publisher for his work. He self-published an earlier fragment of his account, much as he apparently self-published *The Secret of the Saucers* at Amherst Press in Amherst, Wisconsin. Greer founded his own press, Crossing Point, Inc. and had *Hidden Truth—Forbidden Knowledge* produced through the 123PrintFinder, Inc. in California. By contrast, the publication of Hoyle's *The Black Cloud* by Harper & Brothers illustrates the mainstream media's preference for seeing extraterrestrial intelligence as dangerous to humans.

The preparation to write this chapter provided yet another example of the difficulty early twenty-first-century civilization will have in accepting the truth about ET visitation. Acquiring *The Black Cloud* was easy because my own university's library owns a copy, but *The Secret of the Saucers* had to be ordered through the inter-library loan system. Ironically, the book arrived from a highly religiously conservative institution in the eastern United States, bearing a faded stamp in the front matter to this effect:

> TO THE READER
> This book reflects the wealth of knowledge in the world today. X Baptist College includes this knowledge in order to standardize the work [that is, to keep the school on a par with secular institutions] and validate the credits of the college [that is, keep its accreditation]. Use of this volume by X Baptist College is not an endorsement of its contents. The position of the College on the fundamentals of the faith and the separate Christian life is well known.
> X Baptist College

My inquiry into the exact wording of this insertion elicited the following response from a reference librarian at that school:

> Without going down to pull an older book off the shelf, [I believe that] this sounds like a standard disclaimer that many fundamentalist Christian colleges and universities used to put in all of their books. The idea behind the "disclaimer" was that even though we owned the title and had the book on our shelves it didn't mean that the college endorsed the philosophical viewpoint of the book (for instance, a book on evolution). There also were a lot more student conduct rules back then and so if the book had a picture of someone that didn't meet the dress code [the reader could be sure] that we were not "endorsing" such behavior. We have been "X Baptist University" rather than "X Baptist College" since 1984 and as far as I know we have not placed those types of stickers in books since the early 1980s.
>
> One final note. Seeing such a disclaimer in an older book doesn't necessarily mean that this was a book that they particularly disagreed with. As far as I know, it was put into ALL books (except perhaps versions of the Bible). So it has no evaluative function[;] it was just part of standard processing procedure, like adding a date due slip or card pocket.

Angelucci might appreciate the librarian's implication that Jung's *Flying Saucers: A Modern Myth of Things Seen in the Skies*, and indeed *The Collected Works of C. G. Jung* as a whole, would also have been stamped with a disclaimer. The good news in the librarian's reply to my inquiry is that progress is being made toward greater openness—cautionary reminders have not been added to new books for nearly three decades. The bad news is that X Baptist University apparently still affirms the literal interpretation of the biblical creation story over the truth of evolutionary science; surely they would want no part of Greer's assertion that *Homo sapiens* are the result of genetic manipulation by extraterrestrials! As the librarian's reply implies, such accounts as I have investigated in this chapter will probably not receive the full credulity and critical attention that they deserve for quite some time; but just as we are grateful to Jung for expanding our understanding of the unconscious, perhaps one day we will eventually look back to people like Angelucci and Greer and feel gratitude that they helped to bring accounts of extraterrestrial contact into the mainstream. The result of such contact may be greater individuation. Jung suggests that because human beings are "cosmically isolated" "on a tiny speck of a planet in the Milky Way," our self-understanding is limited—we know that we are not animals or trees, but what we *are* "remains obscure." Contact with intelligent species from other planetary systems may lead us deeper into the human condition: "We would need an intimate knowledge of the inhabitants of other planets, inasmuch as they can be compared with men, in order to enable us to form some idea of what man is."[32]

Notes

1 Robert A. Monroe, *Ultimate Journey* (New York: Doubleday, 1994), 47–49. Monroe is not the only author previously considered in this book who acknowledges the possibility of intelligent life elsewhere in the universe. Milton refers to the possibility of extraterrestrial life when he calls "every Starr perhaps a World / Of destind habitation" (7.617–22). He also refers to such "other Worlds" at 3.566. See John Milton, *Paradise Lost*, in *The Riverside Milton*, ed. Roy Flannagan (Boston, MA: Houghton, 1998).

2 Robert A. Monroe, *Far Journeys* (New York: Doubleday, 1982), 230. The "Gathering" is also called Focus 35. See chapter 4, n. 12 for Monroe's system of Focus levels.

3 Monroe, *Ultimate Journey*, 274.

4 Ronald Russell, *The Journey of Robert Monroe: From Out-of-Body Explorer to Consciousness Pioneer* (Charlottesville, VA: Hampton Roads, 2007), 183 and 242.

5 Michael Talbot, *The Holographic Universe* (New York: HarperCollins, 1991), 276–85.

6 I discuss Jung's statement in *A Jungian Study of Shakespeare: The Visionary Mode* (New York: Palgrave Macmillan, 2009), 155, n. 1.

7 Donald E. Keyhoe, *Flying Saucers from Outer Space* (New York: Holt, 1953), 104.

8 Jung sees a synchronistic relationship between an archetype and the vision of a flying saucer (*CW* 10, 593/313 and 780/411). There may be such a relationship in Angelucci's invitation to speak at the Neptunian Club in light of his earlier conversations with an ET known as "Neptune" (Orfeo M. Angelucci, *The Secret of the Saucers* [Amherst, WI: Amherst, 1955], 131). Angelucci prefers the spelling "extra-terrestrials," but I have deleted the hyphen in all cases in the interest of consistency.

9 John Wyndham, *The Midwich Cuckoos* (London, UK: Michael Joseph, 1957).

10 Fred Hoyle, *The Black Cloud* (New York: Harper, 1957).

11 Monroe reports a similar experience of inhabiting another person's body in a chapter called "Reverse Image" (*Journeys Out of the Body*, updated ed. [1971; Doubleday, 1977], 86–100).

12 *The Gods Must Be Crazy*, directed by Jamie Uys (Hollywood, CA: Columbia Tristar, 1980), VHS.

13 "Orfeo M. Angelucci." *Wikipedia*, http://en.wikipedia.org/wiki/Orfeo_Angelucci (accessed July 30, 2012).

14 See Monroe, *Journeys*, chapter 15, "Sexuality in the Second State," 190–202.

15 *MDR*, 252.

16 The book includes an embarrassing error that reflects Angelucci's lack of a higher education. Adam asks him to tell the story in second person, by which they both clearly mean *third* person.

17 Angelucci, *Nature of Infinite Entities* (San Diego, CA: Talk of the Times, 1952), 2.

18 Charles T. Tart. *The End of Materialism: How Evidence of the Paranormal Is Bringing Science and Spirit Together* (Oakland, CA: New Harbinger and Noetic, 2009), 141. Tart's chapter 3, "Ways of Not Knowing: Distortions of Science and Intelligence," discusses "Pathologies of Knowing and Learning" (55–62). Dean Radin mentions similar fallacies in *The Conscious Universe: The Scientific Truth of Psychic Phenomena* (New York: HarperCollins, 1997), chapter 13, "A Field Guide to Skepticism" (205–27). Both authorities are writing about psi-related skepticism, but many of the intellectual traps apply equally well to people's doubts about UFOs.

19 Joseph M. Felser suggests that doomsday thinking results from human beings' separation from nature as a result of the Agricultural Revolution about 10,000 years ago. See *The Myth of the Great Ending: Why We've Been Longing for the End of Days Since the Beginning of Time* (Charlottesville, VA: Hampton Roads, 2011), 51.

20 Desmond Leslie and George Adamski, *Flying Saucers Have Landed* (New York: British Book Centre, 1953), 125.

21 Ibid., 171.

22 Ibid., 211.
23 Keyhoe, *Flying Saucers*, 157–59. Keyhoe writes that "the lone unofficial American report [Adamski's] reads like science fiction, and not too good fiction at that." Keyhoe's reason for not mentioning the affidavits may be that his source was Len Welch's "tongue-in-cheek" account of Adamski's encounter in the Phoenix *Gazette* (November 24, 1952) rather than Adamski's *Flying Saucers Have Landed*, which was not published until 1953.
24 Steven M. Greer, *Contact: Countdown to Transformation—The CSETI Experience 1992–2009* (Crozet, VA: Crossing Point, 2009).
25 Steven M. Greer, *Disclosure: Military and Government Witnesses Reveal the Greatest Secret in Modern History* (Crozet, VA: Crossing Point, 2001) and *Extraterrestrial Contact: The Evidence and Implications* (Crozet, VA: Crossing Point, 1999).
26 Keyhoe's chapter 8, "The Canadian Project," records the author's interaction with Smith and some of Project Magnet's discoveries (*Flying Saucers*, 128–49).
27 The memo, dated August 3, 1962, is reproduced in *Hidden Truth—Forbidden Knowledge* (Crozet, VA: Crossing Point, 2006), 139.
28 Greer, *Hidden Truth*, 25–26, 49, 228, and 261.
29 Ibid., 54.
30 Greer evidently understands "nonlocality" to mean There rather than Here—that is, some nonphysical realm versus the world that is visible to us. As I stated in the introduction, "nonlocality" properly means "acausality."
31 In one of his statements on primitive mentality, Jung opines that Americans are less individuated than Europeans and therefore more vulnerable to unconscious forces (*CW* 18, 341/148). I address his problematic statement in *A Jungian Study of Shakespeare*, 95–96.
32 C. G. Jung, *Letters*, ed. G. Adler and Aniela Jaffé, trans. R. F. C. Hull, vol. 2 (Princeton, NJ: Princeton University Press, 1975), 592–93 and 323.

6

SYNCHRONICITY

Wordsworth's stolen boat episode in *The Prelude*

Even skeptics who give little credence to altered states, out-of-body experiences, and extraterrestrials and who would object to these phenomena as fit subjects for literary interpretation would acknowledge the reality of "synchronicities," which for Jung may involve simultaneity in space in time, separation in time, or separation in place.[1] As he puts it,

> An unexpected content which is directly or indirectly connected with some objective external event coincides with the ordinary psychic state: this is what I call a synchronicity, and I maintain that we are dealing with exactly the same category of events whether their objectivity appears separated from my consciousness in space or in time.
>
> (*CW* 8, 855/445)

Such meaningful coincidences imply that time operates strangely at the quantum level of reality. It is not the arrow that Westerners assume it to be but instead a circle. William Shakespeare's language provides apt illustrations of this contrast. Prospero's phrase in *The Tempest*, "the dark backward and abysm of time" (1.2.50), refers to linear time in which the past is distant; Feste's phrase in *Twelfth Night*, "the whirligig of time" (5.1.376), conveys not only the cycle of life but perhaps also the unity and simultaneity of all action. A very similar contrast appears in William Faulkner's description in "A Rose for Emily" of "the very old men . . . to whom all the past is not a diminishing road but, instead, a huge meadow which no winter ever quite touches.[2] If time is a loop that encompasses past, present, and future, much as all points on the circumference of a circle are equidistant from the center, then the temporal abnormality of synchronicities comes into clearer focus. This chapter investigates the underpinnings of Jung's synchronicity theory in terms that resonate with the One Mind, and then it discusses synchronicity within an overall Jungian reading of William Wordsworth's stolen boat episode in his psychological epic, *The Prelude*.

Jung's synchronicity theory

Within the One Mind/*unus mundus*, there is a holographic relationship among the parts, meaning that each part contains a model of the whole. The point is heavy with implications. First, it follows from an overarching connection between the part and the whole that synchronicity (a part) has a link to a much greater whole, an "'absolute knowledge'—a knowledge unobtainable through normal sensory channels or reasoning."[3] A second implication is "that psyche and matter are two different aspects of one and the same thing" (*CW* 8, 418/215) because the One Mind subsumes "the empirical world of appearances" and its "transcendental background."[4] In other words, the One Mind encompasses the realms that David Bohm calls the implicate and explicate orders. As discussed in the introduction, the explicate order is the realm of classical physics (Newton and Descartes), whereas the implicate order is the realm of quantum physics (Einstein and others). Bohm states, "In the implicate order everything is . . . internally related to everything, everything contains everything, and only in the explicate order are things separate and relatively independent."[5] The statement expresses much the same thing as chapter 2's discussion of Thomas Campbell's "theory of everything," which describes reality as a series of fractals in which consciousness becomes increasingly differentiated. In other words, there are different degrees of consciousness within the One Mind, though it is unitary in nature.

Even within the explicate order, separation is illusory because a physical fractal is a part that contains and connects to the whole, with multiple implications arising. For example, Bohm suggests that, on the level of implicate order, universal causality may be the case. Similarly, F. David Peat observes that "everything that happens in our universe is in fact caused by everything else." Further implications include what Jung calls "a psychically relative space-time continuum" (*CW* 8, 440/231) and, as J. Gary Sparks notes, "the fact that intelligent meaning can reside in and arise from matter." As Sparks goes on to say, "For more and more people, the spirit no longer comes down from above. It emerges up from matter and is there for those who are willing to accept the earth's complications and see the spirit in the storms body and matter throw at us."[6]

For Jung, of course, it is the archetype that bridges the physical and the nonphysical. As if to enact this principle, his treatise, *Synchronicity: An Acausal Connecting Principle* (1952), was originally published in a volume with the work of physicist Wolfgang Pauli. It is not just that the archetype is a nonphysical organizing principle that guides the creation of images in physical manifestation. Pauli knows that mind impinges on matter, just as Jung understands that the archetype has a physical aspect, which he calls psychoid, "an adjective referring to the boundaries of the psyche, one of which interfaces with the body and the physical world and the other with the realm of 'spirit.'"[7] The psychoid realm is not only physical and nonphysical but also neither—some third thing. The result is a complementarity between physics and psychology, which Jung addresses in a difficult statement:

> Microphysics is feeling its way into the unknown side of matter [the quantum but also the mind], just as complex psychology is pushing forward into the unknown side of psyche [the collective unconscious but also matter]. . . . The common background of microphysics and depth-psychology is as much physical as psychic and therefore neither, but rather a third thing [the psychoid], a neutral nature which can at most be grasped in hints since in essence it is transpersonal.
>
> (*CW* 14, 768/538)

Peat's discussion of the psychoid factor illuminates that third thing:

> the psychoid as a spectrum which contains mind and matter at its ends . . . with a whole range of hidden possibilities in between and even beyond. Synchronicity, for Jung, therefore had its origin in a movement of this spectrum which then manifests itself in its two extremes, as the simultaneous manifestation of a pattern of the material and mental realms.[8]

Jung is more helpful in *On the Nature of the Psyche* in stating that "the relative or partial identity of psyche and physical continuum is of the greatest importance theoretically, because it brings with it a tremendous simplification by bridging over the seeming incommensurability between the physical world and the psychic" (*CW* 8, 440/231). Marie-Louise von Franz calls this relationship a "*coniunctio* of matter and psyche"; Michael Conforti refers to "the indivisibility of psyche and matter"; and Jung himself considers the archetypes transgressive, meaning that "they are not limited to the psychic realm."[9] In short, a physical manifestation in the explicate order registers a connection to the unseen implicate order; and the archetype, as a psychoid go-between, illustrates the unity among the divisions within the One Mind. The conclusion, then, is a stark distinction that sets Jung quite apart from his early mentor: Freud is to classical physics, causality, the personal unconscious, and the physical world as Jung is to quantum physics, acausality, the collective unconscious, and the *unus mundus*.

The purpose of the preceding paragraphs has been to sum up the thinking that undergirds Jung's actual theory of synchronicity, to which I now turn. The synchronicity treatise speaks of "synchronism" as "the simultaneous occurrence of two events" (*CW* 8, 849/441). Some are causal and inhabit the realm of classical physics or relate at least to chance, such as streaks in random events. Those that are acausal or quantum are called synchronicities and arise from the archetypes' psychoid nature: "phenomena of simultaneity or synchronicity seem to be bound up with the archetypes," Jung succinctly states (*CW* 8, 841/437); but they also seem to manifest in connection with instinct and emotion. He offers various definitions of synchronicity; here is one of the best: "Synchronicity therefore consists of two factors: *a*) An unconscious image comes into consciousness either directly (i.e., literally) or indirectly (symbolized or suggested) in the form of a dream, idea, or premonition. *b*) An objective situation coincides with this content" (*CW* 8, 858/447). The parts of this *coniunctio* commingle with affectivity and comment on each other in meaningful ways, often relating as well to complexes but arising without any known cause. As Conforti states, "The complex creates a type of antenna so that we can tune into and align with a specific frequency of an archetype"; this, he argues, accounts for "an issue that suddenly manifest[s] in virtually every facet of our lives."[10] But synchronicity, as Sparks emphasizes, is also like dreaming while awake because "*the dream process occurs in the outer world*."[11] Two possibilities thus arise: synchronicity *manifests*, and synchronicity *compensates*.

Although synchronicity is acausal, Jung does speak of a condition that acts as a kind of seedbed by providing context and opportunity for the phenomenon: a lowering of consciousness, as in meditation. For example, he writes, "When . . . the vision arose in Swedenborg's mind of a fire in Stockholm, there was a real fire raging there at the same time, without there being any demonstrable or even thinkable connection between the two" (*CW* 8, 912/481). Jung speculates, "We must assume that there was a lowering of the threshold of consciousness which gave him 'absolute knowledge'" (*CW* 8, 912/481). Elsewhere, he speaks of "an *abaissement du niveau mental*, that is, the overpowering of the ego by unconscious contents and the consequent identification with a preconscious wholeness" (*CW* 8, 430/225). As Stein observes more clearly,

> Often synchronicity occurs . . . when a person is psychically in an *abaissement du niveau mental* (a lower level of conscious awareness, a sort of dimming of sense) and the level of consciousness has dropped into what is today called an alpha state. This means also that the unconscious is more energized than consciousness, and complexes and archetypes are aroused into a more activated state and can push over the threshold into consciousness. It is possible that this psychic material corresponds to objective data outside the psyche.[12]

Even more simply, Jung states that "synchronistic phenomena can be evoked by putting the subject into an unconscious state (trance)" (*CW* 8, 440/232). His essay "The Psychology of Eastern Meditation" mentions how "the Indian" speaks of *dhyāna*, "the sinking and deepening of contemplation" (*CW* 11, 936/570, 938/571), that is, a "*sinking* into meditation" (*CW* 11, 911/560; emphasis in the original); how "meditation . . . is therefore something like a descent into the fountainhead of the psyche, into the unconscious itself" (935/570); and how "the West is always seeking to uplift, but the East seeks a sinking or deepening" (936/570). As Sparks observes, when we go within to perform the work of self-examination, "Events in the outer, physical world itself come to us in moments of resonance, guidance and response."[13] Surely, inner and outer come into even greater synchronicity when one meditates. That may partly account for why Jung states, in connection with "The Tibetan Book of the Great Liberation," that "the meditation our text has in mind seems to be a sort of Royal Road to the unconscious" (*CW* 11, 827/507). The ultimate goal, of course, is *samādhi*, "the state of supernatural calm" (*CW* 11, 917/562); however, in order to make progress in achieving altered states, one must work through "the *kleshas*, the disorderly and chaotic instinctual forces which yoga proposes to yoke" (*CW* 11, 938/571). While meditation and yoga both facilitate inner work by lowering consciousness, the road to enlightenment leads through the personal unconscious and especially the shadow. It follows that a synchronicity's meaning may guide the individuation process.

Wordsworth's stolen boat episode

How might Jung's synchronicity theory be applied to canonical literature; and how, especially, can doing so *expand* his sense of the relationships among nature, archetype, and psyche? What happens to interpretation, for example, if the relationship between the archetype and nature is reversed so that the outer world provides a hinge between the psyche and the archetype? A close reading of Wordsworth's stolen boat episode in *The Prelude* enables an exploration of this possibility. Although Wordsworth's passage does not perfectly match any of Jung's three types of meaningful coincidences, the elements of synchronicity theory are part of a more general Jungian reading that has remained surprisingly absent from the critical discussion. Indeed, Wordsworth's poem is a particularly rich medium for a discussion of the One Mind because "seeing" in Romantic poetry involves a dialectical engagement between psyche and nature.

In both *The Prelude* and "Tintern Abbey," Wordsworth lays out three stages of cognitive development: physical union with nature in early childhood, emotional experience of nature in youth, and an adult stage marked by the "philosophic mind."[14] In the stolen boat episode, he is writing in stage three about an experience in stage two, the emotional stage. The incident is one of the "spots of time" that he discusses and illustrates in book 12—seemingly trivial events that have "a renovating virtue," nourish and repair our minds, and enhance our pleasure (lines 208–18). Directly following this declaration, he describes two such "spots." The first involves seeing the corpse of a murderer who had been hanged in chains and then a "female and her garments vexed and tossed / By the strong wind" (lines 260–61). The second spot of time is a recollection of his father's death at Christmas time in 1783 when Wordsworth was 13 years old. Losing his father "appeared / A chastisement," apparently for the sexual desire that the wind-blown girl has evoked in him; and he "bowed low / To God, Who thus corrected [his] desires" (lines 310–11 and 315–16).

The stolen boat episode is a spot of time that takes place earlier in the emotional stage—perhaps, as Richard Lansdown suggests, when Wordsworth was between four and nine years of age.[15] The boy's sexual desire is essential to an understanding of the theft, as are the spots of time that directly precede the author's brief outing on the moonlit lake. These are both thefts that involve birds, represent the young fellow's relationship to nature in general, and stand in for our own orientation toward the natural world. Wordsworth steals another man's bird and then plunders a bird's nest high up on a wind-swept crag.[16] No bird attacks Wordsworth, and his pain is not a physical wound but instead a pang of conscience. In the first case, he hears "among the solitary hills / Low breathings coming after me"; in the second, he hears "the loud dry wind" (1.300–39 and 337). These experiences illustrate the pattern of infraction and consequence in book 12's description of spots of time, with guilt projected onto the natural world, which then appears to rise up in pursuit. Yet even such disturbing moments are part of "a dark / Inscrutable workmanship" that "reconciles / Discordant elements" and makes up his adult self (lines 340–50). As the subtitle tells us, *The Prelude* is a poem about the "Growth of a Poet's Mind," which is often traumatic at an early age.

The comingling of action and affect also structures the stolen boat episode (1.357–400); here is a brief synopsis. On a summer evening, the youthful Wordsworth finds a small rowboat "within a rocky cave," which may be either a literal cave or a rocky cove with overhanging branches (hence "the covert" at line 387). In order to row the boat straight out into the lake, he fixes his eyes on "a craggy ridge" behind him, keeping it directly over the stern." Then "a huge peak . . . / Upreared its head." As he pulls away from the shore, the mountain that towers over the ridge directly above the cave or cove begins to appear.[17] Ted Holt and John Gilroy describe the scene:

> In daylight he would have been able to see the dividing line between ridge and peak, but the effect of the moonlight was to obscure this detail. In fact, all he saw was the first black silhouetted shape suddenly grow dramatically in bulk as he rowed away and seem to come towards him.[18]

The farther he rows out onto the lake, the larger the peak becomes, and "like a living thing / [it] Strode after [him]." He eventually turns around and, "with trembling oars," rows back to shore. But the terrifying sight of the mountain has psychological consequences that endure well after the return of the boat to its mooring in "the covert of the willow tree": his consciousness suffers "a darkness . . . / Or blank desertion," and the episode on the lake proves to be "a trouble to [his] dreams."

Not surprisingly, the stolen boat episode just described lends itself to Freudian psychological interpretation. To begin with, Wordsworth's theft is "an act of stealth / And troubled pleasure" in retrospect (lines 361–62), which illustrates Freud's idea of the ambivalence of emotions in *Totem and Taboo* because the resulting trauma recalls the way in which violating a taboo makes one unclean.[19] Oedipal conflict erupts; and desire becomes phallic, as, for Thomas Weiskel, it also does in "Nutting," a poem about Wordsworth's rapacious violation of nature.[20] The similarities between the stolen boat episode and "Nutting" suggest that they describe essentially the same psycho-sexual process; redundancy may explain why Wordsworth excised the latter from *The Prelude.* Much as the boy destructively penetrates a clearing in "Nutting," he rows "lustily" toward the center of the lake in his stolen boat, with the contrast between feminine and masculine images suggesting that the episode is an act of compromise as regards the Oedipal dilemma.[21] On the one hand, Wordsworth steals a boat from a cave or "covert" and takes it out onto a moonlit lake, making "small circles" as he rows (feminine). On the other, his oars penetrate the lake; and he rows "an unswerving line" away from "a craggy ridge," until the "huge peak" rears up to frighten him (masculine). It is as if, in stealing another man's boat, the boy enacts inappropriate desire for the maternal feminine; and the return to shore "with trembling oars" suggests a psychological chastisement for inappropriate phallicism. Affect produces action, which leads in turn to a compensating affect. Accordingly, the mountain that rears up and scares Wordsworth has been considered "a totem or father-substitute" (Empson) and "a subconscious symbol of adult authority" (Bateson). The peak, however, never really "upreared its head"; since it is only "as if" that happens, projection evidently occurs. The "huge and mighty forms" that Wordsworth then experiences in the aftermath of his moonlit outing may be the Jungian-sounding "primordial shapes of punishment" (Lansdown), which are all the more appropriate as a substitute for Wordsworth's father.[22] It appears, then, that the stolen boat episode is a key moment in the formation of Wordsworth's superego. Not having learned the inappropriateness of theft in the bird-stealing episode or from the plundering of a mother-bird's nest, he must repeat the same basic lesson at greater intensity in the stolen boat episode: one must not only resist sexual desire but also respect and internalize masculine authority in order to achieve mature self-restraint.

Imagination and inflation. In the first half of the stolen boat episode, various details suggest that the imagination becomes active. Presumably the young Wordsworth has enjoyed reading romances and tall tales. John Beer states that the poet's "childhood reading of giants, in stories such as that of Jack and the Beanstalk" makes him susceptible to fear.[23] But the more important point is that activating his imagination on the water is second nature to him because he has already done so in his reading. Thus he is "*like* one who rows, / Proud of his skill" (my emphasis). The "little boat" becomes "an elfin pinnace," which goes "heaving through the water like a swan." The "huge peak" seems to rear up, "as if with voluntary power instinct" (pronounced in*stinct*, that is, seemingly with a will that is innate in the mountain's basic nature) and to stride after him. Imagining that the boat is elfin and that he is a competent oarsman signals positive inflation, as though the boy is rowing his way into the pages of a romance tale. The appearance of the peak then sparks *enantiodromia*, a swing to negative inflation—guilt, terror, powerlessness, and a harsh snap back to reality.

Synchronicity. As well, the boy's experience shares some of the characteristics that Jung assigns to synchronicities. There is the simultaneous occurrence of a psychological state and a perception—but not an actual occurrence—of something in the natural world. Affectivity is certainly engaged. The experience is meaningful. The father archetype may mediate between the mind and nature. Beer certainly has the archetypes in mind when he writes that "the crucial element in the episode of the stolen boat was that it was an act of guilt, committed in nature and subsequently admonished by forces of nature, acting in conjunction with *innate powers of the mind itself*" (my emphasis).[24] But there may be causality at work rather than coincidence: unconscious guilt is projected onto the peak, whose unexpected and sinister appearance shuts down the boy's romantic imaginings and corrects his positive inflation by eliciting fear. If projection and causality are present, and if the mountain itself really does not do anything, the stolen boat episode cannot be considered a synchronicity in the purest sense. Evidently, the "act of stealth" activates the archetype, which colors the boy's perception of the peak, which leads in turn to negative affects—but that is a causal process. In this respect, the episode is a better fit for Michael Talbot's previously quoted understanding of perception: "The eye/brain is not a faithful camera, but tinkers with the world before it gives it to us."[25] Certainly the point is consistent with the Romantic sense that the mind and nature actively impact each other.

Then again, the peak looms large "as if with *voluntary* power instinct"—as if it does so under its own power rather than in response to the boy's consciousness, which at that moment is enjoying a state of positive inflation and imaginative reverie. The mountain does not actually do anything; it just appears as a *coincidence* of the boy's rowing away from shore. But in an expanded reading of synchronicity, it plays the bridge-like role, becoming the meeting place of the psyche and the father archetype. Whereas archetype is the meeting ground between nature and psyche in a traditional reading, an expanded and more flexible application of synchronicity theory suggests that archetype barges in to meet psyche in the middle ground of nature. In each case, the boy registers the mountain as active; the difference is the degree of agency attributed to the archetype. The coincidental meeting of archetype and psyche in the medium of nature now becomes meaningful to him through fear. Thus stealing the boat is the occasion for, but not necessarily the sole cause of, his belief that the peak strides after him. The episode may still involve some projection, but archetypal intervention is at least equally important. The mountain appears sinister to him because the archetype actively imbues it with energy, animating nature rather than merely amplifying projected guilt.

Archetype and archetypal image. The link between the mountain and the archetype comes into clearer focus in light of the passage's structure. The stolen boat episode is 43 lines long. Twenty lines into the passage, Wordsworth's psyche is still in a state of positive inflation as he imagines his boat's motion through the water to resemble that of a swan. At line 21, he begins to see over the "craggy steep"; and at line 22—exactly halfway through the passage—the "huge peak" rears up. This intrusion of an archetypal image of the father-mountain marks the transition from Wordsworth's engagement with Oedipal feelings from his personal unconscious to the deeper reality of the collective unconscious in the remainder of the passage. In the aftermath of his outing, his psyche is deeply troubled. Here is the description, with emphases added.

> for many days, my brain
> Worked with a dim and undetermined sense
> Of *unknown modes of being*; o'er my thoughts
> There hung a darkness, call it solitude
> Or blank desertion. *No familiar shapes*
> *Remained, no pleasant images* of trees,
> Of sea or sky, no colours of green fields;
> But *huge and mighty forms*, that do not live
> Like living men, moved slowly through the mind
> By day, and were a trouble to *my dreams*.
> (lines 391–400)

The traumatic experience involving the "huge peak" (his engagement with the personal unconscious via the imagination) has opened Wordsworth's psyche to the collective unconscious. The "unknown modes of being" and "huge and mighty forms" are the archetypes. Herbert Lindenberger reaches a similar conclusion by non-Jungian means, stating that "the 'huge and mighty Forms' which pursue the poet for days after the stolen-boat incident exist at once in his own mind, in the external landscape, and . . . in the universal mind as well."[26] This is an excellent statement, for it stresses three crucial points about archetypes: they are innate, they have a physical dimension, and they are subsumed by the One Mind. Of course, archetypes are universal patterns or the potential for representation, not the images themselves. The fact that Wordsworth perceives "no familiar shapes" or "pleasant images" suggests that stealing the boat triggers a direct experience of the archetypes, both while he is awake and in his dreams. The latter illustrate the connection that was made in the introduction between the collective unconscious and Bohm's "implicate order." As Talbot puts it, "Perhaps dreams are a bridge between the perceptual and nonmanifest orders and represent a 'natural transformation of the implicate into the explicate'."[27] At the very least, the stolen boat episode shares with synchronicity the imbrication of mind and matter; and it clearly suggests that dreams are meaningful, as I have stressed in chapter 3's discussion of the wanderer's dream and hallucination in another small boat.

The archetypal basis of experience, especially of synchronicities, has great significance to Jung, whose following statement seems tailor-made for the aftermath of the stolen boat episode:

> The archetypes are formal factors responsible for the organization of unconscious psychic processes: they are "patterns of behaviour." At the same time they have a "specific charge" and develop numinous effects which express themselves as *affects*. The affect produces a partial *abaissement du niveau mental*, for although it raises a particular content

> to a supernormal degree of luminosity, it does so by withdrawing so much energy from other possible contents of consciousness that they become darkened and eventually unconscious. Owing to the restriction of consciousness produced by the affect so long as it lasts, there is a corresponding lowering of orientation which in turn gives the unconscious a favourable opportunity to slip into the space vacated. Thus we regularly find that unexpected or otherwise inhibited unconscious contents break through and find expression in the affect. Such contents are very often of an inferior or primitive nature and thus betray their archetypal origin.
> (*CW* 8, 841/436–37; emphases in the original)

Jung describes precisely what the young Wordsworth experiences. The paternally charged archetype imbues with meaning the archetypal image of the "huge peak," which causes a specific affect (terror). In the aftermath of the outing on the lake, he experiences a lowering of consciousness characterized by the darkening of the content (images disappear), which enables the "huge and mighty forms" to make their presence known to consciousness, especially in dreams. As stated in the previous section on synchronicity, Wordsworth's experience on the lake (his encounter with nature) provides a link between his psyche and the collective unconscious. This troubling aftermath compensates for the inflation that precedes the boy's perception of the "huge peak."

The One Mind. An earlier draft appearing in Wordsworth's Alfoxden notebook enhances the relevance of the passage to this book's study of the One Mind's literary significance.

> unknown modes of being which on earth,
> Or in the heavens or in the heavens and earth
> Exist by mighty combinations, bound
> Together by link, and with a soul
> Which makes all one.[28]

Again, "unknown modes of being" are archetypes; but the alternative passage points to their psychoid nature ("on earth / Or in the heavens or in the heavens and earth"). Jung would prefer this version because it more clearly asserts that the archetypes are the connecting links between the psychological/mental and the physical/natural. They are also organizing principles—they "exist by mighty combinations"—but are subsumed within something even greater, "a soul / Which makes all one," the One Mind. In the editorial commentary that follows the stolen boat episode, the poet drives home the points made in his notebook:

> Wisdom and Spirit of the universe!
> Thou Soul that art the eternity of thought,
> That givest to forms and images a breath
> And everlasting motion, not in vain

By day or star-light thus from my first dawn
Of childhood didst thou intertwine for me
The passions that build up our human soul;
Not with the mean and vulgar works of man,
But with high objects, with enduring things—
With life and nature, purifying thus
The elements of feeling and of thought,
And sanctifying, by such discipline,
Both pain and fear, until we recognize
A grandeur in the beatings of the heart.
(lines 401–14)

Here again is the One Mind ("Wisdom and Spirit of the universe"), which Wordsworth identifies as consciousness ("Thou Soul that art the eternity of thought"). This is the same spirit that in "Tintern Abbey" "impels / All thinking things, all objects of all thought, / And rolls through all things" (lines 100–2). It is the source of, or the Unmoved Mover behind, archetypes and archetypal images ("forms and images"). It plays a creative and pedagogical role in confronting a young boy with emotions ("the passions that build up our human soul") by means of the experience of nature ("enduring things . . . life and nature"), which is not always easy ("pain and fear") so that he develops the proper attitude ("a grandeur in the beatings of the heart").

As regards the One Mind, the stolen boat episode anticipates Wordsworth's culminating vision in book 14 atop Mt. Snowdon where the moon illuminates water vapor: "The Moon hung naked in a firmament / Of azure without cloud, and at my feet / Rested a silent sea of hoary mist" (lines 40–42). The scene appears to him as "the type / Of a majestic intellect" (lines 66–67).

There I beheld the emblem of a mind
That feeds upon infinity, that broods
Over the dark abyss, intent to hear
Its voices issuing forth to silent light
In one continuous stream; a mind sustained
By recognitions of transcendent power,
In sense conducting to ideal form,
In soul of more than mortal privilege.
(lines 70–77)

The moon overlooks Wordsworth, who overlooks the illuminated mist below him: the One Mind is to human consciousness as the latter is to nature. It is also significant that the "mind / That feeds upon infinity" is "intent to hear" the voices issuing forth from "the dark abyss" of nature. Apparently, the One Mind, out of which everything is made, needs nature and the human psyche in order to experience itself. Wordsworth's realization culminates the developmental process of which the stolen boat episode is a crucial piece. His acts of theft and the "low breathings" that pursue him in book 1 make him anti-Romantic insofar as he is at odds with both nature and his own psyche. My father, Francis Fike, explores Wordsworth's anti-Romanticism in his article on the correspondent breeze.[29] Just as he suggests that the death by drowning of Wordsworth's brother shows nature to be dangerous (see "Elegiac Stanzas"), I would argue that the stolen boat episode presents nature as having the capacity for moral chastisement. It is thus "correspondent" to conscience in the same way that imagination corresponds to wind (1.35). Or as Wordsworth states in "Tintern Abbey," nature is "the guardian . . . / Of all my moral being" (lines 110–11). By the time he stands atop Mt. Snowdon, however, he has developed a properly Romantic attitude: achieving both "philosophic mind" and individuation has enabled him to understand that human beings should live in harmony with nature because all of creation participates in the One Mind.

Notes

1 The three types are illustrated in my essay "*Light at Midnight* and the Art of Synchronicity," *Conversations in the Field* 1, no. 7 (2010): 1–8, http://thejungiansociety.org. There I also discusses the underpinnings of synchronicity featured in the following paragraphs.

2 William Faulkner, "A Rose for Emily," in *The Riverside Anthology of Literature*, ed. Douglas Hunt, 3rd ed. (Boston, MA: Houghton, 1997), 259. Philosopher Joseph M. Felser discusses the distinction between time as linear versus circular throughout *The Myth of the Great Ending: Why We've Been Longing for the End of Days Since the Beginning of Time* (Charlottesville, VA: Hampton Roads, 2011).

3 Victor Mansfield, *Synchronicity, Science, and Soul-Making: Understanding Jungian Synchronicity through Physics, Buddhism, and Philosophy* (Chicago, IL: Open Court, 1995), 58. For "the absolute knowledge of the unconscious," see *Synchronicity: An Acausal Connecting Principle* in *CW* 8, 923/489.

4 Marie-Louise von Franz, *On Divination and Synchronicity*, 126.

5 David Bohm, *On Creativity*, ed. Lee Nichol (New York: Routledge,1998), 105. F. David Peat helpfully explains implicate versus explicate in *Synchronicity: The Bridge Between Matter and Mind* (New York: Bantam, 1987), 167ff.

6 David Bohm, *Wholeness and the Implicate Order* (New York: Routledge), 225; Peat, *Synchronicity*, 58; and J. Gary Sparks, *At the Heart of the Matter: Synchronicity And Jung's Spiritual Testament* (Toronto: Inner City, 2007), 117 and 172.

7 Murray Stein, *Jung's Map of the Soul: An Introduction* (Chicago, IL: Open Court, 1998), 234.

8 Peat, *Synchronicity*, 188.

9 See Marie-Louise von Franz, *On Divination and Synchronicity*, 116; Michael Conforti, *Field, Form, and Fate: Patterns in Mind, Nature, and Psyche*, rev. ed. (New Orleans, LA: Spring Journal, 2003), 51; and Stein, *Jung's Map of the Soul*, 201.

10 Conforti, *Field, Form, and Fate*, 24.

11 Sparks, *At the Heart of the Matter*, 52.

12 Stein, *Jung's Map of the Soul*, 211.

13 Sparks, *At the Heart of the Matter*, 14.

14 The phrase "philosophic mind" is from "Intimations Ode," line 187. This chapter uses *Selected Poems and Prefaces by William Wordsworth*, ed. Jack Stillinger (Boston, MA: Houghton, 1965). All citations to Wordsworth's poems appear in the text.

15 Richard Lansdown, "Transitional Objects: The Spots of Time in *The Prelude* of 1799," *The Critical Review* 42 (2002), 19.
16 There is a notable contrast between Wordsworth's bird theft and Loren Eiseley's account of capturing a sparrow hawk in an abandoned cabin in "The Bird and the Machine," in *The Immense Journey* (New York: Random, 1957), 188–89.
17 Based on this topographical information, Mary R. Wedd identifies two possible locations: "Stybarrow Crag, in which case the 'huge cliff' would be Black Crag" and somewhere "near Blowick, probably on the north side, either of Purse Crag or of the Devil's Chimney, in which case the 'huge cliff' would be Place Fell" ("Wordsworth's Stolen Boat," *The Wordsworth Critic* 11 [1980]: 248).
18 Ted Holt and John Gilroy, *A Commentary on Wordsworth's* Prelude *Books I–V* (Boston, MA: Routledge, 1983), 15.
19 Sigmund Freud, *Totem and Taboo*, in *The Standard Edition of the Complete Psychological Works*, ed. and trans. James Strachey, vol. 13 (London: Hogarth, 1966), 1–162. Pages 18–74 deal with taboo and emotional ambivalence.
20 Thomas Weiskel, *The Romantic Sublime: Studies in the Structure and Psychology of Transcendence* (Baltimore: The Johns Hopkins University Press, 1976), 134.
21 For acts of compromise, see *The Standard Edition*, vol. 13, 30–31.
22 William Empson, *Seven Types Of Ambiguity* (London, UK: Chatto and Windus, 1956), 20; F. W. Bateson, *Wordsworth: A Re-interpretation* (New York: Longmans, 1954), 55; and Lansdown, "Transitional Objects," 20.
23 John Beer, *Wordsworth in Time* (Boston, MA: Faber, 1979), 73.
24 Beer, *Wordsworth in Time*, 75–76.
25 Michael Talbot, *The Holographic Universe* (New York: HarperCollins, 1991), 163.
26 Herbert Lindenberger, *On Wordsworth's* Prelude (Princeton, NJ: Princeton University Press, 1963), 90–91.
27 Talbot, *The Holographic Universe*, 63.
28 Quoted in Beer, *Wordsworth in Time*, 74.
29 Francis Fike, "Correspondent Breeze: The Course of a Romantic Metaphor," *Renascence: Essays on Values in Literature* 32 (1979): 3–12.

7

REMOTE VIEWING AND CHANNELING

The sonnets of Shakespeare and "Shakespeare"

Chapter 7 considers two unconventional means of obtaining information that will receive attention from literary critics in the future: remote viewing and channeling. Each phenomenon has some basis in Jung's writings. In *Synchronicity: An Acausal Connecting Principle*, he asks and answers a relevant question in a way that hints at the possibility of remote viewing:

> How could an event remote in space and time produce a corresponding psychic image when the transmission of energy necessary for this is not even thinkable? However incomprehensive it may appear, we are finally compelled to assume that there is in the unconscious something like an *a priori* knowledge or an "immediacy" of events which lacks any causal basis. At any rate our conception of causality is incapable of explaining the facts.
>
> (*CW* 8, 856/4470)

In a similar way, a partial explanation for channeling may lie in the following passage from *On the Nature of the Psyche*:

> This hypothetical "subconsciousness," which immediately becomes associated with a "superconsciousness," brings out the real point of my argument: the fact, namely, that a second psychic system coexisting with consciousness—no matter what qualities we suspect it of possessing—is of absolutely revolutionary significance in that it could radically alter our view of the world. Even if no more than the perceptions taking place in such a second system were carried over into ego-consciousness, we should have the possibility of enormously extending the bounds of our mental horizon.
>
> (*CW* 8, 369/178)

As the first quotation suggests, it is possible to recover data across space-time; and as the second implies, it may even be possible to "download" text from a nonphysical source. These abilities, along with altered states, OBEs, extraterrestrial contact, and synchronicities, are fruits of the One Mind because its primordial consciousness connects all things and *is* all things. This chapter discusses remote viewing and channeling in a literary context. First, the Jungian basis for psi gives rise to an experiment with time involving remote viewing the identity of William Shakespeare's Dark Lady in the Sonnets. Second, an analysis of four additional "Shakespeare" sonnets channeled from the afterlife suggests the potential of tapping into resources beyond even the collective unconscious.

Jung and space-time relativity

Whereas synchronicity is a meaningful coincidence for the perceiver, remote viewing (RV) is an intentional process that may yield information to which the viewer is indifferent. In other ways, though, there is common ground. Synchronicities and RV both depart from time's causal arrow, support the concept of separation-as-illusion, and point toward the overarching unity of the One Mind. RV works because each person's psyche is connected to all that is. As Michael Talbot explains, gaining information psychically "is not so strange when one remembers that in a holographic universe, consciousness pervades all matter" and that it is possible to look backward in time because all information is eternally present and accessible in each fractal of the hologram. Or, as Russell Targ points out, "There is no known spatial or temporal limit to our awareness." Psychic archeology, therefore, is a genuine possibility.[1]

A brief example of psychic archeology will introduce the potential of RV to find answers to intractable historical problems in the distant past. One may be aware of RV through the film *Men Who Stare at Goats*, which takes extreme liberties with the U.S. government's RV unit (1977–1995). But the main character, Lyn Cassady, played by George Clooney, is loosely based on a real person, Lyn Buchanan, who worked for that unit and later published a book called *The Seventh Sense: The Secrets of Remote Viewing as Told by a "Psychic Spy" for the U.S Military*. After getting out of the Army, Buchanan offered his RV skills for hire; and one experience provides a relevant example of using psi to solve a "historical puzzle." He did not know what the target was; he had only four words: "'The question is *why*?'" After a number of remote viewings, he reported a simple answer: "'They didn't have money.'" Initially, the historian who had hired Buchanan was disappointed; but after a year's reflection, he realized that Buchanan had solved the mystery of "'why Aztec and Mayan cities emptied out overnight and [of] what happened to the people.'" The answer that Buchanan had supplied did not mean that the people were poor; it meant that, because they lacked a currency system, they paid their taxes with public service in the cities over two-week periods and then went home to their farms; they were then replaced by another group from the country. Such information, Buchanan argues, comes through the subconscious, but he disagrees with Jung on a fundamental point: "Here, especially, I have realized that the term 'collective unconscious' is totally in error. The collective mind is very conscious, indeed. . . . I submit that the term 'unconscious' should be reserved for deep coma or death."[2]

Let us now explore in greater detail Jung's beliefs on space-time malleability. To begin with, in a statement about J. B. Rhine's paranormal research, Jung regards psychic functioning to be an established fact:

> Anyone who has the least knowledge of the parapsychological material which already exists and has been thoroughly verified will know that so-called telepathic phenomena are undeniable facts. An objective and critical survey of the available data would establish that perceptions occur as if in part there were no space, in part no time.
>
> (*CW* 8, 814/413)

He further maintains that

> every conceivable kind of attempt has been made to explain away these results, which seem to border on the miraculous and frankly impossible. But all such attempts come to grief on the facts, and the facts refuse so far to be argued out of existence.
>
> (*CW* 8, 840/435)

Despite methodological problems with some of Rhine's experiments and the persistence of scientific materialism, Jung's positive estimation of card experiments is not incorrect. Given recent discoveries in quantum physics as discussed by Radin and others, it may be that Jung's point of view on psi heralded a new era in scientific thinking about human potential.

In part neither time nor space—this is the key phrase. Jung writes, "Part of our psyche is not in time and not in space. They are only an illusion [of the explicate order] . . . and so in a certain part of our psyche time does not exist at all" (*CW* 18, 684/287). That "part," of course, is for Jung the collective unconscious, which "must have a spaceless and timeless quality" (*CW* 10, 849/450). He explains that time and space are "limiting factors" on "corporeal man" because of his "low frequency"; but we are also "psychic beings . . . not entirely dependent upon space and time," beings whose "psychic totality reaches beyond the barrier of space and time" (*CW* 18, 753/315 and 1572/695). The dimensions of space and time set boundaries for our physical bodies and presumably for our conscious minds; but the unconscious mind—for Jung, the psychic or spiritual part of the psyche—transcends these boundaries. Certain that he is right about psi, Jung even chides the skeptics in our midst: "The fact that we are unable to imagine a form of existence without space and time by no means proves that such an existence is in itself impossible" (*CW* 8, 814/414). It might be more precise, however, to say not that the collective unconscious is timeless but that it transcends and includes all time—past, present, and future. Lest Jung's statements seem naïvely enthusiastic, it is worth considering their similarity to an extended statement by Charles T. Tart:

> My findings and parapsychological findings on precognition in general have forced me to theorize further that there is another dimension of time

> (and probably of space as well) that some aspect of our awareness can sometimes make contact with. This second dimension acts as the channel for psi information. I theorize that one property of this second dimension of time is that the experienced present of awareness is wider than the experienced present of ordinary consciousness. In my theory of states of consciousness, ordinary consciousness is seen as basic awareness modulated by brain mechanisms and thus tied to ordinary time. . . . The experienced present of the second dimension includes portions of time that from our ordinary point of view are past and future. . . . In electrical engineering terms, we can say that the operation of the brain and nervous system and the ordinary consciousness that results constitutes [*sic*] a high-gain, narrow-band filter dealing with the immediate physical present. This is obviously of high biological significance for our survival. The second dimension of time, which awareness can sometimes work with, is a filter with a much wider band, but its output is ordinarily quite low. . . . Thus, if a percipient wants to use psi, he must tap into the portion of his awareness that deals with this other dimension of time.[3]

Like other things in *The Collected Works*, Jung's theory of time is not without at least one contradiction. When he writes about future time in *Synchronicity: An Acausal Connecting Principle*, he argues that "it would be absurd to suppose that a situation which does not yet exist and will only occur in the future could transmit itself as a phenomenon of energy to a receiver in the present" (*CW* 8, 840/435). But in his essay "On Synchronicity" (1951) he states, in connection with Rhine's experiments with precognition, that future time "can become psychically relative" (*CW* 8, 978/527), which presumably means that a future event *could* transmit itself to someone in the present. I regard the latter as Jung's true position because the following remark in *Synchronicity: An Acusal Connecting Principle* seems to trump all others: "What happens successively in time is simultaneous in the mind of God" (*CW* 8, 967/518, n. 17).[4] If shorn away from a theological context, the remark means that the One Mind contains all events at all times.

Synchronicity is a minor example of psychic functioning, but it provides a link to a more fundamental type: "When an unconscious content passes over into consciousness its synchronistic manifestation ceases; conversely, synchronistic phenomena can be evoked by putting the subject into an unconscious state (trance)" (*CW* 8, 440/232). In other words, to venture into the unconscious is to journey beyond clock time to a realm of temporal relativity, synchronicity, and perhaps even simultaneity. The passage further suggests that a trance state in which one is conscious but turned inward can promote conscious apprehension of unconscious (timeless) material. Jung explains the resulting psi phenomena as follows: "The very diverse and confusing aspects of these phenomena are, so far as I can see at present, completely explicable on the assumption of a psychically relative space-time continuum" (*CW* 8, 440/231).

In "Psychology and Spiritualism" (1948) Jung affirms the possibility of retrieving information across space-time through the unconscious mind.

> In addition, it has been proved by experiment that time and space are *relative* for the unconscious, so that unconscious perception, not being impeded by the space-time barrier, can obtain experiences to which the conscious mind has no access. In this connection I would refer to the experiments conducted [by J. B. Rhine] at Duke University and other places.
>
> (*CW* 18, 747/313; emphasis in the original)

He also states that

> knowledge finds itself in a space-time continuum in which space is no longer space, nor time time. If, therefore, the unconscious should develop or maintain a potential in the direction of consciousness, it is then possible for parallel events to be perceived or "known".
>
> (*CW* 8, 912/418)

In his writings on time, Jung thus establishes a theory of psychic functioning. In order to "see" beyond the veil of space-time, one must achieve an altered state—like Adam in chapter 2 or the wanderer in chapter 3—in which a flicker of consciousness can apprehend unconscious and therefore timeless content. He admits to "many a headache" as a result of such ruminations, but he insists that demonstrating the relativity of space-time "must rank as an event of the highest theoretical significance" (*CW* 8, 813/412–13).

Here are two views of the kind of psychic functioning that Jung describes. The first puts the phenomenon in Jungian terms. RV works when a "data stream" originates in the fourth dimension beyond space-time from the extrapsychic target in the collective unconscious, which is Jung's "vast historical storehouse" (*CW* 18, 280/127). The information flows through the personal unconscious (the medium or the middle stage). Finally, the three-dimensional-oriented conscious mind provides a two-dimensional articulation in the form of a drawing or summary.[5] Everything is eternally present, but in order to gain access to it one must dip down into the transpersonal so that a flicker of consciousness can access the extrapsychic information. Second, from a non-Jungian standpoint, the term "subconscious," meaning an area of the psyche below consciousness, blurs the line between personal and collective. In order to go "out there" or "back then," we need only look "in here," which implies that every human psyche, as Talbot asserts, contains the whole universe—all of space-time. Thus the target is intrapsychic after all. Indeed, holographic field theory's emphasis on fractals explains abilities like RV. If the part contains the whole, and if one can perceive the part, then one can also perceive the whole.[6] Regardless of which view one espouses, the common ground between both Jungian and non-Jungian perspectives on psi is that RV allows access to material that lies below normal conscious awareness and beyond the veil of space-time illusion.

If time, space, matter, and thought are not really separate things but are rather all bound up in the One Mind, then the resulting potential for psychic ability is worth investigating as a tool in literary scholarship. For example, while Shakespeare (we assume) wrote about real people in the Sonnets and was himself one of them, a definitive matching of characters and historical persons has so far been impossible through conventional scholarly means. But the intersection of RV results and traditional theories of identity in the Sonnets may suggest areas where further validation through conventional scholarship should be sought. Rather than claiming that I have identified the Dark Lady, as plenty of previous critics have done, I contend that the data produced by RV of this elusive character suggest the merit of one theory over others and demonstrate some of the strengths and limitations of RV for literary research more broadly.

Hal Puthoff and Russell Targ, who developed RV at the Stanford Research Institute, offer the following definition: "This phenomenon pertains to the ability of certain individuals to access and describe, by means of mental processes, information sources blocked from ordinary perception and generally accepted as secure against such access."[7] RV's "mental processes" involve two essential protocols: the viewer and the monitor must both be blind to the target; and the viewer must report and record but not analyze, for the latter leads to *analytic overlay* (AOL). Obviously, in order for an experiment involving psi to work, a reputable practitioner is needed. For my experiment with time, I hired the services of the world's greatest living remote viewer, Joseph McMoneagle (JM), a veteran of the Army's Stargate program. If someone like him who does not know Shakespeare's works and who is unaware that the Sonnets are the target of blind viewings (I communicated only with his wife) can perceive and record details that match conventional theories and evidence, the results may well be fertile ground for further literary-historical research. Traditional literary scholars—many of whom are unlikely to credit RV's use to augment conventional investigation—will squawk about the CIA's "AIR Report," which purports to debunk RV in keeping with the bias of the traditional intelligence community that sought Stargate's termination. Fortunately, the report has been discredited.[8] In any case, there is enough evidence in the following pages to confirm the Jungian position that a scientific fundamentalism that considers only physical, material reality is untenable. Given the results reported here, it is possible to conclude that a controlled scientific form of psychic investigation may one day help critics negotiate their way out of blind ends in conventional literary-historical scholarship.

Who was the Dark Lady?

Regarding the Dark Lady of the Sonnets, S. Schoenbaum affirms, "This dusky phantom eludes us still." After surveying all the proposed candidates, he adds, "Aemilia Lanyer brings to a close my selective survey of Dark Ladies; the quest, pursued with so much energy, learning, and ingenuity, fizzles out with yet another failure."[9] Stephen Greenblatt qualifies the whole enterprise of determining identity in the Sonnets in his recent biography of Shakespeare:

> It would be folly to take these [sonnets] as a kind of confidential diary, a straightforward record of what actually went on in the relationship between Shakespeare and his deceitful dark lady, whoever she was in real life, or between Shakespeare and the aristocratic young man, whether he was Southampton or someone else, or perhaps an amalgam of multiple lovers.[10]

Dympna Callaghan's conclusion nicely sums up the state of the conventional scholarship: "As readers of the sonnets, we simply have to learn to live with a considerable degree of ambiguity and uncertainty."[11] There is no way to say for certain whom Shakespeare writes about or even when he writes—no way, that is, short of rolling back space-time through psychic functioning, as Jung asserts to be possible. For Jung, time and space are relative from the standpoint of psychic functioning:

> The phenomena of parapsychology . . . point to a relativization of space and time through psychic factors which casts doubt on our naïve and overhasty explanation in terms of [mere] psychological parallelism. For the sake of this explanation people deny the findings of parapsychology outright, either for philosophical reasons or from intellectual laziness. This can hardly be considered a scientifically responsible attitude, even though it is a popular way out of a quite extraordinary intellectual difficulty.
>
> (*CW* 10, 527/270)

Claire Douglas, writing in *The Cambridge Companion to Jung*, frankly acknowledges Jung's enthusiasm about psychic functioning but ads a caveat: "Jung's interest in and knowledge about parapsychology adds a rich though suspect edge to analytical psychology which demands attention congruent with the extended scope of scientific knowledge today."[12]

Two problems thus arise: the mystery of identity in Shakespeare's Sonnets; and Jung's "rich though suspect" assertions about time, space, and psychic functioning. But if, as Russ McDonald puts it, "scholarship (both historical and interpretive) has been notoriously unsuccessful in its attempts to solve the mysteries of the sonnets,"[13] it may be that my experiment with time offers the potential for fresh insight. What follows, however, is not a departure from previous criticism; much that has been previously said is present here. Chapter 7 departs instead from conventional scholarly *method*; it attempts to fit unconventionally gathered information into a conventional scholarly matrix for the purpose of furthering the discussion of the Dark Lady's identity. This old and inveterate problem in

Shakespeare criticism will be approached in a new and potentially illuminating way that is consistent with both Jungian theory and quantum physics.

If the Sonnets are autobiographical, Shakespeare evidently had a mistress who not only was darkly complexioned but also manifested a darkness of character. Schoenbaum offers the following excellent summary of how the Sonnets depict her:

> She is younger than the poet [and older than the young man], musical, raven-haired and raven-eyed, dark-skinned (how dark is not clear), and either unattractive or unconventionally beautiful, depending on the viewer's mood. She is certainly seductive, gives free rein to her appetite, may be married, and is possibly infected with venereal disease. In character she is a *femme fatale*: proud, fickle, overbearing, and deceitful.[14]

Who was she? To begin with, it is fairly certain that she was not Shakespeare's wife, whom he leaves behind in Stratford. Despite Shakespeare's bitter description of her as "the bay where all men ride" and "the wide world's common place" (Sonnet 137), she is probably not Lucy Morgan (Lucy Negro), a brothel owner who had once been a maid to Queen Elizabeth, was older than Shakespeare, and died of syphilis. As K. D. Sethna notes, the Dark Lady may have had gonorrhea, not syphilis, and may have given it to the young man—she may "fire my good one out," as Sonnet 144 mentions. The Dark Lady is probably not Anne Davenant, the wife of John Davenant who owned the Taverne in Oxford where Shakespeare may have stopped on his trips home to Stratford (Greenblatt). Their son William later claimed to be Shakespeare's illegitimate child; but if John did not receive a vintner's license until 1605 (Wilson), it is highly unlikely that Shakespeare would have visited his tavern soon enough for Anne to be part of the events that the Sonnets record. If the Sonnets were written before 1598, she was probably not Elizabeth Vernon, who later became Southampton's wife. She was probably not Mary Fitton, whom Pembroke impregnated, because Fitton did not marry until 1607 (Hubler) and was either a blonde (Wilson) or a brunette with fair skin and grey eyes (Hubler). And besides, Callaghan states that Mary Fitton was "an aristocratic lady who was one of Queen Elizabeth's maids of honor, though a surviving portrait shows her to be a very fair-skinned brunette, and definitely a 'lady' rather than the 'woman' Shakespeare describes." She was probably not Penelope Rich, "the Stella of *Astrophel and Stella*, [who] has also been nominated for the dubious honor, but only because she deserves it" (Hubler). There are other candidates, but the Dark Lady is so elusive that Sethna gives her a fictitious name, Anastasia-Guglielma, and hopes that conventional scholarship will one day match the Dark Lady with a historical person.[15]

This summary, of course, saves for last the likeliest theory, which is that the Dark Lady was Aemilia Lanyer. Aemilia was the illegitimate daughter of Baptiste Bassano and Margaret Johnson, an English woman. That Bassano was "a native of Venice"[16] suggests that Aemilia may have had dark skin.[17] Since he had been a musician in Henry VIII's court, it is possible that Aemilia could be the woman who plays the virginals (spinet) in Sonnet 128. On October 18, 1592, Aemilia married Alfonso Lanyer, not William Lanyer as A. L. Rowse erroneously states.[18] It would be convenient, though, if her husband's name *were* William, for then the pun on "will" (male or female genitalia) in Sonnet 135 would be delicious in the extreme: "Whoever hath her wish, thou hast thy Will, / And Will to boot, and Will in overplus." As Callaghan states, "'Over-plus' means the woman has had sexual possession of the speaker to the point of surfeit and even that the dimensions of his tumescent member have overwhelmed her."[19] In any case, Aemilia was twenty-three in 1593, her husband twenty, Shakespeare twenty-nine, and Southampton nineteen—ages that fit the evidence in the Sonnets about age relationships among the poet, young man, and Dark Lady. Significantly, if Amelia is the Dark Lady, then Leslie Hotson's theory that the sonnets were written to Essex between 1587 and 1589 can be ruled out: she was not married during that period.[20] Moreover, she was promiscuous, we presume, not only with Shakespeare and the young man but also with Henry Carey, Lord Hunsdon, whose patronage helped support Shakespeare's theater company.[21] The connection through Hunsdon explains how they all might have known each other.

While Aemilia Lanyer seems to fit the Sonnets' profile of the Dark Lady, David Bevington sounds a cautionary note:

> All that can be brought to Aemilia Lanyer's candidacy is an argument about probabilities: that the alleged whorish reputation, the courtly favor of the queen, the purportedly dark complexion, and the musicianship are unlikely to be found together in any one woman present on the scene in 1592–94 unless the woman is the "dark lady."[22]

We are left, then, in a state of epistemological quandary: maybe Aemilia is the Dark Lady; maybe she is not. But if Jung is right that space-time can be reduced in the mind's eye to virtually nothing, RV results may match elements in the conventional scholarship, help shift possibility toward probability (or away from it), and add weight (or not) to the case for Aemilia. JM's target was the "Dark Lady in Shakespeare's Sonnet 130," which begins with the line, "My mistress' eyes are nothing like the sun," and describes her as being unconventionally beautiful.

> TARGET: 22405
>
> 1) *Please describe target.*
> 2) *Describe target's kind of work.*
> 3) *Describe target's parent's work.*
> 4) *What nationality are target's parents?*
>
> <u>Question 1</u>: Target is a young woman, approximately 22 to 25 years of age. She is about five feet, four inches tall, with raven hair almost to the waist. She wears her hair twisted in a very complex braid either Spanish

> or French. She has dark brown eyes and high cheek bones and a very dark complexion, like that of a woman who might be Spanish or Northwestern Italian in origin—this is a woman of mystery. At 120 pounds, she would be considered slightly heavy by today's standards, but in her time this would have been highly desirable, as it would have demonstrated breeding and desirability. I have a sense that she is quite capable on a horse or with a sword. She reeks of musk and wine, and her eyes hide the very mystery within which she has encased herself. She keeps her own schedule and to all who know her she is an enigma.
>
> Question 2: I do not see her working. She is the daughter of an aristocrat. She is engaged to a man in government who is constantly absent. She spends her time visiting with friends and partying. She practices her mystery as an exercise—it is what is done in these times. Both men and women are apt to live their lives this way as a form of excitement, to release their boredom.
>
> Question 3: Her father is both a representative of a government as well as an official of some sort from the court of a Queen, probably either the Spanish or the Italian court. He owns considerable property in terms of land and productive farms. He also owns some shipping of sorts, which do trade within the land locked seas (Mediterranean). He is the primary support for the woman in Question 1. She is betrothed to another man who is also involved in the aristocracy. But this man is not yet completely committed to the wedding which has yet to be planned. It is a wedding of convenience, and not one of love.
>
> Question 4: I believe the woman's parents are probably Spanish. There is a 30% possibility that they could be extreme northwestern Italian, but it is difficult to tell. The border region at the time of this event is liquid and difficult to pin down adequately. I would say that they are more than likely Spanish with some Northwestern Italian heritage.

These results are far from proving that Aemilia Lanyer is Shakespeare's Dark Lady, and they contain both meaningless references to her time period and a nonexistent border between Italy and Spain. Also, Lanyer was not an aristocrat by birth or marriage, nor was her father a businessman. She did inherit £100 from Baptiste,[23] but being Hunsdon's mistress does not make her an aristocrat by association, even if he did provide her with £40 per year. These qualifications aside, the results do have some overlap with what we know about Lanyer from the conventional scholarship and are consonant with the possibility that she may have been Shakespeare's Dark Lady. The following five points are staggeringly accurate given the fact that JM knew only that he was investigating a person.

- The target is a "young woman, approximately 22–25 years of age." (Lanyer was 23 in 1592.)

- She has "raven hair," "dark brown eyes," and "a very dark complexion."
- She has a Mediterranean ancestry, and the results specifically mention Italian heritage.
- She enjoys socializing.
- She was involved in a marriage of convenience.

The fact that the results contain both hits and misses teaches us something about the way RV works. Since the information comes from the collective unconscious through the personal unconscious to the conscious mind, which then oversees the transcription of the results onto paper, the image of panning for gold is relevant. By dipping a pan into a stream, one may end up with gold dust or nuggets; but the pan also contains sand, gravel, and a large quantity of water. Their presence does not nullify the existence of gold, but the analogy does provide a clue as to what may be happening when RV results contain inaccuracies.

Channeled text

It seems likely that information available across space-time to a remote viewer reflects, at a minimum, the role of the collective unconscious, which Jung believes to be a transpersonal storehouse of human information—"the deposit of all human experience right back to its remotest beginnings" (*CW* 8, 339/157). But beyond the collective unconscious, there is an aspect of the One Mind that could be called "superconsciousness," which may also be engaged in the RV process. Certainly "the possibility of enormously extending the bounds of our mental horizon" (*CW* 8, 369/178) characterizes RV's potential to achieve conscious retrieval of distant information, but Jung takes a reductive view of superconsciousness in attempting to fit it into his psychological theory. "As a matter of fact," he writes, "this psyche, which in Indian philosophy is called the 'higher' consciousness, corresponds to what we in the West call the 'unconscious'"; and he justifies his view by asserting that there can be no super*consciousness* without an acting subject or ego (*CW* 9i, 506/282–83; Jung's emphasis). This is an unfortunate formulation, for Jung is attempting to make reality conform to his theory rather than properly considering the possibility that the One Mind may contain a dimension that is greater than the unconscious. For Jung, altered states amount to an *abaissement du niveau mental* or lowering. According to psychic archeologist Stefan Ossowiecki, however, superconsciousness is rather "'a higher level of organization [that] requires the necessary presence of a new element—the element of spirit, of trained will."[24] One suspects that this statement characterizes JM's remote viewing of the Dark Lady, as well as Robert A. Monroe's experiences out of the body. Height or depth is a red herring because what lies above or below consciousness is mysterious, and language captures it inadequately. Pinning down the exact nature of expanded awareness is not a prerequisite for talking about how to use it, any more than driving requires an understanding of auto mechanics.

In a previously published essay, I discuss how to marshal subterranean resources and provide various literary examples of mystical composition, including John Milton's *Paradise Lost*.[25] It is possible that the collective unconscious accounts for inspiration (Jung's "visionary mode") and that problem-solving dreams emanate from the personal unconscious. However, if information comes from the superconscious or higher self, a higher being, the Holy Spirit, or a disembodied spirit, then we have the kind of channeling that Jung did in *Seven Sermons to the Dead*. If it is reasonable to assume that a person can gather information distant in time or space, as McMoneagle's work suggests, is it also possible to retrieve *text* from a nonphysical source?

The possibility that a literary text can be channeled from the afterlife, a realm of pure spirit beyond the collective unconscious—would strike most academicians as risible. Yet that is precisely what we encounter in a book that is both dismissed and maligned, Percy Allen's *Talks with Elizabethans: Revealing the Mystery of "William Shakespeare*."[26] Allen's conclusion that "Shakespeare" is a combination of the historical William Shakespeare, Edward de Vere, and Francis Bacon is dismissed by mainstream Shakespeare critics, even as New Historicists harp on the idea that Early Modern texts are cultural productions and even as Stratfordians acknowledge that many of Shakespeare's plots are borrowed. By "maligned," I have in mind Schoenbaum's statement that Allen consulted a spirit medium named Mrs. Hester Dowden who, through her guide Johannes, helped communicate with the three previously named Elizabethans who professed their joint authorship. Schoenbaum then notes, however, that the year after Allen's sittings with Mrs. Dowden took place and four years before *Talks with Elizabethans* was published, Alfred Dodd's *The Immortal Master* used Mrs. Dowden's channeled information to claim exclusive authorship for Bacon. Schoenbaum zeroes in on the inconsistency to dismiss both texts in a sound bite: "Some spooks, it seems, are unreliable."[27] So much for Allen, or so it would appear.

Missing from Schoenbaum's dry critique, however, is the astonishing fact that Allen's book contains four Shakespearean sonnets that were channeled, he claims, through Mrs. Dowden from Edward de Vere, to whom he assigns authorship of the Sonnets. One does not need to wade into the thorny authorship debate in order to recognize that neither Allen nor Mrs. Dowden, nor for that matter Johannes, was a poet. That the sonnets exist means that they came through a channeler from a spiritual source—that is, from a part of the One Mind beyond what Jung acknowledges in his comments on superconsciousness. In Allen's view, at least one of these sonnets (the third that I will discuss) is "surely one of the loveliest in our language," "matches, in poetic quality, the very best Shakespearean sonnets which we possess," and is spiritually "far ahead of them."[28] But even if one views their quality as inferior to the 154 sonnets in Shakespeare's sequence, they are still of higher quality than a nonpoet could achieve. Moreover, they speak in important ways to the nature of time and the afterlife. The purpose here is not to rehash the debate between Stratfordians, Oxfordians, and Baconians, though some of Allen's comments that point to Oxford-as-author do contribute to the explication.

The purpose is rather to introduce and discuss four lovely poems as an illustration of an unconventional means of literary composition and to explore their insights on space-time and the afterlife. Regardless of their provenance, these sonnets exist and deserve an audience.

Here is the first sonnet:

> How dark the murky stream of time that flows,
> Bearing within its bulk both foul and fair;
> All that is gracious to oblivion goes,
> All that is beauteous, precious, and most rare,
> While in some golden realm thy spirit dwells
> Far from the earth—Immortal, beyond Time—
> Terror of Death, nor creeping age compels
> Me to be fearful of thy sure decline.
> Nay, all my love is thine, in perfect joy,
> And all the sweetness that within thee lies
> Age cannot alter, Time cannot destroy;
> A holy fire art thou, that never dies—
> Immortal love, clad in unchanging youth,
> Fair sacrament of Beauty and of Truth.[29]

Allen reads the sonnet's final line in harmony with his contention that the fair youth in the Sonnets, Southampton, is the son of Oxford and Queen Elizabeth. "Fair" is the young man, "Beauty" is the queen, and "Truth" is Oxford. Allen states that "the word 'sacrament' means that Southampton, now, with his earthly parents, in the spirit-world, is the living and 'holy' symbol of the love between Queen Elizabeth, who is *Beauty*, and Oxford, who is *Truth*."[30] Like the authorship controversy, that hypothesis is not one with which I wish to engage; I prefer rather to note that its speaker, who resides in the realm of pure spirit, comments on life and the afterlife. Earthly existence is characterized by linear time ("the murky stream of time"), dualities ("foul and fair"), age, decline, fear, and death. On the other hand, the speaker asserts that death shears away what is "foul" so that only "all that is gracious . . . beauteous, precious, and most rare" goes to a timeless "golden realm" of love and "perfect joy." In line 5, the introduction of direct address ("thy spirit") suggests several alternatives: "thy" may be impersonal and general; it may indicate that a specific living addressee *will* dwell in pure spirit after a time; or perhaps at death the listener will realize that he has already been participating in a realm of expanded awareness in life on an unconscious level. In any case, this immortal part is "a holy fire," which suggests that each soul participates in the Godhead and that it can never be destroyed. Coincidentally, the image anticipates the phrase "sages standing in God's holy fire" in Yeats's "Sailing to Byzantium," another poem that looks ahead to the afterlife.[31] It also appears that each soul in the afterlife experiences "unchanging youth," a point that resonates with the assertion in popular literature that everyone in the afterlife is thirty years old. For example, Monroe reports an experience that supports this point. Setting out to find his late friend, Dr. Gordon, in the afterlife, Monroe is surprised to find not a senior citizen but instead a "thin young man with the big shock of hair."[32]

The sonnet's punctuation, though, is a bit strange. The dash at the end of line 6 functions, I believe, as a period so that the strange punctuation enacts the fragmentation and murkiness of life in our physical world. The next line switches from a general characterization of the afterlife to direct address to a beloved person who still lives in "the murky stream of time." The afterlife is a golden world. "[Therefore, neither] Terror of Death, nor creeping age compels / Me to be fearful of thy sure decline." Why not? Because, as with the general situation described in lines 1–6, so with the addressee's particular case in lines 7–12: though the body is subject to age and time, the soul is immortal, which ensures a continuity of the best parts of the psyche through the barrier of death.

The second sonnet continues a number of the motifs just introduced:

Now is the beauty of thy soul laid bare;
In dust the fairness of thy body lies;
Radiant is thy soul! most chaste and fair,
Clearer than stars spangling the summer skies.
Nothing of thee can wither or can fade,
Nor foul decay touch thy triumphant prime;
For ever shall our souls, no more afraid,
Gaze surely on the passing flight of time.
Bounteous my love enwraps thee all around;
No churl am I; for all I give to thee;
In thee all that in highest Heaven is found
Is thine and mine, sure and eternally.
Thus close entwined, in perfect love and truth,
Endures our spring and our unending youth.

Allen's comment on this second sonnet is that "the poet rejoices once more that in the spirit-world his son's 'triumphant prime' can neither wither, fade, nor decay, and that the shared joys of their 'highest heaven' unite eternally their undying love." Then he continues with his Oxfordian lore: "The last ten words of the sonnet include, '*love*', '*youth*', '*truth*' and '*spring*', of which the two last can be rendered by the words *Vere*, or *Ver*, the Latin for spring."[33] Whereas the first sonnet addresses a living person who fears death, the second sonnet opens with the addressee having made that perilous transition and finding that his soul is "radiant." In other words, the relationship between the first and second sonnets resembles that between "Sailing to Byzantium" and "Byzantium." Presently the speaker celebrates the unchanging nature of the soul in the afterlife. The two souls, now without fear, "gaze surely on the passing flight of time"; they are observers of, not participants in, what the first sonnet calls "the murky stream of time." The rest of the sonnet celebrates the love between the speaker and the addressee: it is total, all-encompassing; and they find in each other heaven's highest bounty—love, truth, and youth—now and eternally. Overall, the syntax is much smoother here, as befits a poem whose addressee has transcended the fragmentation of the physical world.

The third sonnet is written from the same speaker's point of view but with the understanding that the addressee has now been in the afterlife for a while.

> When from the star-strewn heavens I gaze around,
> And mark the narrow compass of the Earth,
> Small as an atom in the sunlight drowned—
> I marvel how within such narrow girth
> My love for thee found sustenance and space;
> The wine too close was housed, too small the cup;
> My precious draught o'erflowed the narrow place,
> Lost all its perfumed flavor, soon dried up.
> Now has my love found her true path of grace;
> Deep in thy soul she hides herself and me.
> Here is no fear of time, of age no trace;
> Forever of restraining fetters free—
> So we enjoy the glory of the sun,
> In sure affinity—for we are one.

Allen comments that

> *Sonnet III* is the best and spiritually the most exalted of the trio, as *Shakespeare*, gazing down from the 'star-strewn heavens' upon this mere atom of our revolving earth, marvels how that draught of so choice vintage—his love for his son—ever found there sufficient sustenance, and space in which to live. He closes, once more, upon the motive that neither of the pair is longer shackled in the fears and fetters of *Age* or *Time*.[34]

Of course, Allen gets in his Oxfordian licks here as well. He states:

> It may justifiably be argued that the use of the word 'love', in the feminine gender, in the ninth line of this third sonnet need not necessarily be interpreted as meaning Queen Elizabeth. I concur; but, after mature consideration, and after long familiarity with the subtleties of Elizabethan minds, I am satisfied that Oxford does refer here to his queen; it being his usual practice to veil cleverly his references to his royal mistress, and to make them "covert" rather than open.[35]

However, the soul is feminine, according to Jung; so the sonnet could mean Elizabeth's soul or anyone else's, male or female. I am more interested in what the poem says about time and the afterlife apart from the possibility of such a historical reference.

Here is my own reading. For a soul accustomed to the afterlife, it seems remarkable that his love for the addressee was possible at all, given the Earth's many restrictions. Then a note of self-condemnation arises: "My precious draught o'erflowed the narrow place, / Lost all its perfumed flavor, soon dried up." His love, being of the soul, ill befitted earthly, physical reality and "soon dried up." Now in the afterlife, where there is no time or restriction of any sort, only freedom, he realizes that he and his love are anchored in the other's soul. The pun on "sun" and "son" in line 13, according to Allen, is deliberate and refers to Southampton as a son, more than it refers to Christ as the Son of God. Whatever may be meant, the sonnet concludes with the notion of unity ("we are one"). The use of "I" and "thee" suggests that individual identity endures physical death, but the final line points to a greater unity that love enables in the afterlife when "the narrow place" of the physical body has been left behind. In other words, the speaker's point of view has transcended the separation that characterizes life on Earth; and his love now teaches him that he and his beloved are One rather than two.

Three sonnets—all channeled from the afterlife. Whether the source is Oxford or Shakespeare or someone or something else is immaterial. The poems exist, and they were transcribed by a woman who was not a poet for a scholar who was a nonpoet as well. Since Mrs. Dowden no doubt relied at least partly on the unconscious as an interface between her conscious mind and the poet's afterlife, the resulting point for our purposes is simple. If the unconscious can help her tap into the mind of a disembodied soul, then something beyond Jung's visionary mode is in play. As in remote viewing, expanded awareness can be harnessed for constructive purposes. Though it sounds strange to readers in the early twenty-first century, what I have described in this chapter in nascent form is the wave of the future. Humanity is evolving toward a greater connection between the conscious mind and unconscious—or one might also say "spiritual"—resources. But channeling is not easy. For example, "Oxford" points out that the sonnets "were given slowly—words being very carefully chosen", and "Bacon" states that the sonnets "were composed at the time they were written. The mind of the writer was used as an instrument only; and, at times, was difficult."[36]

The fourth channeled sonnet in Allen's book appears as an epigraph on the title page. I will conclude with this poem, whose final couplet encapsulates the point that I am making about writing:

> Enshrinèd in this tomb a secret lies,
> Mark ye! The body must to dust decay;
> The soul immortal is, it never dies,
> A living flame that burns by night and day.
> Perchance the ghost that walks the witching night
> May speak true words, and secrets dark reveal,

For memories dwell in souls that seek the light.
Like players on a stage, they live and feel.
Such memories speak the truth; they dare not lie—
The plays they played on Earth they play once more.
E'er the cock crows, and from the Earth they fly,
Learn what you may—your patience they implore.
    Thus from the tomb its secret you may steal,
    Stirring no dust, no bones can you reveal.

The poem conveys the general purpose of Allen's project, which is to tap the memory of spirits in order to solve critical conundrums. The opening line, which states that there is a secret in the tomb, seems to invoke the suspicion that Shakespeare was buried with some of his manuscripts. That possibility, however, winks out in line 3 where the secret appears to be that the soul is immortal, even perhaps that it never sleeps once it has departed from the physical body (lines 2–4). This continuity of consciousness is very much in the spirit of Shakespeare's Sonnet 146. Each poem contrasts the physical body's decay with the soul's immortality, but Allen's sonnet lacks 146's Christian context. Apparently, the dead poet in Eternity realizes that Christian doctrine is not the definitive authority on the afterlife.

The next lines about "the ghost that walks the witching night" contrast with the souls of suicides in *A Midsummer Night's Dream* who "willfully themselves exile from light / And must for aye consort with black-browed night" (3.2.386–87). The soul in the poem is among those "that seek the light," and being a saved soul enables memory of earthly life to abide. As a further consequence, "Like players on a stage, they live and feel." The line obviously recalls Jaques's speech on the Seven Ages of Man in *As You Like It*: "All the world's a stage, / And all the men and women merely players" (2.7.138–39). The stage metaphor heightens the reality of the afterlife, but we remember Hamlet's complaint that players feign passion (*Hamlet*, 2.2.560–66). Beyond "second childishness," there is a stage of human existence in the afterlife characterized by a synergy of actions and emotions or perhaps unity of being. In that heightened state, souls remember their physical lives in perfect detail—"Such memories speak the truth; they dare not lie"—and they can replay what they experienced on Earth. Like the damned souls that Puck mentions, however, those in the sonnet who experience total recall visit us at night when living persons are most receptive to afterlife communication. They seek not to haunt us but to inform us. "Learn what you may—your patience they implore" implies not only the difficulty of "downloading" information from the realm of spirit to the realm of matter but also the sense that we are as eager to learn secrets as spirits are to communicate them. Such souls are a bit like "that affable familiar ghost / Which nightly gulls him [the rival poet] with intelligence" in Shakespeare's Sonnet 86.

In the final couplet, "tomb" has ceased to mean crypt and now stands in for the afterlife in general. "Thus from the tomb its secrets you may steal" means that we may acquire knowledge from the dead who are alive in the spirit world. "Stirring no dust, no bones can you reveal" emphasizes that the sonnet is not describing a physical process like stealing manuscripts from Shakespeare's tomb. The words "dust" and "bones," however, echo of the inscription that he wrote for the stone slab that covers it:

> Good Frend for Jesus Sake Forbeare,
> To Digg the Dust Encloased Heare:
> Bleste Be Y^{e} Man Y^{t} Spares Thes Stones,
> And Curst Be He Y^{t} Moves My Bones.[37]

The sort of inquiry that the sonnet proposes is not the earthly intrusion that Shakespeare hopes to prevent but rather an archeology of mind and spirit. Rather than coming from the collective unconscious the way a text is generated in Jung's visionary mode, the four sonnets, like the information on Shakespeare conveyed in Allen's book, originate in the spirit world and reach consciousness via the unconscious of the channeler. The poems come *through* rather than *from* the unconscious. And the fact that Johannes has to function as a step-down or go-between may mean that "Shakespeare" is on a higher plane where direct contact with living persons is difficult or impossible even for the highly skilled Mrs. Dowden.

Thus it is possible that text can come through a channeler, as *Seven Sermons to the Dead* came through Jung and as Allen's four sonnets came through Mrs. Dowden. It may be, though, that channeling is easier in prose than it is in poetry where diction and form require greater precision. The difference in degree of difficulty may account for why there are already plenty of channeled texts in the New Age community, the foremost being the works that Seth channeled through Jane Roberts, but little poetry.[38] Channeling as a source of *literary* production will still be a hard pill for the mainstream to swallow—but how else to explain the existence of four Shakespearean sonnets in Allen's *Talks with Elizabethans*? Psi ability that is hard to believe in real life, however, is easily enjoyed in fantasy fiction. In the next chapter, we will consider psi phenomena in Robert Jordan's *The Wheel of Time* series to illustrate the potential of the One Mind. Fantasy literature appeals to us, I will argue, precisely because its depiction of psi resonates with a deep and unacknowledged potential within the human condition.

Notes

1 Michael Talbot, *The Holographic Universe* (New York: HarperCollins, 1991), 145, 199, and 200–1; and Russell Targ, *Limitless Mind: A Guide to RV and Transformation of Consciousness* (Novato, CA: New World Library, 2004), xxvi. For a discussion of "quantum interconnectedness" and other discoveries in physics, see Targ's first chapter (3–24). See also Stephan A. Schwartz, *The Secret Vaults of Time: Psychic Archeology and the Quest for Man's Beginnings* (New York: Grosset, 1978).

2 Lyn Buchanan, *The Seventh Sense: The Secrets of Remote Viewing as Told by a "Psychic Spy" for the U.S. Military* (New York: Paraview Pocket, 2003), 166–68 and 120–21. *Men Who Stare at Goats* (DVD, directed by Grant Heslov, 2009; Beverly Hills, CA: Overture Films, 2010, grossly distorts the military's RV program. For accurate accounts, see Jim Schnabel, *Remote Viewers: The Secret History of America's Psychic Spies* (New York: Dell, 1997); Paul H. Smith, *Reading the Enemy's Mind: Inside Star Gate, America's Psychic Espionage Program* (New York: Tor, 2005); Joseph McMoneagle, *Mind Trek: Exploring Consciousness, Time, and Space Through Remote Viewing* (Charlottesville, VA: Hampton Roads, 1997) and *The Stargate Chronicles: Memoirs of a Psychic Spy* (Charlottesville, VA: Hampton Roads, 2002).

3 Charles T. Tart, *PSI: Scientific Studies of the Psychic Realm* (New York: Dutton, 1977), 156.

4 Cf. Augustine, *St. Augustine's Confessions*, trans. William Watts, 2 vols. (Cambridge, MA: Harvard University Press, 1961), 2:235 and 237:

> Nor dost thou in time precede times: else thou shouldest not precede all times. But thou precedest all times past, by high advantage of *an ever present eternity*: and thou goest beyond all times to come, even because they are to come, and when they shall come, they shall be past: whereas thou art still the same, and thy years shall not fail.
>
> (book 11, chapter 13; my emphasis)

Augustine's reference is Psalm 102:27: "But thou art the same, and thy years have no end."

5 An excellent explanation of the RV process appears in Smith, *Reading the Enemy's Mind*, 168–86. Smith and others are convinced "that there must be some sort of timeless repository of facts that could be persuaded to give up its contents when properly stimulated" (182). The collective unconscious may be such a repository.

6 Talbot writes: "Indeed, it quickly became apparent to the ever growing number of scientists who came to embrace the holographic model that it helped explain virtually all paranormal and mystical experiences." Holographic theory accounts for synchronicities as well as "archetypal experiences, encounters with the collective unconscious" (*The Holographic Universe*, 2–3).

7 Harold E. Puthoff and Russell Targ, "A Perceptual Channel for Information Transfer over Kilometer Distances: Historical Perspective and Recent Research," in *Mind at Large: Institute of Electrical and Electronic Engineers Symposia on the Nature of Extrasensory Perception*, ed. Charles T. Tart, Harold E. Puthoff, and Russell Targ (New York, Praeger, 1979), 14. For the story of RV's discovery, see Russell Targ and Harold E. Puthoff, *Mind-Reach: Scientists Look at Psychic Ability* (New York: Delacorte, 1977), 107–19. Targ provides a good overview of RV in *Limitless Mind*, 25–56, and in *Miracles of Mind: Exploring Nonlocal Consciousness and Spiritual Healing* (Novato, CA: New World Library), chapters 1–3.

8 See Edwin C. May, "The American Institutes for Research Review of the Department of Defense's Star Gate Program: A Commentary," http://anson.ucdavis.edu/~utts/may.html (accessed July 10, 2007). May writes in his abstract:

> It will be shown that there is compelling evidence that the CIA set the outcome with regard to intelligence usage before the evaluation had begun. This was accomplished by limiting the research and operations data sets to exclude positive findings, by purposefully not interviewing historically significant participants, by ignoring previous DOD extensive program reviews, and by using the questionable National Research Council's investigation of parapsychology as the starting point for their review.

9 S. Schoenbaum, "Shakespeare's Dark Lady: A Question of Identity," in *Shakespeare's Styles: Essays in Honour of Kenneth Muir*, ed. Philip Edwards et al. (London, UK: Cambridge University Press, 1980), 222 and 236.

10 Stephen Greenblatt, *Will in the World: How Shakespeare Became Shakespeare* (New York: Norton, 2004), 249. Of course, since Greenblatt frequently stresses that Shakespeare wrote in an age when one's lack of confidentiality could lead to his execution, the amalgam theory does not necessarily follow from scholars' inability to identify the characters. The Sonnets may still provide a *veiled* record of Shakespeare's interaction with individual persons.

11 Dympna Callaghan, *Shakespeare's Sonnets* (Malden, MA: Blackwell, 2007), 34.

12 Claire Douglas, "The Historical Context of Analytical Psychology," in *The Cambridge Companion to Jung*, ed. Polly Young-Eisendrath and Terence Dawson (New York: Cambridge University Press, 1997), 28.

13 Russ McDonald, *The Bedford Companion to Shakespeare: An Introduction with Documents*, 2nd ed. (Boston: Bedford/St. Martin's, 2001), 16.

14 Schoenbaum, "Shakespeare's Dark Lady," 226.

15 K. D. Sethna, *"Two Loves" and "A Worthier Pen": The Enigmas of Shakespeare's Sonnets: An Identification through a New Approach* (New Delhi: Arnold-Heinemann, 1984), 129 and 158; Greenblatt, *Will in the World: How Shakespeare Became Shakespeare* (New York: Norton, 2004), 330; John Dover Wilson, *An Introduction to the Sonnets of Shakespeare for the Use of Historians and Others* (New York: Cambridge University Press, 1964), 48; Edward Hubler, *Shakespeare's Sonnets and the Commentators* (New York: Basic, 1962), 18; and Callaghan, *Shakespeare's Sonnets*, 31.

16 David Bevington, "A. L. Rowse's Dark Lady," in *Aemilia Lanyer: Gender, Genre, and the Canon*, ed. Marshall Grossman (Lexington, KY: University Press of Kentucky, 1998), 18.

17 The only mention of her appearance, however, is Simon Forman's reference to a mole on her throat. There is no physical self-description in her poem, *Salve Deus Rex Judaeorum*.

18 A. L. Rowse, *Shakespeare's Sonnets: The Problems Solved*, 2nd ed. (New York: Harper, 1964), xxxvii.

19 Callaghan, *Shakespeare's Sonnets*, 25.

20 Leslie Hotson, *Mr W.H.* (New York: Knopf, 1964), 282.

21 Schoenbaum, "Shakespeare's Dark Lady," 233; and Bevington, "A. L. Rowse's Dark Lady," 21.

22 Bevington, "A. L. Rowse's Dark Lady," 22. Bevington's conclusion is that studying Lanyer's life leads us to discover not that she is the Dark Lady but that she is a Christian poet. Critics regard Lanyer's Christian sensibility as genuine, though perhaps shallow. Rowse implies that the publication in 1611 of her feminist poem, *Salve Deus Rex Judaeorum*, may have been a response to being maligned as the Dark Lady in the Shakespeare's Sonnets, published in 1609 (*Sex and Society in Shakespeare's Age: Simon Forman the Astrologer* [New York: Scribner's, 1974], 104–5). Barbara Kiefer Lewalski considers Rowse's account of Lanyer's life unreliable, suggesting that Forman gives her a bad name because, although flirtatious, she did not have intercourse with him (*Writing Women in Jacobean England* [Cambridge, MA: Harvard University Press, 1993], 216 and 219). Lewalski defers to the biographical summary in Suzanne Woods's introduction to *The Poems of Aemilia Lanyer:* Salve Deus Rex Judaeorum, ed. Suzanne Woods (New York: Oxford University Press, 1993).

23 Woods, introduction, xv, n. 1.

24 Quoted in Stephan A. Schwartz, *The Secret Vaults of Time: Psychic Archaeology and the Quest for Man's Beginnings* (New York: Grosset, 1978), 63.

25 See "The Role of the Unconscious in the Writing Process," *Peer English: The Journal of New Critical Thinking* 1, no. 1 (2006): 45–55.

26 Percy Allen, *Talks with Elizabethans: Revealing the Mystery of "William Shakespeare"* (New York: Rider, 1947).
27 S. Schoenbaum, "Loony and the Oxfordians," in *Shakespeare: An Anthology of Criticism and Theory 1945–2000*, ed. Russ McDonald (Malden, MA: Blackwell, 2004), 11–12.
28 Allen, *Talks with Elizabethans*, 194.
29 Allen does not indent the couplet, but I take this to be an oversight because the other two sonnets end with indented couplets.
30 Allen, *Talks with Elizabethans*, 194.
31 W. B. Yeats, "Sailing to Byzantium," in *Selected Poems and Two Plays of William Butler Yeats*, ed. M. L. Rosenthal (New York: Macmillan, 1962), 95, line 17.
32 Robert A. Monroe, *Journeys Out of the Body* (1971; New York: Doubleday, 1977), 107.
33 Allen, *Talks with Elizabethans*, 194.
34 Ibid., 194.
35 Ibid., 195.
36 Ibid., 192.
37 Quoted in McDonald, *The Bedford Companion to Shakespeare*, 23.
38 See "Seth: The Spiritual Teacher that Launched the New Age," accessed on May 29, 2012, http://www.sethlearningcenter.org/. A helpful overview of the Jane Roberts's work appears in chapter 8 of Joseph M. Felser's *The Myth of the Great Ending: Why We've Been Longing for the End of Days Since the Beginning of Time* (Charlottesville, VA: Hampton Roads, 2011), 133–57.

8

AMPLIFICATION AND QUATERNITY IN ROBERT JORDAN'S *THE WHEEL OF TIME* SERIES

Robert Jordan was a native of Charleston, South Carolina, a Vietnam veteran, and a student of history (especially the Civil War)—all of which helps illuminate the emphases on history and battle in *The Wheel of Time*.[1] He seems to have gotten his wish to keep writing until his casket was nailed shut because the massive series was unfinished at the time of his death in 2007. Brandon Sanderson, who teaches creative writing at Brigham Young University, ghost-wrote the twelfth and thirteenth books. A fourteenth, which will complete the series, is forthcoming in 2013.

The present chapter is the first of two case studies that cap off this book. I chose *The Wheel of Time* because the series provides relevant examples of the themes and topics addressed previously. That good fit is particularly evident when Loial the Ogier makes a comment to the series' main character, Rand al'Thor, that illustrates unity via the One Mind:

> Everything is . . . linked, Rand. Whether it lives or not, whether it thinks or not, everything that *is*, fits together. The tree does not think, but it is part of the whole, and the whole has a—a feeling.
>
> (2.237; ch. 15)[2]

However, two matters that have figured prominently in previous chapters receive minimal attention in chapter 8. First, the problem of materialism is not relevant because everyone in Jordan's fictional universe acknowledges that Spirit is an element along with Earth, Air, Fire, and Water. Belief perseverance, when it does arise, reflects a negative evaluation of channeling the One Power, not an insistent denial that it is possible to do so. The best example is the Children of the Light who consider the Aes Sedai to be "witches" and Darkfriends but do not doubt that Aes Sedai can do what they claim. Materialism is such a patently false assumption that it never receives mention, much less serious consideration. A second matter—the possibility of life on other planets—seems to be on the tip of Moghedien's tongue in one of her conversations with Nynaeve: "'travel to other worlds, even worlds in the sky. Do you know that the stars are . . . '" (4.909; ch. 54). The ellipsis, which is part of the text, suggests that she resists a direct affirmation that the One Power could be used to visit other inhabited planets; but the point is on her mind.[3] Meanwhile, the schools that Rand founds enable the birth of modern astronomy. As Headmistress Tarsin notes, "'Kin Tovere constructed his big looking glass [telescope]. You can see the moon through it plain as your hand, and what he claims are other worlds, but what is the good of that?'" (9.79; prologue). Within the characters' own world, however, portal stones and *ter'angreal* transport them to alternate versions of reality or to other worlds, if not other planets. With plenty of such destinations in *The Wheel of Time*, there is no need for anything extraterrestrial.

Unlike materialism and life on other planets, all of the major emphases in previous chapters are present; and some of them are highly relevant. The traditional Jungian approach of chapter 1 (shadow and anima) and the connectedness at which "Young Goodman Brown" hints correspond to the series' central conflict with the Dark One, the main characters' contra-sexual relationships, and the philosophy of oneness expressed by Loial. All things are connected via the One Mind, including a series of removes, as in *Paradise Lost*, from the Creator to physical matter. As with Adam and the wanderer, altered states, especially something very similar to Robert A. Monroe's out-of-body state, receive a great deal of attention. Synchronicity parallels Jordan's treatment of luck, chance, and the effect of being *ta'veren*. Space-time relativity and various psychic feats that call to mind remote viewing are commonplace in *The Wheel of Time*.[4] Since Jordan deals with almost all the major emphases in this book, his series provides an appropriate way to illustrate the implications of the One Mind for fiction; to model literary criticism based on that premise; and to bring our argument to a climax, though not a close.

Genre and Jung

The Wheel of Time is a sprawling psychological epic fantasy, and it makes sense to begin with a comment on each of these characteristics. Even its extreme page count, which rivals *The Collected Works of C. G. Jung*, belies the breadth of the Jordan's project. The point of view sprawls to include dozens of characters—good and evil, major and minor. Jordan tells the story primarily from the viewpoints of the eight main characters: Rand al'Thor, the Dragon Reborn; his childhood friends, now his comrades in arms, Perrin Aybara, who becomes a Wolfbrother, and Mat Cauthon, a gambler who remembers the Old Tongue and hundreds of past lives as a military commander; Nynaeve al'Maera, the "wisdom" of Rand's home village who becomes the most powerful Aes Sedai (female channeler of the One Power, trained at the White Tower in Tar Valon) since the Age of Legends; Egwene al'Vere, Rand's childhood sweetheart, who becomes the Amyrlin Seat, the leader of the seven Ajahs of the Aes Sedai; and three women who fall in love with Rand and eventually link to him psychically through "bonding": Elayne Trakand (Daughter Heir to the Lion Throne of Andor who also becomes a powerful Aes Sedai), Min Farshaw (a reader of auras who foretells the future), and Aviendha (an Aiel Maiden of the Spear who becomes a Wise One-in-training, and later a Wise One; she too can channel).[5] *The Wheel of Time* is also told from the points of view of various secondary characters, the most prominent being Thom Merrilin, the gleeman;[6] Siuan Sanche, the deposed Amyrlin Seat; leaders of the Children of the Light (pejoratively called White Cloaks), an itinerant army that violently enforces its own conservative ideology; and some of the Forsaken (thirteen male and female Aes Sedai from the Age of Legends who have received immortality in exchange for their service to the Dark One). The series sprawls not only because of this proliferation of points of view but also because Jordan describes actions and settings in great detail. Within multiple plots, the books feature, for example, the minutia of the characters' meals and lodging during their travels through numerous nation states; consequently, the weaving of narrative fabric in each book takes hundreds of pages (it is a great relief to the reader when the rediscovery of Traveling minimizes the trudging to and fro). After the first seven books, however, little that is unique is introduced; therefore, this chapter focuses on the series' first half. In other words, despite a wealth of ideas that are relevant to the present study, *The Wheel of Time* is often storytelling for its own sake, sometimes in excess.

As befits a multivolume work with multiple points of view, *The Wheel of Time* is epic in scope. According to Gary K. Wolfe, the term "epic fantasy" is used in reference to "almost any multivolume fantasy work."[7] *The Wheel of Time* is epic in the adjectival sense simply because it is very long, but it is also an epic in the traditional nominative sense. Jordan obviously considers it as such when he refers to "'the topless towers of Cairhien'" (1.84; ch. 6). In keeping with the Marlovian allusion, the series' martial activity is Iliadic, for Rand's objective is to unite the world, by conquest if necessary, in preparation for Tarmon Gai'don, the Last Battle. The series also includes an Odyssean emphasis on romantic relationships among the main characters, particularly Rand and his three women. As well, epic tells the story of one action—in this case, the (one hopes successful) fight with the Dark One—while including history, as in Ezra Pound's well-known definition. For example, characters frequently compare themselves to legendary figures in books; references to the Age of Legends and especially to the Breaking of the World recall the actions of Lews Therin Telamon, the former Dragon, who begins speaking in Rand's head after he learns to channel the One Power; Rand's visions among the column *ter'angreal* in Rhuidean reveal the history of the Aiel, particularly the fact that these war-like people are directly related to the Tuatha'an, the Traveling People, who embrace pacifism; and there are frequent references to more recent events such as the senseless felling by Laman Damodred of *Avendoraldera*, a great tree grown from a cutting of *Avendesora*, the Tree of Life. Moreover, the circularity of time makes history a kind of character in its own right. The series is set in the Third of the Seven Ages, all of which repeat, which is why Rand painstakingly consults history books like *The Karaethon Cycle* and *The Prophecies of the Dragon* for insights into his mission.

The nature of *The Wheel of Time* as fantasy, especially in relation to Jungian psychology and theories of fantasy, requires a more extended analysis. What does Jung say about fantasy? As John Aquino explains, Jung associates fantasy with "the primitive mind" and "infantile memories."[8] Aquino's source is the essay "Approaching the Unconscious" in *Man and his Symbols*, where Jung writes, "Most of us have consigned to the unconscious all the fantastic psychic associations that every object or idea possesses." The statement, however, does not accurately address what Jung means by the primitive mentality. A later passage cited by Aquino mentions the "primitive instincts" and "infantile memory" without any mention of fantasy; Jung is simply discussing children's psychology.[9] Elsewhere, he is more helpful in associating fantasy and imagination.

> Fantasy as imaginative activity is, in my view, simply the direct expression of psychic life, of psychic energy which cannot appear in consciousness except in the form of images or contents, just as physical energy cannot manifest itself except as a definite physical state stimulating the sense organs in physical ways. . . . We could therefore say that fantasy in the sense of a fantasm is a definite sum of libido that cannot appear in consciousness in any other way than in the form of an image. A fantasm is an *idée-force*. Fantasy as imaginative activity is identical with the flow of psychic energy.
>
> (*CW* 6, 722/433)

Jung clarifies the word "fantasm" as follows: "By fantasy in the sense of *fantasm* I mean a complex of ideas that is distinguished from other such complexes by the fact that it has no objective referent" (*CW* 6, 711/427). Obviously, fantasy-as-imagination or fantasm-as-complex could easily result in creative activity, as W. R. Irwin rightly notes. Irwin quotes Jung as stating that fantasy "'is the creative activity whence issue the solutions to all answerable questions'" and that active fantasy is "'the principal attribute of the artistic mentality.'" Irwin himself states that Jungian fantasy "resembles the intellection that can lead to literary fantasy" insofar as it relates to "the artistic potential of emanations from the collective unconscious." Irwin further states that "the process described by Jung is one source of what I have called 'the fantastic,' and his phrase for such constructs, that they 'correspond to no external state of affairs,' goes far toward defining 'the fantastic.'"[10] But could not the same be said of fiction in general? Jung's theory of fantasy may not apply to fantasy literature as specifically as Irwin maintains.

A final distinction, according to Jung, is between active fantasy and passive fantasy. Active fantasy is evoked by intuition and is compatible with unconscious content; so active fantasy means that what arises is in sync with the unconscious. But passive fantasy, because it pits consciousness against the unconscious, needs "conscious *criticism*, lest it merely reinforce the standpoint of the unconscious opposite" (*CW* 6, 712/428 and 714/429; emphasis in the original).[11] Active fantasy manifests a compensatory relationship with the unconscious, whereas passive fantasy involves criticism that suggests opposition between consciousness and the unconscious. Either type might result in artistic productivity, but nothing in Jung's sometimes-mercurial statements about fantasy illuminates fantasy *literature* to any great degree, much less provides a means of understanding Jordan's relationship to the genre. Indeed "fantasy as imaginative activity" does not necessarily lead to a literary product at all; and a literary product, though imaginative and reflective of psychic life, might not involve the kind of elements that characterize fantasy literature. How, then, does Jordan's series fit into the theories of fantasy that various critics put forward in the 20th century?

Theories of fantasy and the fantastic

Fantasy is a genre, and the fantastic is the mode that it employs. As Wolfe notes, fantasy is "a fictional narrative describing events that the reader believes to be Impossible," that is, set in opposition to materialism.[12] The fantastic is whatever transgresses the laws of nature as we know them; and fantasy thus presents the impossible, a point on which nearly all theorists agree. For our purposes, one of the earlier, less well-known theorists is the most helpful because many of his assertions precisely characterize *The Wheel of Time*. Witold Ostrowsky (1966) asserts that the fantastic in literature involves transgressing one or more laws of "the empirical world and/or their pattern" such as matter, space-time, causality, and consciousness. He cites examples like "superhuman knowledge," "consciousness able to live apart from any body," "everlasting youth," and "an ability to leave one's body or to enter someone else's." Such phenomena, he states, "exist in their literary form as products of the imagination or fantasy and for this reason are called fantastic." As well,

> Any heightening of mental powers means their emancipation from matter and space. This is evident in cases of seeing and acting at a distance or of physical translocation by the power of will. Knowledge of the future or of the unrecorded past, memory of previous incarnations . . . unusual longevity or immortality are all based on a rearrangement of the typical relations between mind, matter and time.[13]

In Jordan's series, past/present, dream/reality, and even man/beast are not binary categories but rather imbrications. In addition, the Ways and the rediscovery of Traveling show space-time relativity; there is great longevity on the part of women who can channel the One Power; several characters have the talent of Foretelling; reincarnation is a given; past-life memories are possible to achieve; and various characters have out-of-body experiences in the World of Dreams. Ostrowsky's theory fits *The Wheel of Time* so well that it is almost as if Jordan had the article open in front of him as he planned his novels.

The next significant critic of the fantasy genre, Tzvetan Todorov (1973), echoes Ostrowsky in stating that "the physical world and the spiritual world interpenetrate;

their fundamental categories are modified as a result. The time and space of the supernatural world . . . are not the time and space of everyday life." In addition, "the fantastic is that *hesitation* experienced by a person who knows only the laws of nature, confronting an apparently supernatural event" (my emphasis). The fantastic, for Todorov, is not only the events that violate natural law as we understand it but also the reader's response to the impossible. He does mention "the description of a fantastic universe, one that has no reality outside language,"[14] but his emphasis on the reader's response to portrayals of our own world diminishes the usefulness of his study for Jordan's alternative universe.

The next two studies, both published in 1976, seem to echo each other's conclusions on fantasy and the fantastic; and at least one of them aligns with Todorov's emphasis on reader response. For Eric S. Rabkin, fantasy offers an alternative by reversing and thus violating the "ground rules" of our world. The fantastic is the resulting "emotional affects" or "quality of astonishment" (akin to Todorov's "hesitation") that we feel as we read. Again, fantasy is the genre, whereas the fantastic means not only the "structural properties" that involve "the direct reversal of ground rules" (that is, the impossible) but also the reaction elicited in the reader.[15] Irwin simultaneously reaches a very similar conclusion that "fantasy is a story based on and controlled by an overt violation of what is generally accepted as possibility; it is the narrative result of transforming the condition contrary to fact into 'fact' itself." Fantasy "presents the persuasive establishment and development of an impossibility, an arbitrary construct of the mind with all under the control of logic and rhetoric"; thus the fantastic is "the factitious existence of the antireal."[16] For both Rabkin and Irwin, fantasy is a genre in which the laws of nature are reversed; and the fantastic refers to the actual machinery that effects the reversal. For Rabkin at least, the fantastic elicits a specific reader response.

In light of this definition of fantasy—literature in which the laws of nature are violated—it is clear that we have already discussed literary texts that include fantastic elements. In "Young Goodman Brown," the devil claims to have traveled sixteen or more miles from Boston to Salem in fifteen minutes—apparently he has flown, which is impossible. Just as Brown speaks with the devil, Eve speaks with Satan in *Paradise Lost*; she and Adam also interact with angels. Frederick Henry, injured by an explosion, finds his consciousness outside his body. In *The Midwich Cuckoos* the extraterrestrial children use their mental powers to compel others. Finally, the young doctor in *Sun of the Son* travels off world with extraterrestrials, plunges into the sun on an alien spaceship, and uses a nectar to share enhanced consciousness with the novel's Angelucci character.

Postdating Rabkin and Irwin, other theorists use terminology relevant to *The Wheel of Time*, starting with Marshall B. Tymn and his co-authors in 1979. Low fantasy, the kind that Todorov mainly discusses, is set in our own world, whereas high fantasy, the kind that writers like Jordan and Tolkien create, is set in a made-up or secondary world. (Irwin uses the term "total mythologies" to describe stories that take place in this type of created universe.) Wolfe nicely defines the key terms as follows: the distinction is between "[high] fantasy set in a fully imagined Secondary world . . . [and] Low Fantasy which concerns supernatural intrusions into the 'real' world."[17] Jordan achieves an interesting homology within his fictional world as follows: our own primary world of consensus reality is to the secondary world of the series (the world of high fantasy) as that secondary world is to alternative universes within it such as World of Dreams (the astral plane or spirit world). In other words, the world of *The Wheel of Time* becomes its own consensus reality and takes on greater verisimilitude to the extent that other dimensions violate its ground rules.

High fantasy—in Jordan's case, "all-ages high fantasy"—has three characteristics: noble characters, archetypes, and elevated style.[18] First, Jordan's characters rise from humble origins to noble positions. Rand, for example, begins book 1 as a sheepherder but eventually is crowned King of Illian (thus he wears the Crown of Swords to which the title of book 7 refers). Similarly, the Aiel call him the *Car'a'carn*, the chief of chiefs. Meanwhile, Perrin and Mat become great military leaders—lords, though they dislike the appellation; Mat also becomes Prince of the Ravens when he marries Seanchan royalty—while Egwene and Nynaeve ascend to prominence among the Aes Sedai. Second, the series obviously also incorporates archetypes and their associated images. Most notably, the Dark One gives the archetype of evil a malevolent personality and intent. Evil actually walks the land in the form of the Forsaken, and the Ways are polluted by a pure evil called the Black Wind (*Machin Shin*).[19] Jordan is also intrigued by female types and by the warrior archetype, hence the depth of description he gives to the Aiel Maidens of the Spear. In great contrast to Jung's essentialism, in which women are Eve, Mary, Helen, or Sophia, Jordan's imagination seems stuck on women who are leaders, commanders, Amazons, bullies, or some combination of these types. The third criterion, high style, is hard to see in *The Wheel of Time*. Ordinarily Jordan's style is brisk, economical, and down-to-earth; it is occasionally beautiful but even then not elevated.[20]

A couple of other less well-known theorists also deserve mention. *The Wheel of Time* fits most of the six characteristics of fantasy that John H. Timmerman sets out: traditional story, common characters and heroism, another world, magic and the supernatural, struggle between good and evil, and a quest. Regarding the other world, he notes that it is created whole (true enough in Jordan's case) but that it matches reality and is not "an escapist world but a world in which we live."[21] Also, Brian Attebery suggests that fantasy literature is comic.[22] Indeed, each book culminates in a battle in which the forces of the Light triumph over the representatives of the Dark One, especially the Forsaken. One assumes that book 14 will feature a comic ending for the overall series—the defeat of the Dark One and perhaps a happy ending for Rand, despite the prophecy that his blood must be shed at the Last Battle.

We may turn now to Jordan's own comments on fantasy for an introduction to his insights into the genre. His comments are quoted in the previously mentioned article in *Locus*.[23]

> In fantasy, we *can* talk about right and wrong, and good and evil, and do it with a straight face. We can discuss morality or ethics, and believe that these things are important, where[as] you cannot in mainstream fiction. It's part of the reason why I believe fantasy is perhaps the oldest form of literature in the world, at least in the western [*sic*] canon. You go back not simply to *Beowulf* but *The Epic of Gilgamesh.*

It is hard for a serious student of literature to digest this comment with a straight face. Does Jordan really mean to imply that authors who do not write fantasy cannot talk about right and wrong, morality and ethics, or believe that such themes are important? Do not countless authors deal with those same themes apart from creating a genre in which things violate natural laws? Fantasy literature does not have a lock on matters of central concern to humans, but perhaps he means that the fantasy genre's machinery (the fantastic) enables a more direct way of portraying good and evil. It may also be that fantasy is a more inclusive genre than one may commonly believe, as he suggests in his next comment:

> And it survives pervasively today. People in the field of science fiction and fantasy are willing to accept that the magic realists are fantasy writers, but to the world at large, "Oh no, that's not fantasy, that's literature." Yes it *is* fantasy. And a lot of other things, that are published as mainstream, really are fantasy but not identified as such. We really have quite a pervasive influence.

His point about fantasy's inclusiveness might be better framed as follows: within a genre like the short story ("Young Goodman Brown"), the epic (*Paradise Lost*), or the novel (*Son of the Sun*), authors may use fantastic elements to various degrees to achieve their narrative and thematic goals. The truth of that point, however, does not mean that only writers of fantasy can discuss themes related to the human heart and mind. Then Jordan makes a very reasonable, but not original, point:

> I hope [fantasy's "pervasive influence" is] for the good, because there is a human *necessity*. Terry Pratchett postulated something, and I don't know whether or not it's original to him, but it seemed a very interesting point. He said that we believe in fantasies, in things that don't exist, and that the ability to believe in things that don't exist, such as those in fantasy, prepares us to believe in other things that don't exist, like justice and mercy.

Fantasy's presentation of the impossible, replete with violations of natural law, requires a mental agility that lends itself to contemplation of themes that matter in our primary world. In this sense, fantasy literature plays a pedagogical role in society, at least if the text stirs readers to contemplate virtue. But Jordan claims for fantasy what far more astute critics, foremost among them Sir Philip Sidney, attribute to art in general. In Sidney's well-known dictum, literature delights its readers in order to teach them to affirm moral virtues of various sorts.

Although Jordan's claims about fantasy are both poorly informed and insufferably grandiose, they do point toward the concept that I want to emphasize in the following analysis of *The Wheel of Time*. It is not merely that one unreal thing promotes consideration of another unreal thing. More than that, fantasy literature increases the wattage of human capacity: the real becomes hyper-real. In other words, fantastic elements *amplify* genuine human capacity by means such as personifying archetypes, intensifying a process like dreaming, and dramatically increasing the potential of the mind, as Ostrowski observed in the 1960s. Of course, this is not amplification as Jung understood it—a piling on of associative detail in order to establish the meaning of an image from a dream or vision. As Daryl Sharp explains, Jungian amplification is "a method of association based on the comparative study of mythology, religion and fairy tales, used in the interpretation of images in dreams and drawings."[24] Jung uses the technique, for example, in *Symbols of Transformation* (*CW* 5) in order to gloss Miss Frank Miller's experience of psyche and in *Flying Saucers: A Modern Myth of Things Seen in the Skies* to establish the saucer shape as an image of wholeness. In the sense of the hyper-real, amplification in the present study goes hand-in-hand with the fantastic in order to heighten intensity and to portray psyche more vividly. What is writ small in the real or primary world is writ large in a secondary world; what is latent in us takes on "a local habitation and a name" in a secondary world, to borrow Shakespeare's memorable phrase from *A Midsummer Night's Dream*. Fantastic elements in literature, far from constituting a black-and-white alternative to our world and violating natural law, seize on something true about us and emphasize it. The result is myth—a story, as Jung understood, that tells us what we do not know about our own psyche.[25]

A purpose of this chapter, then, is to show that *The Wheel of Time* depicts an amplification of what is dim or nascent in us at the present moment in time. Perhaps witnessing the seemingly impossible in the amplified secondary world of fantasy may inspire us to consider what is *not* impossible in our own. Still, Jordan's use of fantastic elements does break *some* ground rules. So far as anyone knows, we cannot use the mind to light a candle, for example. But in fantasy even violations of natural law function as amplifications and reminders of the often-unacknowledged potential of the human mind and of the One Mind in which everything participates. Of course, a reader's response to *The Wheel of Time*'s many volumes may include compensation. An average person with a mundane life may start having dreams about Rand, a sheepherder who discovers that he can channel the One Power that turns the Wheel of Time. But just as Jordan's series is about characters who discover that they have hidden talents, we too may discover and develop our own. Often one discovers a talent for healing, travel, illusion, compulsion, dreaming, or foretelling. In Jordan's series, these talents become Healing, Traveling, Illusion, Compulsion, Dreaming, and

Foretelling: amplifications that call attention to the readers' own talents, gifts of the spirit that do exist in our primary world but often lie fallow in the unconscious. In this fashion, fantasy provides a vision of human possibility amplified to the point of exaggeration or even unreality, until it dawns on readers that fantastic-seeming manifestations of the One Mind may actually be natural in the sort of undiscovered, underestimated, and quite wonderful ways that this book has explored.

Quaternity and cosmology

The role of amplification is present in multiple details below, but we turn first to the concept of quaternity from chapter 1 and the transcendental monism from chapter 3.[26] Both serve as organizing principles in an analysis of Jordan's cosmology in *The Wheel of Time*, a cosmology that strongly supports Loial's affirmation of unity and oneness in his statement that all things are linked. Like Milton in *Paradise Lost*, Jordan includes a history of the cosmos from creation *ex Deo* to a series of lesser nonphysical forces, physical matter, human beings, the forces at work in the world, and the artifacts that arise from human ingenuity. In this series of removes, the Jungian concept of quaternity serves as a structural principle: the universe originates in the Creator/Light (Father) who imprisons the Dark One (Satan) and provides the True Source (Holy Spirit) to assist the Dragon Reborn, the Promised or Chosen One (Son) (1.758, ch. 51; and 2.681, ch. 50).

The Creator. Jordan affirms at various points that there was a "moment of creation" and that the universe originates in the Creator, who is said to be Light (2.681; ch. 50). He is omnipresent in multiple created worlds (3.239; ch. 21) because everything is made out of primordial energy. Jordan subtly underscores the true nature of the Creator by assigning incorrect conclusions to the Forsaken. Rahvin, for example, considers "the protection of his bonds and oaths [to the Dark One as] ties to what he knew as a greater power than the Light, or even the Creator" (5.29; prologue). The statement is wrong on two counts: there is no hierarchical relationship between the Creator and the Light because they are one and the same, and it is certain that the Creator is more powerful because he imprisoned the Dark One beyond time at Shayol Ghul at the moment of creation.[27] A subtler misconception appears in Heather Attrill's claim that "the Creator, having set the cosmic loom in motion, appears to stand outside and to play no obviously active part. Jordan thus suggests that in his world humanity can expect no miracles or interventions."[28] Instead, as Sammael, another of the Forsaken, correctly realizes, the war between the Creator and the Dark One involves "human surrogates" (6.175; ch. 6).[29] A moving illustration in book 1 both illustrates Sammael's point and qualifies Attrill's. Rand, filled with untainted *saidin* drawn from the Eye of the World, searches for Ba'alzamon (Heart of the Dark in the Trollocs' language; the Dark One's physical manifestation in the Forsaken named Ishmael). Notably, the exchange is one of only two times italicized all caps ever appear in the first thirteen books.

> "The Light blind you, Ba'alzamon! This has to end!" [Rand cries.]
> *IT IS NOT HERE.*
> It was not Rand's thought, making his skull vibrate.
> *I WILL TAKE NO PART. ONLY THE CHOSEN ONE CAN DO WHAT MUST BE DONE, IF HE WILL.*
> "Where?" He did not want to say it, but he could not stop himself. "Where?"
> *NOT HERE.*
> Through the mist, as from the far end of the earth, came a cry. "The Light wills it!"
>
> (1.758; ch. 51)[30]

The exchange makes it clear that the forces of the Light must combat the forces of the Dark on their own with no direct help from the Creator, as Attrill would agree. The Creator does not reach out to pull Rand out of a hole, as Moridin does in Shadar Logoth (7.846; ch. 41).[31] But Pedron Niall, a leader of the Children of the Light, incorrectly thinks that "the Creator had abandoned mankind to its own devices long ago" (6.62; prologue); for at the critical moment when Rand first wields the One Power there is a miracle of intervention in the form of guidance. Ironically, though, he seems to have forgotten about the Creator's intervention in a later book: "The Creator had made the world and then left humankind to make of it what they would, a heaven or the Pit of Doom by their choosing" (10.558; ch. 24).

The Dark One. At first, Jordan and his co-author Teresa Patterson seem to arrogate more power to the Dark One than his imprisonment would seem to justify. He is "a being with godlike abilities, perhaps on a level with the Creator's. Many scholars believe him to be the complete antithesis of the Creator." They then qualify the claim by stating, "He does not, however, have the ability to break free of his prison without assistance from our world."[32] Perhaps he is a being with god*like* abilities, but his imprisonment attests that he is not the Creator's equal. The point about antitheses, however, is exactly right. The Creator, as his name implies, brings about order, goodness, and balance; the Dark One seeks chaos through destruction and promotes evil, from which he takes his name, Shai'tan. A similar dynamic plays out in the opposition between the Dark One and the forces of the Light. When Ba'alzamon tells Rand that they "'are tied together as surely as two sides of the same coin,'" Rand immediately responds by calling him the "'Father of Lies'" (2.242; ch. 15). Yet the balance implicit in the statement contains some truth. The Dark One's goals are to break free from his prison, destroy time, and remake the world and all Seven Ages in his own perverted image. As an Aes Sedai named Verin Mathwin explains, "'The Dark One is the embodiment of paradox and chaos, the destroyer of reason and logic, the breaker of balance, the unmaker of order'" (3.239; ch. 21). Although still confined, he has begun to touch the world, as the perpetual summer attests: "He had strained from his prison to touch the world enough to fix the seasons in place" (8.83; ch. 2).

Rand and his friends, on the other hand, attempt to thwart the Dark One at every turn. For example, Nynaeve, Elayne, and other female channelers, using the Bowl of the Winds, nudge the cycle of the seasons back into motion, much as Rand's victory in *The Eye of the World* brings spring out of winter (1.777; ch. 53). If human agency can undo or curb the work of the Dark One, then he cannot be a force equivalent to the Creator. But he is pretty clearly the second person in Jordan's quaternity, unlike Satan who is the fourth person in Jung's.

The One Power. Occupying the third position is the True Source, an infinite and omnipresent "driving force of the universe, which turns the Wheel of Time" (1.798; glossary). The One Power is drawn from the True Source (1.105; ch. 8), suggesting a hierarchical relationship between the two. There is also the Dark One's so-called True Power, but Jordan does not make it clear whether the Dark One has tapped into the One Power and perverted it or whether the True Power is a different strain of energy altogether (7.452; ch. 20). Regardless of its provenance, the True Power is lower in the hierarchy than the Creator, though vaster and more powerful than the One Power (12.450; ch. 29). The important thing is that it is possible for a Forsaken to draw upon it for evil purposes, though its regular use causes black flecks called *saa* to swim across the eyeballs and is "a drug more addictive than *saidin*, more deadly than poison" (9.317; ch. 13).

Saidin is the male half of the One Power, *saidar* the female half. Moiraine Damodred, the Aes Sedai who guides the main characters in the early books, offers the following helpful explanation of the One Power in *The Eye of the World*:

> "The One Power . . . comes from the True Source, the driving force of Creation, the force the Creator made to turn the Wheel of Time." She put her hands together in front of her and pushed them against each other. "*Saidin*, the male half of the True Source, and *saidar*, the female half, work against each other and at the same time together to provide that force. *Saidin*"—she lifted one hand, then let it drop—"is fouled by the touch of the Dark One, like water with a thin slick of rancid oil floating on top. The water is still pure, but it cannot be touched without touching the foulness. Only *saidar* is still safe to be used."
>
> (1.168; ch. 12)

The fact that the two halves push against one another implies a balanced tension that lies at the heart of Creation and has an important effect. "The male and female halves of the True Source were alike and unalike, attracting and repelling, fighting against each other even as they worked together to drive the Wheel of Time" (9.637; ch. 35), which is the next remove from the Creator.

The Wheel of Time. Attrill points out that time is a wheel in Hindu mythology,[33] and the metaphor calls to mind the way in which Monroe (chapter 4) uses rings to describe the nonphysical universe. As the wheel image suggests, time is circular, which is why Rand seeks guidance in history and prophecy, especially *The Karaethon Cycle* and *The Prophecies of the Dragon*: what once was will be again. After founding a school in Cairhien to promote scientific research, Rand consults with his lead academician, Herid Fel, on time's circularity.

> Snatching his pipe out, Herid drew a circle in the air with the stem. "The Wheel of Time. Ages come and go and come again as the Wheel turns. All the catechism." Suddenly he stabbed a point on that imaginary wheel. "Here the Dark One's prison is whole. Here, they drilled a hole in it, and sealed it up again." He moved the bit of the pipe along the arc he had drawn. "Here we are. The seal's weakening. But that doesn't matter, of course." The pipestem completed the circle. "When the Wheel turns back to here, back to where they drilled the hole in the first place, the Dark One's prison has to be whole again."
>
> (6.415; ch. 18)

Characters' frequent adage, "'the Wheel weaves as the Wheel wills,'" deserves scrutiny in light of Fel's explanation of time's circularity. If time is one vastly complicated wheel, then some kind of inscrutable cosmic cycle accounts for things beyond human control and understanding. There is no will behind time, only a motion powered by the opposing forces of *saidar* and *saidin*. Events happen because, as the wheel turns, they come around again. For example, certain souls are "bound to the Wheel" (2.661; ch. 47), which means that they reincarnate over and over again. The concept is best illustrated by Birgitte Silverbow, who is ripped out of the World of Dreams as a fully grown woman, and her love interest, Gaidal Cain, whom she meets in each of her lifetimes. Two others who appear to be bound to the wheel are Rand and Mat. Both experience anamnesis from past lifetimes, and ancient memories frequently provide useful guidance and know-how, especially in battle. Rand and Mat remember because the one wields *saidin* and the other has *saidar* applied to him. Mat later has a near-death experience in Rhuidean; and the Eelfinn either unlock some of his past-life memories or insert other men's memories into his own. In other words, because the One Power amplifies to the point of recollection the past-life knowledge that is locked in the unconscious mind, characters' reincarnations demonstrate the circularity implicit in the wheel image.

The Pattern. Along with the wheel, there is one other important image that expresses the effect of cosmic forces on human lives: the loom. The combination is a bit of a mixed metaphor: the One Power drives the wheel that weaves the Pattern of men's lives (wheels cannot weave). But there is a significant correspondence between this cosmic weaving of people's lives and the weaving that they do with *saidar* and *saidin*. Channelers use the One Power by weaving together combinations of the five elements. Much as an artist is often said to be a co-creator with God (like Eiseley in chapter 1), channelers are co-creators with the Creator who made the universe out of himself and who allowed opposing forces to set the Wheel of Time in motion. A much younger Moiraine correctly states in *New Spring* that "'the Pattern is the work of the Light'" (223), but this is true only indirectly. Moveover, the principle of balance that obtains in the macrocosm between *saidar* and *saidin* also governs individual lives, which are woven of threads both good and evil.[34] As Moiraine explains to Perrin, "'There are many threads woven in the Pattern, and some are as black as the Shadow itself'" (3.511; ch. 44). In summary, as we descend down the Scale of Being, we have the following set of removes: Creator, True Source, One Power, Wheel of Time, Pattern, Age Lace or Great Pattern (which is formed of Ages), and finally the Pattern of an Age (3.238; ch. 21). There are seven ages, and Jordan's series takes place in the Third Age, "an Age yet to come, an Age long past," as he states at the beginning of chapter 1 in each book. The events that *The Wheel of Time* depicts have happened before and will occur again.

Balefire. Although it sounds as if the Pattern is completely deterministic, there are ways of affecting it, especially if one uses the One Power. Moiraine espouses determinism in stating, "'What is, is. What is woven already is past changing.'" Later she adds, "'What is already woven cannot be undone'" (1.578 and 665; ch. 38 and 44). This is not the whole truth of the matter. In *The Fires of Heaven*, when she uses balefire to destroy Darkhounds, she alters the Pattern quite dramatically. She explains its use to Rand as follows:

> "When anything is destroyed with balefire, it ceases to exist *before* the moment of its destruction, like a thread that burns away from where the flame touched it. The greater the power of the balefire, the further back in time it ceases to exist. The strongest I can manage will remove only a few seconds from the Pattern. You are much stronger. Very much so.... For as far back as you destroyed the creature, whatever it did during that time *no longer happened*. Only the memories remain, for those who saw or experienced it. Only what it did before is real, now."
>
> (5.167; ch. 6)

Rand's strength in the power is the reason why Moiraine and later Cadsuane Melaidhrin, the oldest living Aes Sedai, advise him never to use balefire. Reportedly, it was used in the past to wreak such destruction that the Pattern nearly could not recover. Rand does use it, however, to good effect in destroying the souls of some of the Forsaken (otherwise, their souls transmigrate into living bodies and continue to cause trouble: their ability to do this is one reason why the Dark One is called the Lord of the Dead), and Rand even rains balefire down on an entire town in book 12, chapter 37, in order to eradicate the female Forsaken known as Graendal (she escapes just in time, but the blast kills another Forsaken, Halima/Aran'gar).

Ta'veren. Another means of affecting the Pattern seems more in line with a deterministic reading: namely, the effect that *ta'veren* such as Rand, Perrin, and

Mat have on others. As "'centerpoints of the weaving'" (2.35; ch. 3), they can "bend lives around [them] into the shape *the Pattern required*" (6.40, prologue; my emphasis). Yet the narrator also states that a "*ta'veren* [is] one of those rare individuals who, instead of being woven into the Pattern as the Wheel of Time chose, forced the Pattern to shape itself around them, for a time at least" (4.37; ch. 1). Which is it? Do *ta'veren* bend the Pattern, or does the Pattern force *ta'veren*? Apparently the answer is both. Loial, who is a great reader of scholarly books, offers a well-informed answer:

> "As the Wheel of Time weaves us into the Pattern, the life-thread of each of us pulls and tugs at the life-threads around us. *Ta'veren* are the same, only much, much more so. They tug at the entire Pattern—for a time, at least—forcing it to shape around them. The closer you are to them, the more you are affected personally. . . . But it doesn't only work one way. *Ta'veren* themselves are woven to a tighter line than the rest of us, with fewer choices."
>
> (3.47; ch. 2)

In other words, *ta'veren* amplify the kind of influence all persons have on those around them; but the stronger the *ta'veren*, the fewer choices he has; and the more powerful are his effects on others. Ironically, men like Rand, Perrin, and Mat, whose mere presence can change others' lives, have fewer options of their own. They change the fate of others, but the Pattern chooses the fate of a *ta'veren*. Rand, who can channel the One Power, which stands above the Wheel that weaves the Pattern, is not a master of his own fate—a bit like a president who has great impact on others but whose office imposes limits on his own personal freedom of choice. A *ta'veren*'s impact can be immense. For example, Rand can sway a negotiation in his favor by his very presence; and his passing through a town causes a string of weddings or a rash of murders. He thus stands in a particular place in Jordan's cosmology: lower than the Wheel of Time and the Pattern but higher than lesser forces such as fate, chance, and luck. As Elayne rightly says of Mat, "'He alters the Pattern, alters *chance*, just being there, I'm ready to admit we need luck, and a *ta'veren* is more than luck'" (7.320; ch. 13). Or as Verin observes, "'Coincidence is how being *ta'veren* works. . . . Random chance randomly works in your favor'" (12.555; ch. 36). Mesaana, one of the female Forsaken, has a similar thought about Rand: "Lews Therin had made his own luck as a mint made coin. In her opinion it seemed that so far Rand al'Thor did the same" (6.69; prologue).

Lesser forces. It may be pleasant to think that one can bend the Pattern to some extent; but as we move down the cosmological ladder, fate (synonymous with destiny) becomes a more puissant and deterministic force.[35] Fate is the outcome that the Wheel wills, what is "fated [or determined] by the Pattern" (5.575; ch. 36); therefore, it is "'what must and will be'" (5.147; ch. 5). Fate is indifferent to human wishes—"'The Pattern doesn't much care what we want,'" as Min observes (2.560; ch. 39). Nor can it be forced, which is why one must not fight it. As Bair, an Aiel Wise One, says to Egwene,

> "You must learn to ride fate. Only by surrendering to the Pattern can you begin to have some control over the course of your own life. If you fight, the Pattern will still force you, and you will find only misery where you might have found contentment instead."
>
> (5.147; ch. 5)

Moiraine frames the same point more sternly in advising Rand against trying to force a prophesied outcome:

> "Prophecy is most dangerous when you try to make it happen. . . . The Pattern weaves itself around you, but when you try to weave it, even you cannot hold it. Force the Pattern too tight, and pressure builds. It can explode wildly in every direction. Who can say how long before it settles to focus on you again, or what will happen before it does?"
>
> (4.831; ch. 50)

As he wisely realizes in book 12, "'My power and influence are meaningless against fate'" (105; ch. 5). Since the Pattern determines the major course of a person's life, it is treacherous to stray from the predetermined path, as Rand discovers when he views alternate scenarios for his life. Not affirming his role as the Dragon Reborn results in madness, disaster, or death in every case (see 2.527–32; ch. 37, "What Might Be").

Mat provides perhaps the best illustration of the power of fate in regard to finding his wife. When a *ter'angreal* takes him to another world in book 4, the Aelfinn inform him that he is fated to marry the Daughter of the Nine Moons, a title no one has ever heard of because her people live on another continent across the Aryth Ocean. For many books, Mat is the consummate gambler, riding chance like a wave; and the more random the risk, the greater luck he enjoys. The massive application of *saidar* to Heal the corruption leached into him by the dagger he picks up in Shadar Logoth amplifies his luck to such an extent that, in a single night, he gambles successfully, falls safely from a great height, and meets up with Thom Merrilin. In similar ways, for many books, he reaps the benefit of his amplified luck; but when someone in his presence suddenly identifies Tuon, the tiny Seanchan princess (later the Empress Fortuona Athaem Devi Paendrag), as the Daughter of the Nine Moons, Mat's reaction illustrates the way in which one must accede to fate: "'She is my wife,' he said softly" (9.588; ch. 31). The Seanchan, of course, are an enemy to all nations: they use leashed women who can channel to try to retake territory lost in an ancient war to Artur Hawkwing, which is why their arrival is called The Return. The Daughter of the Nine Moons, therefore, is the last person whom Mat would want to wed;

but he stoically accepts his fate, knowing that to do otherwise would be to court disaster.

> Try to run away, and the Pattern pulled you back, often roughly; run in the direction the Wheel wove you, and sometimes you could manage a little control over your life. Sometimes. With luck, maybe more than any expected, at least in the long haul.
>
> (5.726; ch. 45)

He and Tuon have free will in the small things—how to treat each other, which way to turn at a fork in the road—but their togetherness has been fated. It will be and must be. Consequently, as the narrator says from Mat's point of view, "When fate gripped you by the throat, there was nothing to do but grin" (10.631; ch. 29).

Coincidence. The heavy influence of fate—of the Wheel and the Pattern—alters the Jungian concept of synchronicity. The coincidence of inner image and outer event appears to be a causal rather than acausal phenomenon. Nynaeve puts it most succinctly: "'Coincidences *do* happen. The Wheel weaves as the Wheel wills, as you may have heard'" (5.641; ch. 40). The causal nature of coincidences is also on Verin's mind when she informs Rand that "'the Wheel of Time weaves us all into the Pattern as it wills . . . but sometimes it provides what we need before we know we need it'" (2.454; ch. 31). Similarly, when Perrin has a chance encounter with Raen, the leader of a band of Tinkers, whom he met on a previous occasion, the narrator states, "Coincidences made him uneasy; when the Pattern produced coincidence, the Wheel seemed to be forcing events" (4.674; ch. 41). Perrin is also the recipient of one of the series' more endearing coincidences. When Min tells him that she sees a falcon in his aura, he knows that a falcon will be important at some future moment. Auras, like a preview of coming attractions, provide glimpses of what the Pattern has in store for people; and she can read people with dazzling accuracy because she is foretelling fate. In *The Dragon Reborn*, when Perrin meets Zarine Bashere who says that she will call herself Faile (falcon), the narrator states, "He stiffened and almost missed the first step of the ladder. *Coincidence.* He made himself go down without looking back toward her. *It has to be. . . . Min, why did you have to go seeing things?*" (3.406; ch. 35; emphasis in the original). Perrin has just met his future wife. As these examples illustrate, though there are coincidences aplenty in *The Wheel of Time*, they are synchronous in the Jungian sense only because they are meaningful and full of affect; but they arise causally because the Wheel weaves the Pattern from human lives. Fate acts upon persons, and coincidences are predetermined; they are not the universe's sly wink but rather its expected fulfillment of a sometimes-foretold necessity.

Free will. The series' pervasive determinism, however, should not obscure the fact that free will is still a necessary and relevant force in Jordan's secondary world. The best example is Rand's interaction with Ba'alzamon before learning from Asmodean (another Forsaken) how to shield his dreams. The Dark One appears in Rand's dreams and tempts him by offering all the power in the world, so long as he will pledge fealty. Such a pledge, if coerced, would be meaningless, as Rand well knows: "'If you could just take me, why haven't you? Because you cannot. I walk in the Light, and you cannot touch me!'" (2.242; ch. 15). Although there is a complicated procedure known to be capable of forcing a person to become a Darkfriend, there is no example of it in the series thus far. Darkfriends, though, have gone over to the Shadow of their own free will. Thus the Chosen, or Forsaken, serve the Dark One not only because they have *been* chosen but also because they *have* chosen. Walking in the Light is humans' default setting, as a familiar expression implies: being "clad in the Light" is a euphemism for nakedness. It makes sense that no one is born a Darkfriend because the Creator, who *is* Light, is connected to humans by the series of removes that we have been charting: the True Source, the One Power, the Wheel of Time, the Pattern, the Age Lace, and the physical world into which one is born.[36] Loial rightly notes that all things on the physical plane are connected, but it is equally true that all physical things link to the nonphysical removes that lead back to the Creator, who makes all that is, out of himself. Those who go over to the Dark One do so by free will, and that shift from Creator to Dark One abrogates humans' basic link to all that is good. Although there is no organized religion in *The Wheel of Time*, a connection to the Creator is inherent in everyone. Only an act of free will can undo it.

Cosmological implications

Unity. The cosmology just surveyed is heavy with implications for a reading of Jordan's series. The most significant concept is unity: everything is connected because it proceeds from the Creator. A few examples bear witness to the implications. In *New Spring*, the narrator notes that "*Your* carneira [first lover] *wears part of your soul as a ribbon in her hair forever*" (217). A man and a woman are united, to begin with, simply because of the way the universe emerges from the same source; but sexual relations bond them even more intimately. Similarly, the Warder bond amplifies the connection between two persons, usually an Aes Sedai and her male protector, much as "linking" is a way to use the One Power to pool the might of two or more channelers.[37] Dreams also provide a link between persons; and in the spirit of amplification, a channeler's dreams can actually affect others' dreams (*New Spring* 96). Perhaps the best example of unity-in-dreams is the "wolf dream," the wolves' version of the World of Dreams, in which Perrin reaches out to communicate with his vulpine brethren. As well, the unity of diverse peoples is not only a major theme of *The Wheel of Time* but also Rand's specific goal in trying to unite the nations into one force to face the Dark One at the Last Battle. His efforts are the opposite of the Way of the Leaf, the unrealistic pacifism practiced by the Tuatha'an, the Travelling People. If all things are a unity, then to make war against the Other is to fight oneself and to violate the basic nature of reality. Unfortunately, the Way of the Leaf disregards the shadow within all persons as well as the Shadow whose minions stalk the land. But even the Tuatha'an, the most peaceful people, are one with the Aiel, the most martial people. As the column *ter'angreal* in Rhuidean reveals to Rand and to leaders among the Aiel, they too followed the Way of the Leaf in ancient times. Unity is the truth of the human condition, separation an ego-driven illusion.

Time's circularity. Another set of implications centers on the effect of time's circularity on the development of technology. Jordan states, "If you want to imagine what the period is, imagine it as the late 17th century without gunpowder."[38] First, the point about gunpowder is not strictly true because the Illuminators (fireworks experts) use an explosive powder to fuel their devices. Mat realizes at more than one point that it has untapped potential to fire projectiles in battle (9.332–33, ch. 15; and 11.213–15, 453, and 709, ch. 8, 21, and 34). Jordan's societies do seem to have gunpowder but do not use it in war until late in the series. In book 13, Mat convinces Elayne (now Queen of Andor) to have her bell founders forge "dragons" (cannons), which will presumably play a role in the Last Battle. As befits the seventeenth century, however, science has not advanced enough to enable comprehension of the fossilized remains of an ancient fish's skull (3.533; ch. 46) and bones of dinosaur-like creatures that no living person has ever seen (4.209; ch. 11). Similarly, Rand himself, unaware that the atmosphere becomes thinner the higher one climbs up a mountain, attributes others' shortness of breath to fear (5.370; ch. 20).[39] And besides, characters use privies, chamber pots, and midden heaps. These and many other details illustrate Jordan's sense of late seventeenth-century technology. A clock, a catapult, spy glasses called "looking glasses," and matches called "firesticks" are the extent of human technology as the series opens. Inventors at Rand's schools, however, are developing a plow on wheels, a hay harvester, harrowers, reapers, viaducts, drains and sewers, ways to pave roads, balloons, wing warping, hang gliders, telescopes, steam locomotives, applications for methane gas, electricity, and batteries (6.411–12 and 880, ch. 18 and 50; and 9.78–79, prologue).[40] His scholars are rediscovering the technology that leads to trains, planes, and automobiles—all of which existed in the past and will reemerge in the future. In other words, like time itself, technological development is circular, as Rand's Rhuidean visions reveal. There he witnesses "jo-cars and jumpers, hoverflies and huge sho-wings," and a bit later "armored jo-cars" along with a hoverfly, "a deadly black metal wasp containing two men." A few pages further still, he sees "a great white sho-wing [that] darted across the sky, carrying citizens to Comelle or Tzora or somewhere" (4.430–31 and 435; ch. 26). Elsewhere, he recalls having seen "great cities of impossibly tall buildings shining in the sun, with shapes like beetles and flattened water-drops speeding along the streets" (6.427; ch. 19).[41] Rand's visions are of a technological society similar to our own, complete with mega-cities, sky scrapers, automobiles, airliners, attack helicopters, tanks, and fighter planes.[42] The visions portray an Age whose engineering vastly exceeds that of the Third Age, whose inventors are quickly moving toward such sophistication. Because time is circular, so are human inventions, with the apparent exception of creatures brought into existence by genetic engineering. Although biological technology has been lost, beings created through its use such as Draghkar, Gholam, Myrddraal, and Trollocs continue to inhabit the land and to threaten humans.[43]

Knowledge of the One Power also appears to be cyclical, for much lore from the Age of Legends is rediscovered in the course of the series. But the Forsaken possess superior knowledge that has been lost to the Aes Sedai. For example, Asmodean teaches Rand how to bend light (Illusion or the Mirror of Mists) in order to disguise or hide himself. Semirhage is aware that the brain contains pain and pleasure centers when she uses Spirit and Fire to stimulate a woman's pain centers (6.184; ch. 6), much as a neurosurgeon might do with an electrode. And Graendal notes the possibility, as in cosmetic surgery, of "removing the burned furrow that slanted across his face [that of Sammael, another Forsaken]" (6.181; ch. 6), a remarkable claim given the commonly held maxim that one cannot Heal what has already been Healed. In addition, the Forsaken have devices that approximate the beginnings of electronic navigation and communication. A callbox (*nar'baha*) creates a wayline that enables the Forsaken to find its activator, and rechargeable traveling boxes allow those who cannot channel to create a gateway. Ancients also knew how to make Heartstone (*cuendillar*), a material so hard that it actually absorbs energy from any kind of attack. Seals made of this material hold the Dark One in his tomb at Shayol Ghul. Knowledge of how to make Heartstone was lost to the Aes Sedai, but Moghedien provides enough clues that Egwene manages to rediscover the weave for making it (10.427–28; ch. 17). Egwene also rediscovers Traveling and Compulsion. Since the latter is forbidden, she learns the weave only to figure out how to counteract it (10.671; ch. 30).

Space-time relativity. Jordan's statement about a late seventeenth-century setting is somewhat ironic because the One Power allows miraculous amplifications like bending light with the mind, instantaneous Healing of wounds that would otherwise be fatal, and taking advantage of space-time relativity. Regarding the latter, since humans participate in the energy of the Creator, a part of them exists outside of space-time; therefore, by combining the human mind and the One Power, it is possible, as Ostrowski mentions, to transcend the restrictions of the everyday world. By means of Skimming, Traveling through gateways, using portal stones, and journeying through the Ways, it is possible to relativize or eliminate space.[44] Various other details display the relativity of time. First, Ostrowski's idea about longevity relates to "the slowing," which is the way that female channelers' aging process slows down between the ages of twenty and twenty-five (7.488 and 521; ch. 22 and 24). Jordan is fond of mentioning the result of this process, the Aes Sedai's "ageless faces." Second, the World of Dreams enables travel in the astral body over vast distances at the speed of thought (Ostrowski's notion of consciousness apart from the body); but the amount of time spent there might be greater or less than what transpires in the waking world.[45] In fact, "one hour might pass in the waking world while you spent five or ten in the World of Dreams, but it could just as easily be the other way around" (9.497; ch. 26). It is also possible to enter *Tel'aran'rhiod* bodily, which enables fast passage to distant locations, as Egwene does when she travels to Salidar to join the rebel Aes Sedai.

Other dimensions. The Wheel of Time amplifies and illustrates the notion that there may be other dimensions by having characters actually travel there by various means. This is essentially the "many-worlds theory" of quantum physics. Portal stones can take one to alternate or potential worlds, as Rand discovers when Lanfear, one of the female Forsaken, channels him and his companions into an alternate dimension while they sleep. The stones bear the following inscription: "'From Stone to Stone run the lines of 'if,' between the worlds that might be" (2.217; ch. 13). According to Selene (Lanfear), as stated by Loial, "'The Pattern has infinite variation . . . and every variation that can be, will be'" (2.258; ch. 16). Apparently, there is an alternate world for every possible permutation of history. By traveling via portal stone, one can visit the world as it would be if major events had played out differently, much like our being able to see American society following an Axis victory in World War II. Everything that can happen does happen; therefore, Rand finds some alternate realities to be very similar to his own, while others differ significantly. When characters experience a world that is secondary to their own, their world takes on greater verisimilitude in relation to our own. The secondary world of Jordan's imagination becomes primary in relation to the multiplicity of alternate worlds, especially in light of Verin's ultimate amplification. As she mentions,

> "Some in the Age of Legends apparently believe[d] that there were still other worlds—even harder to reach than the worlds of the Portal Stones. . . . Perhaps the Wheel of Time weaves a still greater Pattern from worlds."
>
> (3.238–39; ch. 21)

Besides portal stones, *ter'angreal* make it possible to enter alternate worlds such as the realms of the Aelfinn and the Eelfinn, and those encountered by women who test for Accepted at the White Tower. As Sheriam Sedai states, "'The ancients said there were many worlds. Perhaps this *ter'angreal* takes you to them'" (2.342–43; ch. 23). Nynaeve, for example, encounters a world that matches her heart's desire. There, she finds that she is married to Lan Mandragoran and that they have a child. It takes all of her will to return, and that is the point: one must want to be Aes Sedai more than anything else in the world.[46]

The World of Dreams is where these alternate worlds come together. According to the narrator, *Tel'aran'rhiod* is

> a reflection of the real world. Perhaps of all worlds; some Aes Sedai claimed that there were many worlds, as if all variations of the Pattern had to exist, and that all those worlds together made up a still larger Pattern.
>
> (6.194; ch. 7)

Earlier, Verin accentuates the idea that the World of Dreams is a connector:

> "The point is that there is a third constant besides the Creator and the Dark One. There is a world that lies *within* each of these others, inside all of them at the same time. Or perhaps surrounding them. Writers in the Age of Legends called it *Tel'aran'rhiod*, "the Unseen World." Perhaps "the World of Dreams" is a better translation."
>
> (3.240; ch. 21)

Moreover, as Egwene discovers, just as the World of Dreams enables access to all places on the planet, there is an intermediate dimension—"the space separating the waking world from the World of Dreams"; it looks like "an ocean of stars" (7.229; ch.10)—that enables access to the dream of any person in any world. It is described as "the infinite space between reality and dreams" (10.486; ch. 20). By placing such great emphasis on alternate worlds ranging from those accessed through *ter'angreal*, the World of Dreams, and some kind of matrix of dreams, *The Wheel of Time* suggests that reality is not what it seems. If "'reality is illusion'" (*New Spring* 123), then life is a dream, and death is an awakening. According to Amys, one of the Aiel Wise Ones, "'Life is a dream from which we all must wake before we can dream again'" (5.142; ch. 5).

Psychic functioning. Like access to alternate dimensions, the series' treatment of psi is an implication of the unity of all things through the Creator (or analogously the One Mind). *The Wheel of Time*, in fact, includes a range of psi that would boggle the most adept yogi in India, much of it possible without access to the One Power.[47] The amplification lies partly in the preponderance of psychic feats throughout the series. Let us consider four examples. First, it is likely that Jordan draws heavily on Eastern practice of meditation for at least one of the psychic states that characters achieve: *ko'di*, the Oneness, or the Void (*New Spring* 18 and 216). Lan describes it to Rand this way: "'Blank your mind, sheepherder'" (1.177; ch. 13). By surrendering all distractions through intense focus on an image such as a flame or a flower bud, one achieves a calm state of expanded awareness and passive receptivity. The ability to enter the Void improves with practice, and it is this altered state that serves as a foundation for various psychic feats such as channeling and the trick of distancing oneself from heat or coldness.

With practice, one can enter the Void at will; but Foretelling, a second type of psychic functioning, is unpredictable, potentially dangerous, difficult to interpret, and sometimes ironic. The foremost example is Gitara Moroso's Foretelling of the Dragon's rebirth, which strikes without warning and proves such a shock that it kills her (*New Spring* 28–29 and 125). Elaida Sedai, the false Amyrlin, Foretells that the White Tower will be reunited and that Rand will "'face the Amyrlin Seat and know her anger'" (7.18; prologue). Naturally, Elaida assumes that she is that Amyrlin, but by the end of *The Gathering Storm* (book 12) she is abducted by the Seanchan. Apparently, it is possible to draw a false conclusion about a true Foretelling. The Tower is reunited under Egwene as Amyrlin, and presumably it is her anger that Rand will encounter in book 14. Finally, there is a close connection between Foretelling and precognitive Dreaming. As the narrator observes, "Dreaming was closely linked to Foretelling; the future, and events in other places, could appear in a Dreamer's dreams" (3.307; ch. 26). Egwene sees, for example, Perrin's involvement with two women: "Perrin with a falcon on his shoulder [Faile], and Perrin with a hawk [Berelain]," as well as Mat's hanging in Rhuidean and his connection to the Seanchan (3.290–91; ch. 25). In a later dream, she also sees the Seanchan's attack on the White Tower that leads to Elaida's abduction (10.494–95; ch. 20). Yet there is a significant difference between dreams and Foretellings: "Dreams were not Foretellings—they didn't show what *would* happen, but what *could*" (12.75; ch. 3).

Like Foretelling, the third example of psi sans the One Power is also a kind of precognition that illustrates the relativity of time and the mind's ability to transcend the present moment. Unlike Foretelling, however, it is always on and is not dangerous. Alone among all the characters in the series, Min is able to see images and auras around others, especially those who can channel the One Power and particularly Birgitte, a nonchanneler, whose multiple past lives may account for the intensity of Min's viewings (9.297; ch. 12). An Aiel Wise One named Melaine describes Min's talent as being "'like interpreting the dream without dreaming'" (6.751; ch. 41). The images may represent pieces of the Pattern (1.215; ch. 15); and when she knows what an image means, her prediction always comes true. Naturally, a woman with Min's ability is a great help to Rand as he makes his way toward the Last Battle; but her readings include personal matters as well. For example, she foresees that Rand will be intimately involved with three women, including herself; that he will encounter a dangerous and impossibly beautiful woman (Lanfear); that he will lose a hand; that his personality will merge with that of Lews Therin, the madman in his head; and that he will "fail without a woman who was dead and gone" (Moiraine) (7.696; ch. 35).[48] Sometimes Min sees contrasting outcomes, as she does for Egwene and her sweetheart Gawyn Trakand, Elayne's brother: "Gawyn kneeling at Egwene's feet with his head bowed, and Gawyn breaking Egwene's neck, first one then the other, as if either could be the future" (4.786–87; ch. 47).

Fourth, if dreaming of future events is an intrapsychic phenomenon, its extrapsychic cousin is dreaming oneself into *Tel'aran'rhiod*, a realm that has existed as long as the Wheel of Time, which makes it a logical place for Birgitte to wait between her many incarnations. Accessible without the One Power, especially to a person who has the right kind of *ter'angreal*, the World of Dreams—a realm of pure spirit and thus a secondary world within a secondary world—is akin to the astral plane that Monroe explores. Of course, the laws of nature differ from those in his encounters and from those in the main world that Jordan creates. For one thing, places, objects, and wild creatures have a reflection in the World of Dreams with one exception, Ogier *stedding* (a Dreamer cannot enter a *stedding*) (4.387; ch. 23). Strangely, living persons cannot be seen while one is out-of-body in *Tel'aran'rhiod* except when their normal dreams briefly touch it, in which case they are vulnerable to such dangers as a nightmare that has taken on a life of its own: thoughts on the astral plane can be parlous, as Monroe would agree. For example, since what happens to a person's astral body in the World of Dreams also happens to the physical body, it is easy enough to assassinate persons as they sleep.[49] The narrator comments on the key paradox:

> In the Unseen World, what happened was real, in a strange way. Nothing that happened there affected what was—a door opened in the World of Dreams would still be shut in the real world; a tree cut down there still stood there—yet a woman could be killed there, or stilled.
>
> (4.204; ch. 11)

Nynaeve uses this link between a person's astral and physical bodies to capture Moghedien. In the World of Dreams, Nynaeve forces the Forsaken to drink a sleeping potion, which keeps her physical body asleep long enough for Nynaeve to find her and capture her with an *a'dam* (a Seanchan leash). The World of Dreams can also be dangerous if one enters it physically through a gateway. The Aeil dreamwalkers believe that doing so is evil and that it exacts a toll on one's humanity (6.634; ch. 32). Nevertheless, Rand seems none the worse for wear as a result of going there bodily to hunt Ba'alzamon and later Rahvin (3.653, ch. 55; and 5.935, ch. 55).

Other than the extreme dangers, Jordan's World of Dreams has a great deal in common with contemporary lore on the out-of-body experience (OBE). It is possible to be in a trance, experience the Unseen World, yet ride a horse in the real world or use one's voice to report one's discoveries (6.632; ch. 32). It is possible to enter *Tel'aran'rhiod* by becoming lucid in a dream (5.420; 24). Other similarities are that sleep during one's visit to the World of Dreams is not as restful as normal sleep and that false awakenings are possible (4.572; ch. 35). Even though no one doubts the reality of this higher realm, it is still important to seek validation in shared experience, much as with astral exploration in our own universe, as Nynaeve and Elayne discover when "it quickly became clear that Egwene had said the same things in both their dreams, and that left little room for doubt" (5.756; ch. 47). If two persons share an OBE and both report the same things, then it takes on verisimilitude and must not be a figment of the imagination. But care must be taken not to enter the Dream too fully or for too great a time. As Moiraine states, "'A Dreamer sends only a part of herself'" (3.626; ch. 53). Or as Amys counsels, "'When a Dreamwalker enters the World of Dreams in her sleep, only a tiny bit of her remains with her body, just enough to keep her body alive'" (5.817; ch. 49). If a person enters the Dream too fully or stays out-of-body too long, she will die (4.389; ch. 23). That is the truth of OBE in our world as well.

The One Power, not the Holy Spirit

As the previous section illustrates, *The Wheel of Time* depicts, in amplified form, an array of psychic functioning that human beings are capable of in the real world.

The amplification increases many-fold when the One Power is applied. To begin with, not every person is capable of channeling it; persons who can channel fall into two categories. Those who are born with the "spark" will begin channeling whether they want to or not. If they do not learn how to handle the Power, it will drive them insane and eventually kill them. Others will never channel unless they make an effort to learn. The relationship between *damane* and *sul'dam* is the best illustration of the difference between the two categories. Among the Seanchan, *damane* ("leashed ones") are born with the spark, whereas *sul'dam* (their handlers) have the capacity to learn to channel, though Seanchan culture does not recognize this potential. Among the series' main characters, Rand, Nynaeve, and Egwene are all born with the spark; fortunately, all of them successfully learn to handle the Power, though Nynaeve has a difficult block to overcome along the way.

As previously noted, the One Power has two halves: the female part, *saidar*; and the male part, *saidin*. The ancient symbol of the Aes Sedai—similar to the yin/yang symbol but without the inset circles—represents the fact that the two halves of the Power push against and balance each other. As Attrill writes,

> The ancient symbol of the Aes Sedai in the Age of Legends was a circle, half white and half black, with the colours separated by a sinuous line, representing the equal and opposing balance of *saidin/saidar* that make [*sic*] up the two halves of the True Source.[50]

The white is for women, the black for men, hence the White Tower and the Black Tower. In the words of Mazrim Taim, whom Rand recruits to train male channelers, the purpose of "'the Black Tower [is] to balance the White Tower'" (6.760; ch. 42). The Asha'man ("guardians" in the Old tongue), the male channelers who train at the Black Tower, wear the ancient Aes Sedai symbol on their cloaks, perhaps foreshadowing of the gender balance that their presence is helping to bring about (8.406–7; ch. 21). For example, the rebel Aes Sedai begin moving toward an alliance with the Asha'man in book 10.

However, the absence of inset circles corresponding to anima and animus—the feminine in men, the masculine in women—implies that individuation is the series' grand theme and that cosmic forces amplify the process. In fact, Jordan's description of the two halves bears the stamp of essentialism that must be worked out if true balance is to be achieved. *Saidar* and *saidin* are so different that Siuan likens the futility of a woman's attempt to teach a man to channel to a bird's attempt to teach a fish to fly (*New Spring* 97). On the one hand, women must surrender to *saidar*, and *not* surrendering fully is why Nynaeve cannot channel except when she is angry. In nearly drowning, "she surrendered completely" and finally overcomes her block (7.626; ch. 31). Channeling *saidar* is likened to an embrace (5.91; ch. 2) and to "being one with the Light, a glorious ecstasy" (3.140; ch. 10). On the other hand, men do not surrender to an embrace when they channel *saidin*; instead they must fight for survival in "a war without mercy" (5.91, ch. 2; and 6.112, ch. 3). "Always, *saidin* had to be conquered, forced . . . but let it slip anytime, anywhere, [and it] could kill you" (8.481; ch. 24). "It was like riding a bull driven mad by redwort, or swimming naked in a river of fire churned to rapids by jagged boulders of ice" (5.710; ch. 44). In other words, the two halves of the One Power match traditional gender expectations: *saidar*, passivity, surrender, femininity; *saidin*, activity, battle, masculinity. As the narrator notes, "There was no forgiveness or pity in the male half of the Power" (9.629; ch. 35). "Alongside the turmoil of *saidin, saidar* was a tranquil river flowing smoothly" (9.636; ch. 35). The contrast even extends to the different means by which men and women achieve Traveling. Women must see two places as an identity; men bend the Pattern and bore a hole from one end to the other. Several other differences between men's and women's abilities strengthen the gendered nature of the two halves of the One Power. Men are stronger in Earth and Fire, while women excel with Air and Water; men and women are said to be equal in their ability to channel Spirit (4.153; ch. 7). Women develop their ability slowly, but men leap from one degree to another. And although some women are stronger in the Power than men, it is generally the case that men are stronger channelers than women, much as men's bodies are usually stronger than women's.

Channeling is more dangerous for men partly because of the Dark One's taint on *saidin*.[51] At Shayol Ghul, ancient Aes Sedai had sought a new source of Power not subject to male/female divisions. Using *saidar* and *saidin*, they bored a hole where the Pattern was thinnest in an illustration of what Attrill calls "human lust for selfish power."[52] Their poorly informed effort to transcend the two halves' mutual exclusivity is the cosmic equivalent of skipping over individuation. Their goal is not the unity of the two halves of the One Power but some other source that men and women can both use. They do not realize that they are attempting to tap what Jordan calls the True Power, the Dark One's version of the One Power, which is much like the dark half of the Force in *Star Wars*. Their strategy is worse than trying, as Goodman Brown does, to do anima work before shadow work—the "master-piece" before the "apprentice-piece" in Jung's terms (*CW* 9i, 61/29). In their attempt to achieve a unified power, they enable Shadow to influence the world. The Dark One does not escape through the Bore, but his touch throws society into chaos. Wielding *saidin*, Lews Therin and his one hundred *male* companions then use *cuendillar* disks that bear the Aes Sedai symbol to reseal the Bore and to trap inside it the thirteen Forsaken, who conveniently happen to be meeting there. The omission of female channelers—the use of "*brute force*"—is evidently what enables the backblast from the sealing to taint *saidin* (12.347, ch. 22; and 731, ch. 47).[53] In Rand's experience, "the flow from *saidin* [is now] sweeter than honey, ranker than rotted meat" (3.419; ch. 36). The taint drives Lews Therin and his men immediately insane and causes the eventual insanity of all other male Aes Sedai. As a result, they commit an atrocity called the Breaking of the World. For thousands of years, the Red Ajah of the Aes Sedai has sought out and "gentled" men who can channel, lest madness drive them to wreak similar havoc. The Reds thus enact, in a form amplified by the One Power, an imbalance between the sexes. Meanwhile, the black half of the ancient symbol of the Aes Sedai has been perverted like the swastika. It is now called the Dragon's Fang and is scrawled on the front doors of suspected Darkfriends, though Min views a time when the Dragon's fang has become "'a sign of victory and hope'" (13.403; ch. 25).[54]

Rand's first experience with *saidin*, however, is very positive because he taps into an ancient reservoir called the Eye of the World, created for an hour of dire need. The difference between tainted *saidin* and what is contained in the Eye is like the difference between the air emitted from a smoke stack and a tank of liquid oxygen. The Power stored there is so great that the Dark One hopes to use it to break free from his prison—to "'blind the Eye of the World, and slay the Great Serpent, kill time itself'" (1.640; ch. 42); for as Moiraine states, "'There is enough power in the Eye of the World to undo his prison'" (1.649; ch. 43). Fortunately, Rand gets there first and uses the *saidin* stored in the Eye to turn the tide of a distant battle, to kill Aginor and Balthamel (two of the male Forsaken), and to wound Ba'alzamon.

Besides storing pure *saidin*, the Eye participates in a pattern of imagery in book 1. Ravens lend their eyes to the Dark One so that he can spy on the forces of the Light; when Perrin becomes a Wolfbrother, his eyes turn yellow; his fellow Wolfbrother, Elyas Machera, identifies Hawkwing's "eye" (the remnant of a monument) in a chapter called "Eyes Without Pity" (ch. 29); Mat dreams that Ba'alzamon took his eyes (1.494; ch. 33); and "Ba'alzamon's eyes roared like two furnaces" (1.760; ch. 51). These eye images relate in various ways to one's conscious identity, and the Eye of the World is no exception. As Jung observes. "The eye may well stand for consciousness (which is in fact an organ of perception), looking into its own background" (*CW* 9i, 593/337). In that spirit, channeling the Power stored in the Eye of the World touches off Rand's self-discovery as the Dragon Reborn. Here at the climax of book 1, he is intuitively aware of the uses of *saidin*; however, only later does he begin to hear Lews Therin's voice in his head and to remember things from the madman's lifetime, including multiple ways to use the Power (4.153; ch. 7).

The One Power furthers the individuation not only of Rand but also of his friend Mat, though under vastly different circumstances and with different effects. Mat's anamnesis then takes a dramatic turn as a result of his experience in Rhuidean. Book 1 foreshadows Mat's expanded awareness when he says, "'It's as if some dead man was speaking with my mouth'" (1.278; ch. 19). But he must experience a great ill before *saidar* begins to open him to the truth about many past lives. The dagger that Mat surreptitiously picks up in Shadar Logoth poisons his psyche with evil and nearly kills him. Moiraine's Healing does not cure this condition, but later a group of Aes Sedai Heal him with a massive dose of *saidar* in Tar Valon. This treatment's immediate and long-term consequence is that his luck skyrockets. More importantly, Mat becomes a kind of lightning shaman (Native Americans' term for those whose psi has been amplified by a lightning strike): the Healing begins to open his conscious awareness to memories from thousands of past lives. Even while he is being Healed, he utters the ancient war cry of Manetheren and rebukes the Aes Sedai in the Old Tongue, which he has never studied (3.211; ch. 18). Siuan comments, "'I believe the past and the present were one. He was there, and he was here, and he knew who we were'" (3.213; ch. 18). It is the Aes Sedai's application of the One Power (a force beyond time) that reveals this unity of time and enables Mat's past lives to emerge into consciousness. Past and present are simultaneous. Ancient man lives in modern man.

In Jordan's universe reincarnation is such a given that it is even part of a formulaic prayer: "'May the Light illumine Tamra's soul, brightly as she deserved, and may she shelter in the Creator's hand until her rebirth'" (*New Spring* 196). As the narrator puts it in the spirit of amplification, "everybody was someone reborn, a hundred someones, a thousand, more. That was how the Pattern worked; everyone died and was reborn, again and again as the Wheel turned, forever without end" (7.167; ch. 7). According to Moiraine, "'Men wear many names, many faces. Different faces, but always the same man'" (1.29; ch. 2). Or as Thom emphasizes, "'The dead can be reborn, or take a living body, and it is not something to speak of lightly'" (1.278; ch. 19).[55]

In Mat's case, despite hints of anamnesis early on, a force even greater than *saidar* is required to unlock past-life memories—his own death in Rhuidean. Mat himself believes that the Aelfinn have used other men's memories to fill up the holes in his own left by the tainted dagger, but it is more likely that the Aelfinn hang him so that he can remember his own past lives. Revived by Rand, Mat can consciously speak and read the Old Tongue; and because many of his previous lives centered on martial activity, he intuitively knows how to maneuver men on a battlefield to maximum advantage, becoming one of Rand's most trusted commanders. Mat's psychological situation is described as follows:

> In one part of his mind he knew he had been born in the Two Rivers twenty years before, but he could remember clearly leading the flanking attack that turned the Trollocs at Maighande, and dancing in the court of Tarmandewin, and a hundred other things, a thousand. Mostly battles. He remembered dying more times than he wanted to think of. No seams between lives anymore; he could not tell his memories from the others unless he concentrated.
>
> (5.112–13; ch. 3)

Mat thus experiences something similar to the effect of Lews Therin in Rand's head but not the melding that they eventually achieve. His own words sum up the situation in which he sometimes finds himself: "'I am lost in my own mind'" (4.607; ch. 37).

For all the One Power's marvelous characteristics, the taint on *saidin* becomes so serious for Rand that he may not make it to the Last Battle unless he takes drastic measures. His scholar-friend Harid Fel advises him, not very helpfully, that the cleansing will require "'sound principles, in both high philosophy and natural philosophy'" (8.306; ch. 14). The narrator considers Fel's answer to be a riddle; and when Rand does cleanse the source, there is no indication that he has followed his mentor's advice. Could it be, however, that the difference between natural and high philosophy is akin to the difference between classical and quantum physics? Could it also be that Rand stumbles upon a key to the riddle by accident? The latter possibility relates to two wounds that he sustains—one from Ba'alzamon's sword, the other from Padan Fain's dagger (the one that previously infected Mat).[56] The first is a Christ-like wound in the side that never completely heals; the second would have killed him if not for the Healing offered by Samitsu Sedai and Damer Flinn.[57] The two wounds overlap: "The cut from Fain's dagger . . . ran right across the old round scar" (7.725; ch. 36). Samitsu saves Rand's life, but Flinn's Healing is more effective. He first notices that two kinds of darkness have infected Rand, and then effects Healing as follows:

> "I sort of sealed them away from him, for a time, anyhow. It won't last. They're fighting each other, now. Maybe they'll kill off each other, while he heals himself the rest of the way. . . . On the other hand, I can't say that they won't kill him. But I think he has a better chance than he did."
> (7.737; ch. 36)

Just before Rand and Nynaeve begin their attempt to cleanse the source, the narrator notes that "the slash given by Padan Fain's dagger . . . did not beat together with the pulsing of the larger wound it cut across, but rather against it, alternating" (9.633; ch. 35). In a similar way, the cleansing of *saidin* involves pitting one evil against the other—the Dark One's taint and the evil that infects Shadar Logoth. The setting is particularly appropriate because, as Vandene Sedai tells Moiraine in an earlier book, "'The hate that killed Shadar Logoth was hate they thought to use *against* the Dark One'" (2.328–29; ch. 22).

As in ancient times, male and female channelers—Rand and Nynaeve, linked—work together, using the Choedan Kal, two access keys to the most powerful *sa'angreal* ever constructed, devices so powerful that Lanfear believes that they could be used to challenge the Creator. The conduit that Rand creates—made of *saidar* and joining *saidin* and Shadar Logoth—is the beginning of Fel's "high philosophy," the quantum, for the conduit "covered distance beyond his imagining, and had no length at all" (9.637; ch. 35). But it is natural philosophy, the classical physics governing natural law, that comes into play next. Since *saidar* and *saidin* cannot mix, the *saidin* that is run through the conduit "squeezed in on itself, away from the surrounding *saidar*; and the *saidar* pushed it from all sides, compressing it further, making it flow faster" (9.637; ch. 35). Then *saidin* touches Shadar Logoth, slowly creating a black dome of taint that eventually towers two miles above the city. The narrator notes that "the dome boiled with stygian fire" (9.654; ch. 35), which recalls the "'lake of fire and molten rock'" at Shayol Ghul "'that holds the Great Lord of the Dark in its endless depths'" (5.368; ch. 19), a detail surely borrowed from book 1 of *Paradise Lost*.[58] When "the dome collapsed in on itself in the space of a heartbeat, to a pinpoint, to nothing" (9.654; ch. 35), Shadar

Logoth is no more; in its place is a hole "'approximately three miles across and perhaps a mile and a half deep'" (10.467; ch. 19). Rand has solved Fel's riddle: the One Power is used to skim the taint from *saidin* (natural philosophy, classical physics), and then the two opposing evils cancel each other out (high philosophy, quantum physics). The latter process mimics at the macro level the paradoxical phenomenon of "pair annihilation" at the subatomic level: both becomes neither. More importantly, men and women now have the chance to achieve balance because they are now on equal footing; and the act of cleansing is itself a fitting example of how the two sexes may once again do great things when they work in harmony. Besides calling on more of the One Power than anyone has in the history of the world, Rand and Nynaeve serve as an image of psychic integration that will set a new tone for generations to come. As the Green Man states, "'the greatest Aes Sedai works were always done so, joining *saidin* and *saidar*, as the True Source is joined'" (1.744, ch. 50; cf. 2.360, ch. 24). The Age of such wonders has returned.

The Dragon Reborn, not the Light made flesh

Although Rand occupies the place of the Son in Jordan's quaternity, he is fully and exclusively human and no more divine than any other character. However, Attrill's statement that "Rand is largely a secularised Christ figure" needs further exploration, starting with the story of his birth and early years.[59] Rand's biological mother is Tigraine, the Daughter Hier of Andor, who goes to study at the White Tower where Gitara Moroso tells her that if she does not become an Aiel Maiden of the Spear, disaster will engulf the world (6.384–86; ch. 16). She goes into the Aiel Waste where she becomes a Maiden and gets pregnant by Rand's biological father, an Aiel clan chief named Janduin. Following her journey into the Waste, Laman Damodred cuts down *Avendoraldera*, a great tree that began as a cutting of the Tree of Life and a gift from the Aiel.[60] Their retaliation, known as the Aiel War, brings Tigraine (renamed Shaiel) to the environs of Tar Valon. As *New Spring* opens, after Gitara Sedai foresees Rand's birth on Dragonmount, the peak that rises from Lews Therin's final act of destruction in his madness and despair, the Amyrlin tasks Moiraine and Siuan with finding the infant boy. For a generation, they keep secret his adoption by Tam al'Thor, a young soldier who happens to be in the area. Tam takes the boy home to the Two Rivers where he and his wife, Cari, raise him as their own son—a fortunate move because the Black Ajah is "'killing any man or boy who *might* be able to channel'" (*New Spring* 330), much as Herod commits genocide in an attempt to kill the baby Jesus. Cari's premature death deepens the separation between Rand and the maternal, which may partly account for why he overcompensates later on by being with three women. He grows up on Tam's farm and becomes a sheepherder, but he is destined to become not only a shepherd of nations but also a sacrificial lamb. As the prophecies say, "His blood on the rocks of Shayol Ghul, washing away the Shadow, sacrifice for man's salvation" (4.99; ch. 3). Book 1 opens with the arrival of Moiraine and

Lan in the Two Rivers. That night, Trollocs attack. Moiraine and her Warder lead Rand, Perrin, Mat, and Egwene away from their homes; Nynaeve joins them en route. Thus begins *The Wheel of Time*.

Like the idea of blood sacrifice and the wound in his side, Rand is described in ways that call Christ to mind but point to humanity rather than divinity. Gawyn Trakand, who believes that Rand is responsible for the death of his mother, Queen Morgase of Andor, says, "'I do not care if he is the Creator made flesh'" (6.510; ch. 25).[61] Unlike Gawyn, Masema, the insane Prophet of the Lord Dragon, believes that Rand genuinely *is* the Light made flesh (8.580, ch. 30; and 9.90, ch. 1). A parody of John the Baptist, Masema surrounds himself with "disciples" (5.618; ch. 39) and casts Nynaeve as a kind of Mary-figure: "'Blessed are you among women, Nynaeve al'Maera, none more so save the blessed mother of the Lord Dragon herself, for you watched the Lord Dragon grow. You attended the Lord Dragon as a child" (5.617; ch. 39). In the mouth of a madman, however, such comments deconstruct themselves. Rand is prophesied to die at the Last Battle as a warrior and military leader—a mortal, not a god. Yet, structurally, his story bears elements of Christ's journey, particularly the temptation by Satan in the wilderness. Ba'alzamon tempts him in his dreams with infinite power if he will only pledge fealty to the Dark. Later, Rand encounters Lanfear, disguised as Selene, and resists her offers of immortality, wealth, power, and glory.[62]

If the Christ allegory does not hold up, then how are we to understand Rand's journey through *The Wheel of Time*? An answer suggests itself: the series is the story of his individuation from naïve youth to over-hard man, to his bonding with his three loves (Elayne, Aviendha, and Min), and to a melding of himself and Lews Therin. First, an excellent example of amplification occurs after Rand rejects Berelain's sexual advances in *The Shadow Rising*. A cock crows suggestively outside, and then "three duplicates of himself" step out of mirrors and attack him (4.81; ch. 2). He is experiencing a random phenomenon known as a "bubble of evil" or what the chapter title calls a "whirlpool" in the Pattern, but it is hard to ignore the possibility that his repressed sexuality springs to life and attacks him. In a bow to psychological integration, he eventually overcomes these reflections by absorbing them into himself (4.78–83; ch. 2). Around the same time, he begins his romantic relationship with Elayne, which is the beginning of his avoidance of Goodman Brown's fate. Eventually, he is intimate with all three of his women, though he sees himself as a lecher and worries that he has been too violent with Min. "Images of himself flashed in his head; him tearing at her clothes, forcing himself on her like a mindless beast." When he expresses bitterness and sorrow for his actions, she replies, "'You listen to me, you wooden-headed numbskull. . . . What we did, my innocent lamb, was comfort one another'" (7.668–69; ch. 33). By fully affirming his sexuality with an understanding partner, and through his bonding to the three women, he makes significant progress with his anima.

Cadsuane understands, however, that not all is well with Rand; and Min foresees that Cadsuane has something very important to teach him and all the

Asha'man. Rand believes that he must harden himself in preparation for the Last Battle. Min says, "I can feel him changing. If he was a stone before, he's iron now!" (9.624; ch. 34). When the narrator comments that Rand "was steel, and to his surprise, still not hard enough," it is as if he is taking on the pitilessness of *saidin* (9.629–30; ch. 35). "Where he had once been steel, he became something else. From now on, he was *cuendillar*" (12.356; ch. 22). Cadsuane strongly disapproves:

> "he can do whatever his heart desires, anything at all, as long as he lives to reach Tarmon Gai'don [the Last Battle]. And as long as I can be at his side long enough to make him learn how to laugh again, and cry. . . . He is turning into a stone . . . and if he doesn't relearn that he's human, winning the Last Battle may not be much better than losing."
>
> (9.495, ch. 25; cf. 8.279, ch. 12)

She knows, however, that he will reject any direct attempt to teach him. So what does she do? Like so many other women in the series, she attempts to bully him, as if being hard is the key to softening him and promoting anima integration. She does curb some of his rudeness, but she also supplies a target for projection of negative anima.

Ultimately, Rand's transformation to a more unified personality has very little to do with Cadsuane's ministrations. His solution is not to bend to the will of a bossy, centuries-old Aes Sedai but rather to integrate Lews Therin's past-life personality with his own consciousness. This is a slow process not without setbacks, the main problem being that "Rand hadn't been willing to see Lews Therin as part of himself" (12.351; ch. 22). Afraid of Lews Therin, Rand erroneously believes that he must keep the madman at bay. But progress toward individuation is slowly made: "In some ways, Lews Therin seemed more solidly part of him since [the cleansing of *saidin* at] Shadar Logoth" (10.549; ch. 24). Eventually, "The madman didn't sound as crazy as he once had. In fact, his voice had started to sound an awful lot like Rand's own voice" (12.752; ch. 49). Then, at the end of book 12, he hears Tam's voice in his head, asking why Rand goes to battle.

> *Why?* Rand thought with wonder. *Because each time we live, we get to love again.* That was the answer. It all swept over him, lives lived, mistakes made, love changing everything. He saw the entire world in his mind's eye, lit by the glow in his hand. He remembered lives, hundreds of them, thousands of them, stretching to infinity. He remembered love, and peace, and joy, and hope.

Then, after a massive display of Power on Dragonmount that destroys the great *sa'angreal* that he had used with Nynaeve to cleanse *saidin*, he knows "that he would never again hear Lews Therin's voice in his head. For they were not two men, and never had been." Looking up at the clearing sky, "he let out a deep-throated laugh, true and pure" (12.759–60; ch. 50). Later, he weeps (13.199; ch. 13). He finally achieves the change that Cadsuane hopes for, and it precisely opposes the despair that the Dark One fostered in ancient times when he stood next to Lews Therin ("Kinslayer") as he murdered his family (1.204–5; ch. 14). Rand achieves not the strength of stone or steel or *cuendillar* but "'the strength of the wind'" (13.202; ch. 14).

Rand himself credits those who are around him but also *in* him for his ability to survive until this all-important transformation takes place. He says to Min,

> "I feel more like myself than I ever did as Lews Therin, if *that* makes any kind of sense. It's because of Tam, because of the people around me. You, Perrin, Nynaeve, Mat, Aviendha, Elayne, Moiraine. *He* tried very hard to break me. I think if I'd been the same as I was so long ago, he would have succeeded."
>
> (13.749; ch. 51)

Inside him are the good father (Tam), the wolf (Perrin), the trickster/gambler (Mat), the single-minded crusader for the Light (Moiraine), the no-nonsense village wisdom (Nynaeve), and feminine figures who represent other values. Min is the psychic in touch with her sexuality who steers him away from self-loathing; Aviendha, the warrior-maid who helps him to learn Aiel ways; and Elayne, the future queen who teaches him about leadership. All three teach him about love. It is because of his father, his friends, and his lovers that Rand survives long enough for his psyche to be "'reforged'" into a well-balanced whole (13.82; ch. 3).

Individuation in *The Wheel of Time*

The objective of this chapter has been to show that Jordan's series amplifies psychological processes in order to awaken readers to the truth about their own potential through unity with the One Mind. In effect, the author has the same message for readers that Lanfear has for Rand: "'You half-use the smallest fraction of what you are capable of'" (4. 193; ch. 10). That, I have argued, is why fantasy literature appeals to us. In the spirit of amplification, the series also enacts the individuation process by using not only individual characters like Rand but also whole groups, even nations, particularly the Aes Sedai and the Children of the Light. Aes Sedai who are out of touch with their animus become members of the Red Ajah and spend the rest of their lives hunting and gentling men who can channel. "The Red did attract women who were naturally suspicious of men . . . not many women could belong to the Red for long without taking a jaundiced view of all men" (7.660; ch. 32). The reverse is true as well: "Hunting men who could channel led Red sisters to look askance at all men, and a fair number hated them" (11.536; ch. 25). Galina Casban, the Aes Sedai in charge of kidnapping Rand, is a prime example, as the narrator explains: "At least there were no men present, a small mercy. Men made her skin crawl, and if one could see her now, less than half clothed . . ." (7.803; ch. 40). Now that *saidin* has been cleansed, the Reds will presumably have to come to terms with men by moving toward the Green Ajah's embrace of men and the individuation implied by the Amyrlin's stole, which includes the colors of all seven Ajahs.[63] But for now, the Reds are apparently as out of touch with their animus as the men who compose the Children of the Light are with their anima.[64] In particular, the Children of the Light have a connection to the kind of sexual repression that Rand avoids. Their founder, Lothair Mantelar, condemns sexuality in his book *The Way of the Light*:

> "Therefore abjure all pleasure, for goodness is a pure abstract, a perfect crystalline idea which is obscured by base emotion. Pamper not the flesh. Flesh is weak but spirit is strong; flesh is useless where spirit is strong. Right thought is drowned in sensation, and right action hindered by passions. Take all joy from rightness, and rightness only."

In Min's correct view of this text, "it seemed to be dry nonsense" (4.282; ch. 17). But whether it is nonsense or not, the White Cloaks project their dysfunctional relation to the anima on the world in general and the Aes Sedai in particular, believing the latter to be "witches" and declaring any woman who can channel to be a criminal. The White Cloaks are "a military body answerable only to itself" (4.621; ch. 38); in their view, it is illegal even to study at the White Tower.

The Children of the Light also illustrate what is wrong with the kind of thinking that Jordan may wish to criticize in our own society. Attrill's summary is helpful here. They are

> preachers turned soldiers—pseudo-religious zealots whose extreme and often illogical actions actually put them on the side of the Dark. They have attitudes similar to those of Reformation period "Protestants", being moralistic, militaristic, heavy-handed, bigoted, and fanatical. Always looking for scapegoats and prepared to use violence and torture to instill fear in the name of "Light", they manifest a sad and often brutal perversion of religion. They must parallel for most readers the Puritans and other splinter sects such as the Klu Klux clan [*sic*]. Jordan, in looking at their "excess", is perhaps showing that it is the horrible inheritance to American society from Puritanism, which has continued repercussion in contemporary society, although it is certainly not new for a society to do "evil" in the name of "good".[65]

Attrill might have added that their interrogation technique, putting persons to the question, recalls the Spanish Inquisition and that they call to mind all those throughout history who have burned books. They illustrate the fact that the foremost intellectual impediment in Jordan's series—the great enemy of the balance that is paramount—is not materialism but belief perseverance combined with illogic. As the narrator observes in *New Spring* of persons in general, "People had a way of folding what they saw into what they knew and what they wanted to believe" (329). The Children of the Light illustrate circular, black-and-white reasoning par excellence (3.457; ch. 29), the sort of cognitive traps that Dean Radin and Charles T. Tart identify (see introduction). If the Children walk in the Light, then those who disagree with them must be Darkfriends. As one of them says, "'Only where the Shadow of the Dark One reigns are the Children denied, yes?'" (1.253; ch. 17). The White Cloaks are so eager to project their shadow onto wolves, women, and anyone who disagrees with them that they are blind to the fact that Padan Fain has infiltrated their ranks and is influencing policy. Thinking that they only see the Light, they unknowingly partner with the Dark.

The Children of the Light's conclusions about the world reflect their own twisted assumptions. Along with the White Cloaks' beliefs about the Aes Sedai, they believe that wolves are "'creatures of the Dark One,'" as their leader Geofram Bornhald says to Perrin (1.452; ch. 30). Nothing could be further from the truth. The wolves have a great hatred for Trollocs, team up with Perrin to fight on the side of the Light, have their own pejorative name for the Dark One (Heartfang), and plan to be present at the Last Battle. The wolves are not only highly positive but also the most Jungian creatures in *The Wheel of Time*, for they experience a type of collective memory that is precisely akin to the collective unconscious. As Elyas tells Perrin, "'Every wolf remembers the history of all wolves, or at least the shape of it'" (1.342; ch. 23). Similarly, "'Wolves have long memories. What a wolf knows is never really forgotten while other wolves remain alive'" (10.225; ch. 8). And "wolves all remembered everything that one of their kind knew" (13.263; ch. 18). They are telepathic, and Perrin can communicate with them psychically over great distances as well as interact with them in the Wolf Dream. But from Perrin's initial vantage point, the wolves present a threat to his identity as a human being and to his sanity. "He needed to make peace with the wolf inside himself, the beast that raged when he went into battle" (12.280, ch. 17; and 327, ch. 21). His greatest fear is that he will turn into an animal, like Noam, the man he encounters who has transformed, psychologically at least, into a wolf because he is unable to find the right balance between his humanity and his animality. Perrin fears a similar outcome for himself, especially as regards his own shadow. Smelling Fain, "He had wanted to rip through the bars of the cell and tear the man apart; and finding that inside himself had frightened him more than Fain did" (2.227; ch. 14).

One benchmark of his emerging balance is his friendships with the Tinkers or *Tuatha'an* (unrealistic pacifism) and the Aiel (honor-driven bellicosity). Another is that he discards his axe and takes up a hammer, which can be used for either killing or creating. Eventually he balances both his human personality and his telepathic link to the wolves, illustrating Jung's statement that "nature *must not* win the game, but she *cannot* lose" (*CW* 13, 229/184; emphasis in the original). Perrin, an apprentice blacksmith as the series opens, does a good bit of the "apprentice-piece" before the "master-piece": by integrating his shadow (amplified as his inner wolf), he is then able to embrace a proper relationship with Faile. In a way that Goodman Brown cannot achieve, his marriage helps him in turn with his continuing shadow work. He finds his balance and can say, "'I am who I am. Finally'" (13.619; ch. 40). His journey comes full circle when he realizes that he may not have been at risk of losing his humanity after all; for in the World of Dreams, he discovers that Boundless (Noam) picked the wolf-identity intentionally (13.834; epilogue).

In conclusion, we have seen how the fantastic elements in a fantasy series dovetail with the quaternity (chapter 1), monistic cosmology (chapter 2), and the psychic phenomena in subsequent chapters. Jordan's characters perform wonderful psychic feats, which underscore the reader's own mind's ability to transcend space-time. One more piece remains in this book's argument. When a writer himself is psychic, what effect does his expanded awareness have on the text? The final chapter considers this question in connection with William Blake's *Milton*.

Notes

1 "Robert Jordan" is a pen name. The author's real name is James Oliver Rigney, Jr. See "Robert Jordan: The Name Behind the Wheel," *Locus* 44, no. 3 (2000): 6.

2 As of the fall of 2011, *The Wheel of Time* series consisted of a prequel and thirteen volumes, all published in New York by Tor Fantasy: *New Spring: The Novel* (2004); book 1, *The Eye of the World* (1990); book 2, *The Great Hunt* (1991); book 3, *The Dragon Reborn* (1991); book 4, *The Shadow Rising* (1993); book 5, *The Fires of Heaven* (1993); book 6, *Lords of Chaos* (1994); book 7, *A Crown of Swords* (1996); book 8, *The Path of Daggers* (1998); book 9, *Winter's Heart* (2000); book 10, *Crossroads of Twilight* (2003); book 11, *Knife of Dreams* (2005); book 12, with Brandon Sanderson, *The Gathering Storm* (2009); and book 13, with Brandon Sanderson, *Towers of Midnight* (2010). Book 14, *A Memory of Light* (2013), ghostwritten by Brandon Sanderson, was published too late to be considered here. I have used paperback editions for books 1–6 and cloth editions for books 7–13. In-text citations refer to book, page, and chapter numbers.

3 There is also some awareness of meteors: "There was talk of a gigantic stone from the sky having struck the earth far to the north in Andor, destroying an entire city and leaving a crater" (13.100; ch. 4).

4 For example, the three *ta'veren*—Rand, Perrin, and Mat—see colors when they think of each other. Sometimes an image forms, and the effect seems to be amplified when the One Power is being channeled (10.152, ch. 3, final par.; and 236, ch. 8).

5 These characters and many others are catalogued in the only major article on *The Wheel of Time* currently listed in the MLA Bibliography: Heather Attrill, "Lore, Myth and Meaning—for Post-Moderns: An Introduction to the Story World of Robert Jordan's *Wheel of Time* Sequence," *Australian Folklore: A Yearly Journal of Folklore Studies* 18 (2003): 37–76. Since Attrill's main purpose is to describe Jordan's characters and their world, the article distills her main source, Robert Jordan and Teresa Patterson's *The World of Robert Jordan's* The Wheel of Time (New York: Tor Fantasy, 1997). Despite great breadth of description, Attrill does have a number of excellent insights into the series; and this chapter appropriately credits her work below. For example, in a remark that resonates with the Jungian rubric of *The One Mind*, she comments on "Jungian extensions of the notion of the road as a place of intersection with the world

of the possible through imagination " (43). One correction is in order, however. Perrin's wolf name is Young Bull, not Little Bull, as Attrill has it (54).

6 Attrill claims that Jordan "likens himself to an Old Testament God who has control of his characters" and Jordan's universe to "a cosmic chess board with Jordan (as Creator) setting up the pieces for moves that will be played out in the future" (69–70). I would suggest that Jordan also parallels the role of the gleeman, a traveling bard. The author tells a story that includes a gleeman who also tells stories.

7 Gary K. Wolfe, *Critical Terms for Science Fiction and Fantasy: A Glossary and Guide to Scholarship* (New York: Greenwood, 1968), 31.

8 John Aquino, *Fantasy in Literature* (Washington, DC: National Education Association, 1997), 10–11.

9 C. G. Jung, "Approaching the Unconscious," in *Man and His Symbols*, ed. C. G. Jung et al. (Garden City, NY: Doubleday, 1964). The quotation appears on 43 and 45. Jung discusses child psychology on 99. For an explanation and critique of Jung's theory of the primitive, see chapter 4 in my previous book, *A Jungian Study of Shakespeare: The Visionary Mode* (New York: Palgrave Macmillan, 2009), 89–98.

10 W. R. Irwin, *The Game of the Impossible: A Rhetoric of Fantasy* (Urbana, IL: University of Illinois Press, 1976), 6–8. Irwin is using H. Godwin Baynes's translation of *Psychological Types or The Psychology of Individuation* (New York: Pantheon Books, 1962). The passage that begins "Fantasy as imaginative activity" appears on 69 (see *CW* 6, 78/52). The clause "corresponds with no external state of affairs" appears on 573 (see *CW* 6, 711/427). The phrase "principal attribute of the artistic mentality" is from 580 (see *CW* 6, 720/432).

11 See also Daryl Sharp, *C. G. Jung Lexicon: A Primer of Terms & Concepts* (Toronto, Canada: Inner City, 1991), 54–55.

12 Wolfe, *Critical Terms for Science Fiction and Fantasy*, 38 and 21. Pages 38–40 summarize the most important definitions of fantasy from E. M. Forster in 1927 to Kathryn Hume in 1984. The list also includes J. R. R. Tolkien and several theorists from the 1970s mentioned below.

13 Witold Ostrowski, "The Fantastic and the Realistic in Literature: Suggestions on How To Define and Analyze Fantastic Fiction," *Zagadnienia Rodzajów Literackich* 9, no. 1 (1966): 57, 85, and 59. One correction is necessary: the author inaccurately locates "elves" in *A Midsummer Night's Dream* on page 64.

14 Tzvetan Todorov, *The Fantastic: A Structural Approach to a Literary Genre*, trans. Richard Howard (Cleveland, OH: Press of Case Western Reserve University, 1973), 118, 25, and 92.

15 Eric S. Rabkin, *The Fantastic in Literature* (Princeton, NJ: Princeton University Press, 1976), 41 and 29–30. Rabkin is aware of the sort of "lay definition" of fantasy that traditional psychologists propose. As for Jung, fantasy reflects infantile impulses: for Piaget, this is the "illusion of central position"; for Freud, it is "'the omnipotence of thought,' the fantasy that, should one think something, it will come to pass" (29–30). Rabkin generalizes insufficiently about Jungian and Freudian dream analysis on 226.

16 Irwin, *The Game of the Impossible*, 4 and 8–9.

17 Marshall B. Tymn et al., *Fantasy Literature: A Core Collection and Reference Guide* (New York: Bowker, 1979), 5; Irwin, *The Game of the Impossible*, 156; and Wolfe, 52.

18 Tymn et al., *Fantasy Literature*, 24 and 7.

19 The Black Wind—according to Verin, "'the essence of madness and cruelty'" (2.480; ch. 33)—is one of the consequences of the Dark One's taint on *saidin*. The polluted form of *saidin* was used to "grow" the Ways; therefore, over time, they went from brightly lit to completely dark. Moiraine's comment is instructive: "'As Loial said, the Ways are living things, and all living things have parasites'" (1.687; ch. 45). It is doubtful, however, that the Ways would have a parasite if *saidin* were untainted. In any

case, the taint's effect on the Ways is similar to the slow way in which it affects a man who can channel: the madness usually takes time to manifest.

20 Attrill's only comment on Jordan's style is that the series "is not without stylistic flaw" ("Lore, Myth and Meaning," 37). In the earlier novels, Jordan is sometimes guilty of an egregious typo like "calvary" for "cavalry" (8.588; ch. 30) and dangling modifiers like this one: "Waiting at the bottom of the ridge, minutes passed like hours" (1.425; ch. 29). He apparently does not know the difference between "compared to" and "compared with," or the fact that persons are "hanged" rather than "hung." And one frequently finds that words have been omitted, despite professional proofreading. Jordan is actually a much better poet and song writer than he is a prose stylist—his lyrics are often quite fine. Yet, on rare occasions, prose descriptions are equally beautiful. For example, the description of the Green Man's death is lovely (1.751–52; ch. 50); but the finest writing comes when Jordan expresses the complexity of wolves' names:

> Two Moons was really a night-shrouded pool, smooth as ice in the instant before the breeze stirred, with a tang of autumn in the air, and one moon hanging full in the sky and another reflected so perfectly on the water that it was difficult to tell which was real.
>
> (6.946; ch. 54)

Another example is the description of Morning Mist's name (3.79; ch. 5).

21 John H. Timmerman, *Other Worlds: The Fantasy Genre* (Bowling Green, OH: Bowling Green University Press, 1983), 4 and 49–50.

22 Brian Attebery, *Strategies for Fantasy* (Bloomington: Indiana University Press, 1992), 15.

23 "Robert Jordan: The Name Behind the Wheel," 76. All of Jordan's statements appear in quotation marks in the article.

24 Sharp, *Jung Lexicon*, 15.

25 For Jung's understanding of myth, see my reading in *A Jungian Study of Shakespeare*, 43–46.

26 Trinity is also a useful concept for understanding *The Wheel of Time*. As Attrill points out, Karl-Johan Norén believes that Rand, Perrin, and Mat are a kind of trinity based on "the classical Hindu pattern of Destroyer-Builder-Preserver, with Rand as the Destroyer, Perrin as the Builder, and Mat as the Preserver" ("Lore, Myth and Meaning," 52). Norén's point appears in "The Rand-Mat-Perrin tripod," http://hem3.passagen.se/kjnoren/jordan/tripod.html.

27 It is a bit confusing when Lanfear recalls the lifetime of Lews Therin Telamon as being "'three thousand years ago and more, well before the Breaking of the World, before the Great Lord was imprisoned, before so much'" (5.33; prologue). Nynaeve seems equally confused about the order of events: "*The Dark One and all the Forsaken are bound in Shayol Ghul, bound by the Creator in the moment of creation*" (3.611; ch. 51). Only the Dark One was imprisoned at the moment of Creation; the Forsaken were imprisoned in the Age of Legends when Lews Therin Telamon and his Hundred Companions sealed them up in the Bore (3.24; prologue; and 2.xxi; prologue). Verin offers an interesting corollary to the Dark One's imprisonment in *The Dragon Reborn*:

> "There is one Creator, who exists everywhere at once for all of these worlds. In the same way, there is only one Dark One, who also exists in all of these worlds at once. If he is freed from the prison the Creator made in one world, he is freed on all. So long as he is kept prisoner in one, he remains imprisoned on all."
>
> (3.239; ch. 21)

Therefore, freeing the Dark One from his prison in one world does and does not free him in other worlds. This could be an example of the paradox that he represents. Certainly, it is hard to believe that Verin, an Aes Sedai of the Brown Ajah and therefore a scholar, would lapse into such a blatant contradiction. Another possibility is that Jordan just nodded.

28 Attrill, "Lore, Myth and Meaning," 63.

29 Note that the Creator is to Rand as the Dark One is to Moridin, the Nae'blis, "'the Great Lord's Regent on Earth'" (8.264; ch. 12).

30 The other time italicized all caps are used is when Rand channels the True Power to escape capture by Semirhage (12.354; ch. 22). "It is *HIM*" refers to the Dark One.

31 Moridin is the Forsaken known as Ishmael in a new body (11.142 and 147; ch. 3). He is the "'Nae'blis,' the one who would stand above all others, only a half step below the Great Lord himself after the Last Battle" (Jordan and Patterson, *The World of Robert Jordan's* The Wheel of Time, 49). It is clear that Ba'alzamon = Ishmael = Moridin (12.236; ch. 15). In other words, Ba'alzamon (the Dark One) uses Ishmael's physical form. When Rand kills Ishmael's physical body, the spirit of the Forsaken inhabits another and becomes known as Moridin.

32 Jordan and Patterson, *The World of Robert Jordan's* The Wheel of Time, 49.

33 Attrill, "Lore, Myth and Meaning," 38. The Great Serpent biting its own tail, "an even older symbol for eternity than the Wheel of Time," appears on the rings that Aes Sedai wear (3.58; ch. 3).

34 "*Ta'maral'ailen*" is the word for the Web that the Pattern weaves around an individual person (2.516; ch. 36). Loial uses *ta'maral'ailen* to refer to the impact that a *ta'veren*'s presence has on those around him (1.554; ch. 36).

35 Attrill makes a related comment on Jordan-as-author: "As he likens himself to an Old Testament God who has control of his characters, he therefore posits a pre-determined world. The Wheel weaves as Jordan wills" (69).

36 There is one more remove that is briefly mentioned above—*angreal*, *sa'angreal*, and *ter'angreal*. All are created through the use of the One Power, which "'only a living mind can wield'" (1.272; ch. 18), and all stand in the same relation to human intelligence as computers do in our own world. Objects in the first two amplify a person's ability to channel the One Power; those in the third perform specific functions and break down into two categories. One type, of which the Oath Rod is the foremost example, works when the One Power is applied. The second type, exemplified by the ring *ter'angreal* that enable access to the World of Dreams, as well as doorframe *ter'angreal* like the one in Rhuidean, work without the application of the One Power.

37 The warder bond is described as a kind of male/female *coniunctio* in *New Spring*:

> A sister and her bonded Warder could sense each other's emotions and physical condition, and each knew exactly where the other was, if they were close enough, and at least a direction if they were far apart, but this seemed on the order of reading minds. Some said that full sisters could do that.
>
> (89)

The bond, however, amplifies grief sustained at the death of a Warder. Often an Aes Sedai will grieve deeply for months; sometimes death ensues. On a lighter note, the bond also communicates drunkenness, as when Elayne feels Birgitte's intoxication (7.469; ch. 21). The bonding can be male/female, male/male, or female/female. In addition, one channeler can bond another. Same-sex bonding appears to amplify the psychic connection.

38 "Robert Jordan: The Name Behind the Wheel," 76.

39 Writing from Rand's point of view, however, the narrator mentions the thinness of the air on Dragonmount (12.755; ch. 50). The inconsistency may be due to the fact that Sanderson ghost-wrote the later volume.

40 Engineers make swift progress on the "steamwagon" or "steamhorse." In book 11 Doni notes, "'Four of them hitched together, one behind the other, pulled a hundred wagons all the way from Cairhien'" (441; ch. 21).

41 Other than Rand's visions of the past that will come again, there are the memories of the Forsaken. One of them, Graendal, remembers "shocklances," apparently a Taser-like weapon (9.313; ch. 13).

42 There is also mention of a "lift" (elevator) in book 10 (505, ch. 21).

43 A Trolloc is a chimera, a hybrid of human and animal. It is a killing machine that plays the same role as the Orcs in J. R. R. Tolkien's *The Lord of the Rings*. Myrddraal are most remarkable because they are slightly out of phase with space-time and have power to affect the human mind directly.

44 Like *Tel'aran'rhiod*, the Ways are a secondary world within Jordan's secondary world. As such, the Ways illustrate Rabkin's idea that the "ground rules" are broken. As Elayne recalls, "'Elaida says the rules of nature do not hold in the Ways. At least, not the way they do outside'" (2.559; ch. 39). They are described as "a strange world somehow outside time, or maybe alongside it" (10.552; ch. 24). As for gateways, Jordan implies that the quantum dimension is being engaged. In the narrator's words, "The One Power had little to do with gateways, really; only the making. Beyond, was something else. A dream of a dream, Asmodean called it" (5.910; ch. 54).

45 For examples of traveling at the speed of thought, see the following passages. Egwene travels in the blink of an eye to the Aiel Waste (4.214, ch. 11). Perrin has a different experience of speed as the landscape blurs around him (4.459; ch. 28). Either the characters move, or the World of Dreams moves around them, for it "was almost infinitely malleable" (6.205, ch. 7).

46 Similarly, Aiel women who wish to become Wise Ones use a *ter'angreal* in Rhuidean to see the possible lives to which contrasting choices may lead (10.282; ch. 10). Moiraine uses the knowledge gained from this device to determine how to handle Rand and how to attack Lanfear.

47 A minor example is Aviendha's talent with psychometry, the ability to touch a *ter'angreal* and "read" its power. In book 11 she determines that one "held music, hundreds of tunes, perhaps thousands," that another "was for talking to people a long way off," and that a third "holds thousands and thousands of books" (342–43; ch. 15). Obviously, these objects of power are analogous in our own culture to the iPod, the cell phone, and e-book readers.

48 In book 13, Moiraine is recovered from the realm of the Aelfinn and the Eelfinn by Mat, Thom, and Noal, who is revealed to be the legendary traveler Jain Farstrider.

49 Non-Dreamers briefly touch the World of Dreams, but in that moment they become vulnerable, which is why some people die in their sleep. Another phenomenon relates directly to Jung's belief that the unconscious compensates for consciousness. For example, "A Tairen woman dreaming, a High Lady or dreaming herself as one. She might be plain and dumpy, a farmwife or a merchant, awake" (7.236; ch. 10).

50 Attrill, "Lore, Myth and Meaning," 68.

51 Jordan and Patterson summarize the events that lead up to the tainting of *saidin* in *The World of Robert Jordan's* The Wheel of Time, 40–47.

52 Attrill, "Lore, Myth and Meaning," 68.

53 Rand states, "'The last time I tried to seal the Bore, I was forced to do it without the help of the women. That was part of what led to disaster'" (12.83; ch. 3). The sealing of the Bore was a botched job, which is why Harid Fel's recommendation is "to clear rubble before you can build" (12.240 and 244; ch. 15). Rand must break the remaining seals before further action can be taken to contain the Dark One, but dealing with him this

time must involve men and women. The need for gender balance is apparent in a similar formulation: "Rand needed to be in a circle with two women before he could safely wield the sword that was not a sword [*Callandor*]" (13.732 and 744; ch. 47 and 48).

54 The white half of the symbol is called the Flame of Tar Valon.

55 When Rand kills Rhavin with balefire, the Forsaken ceases to exist and cannot take another body. Persons killed in any other way can reincarnate as walk-ins. "Transmigration" is the word that the narrator uses for this process (9.318; ch. 13). For example, Halima, a stunning woman who insinuates herself into the rebel Aes Sedai camp at Salidar, is a male Forsaken named Aran'gar. She eases Egwene's migraine headaches with scalp massage; however, she actually causes them in the first place, but none of the Aes Sedai know this because they cannot perceive the use of *saidin*. Presumably that is why Egwene's "dreams were always troubled after one of Halima's massages" (10.481; ch. 20).

56 Padan Fain illustrates amplification in the way that he began as a simple Darkfriend but was remade and distilled at Shayol Ghul, then reborn at Shadar Logoth (5.364–65; ch. 19). He now goes by other names—Mordeth and Ordeith.

57 Attrill makes the Christ connection to Rand's wound and also sees the legend of the Fisher King in the background ("Lore, Myth and Meaning," 60).

58 For other references to the lake of fire, see 6.183, ch. 6; and 7.527, ch. 25.

59 Attrill, "Lore, Myth and Meaning," 60.

60 The felling of *Avendoradera* receives conflicting explanations. The narrator states, "Tigraine went to the Waste in secret, which made Laman Damodred cut down *Avendoraldera*, a gift of the Aiel, to make a throne, an act which brought the Aiel across the Spine of the World to kill him" (6.386; ch. 16). But Jordan and Patterson offer an alternative explanation:

> Plots were born to unseat Laman, and he hatched his own schemes to counter them. As a minor part of one of his schemes, Laman cut down *Avendoraldera* to make a throne which could never be duplicated, it was thought. The tree was cut down, and the avalanche began.
>
> (*The World of Robert Jordan's* The Wheel of Time, 121)

Perhaps Jordan nods here.

61 See also Min's sense, as she beholds Rand holding *saidin*, that the One Power was "made incarnate in the man Rand al'Thor" (12.574; ch. 37).

62 For immortality, see 4.181, ch. 9; and 2.244, ch. 15. Lanfear wants Rand to rule the world with her and to replace both the Dark One and the Creator. For wealth, power, and glory, see 3.226, ch. 20.

63 In this respect, the Amyrlin resembles Prince Arthur in Edmund Spenser's *The Faerie Queen*. Arthur's virtue is magnanimity, which presumably encompasses all the main virtues that Spenser uses to structure the poem. In a similar way, the Amyrlin participates in all seven Ajahs.

64 Besides the female bullying previously mentioned, a further indication that the sexes are out of balance is the marriage knife in Ebou Dar. Jordan and Patterson explain that "when a couple marries, the man gives the woman the knife as part of the ceremony. He then requests that she use it to kill him should he ever displease her" (*The World of Robert Jordan's* The Wheel of Time, 266).This practice is the exact inversion of the way Odysseus draws his sword and rushes at Circe, then exacts a promise that she will not make him feel like a weakling unmanned (*Odyssey*, book 10).

65 Attrill, "Lore, Myth and Meaning," 48–49. Like members of the Ku Klux Klan, the White Cloaks wear conical helmets, though the headgear does not cover their faces (5.787; ch. 48).

9

"SUBLIME ALLEGORY"

Ways of seeing in Blake's *Milton*

William Blake's visionary epic *Milton* surpasses in difficulty any work considered in the previous chapters. While the central character, the dead poet John Milton, is clearly recognizable, what happens in the poem's two books and forty-three plates yields significant meaning only to readers who possess specialized knowledge of Blake's unique mythology. Fortunately, previous analyses of the poem, especially those by Northrop Frye and Harold Bloom, help build a foundation for the reading that I wish to propose.[1] This chapter begins with the basic similarities between Blake's system of thought and Jung's psychology, adumbrates Blake's cosmology and the poem's organizational scheme, and then presents an analysis of the poem's main actions with emphasis on Jungian interpretation. On that foundation, Blake's life and letters are used to argue that *Milton*, as a metaphysical statement by a psychic writer, proposes ways of seeing that are consistent with many of the conclusions reached in chapters 1 through 8.

The proposed reading of *Milton* is in sync with Frye's claim that two of Blake's statements—"There is No Natural Religion" and "All Religions are One"—sum up "the whole of [his] thought if they are understood simultaneously" (E 1–2).[2] Blake asserts in these statements, as I have argued throughout, that materialism and separation are illusions and that unity ought to be humankind's starting assumption. That such unity may arise from a common consciousness undergirding even Jung's collective unconscious is in accord with Kathleen Raine's statement in *Blake and the New Age*: "there are many indications that mind, not matter, is once again being considered as the first principle of the universe in which we find ourselves but of which we can know so little."[3] In that spirit, the case study in this final chapter completes the volume by illustrating an author's engagement with phenomena related to the One Mind.

Blake and Jung

Strangely, Blake's Jungian critics are silent on the small number of references in *The Collected Works* to Blake's poetry, prose, and art. Jung's direct statements about Blake therefore provide a suitable starting point. Although Jung's knowledge of British literature was sketchy at best, he did have some exposure to Blake's life and works. When Jung speaks of "this 'blissful' feeling, this ecstasy of love," he glosses his remark in a footnote by quoting *The Marriage of Heaven and Hell*: "Energy is eternal delight" (*CW* 6, 422/248–49; n. 159; E 34). The proverb, from a section called "The voice of the Devil," is the contrary of the notion a few lines earlier "that God will torment Man in Eternity for following his Energies." Although energy is delightful, it can cause problems because there are those who would oppose it through the exercise of reason, as the next proverb makes clear. "Those who restrain desire, do so because theirs is weak enough to be restrained; and the restrainer or reason usurps its place & governs the unwilling." As we shall see, reason-as-restrainer is highly relevant to *Milton*. Nothing else in *The Collected Works* links Blake and Jung on the subject of love or energy; but Jung does make a variety of remarks about Blake that fall neatly into three categories: visual art, mysticism, and psychological types.

Visual art. Jung makes two references to images in Laurence Binyon's *The Engraved Designs of William Blake*.[4] Jung mentions Blake's "Jacob's dream" while discussing the dream imagery of the stairs in terms of ascent and descent (*CW* 12, p. 54; fig. 14, p. 55). Later, as an illustration of the idea that "the anima, having already anticipated the *solificatio*, now appears as the psychopomp, the one who shows the way," he reproduces "The soul as a guide, showing the way," Blake's illustration for Dante's *Purgatorio*, canto 4 (*CW* 12, 74/58; fig. 19, p. 61). If Jung saw these images, it is likely that he also saw the three images from *Milton* that Binyon includes. It is unlikely, however, that Jung ever attempted to read the poem; and we will never know what he might have thought of its visual artifacts in Binyon's anthology.

Mysticism. Jung does refer several times to the mystical dimension of Blake's life and work. In "Psychology and Literature," Jung wonders about the provenance of art:

> The primordial experiences rend from top to bottom the curtain upon which is painted the picture of an ordered world, and allow a glimpse into the unfathomable abyss of the unborn and of things yet to be. Is it a vision of other worlds, or of the darkness of the spirit, or of the primeval beginnings of the human psyche? We cannot say it is any or none of these.
>
> (*CW* 15, 141/90–91)

Then he quotes these lines from Goethe, which bear directly on the One Mind: "Formation, transformation, / Eternal Mind's eternal recreation." The lines reappear in *Memories, Dreams, Reflections* in the context of Jung's discussion of mandalas: "Only gradually did I discover what the mandala really is: 'Formation, Transformation, Eternal Mind's eternal recreation.'"[5] In the next paragraph of

"Psychology and Literature," he notes that the type of vision he has described appears in Blake's paintings and poetry. Moreover, Jung laments the intellectual life of the present day, as does Blake in *Milton*:

> Our attempts have, with few exceptions, all stopped short at either magic (mystery cults, amongst which we must include Christianity) or intellectualism (philosophy from Pythagoras to Schopenhauer). It is only the tragedies of Goethe's *Faust* and Nietzsche's *Zarathustra* which mark the first glimmerings of a break-through of the total experience [that is, of wholeness] in our Western Hemisphere. And we do not know even today what these most promising of all products of the Western mind may at length signify, so overlaid are they with the materiality and concreteness of our thinking, as moulded by the Greeks.
>
> (*CW* 11, 905/554–55)

In a note on the first sentence, Jung adds, "In this connection I must also mention the English mystic, William Blake. Cf. an excellent account in Percival, *William Blake's Circle of Destiny*" (n. 41).[6]

Psychological types. Elsewhere, Jung notes that "the English mystic William Blake says: 'These two classes of men are always upon earth . . . the Prolific and the Devouring. . . . Religion is an endeavour to reconcile the two'" (*CW* 6, 460/272). The reference is again to *The Marriage of Heaven and Hell*:

> Thus one portion of being, is the Prolific. [T]he other, the Devouring: to the devourer it seems as if the producer was in his chains, but it is not so, he only takes portions of existence and fancies that the whole.
>
> But the Prolific would cease to be Prolific unless the Devourer as a sea recieved the excess of his delights.
>
> Some will say, Is not God alone the Prolific? I answer, God only Acts & Is, in existing beings or Men.
>
> These two classes of men are always upon earth, & they should be enemies; whoever tries to reconcile them seeks to destroy existence.
>
> (E 40)

Prolific and Devourer do not refer to literal producing and consuming; rather they are metaphors for contrasting orientations toward life. Whereas the Prolific expands his personality within a given moment, the Devourer sits back and sees the "bigger picture." Insofar as Prolific and Devourer are more like participant and observer, active sender and passive receiver, the essential nature of the Prolific is defined against that of the Devourer: they are contraries. Being Prolific—or for that matter Devouring—is thus a matter of human personality, not divine agency. The Prolific and the Devourer "are always upon earth" and surely within each psyche as well. To reconcile or merge them would be to defeat progress by turning dynamic contraries into sterile negations. Jung's own reading of Prolific and Devourer zeroes in on the psychological dimension of Blake's categories. For Jung, Prolific is to extroversion as Devourer is to introversion.

> It is sufficient to note that the peculiar nature of the extravert constantly urges him to expend and propagate himself in every way, while the tendency of the introvert is to defend himself against all demands from outside, to conserve his energy by withdrawing it from objects, thereby consolidating his own position. Blake's intuition did not err when he described the two classes of men as "prolific" and "devouring." . . . The one achieves its ends by a multiplicity of relationships, the other by monopoly.
>
> (*CW* 6, 559/332)

Although Jung's references to Blake are not far-reaching, they do point toward the basic similarities between the poet's system and Jung's analytical psychology that have been noticed by Blake's Jungian critics.[7] Most fundamentally, both Blake and Jung oppose materialism and believe that the imaginative experience of the collective unconscious is objectively real. Deriving poetic and artistic inspiration from it makes Blake a practitioner of Jung's "visionary mode," though Raine suspects that Blake's work may have been more derivative than is commonly recognized.[8] In addition, Blake and Jung map the psyche, its breakdowns, and its movement toward wholeness. Albion (England, Humanity) corresponds to the Jungian Self, and for both men the quaternity symbolizes wholeness. Blake's Spectre corresponds to Jung's shadow. As Harold F. Brooks explains, "The Spectrous in Blake comprehends a great deal of what in Jung is represented by the Shadow (not to be confused with the Shadow [physical body] in Blake)."[9] Similarly, Blake's Emanation is Jung's anima; and both agree that a man's shadow integration must precede a contra-sexual relationship. Jung's statement about the "apprentice-piece" and the "master-piece" (*CW* 9i, 61/29) echoes Blake's sense that a man must address his Spectre before engaging with his feminine Emanation (anima). The following lines succinctly dramatize the disconnection between shadow and anima, as well as the need for inner work to begin with the shadow:

> My Spectre around me night & day
> Like a Wild Beast guards my way.
> My Emanation far within
> Weeps incessantly for my Sin.
>
> (E 475)

Further difficulties arise within the psyche from Blake's concept of selfhood (in Jung, ego + persona) and its conformity to external authority; from the presence of negations instead of contraries (in Jung, repression rather than compensation);

Blake	Urizen/Satan	Luvah/Orc	Los/Urthrona	Tharmas
Jung	Thought	Feeling	Imagination	Sensation/body

Figure 9.1 Blake's mythology and Jung's psychology.

and from overemphasis on reason. Imbalance arises when thought and feeling are in conflict. Brooks explains that "Satan is nothing other than the State of Urizen [reason] and Orc [feeling] at war as Negations."[10] Blake addresses this imbalance in *Milton,* which describes the process of rebalancing the psyche through "self-annihilation" or what Jung would call individuation. Figure 9.1 clarifies the divisions of the psyche within the two systems.

W. P. Witcutt takes the typology a step further by identifying Blake's personality type as "the intuitive introvert [who] is . . . an inhabitant of two worlds." Los (Imagination) is Blake's dominant function, Tharmas (body) his "most repressed function." (This combination helps explain Blake's great emphasis on the transformational power of sexuality.) Blake's personality type makes him capable of "double vision," the ability to see the concrete world through the lens of the Imagination:

> For double the vision my eyes do see,
> And a double vision is always with me.
> With my inward Eye 'tis an old man grey;
> With my outward, a Thistle across my way.[11]

Witcutt adds that "the great value of Blake's poetry is that it provides a kind of outline of the unconscious mind." The many parallels charted above support this point, but the critic's next comments deserve critique:

> Blake explored this strange region more thoroughly than any before or since, and what is more, he knew what he was doing. . . . Blake is the only one who has ventured as far as they [madmen in asylums] and yet remained sane.[12]

Of course, when Witcutt published his book in 1946, information about Jung's nervous breakdown in 1913 would not have been widely available. But my study makes it obvious that Blake was not the "only one" who explored the far reaches of inner space "yet remained sane." Robert A. Monroe certainly did it, as did Jung himself. Witcutt should at least have noted that Emanuel Swedenborg explored even more deeply than Blake did. In any case, the many similarities between Blake's system and Jung's psychology may arise, in part, from shared experiences of exploring psyche's depths.

Milton: A Jungian analysis

It will help to begin with the basic cosmology and organization that Blake creates in his poem. The three major realms are Eden, Beulah, and Ulro. Eden is Eternity, the afterlife; Beulah, named after the Earthly Paradise in John Bunyan's *Pilgrim's Progress*, an in-between state that corresponds, as S. Foster Damon notes, to the subconscious;[13] and Ulro, the material world of space-time. Obscure though Blake's terminology may be, his cosmology anticipates Jung's divisions among the pleroma, the collective unconscious, and matter: the realm of pure spirit, the quantum, and the physical. The poem's organization is also more straightforward than its mythology suggests. As Jack Lindsay points out, book 1 includes the Song of the Bard followed by Milton's descent, while book 2 features the Song of Beulah followed by the descent of Ololon (the dead poet's Emanation). Each descent ends in a union: of Milton and Blake in book 1, of Milton and Ololon in book 2; and each book ends with a vision: of the physical world in book 1, of Eternity in book 2.[14] As these details suggest, what may seem like a wilderness of self-created mythology actually has a carefully crafted setting and structure.

Plate 23 sums up the poem's main action in the following lines: "This mighty one is come from Eden, he is of the Elect, / Who died from Earth & he is returnd before the Judgment" (E 119). Milton returns, but why, how, for what purpose, and with what implications and consequences? A detailed comment on plates 1 and 2 (E 95–96) suggests some preliminary answers. Plate 1's prose preface states that Milton was "curbd by the general malady & infection from the silly Greek & Latin slaves of the Sword." Blake then calls on "Young Men of the New Age" to embrace the same transition that Milton will make in the poem, from reason to Imagination as inspired by "those Worlds of Eternity; in Jesus our Lord" (the Bible). In other words, the preface establishes *ways of seeing* as central themes of the poem.[15] Plate 1 then presents the famous poem "And did those feet in ancient time," known today simply as "Jerusalem." In the past, Albion (England) was in proper sync with Jerusalem (its Emanation); however, in the present day "these dark Satanic Mills" proliferate, presumably because of the presence of reason-driven greed and the absence of the kind of Imagination that the prose passage emphasizes. The line describes what William Wordsworth calls "getting and spending," but in Blake the situation is not even "a sordid boon"; it is merely sordid.[16] So when Blake states that he "will not cease from Mental Fight, / . . . Till we have built Jerusalem, / In England's green & pleasant Land," he implies that his overall purpose in describing the dead poet's shift from reason to Imagination and union with his own feminine side is to bring about a similar transformation among the English people. Blake hopes to shift his country's ways of seeing from Neo-Classical to Romantic by writing a poem about how Milton transforms both himself and Blake. Insofar as reason must no longer dominate Imagination but must instead be brought into the wholeness of the Self, the epic concerns the individuation process. At the same time, Blake is rewriting *Paradise Lost*, as Peter Ackryod observes:

> He wished to change the epic of the Fall into the prophecy of man's faculties restored, and in so doing allow Milton to re-enter the world, where he might reclaim Satan as part of his own self.[17]

In plate 2, Blake invokes the daughters of Beulah, asking them to activate his Imagination, "The Eternal Great Humanity Divine," so that he can tell the story of Milton's descent from Eternity to his garden in Felpham, located on England's southern coast. The question at issue is then directly asked: "Say first! what mov'd Milton, who walkd about in Eternity / . . . Viewing his Sixfold Emanation [Ololon] scatter'd thro' the deep / In torment! To go into the deep her to redeem & himself perish?" (E 96). Milton's feminine Emanation is sixfold because it represents his three wives and three daughters, but the Emanation may also be considered his poetry. He must be united with Ololon just as Blake wants to reunite Albion and Jerusalem; and it is "A Bards prophetic Song," which begins at the end of plate 2, that motivates the dead poet's descent. What, then, does Milton learn from the Bard's song?

The simplest answer is that the Bard's song makes Milton aware of psychological imbalance—his own and English society's. Plate 3 uses retrospective narration to describe the disintegration of the national psyche. Los (Poetry, Imagination, Poetic Genius, "the father of any civilizing impulse" [Bloom, *Visionary*]) separates into male and female because of the fall into Experience. Other problems include the sealing up of the senses; the emphasis on reason; Orc ("physical passion" [Saurat], "the natural man" [Bloom, *Apocalypse*], revolution [Damon]); the Shadowy Female ("this material world" [Damon]); and the rise of Satan/Urizen (reason), who is "in chains of the mind lock'd up," recalling the "mind-forg'd manacles" in Blake's "London" from the *Songs of Experience* (E 26–27).[18]

Just as these personified forces disrupt the Imagination of Blake's Age, his personal circumstances prove detrimental to his own artistic production. The mention in plate 4 of "Corporeal Friends [who] are Spiritual Enemies" (E 98) refers to William Hayley, Blake's patron during his years at Felpham, who did not understand Blake's poetic vision. In a letter to Thomas Butts written on April 25 1803, Blake speaks of the black-and-white thinking that results when one doubts his friends:

> Christ is very decided on this Point: "He who is Not With Me is Against Me." There is no Medium or Middle state; & if a man is Enemy of my Spiritual Life while he pretends to be a Friend of my Corporeal, he is a Real Enemy—but the Man may be a friend of my Spiritual life while he seems the Enemy of my Corporeal, but Not Vice Versa.[19]

Hayley, who had been Blake's patron and agent, was a friend in the material sense but an enemy of Blake's artistic vision. A perfect example of the misfit between poet and patron centers on the latter's reaction to *Milton*. As Blake wryly notes in a letter to Butts on July 6, 1803, "He [Hayley] knows that I have writ it, for I have shewn it to him, & he has read Part by his own desire & has looked with sufficient contempt to inhance my opinion of it."[20]

Hayley is a Satan-figure in Blake's life, and the poet's discontentment with his patron relates to the Three Classes of Men, a psychological system that encompasses much of the conflict that also animates *Milton*. Each class has mythological and/or real-life representatives: the Elect (Satan/Hayley); the Reprobate (Rintrah and other fiery prophets like Jesus); and the Redeemed (Palamabron/Blake). In plate 25, the key point is that "in every Nation & every Family the Three Classes are born" (E 122). Bloom adds that "all three classes are in every man, but one class or another is dominant at one particular time or stage of his development."[21] One is not wrong here to think of Freud's division of the psyche into the superego (Elect), ego (Redeemed), and id (Reprobate): Freud's categories capture the essential qualities of the Three Classes of Men. The Elect embrace reason and moral virtue and consider the Reprobate, in Frye's words, "dangerous nuisances."[22] Meanwhile, the Redeemed—like the ego within the psyche—are those who try to effect an imaginative transformation of society from within. Like the Reprobate, they stay true to their own vision; unlike the Reprobate, they do not create excessive conflict. The Redeemed are mediators but only in a sense, for the relationships among the Classes are complicated by two terms in Blake's vocabulary: negation and contraries.

The Marriage of Heaven and Hell states that "Without Contraries is no progression" (E 34). Contraries like Reprobate and Redeemed participate in a dynamic struggle, whereas a negation like the Elect seeks opposition for its own sake, with no progress resulting. That is, the goal of the Elect is to shut down the other parts of the psyche, family, or body politic. For example, in *Milton* "The idiot Reasoner laughs at the Man of Imagination / And from laughter proceeds to murder by undervaluing calumny" (E 131). Whereas Rintrah and Palamabron are plowman and harrower, complementary roles that lead to planting and harvest, Satan, as Bloom notes, is a miller who "grinds down created life."[23] Apparently, the Elect affect the Redeemed and the Reprobate to different degrees: the Reprobate "never cease to Believe" in spite of the opposition, but the Redeemed "live in doubts & fears perpetually tormented by the Elect." Yet "the Elect must be saved [from] fires of Eternal Death, / To be formed into the Churches of Beulah that they destroy not the Earth" (E 122). "Saved" is the key word. The assertion that reason must be completely subverted is false; instead Imagination must temper moral law and reason so that the Elect cease to be a negation. In a Jungian nutshell, the dynamics among the Three Classes of Men are Blake's way of suggesting the need for psychological balance conducive to individuation.

A key episode in *Milton* presents an allegory of what happens when reason attempts to take over the role of Imagination. Upon Satan's request, Los gives him the Harrow of the Almighty (Poetry or perhaps Blake's engraving tool), which belongs in the hands of artist-figure Palamabron, who in turn takes over Satan's mills. Evidently, both do a poor job. Palamabron laments, "My horses hath he maddend! and my fellow servants injur'd." When Satan returns to the mills, he discovers the "servants of the Mills drunken with wine and dancing wild / With shouts and Palamabrons songs, rending the forests green / With ecchoing confusion, tho' the Sun was risen on high." Therefore, Los decides to "let each his own station / Keep" (E 101). Bloom sums up the moral of the story by stating, "If Palamabron embraces Satan then he allies himself with a negation, not a contrary, and no cultural progression is possible."[24] As well, if the mills are "Hayley's manufacturing system for churning out verses and art,"[25] then perhaps the workers' reactions to Palamabron are Blake's fantasy of liberation from the daily grind imposed on him by his patron. In any case, the artist is no more adept at running a factory than an embodiment of social convention like Hayley is at creating great art. Slipping into each other's roles (in Jung, *enantiodromia*, a swing to the opposites) is insufficient; a more profound transformation is necessary.

Various details then further the sense of separation among aspects of the psyche. At a solemn assembly, Satan rages at Palamabron in an attempt "To pervert the Divine Voice," the Imagination (E 103). Leutha, Satan's Emanation, offers herself as a ransom for Satan's sin, though, in a show of psychic disintegration, she "stupefied the masculine perceptions / And kept only the feminine awake." She describes Satan's attempt "To devour Albion and Jerusalem the Emanation of Albion / [by] Driving the Harrow in Pitys paths" (E 105–6). Then Elynittria, Palamabron's Emanation (Blake's wife), soothes Leutha and brings her to Palamabron's bed in a prefiguration of the union of male and female that concludes the poem. Thus ends the song of the Bard who merges with Milton, as Milton will soon merge with Blake.

In an important passage, Milton realizes that both he and the English nation are guilty of the imbalance and separation enacted by the Bard's description of the Three Classes of Men. Milton now prepares to take action.

> And Milton said, I go to Eternal Death! The Nations still
> Follow after the detestable Gods of Priam; in pomp
> Of warlike selfhood, contradicting and blaspheming.
>
> I will arise and look forth for the morning of the grave.
> I will go down to the sepulcher to see if morning breaks!
> I will go down to self annihilation and eternal death,
> Lest the Last judgment come & find me unannihilate
> And I be seiz'd & giv'n into the hands of my own Selfhood
>
> What do I here before the Judgment? without my Emanation?
> With the daughters of memory, & not with the daughters of inspiration[?]
> I in my Selfhood am that Satan: I am that Evil One!
> He is my Spectre! in my obedience to loose him from my Hells
> To claim the Hells, my Furnaces, I go to Eternal Death.
>
> (E 108)

The Bard's Song sparks various realizations and convictions on Milton's part. By embracing selfhood (ego, persona), the classics over the Bible, and memory over inspiration (Imagination), Milton and the national psyche align with the Elect's emphasis on reason and moral law. Rather than continuing to exist in such a state of negation, he must confront Satan, his Spectre or Jungian shadow—especially reason, Puritanism, and an improper emphasis on chastity[26]— before he can be united with his feminine Emanation, much as Jung maintains that a man must do shadow work before attempting anima work. In order to reintegrate his psyche, Milton must travel to the "the grave" and "eternal death" (the physical world), where he will "claim the Hells, my Furnaces." These furnaces, which sound like the mills that Satan supervises, represent anything that goes against the Poetic Spirit. Milton must not only acknowledge his inner faults but also confront the societal consequences that his life's work helped bring about. The result will be "self annihilation," not any kind of destruction but rather a purgation of selfhood and a rebalancing of the psyche so that reason, passion, and Imagination—the Elect, Reprobate, and Redeemed, all three—become contraries capable of compensation and progress. Ronald L. Grimes clarifies the concept of self-annihilation by stating that it

> is not the same as self-destruction. To simplify, annihilation of the selfhood is a means for the redemption of the identity, which is the self-in-community. . . . One is reconciled to his fellow, his other, as he is reconciled to himself and vice versa.[27]

Because Milton realizes that he has some unfinished inner work, he "beheld his own Shadow . . . and he enterd into it" (E 108). The Shadow here must be a corporeal body, much as Blake, in his December 11, 1805 letter to Hayley, mentions "that faint Shadow call'd Natural Life."[28] Milton's strikingly beautiful and important statement is made all the more powerful by an overlooked allusion to Luke 15:18. "I will arise and look forth" echoes the prodigal son's realization of fault and his determination to reform: "'I will arise and go to my father. '"[29] But instead of begging forgiveness for his waywardness, Milton must confront and overcome Satan/Urizen in preparation for uniting with his Emanation, Ololon.

While the immortals perceive Milton as sleeping on a couch, another part of him enters "the Sea of Time & Space" through a trans-dimensional vortex (E 109–10), eventually entering Blake's left foot (left signifying a material event that takes place in historical time, foot signifying an altered stance).[30] As Milton travels through the land and notices examples of law, Los initially misunderstands Milton's mission, fearing that "Satan [natural religion, materialism] shall be unloosd upon Albion" (E 111). Given Milton's transcendental monism, discussed in chapter 2, which is far from a pernicious materialism, Los's remark reflects how badly Milton needs to return in order to straighten out his corrupted legacy. Then Milton and Urizen engage in a wrestling match. Bloom provides helpful background on the geographical references: in the Valley of Beth Peor

(Moses's burial place), near the River Arnon (associated with the Red Sea in Numbers 21:14 and implying escape from bondage), Urizen and Milton engage in a wrestling match that signifies "the body of law striving with the human form divine."[31] Urizen pours icy water on Milton's brain, but Milton remolds Urizen with "the red clay of Succoth" (E 112). Bloom notes that Succoth is the place where Jacob (another wrestler) builds a house in Genesis 33:17; but Victor N. Paananen incorrectly states, "Since Succoth is the place to which Jesus went after the Crucifixion, Milton is trying to shape Urizen into the resurrected Humanity."[32] Although the latter part of the assertion is a nice point, there is no record of Jesus's going there after the resurrection. In John 1:14 the word is used to mean "dwelling"; and in John 7:1–13, Succoth is an event, the Feast of the Tabernacles, a harvest festival renowned for joy and celebration, which ties in with the poem's frequent mention of the harvest. Insofar as harvest is concerned, remolding Urizen becomes even more a sign of positive transformation for Milton and for the nation. Milton then enters Blake's left foot (the motif repeats a number of times), and Blake binds a sandal on it to symbolize his union with Los—the union of the corporeal and the Imaginative/prophetic. As Milton remolds Urizen into Divine Humanity, Milton's entrance into Blake's left foot and the binding on of a sandal signify heightened vision: Milton's poetic spirit now lives again in Blake the poet, with heightened vision on Blake's part.[33]

The rest of the poem's events can be briskly summarized. As a further result of the wrestling match, Albion no longer "lies enbalmd" (E 113) but begins to stir. And now Ololon decides to descend as well. As Blake binds on his sandals (plural this time), Los enters his soul: "I became One Man with him," says Blake (E 117). This merging signals an enhanced sense of vision that contrasts with a list of ills of which "Milton's Religion is the cause" (E 117): Voltaire, Rousseau, and the perversion of Swedenborg's visions (George Whitfield and John Wesley, however, play a positive prophetic role). After Ololon descends, Milton says that his Spectre hunts his Emanation, another parallel to Jung's sense of the "apprentice-piece" and the "master-piece." Ololon descends in the pulsation of an artery, the instant of an artist's inspiration, to Blake's garden at Felpham, appearing to him as a twelve-year-old virgin. In his greeting to her, Blake calls his wife "my Shadow of Delight" (E 137). Milton also descends to Blake's garden and states his purpose: "to teach Men to despise death & go on / In fearless majesty annihilating Self" (E 139). Echoing a motif from *Paradise Lost*, the Starry Seven (the seven Angels of the Presence or the seven Eyes of God)[34] call out to Albion to wake up, telling him to "reclaim thy Reasoning Spectre. Subdue / Him to the Divine Mercy, Cast him down into the Lake / Of Los, that ever burneth with fire" (E 140). As Albion rises and Urizen faints, the allegory is clearly of the tempering of reason by Imagination.

Then Milton voices some bad psychology:

> The Negation must be destroyed to redeem the Contraries
> The Negation is the Spectre; the Reasoning Power in Man

> This is a false Body: an Incrustation over my Immortal
> Spirit; a Selfhood, which must be put off & annihilated alway [*sic*]
> To cleanse the Face of my Spirit by Self-examination.
>
> (E 142)

Negation = Spectre = Reason = Selfhood (ego, persona): all this must be wiped away, says Milton, in order to liberate Spirit. That is *enantiodromia*. Like the Jungian shadow, reason should not be destroyed, nor can it be. And besides, the imperative that Milton voices is out of sync with the idea of casting the Spectre onto the burning lake of the Imagination and Blake's previously quoted sense that "the elect must be saved [from] fires of Eternal Death / To be formed into the Churches of Beulah that they destroy not the Earth" (E 122). Negative qualities must be *integrated*, not banished. Milton also seems to exaggerate the case in his proclamation in plate 41.

> I come in Self-annihilation & the grandeur of Inspiration
> To cast off Rational Demonstration by Faith in the Saviour
> To cast off the rotten rags of Memory by Inspiration
> To cast off Bacon, Locke & Newton from Albions covering
> To take off his filthy garments, & clothe him with Imagination
> To cast aside from Poetry, all that is not Inspiration. . . .
>
> (E 142)

The imagery of new clothing recalls Milton's remolding of Urizen with red clay; however, what Blake advocates is not the elimination of reason from the psyche (if that were even possible, it would lead to further imbalance) but a realignment of the artistic and national psyche with Imagination. If Urizen and Tharmas are properly balanced, Satan (the negation that results from imbalance) ought to disappear. There must be a new orientation toward reason; instead of a black-and-white negation between those faculties, they must become contraries capable of spurring progress (Jung's compensation) in each other. Milton's self-annihilation enables the final union of Milton and Ololon and vice versa; each constitutes and enables the progress of contraries.

Blake's fourfold psychic vision

Blake's fourfold understanding of vision ranges, literally, from here to Eternity—from scientific materialism's denial of anything beyond the physical world to the human afterlife. The four types of vision appear in his letter to Butts on November 22, 1802 and are helpfully explicated by John Beer and others.[35]

> Now I a fourfold vision see,
> And a fourfold vision is given to me;
> 'Tis fourfold in my supreme delight

And threefold in soft Beulah's night
And twofold Always. May God us keep
From Single vision & Newton's sleep.

Single vision refers to a focus on the world of generation; as Beer says, it is "the dead vision of contemporary mathematical rationalism." That is, single vision means seeing only with the physical senses: the gathering of concrete data. In twofold vision, Beer explains, an artist's imagination enables him to see the "inner significance" of things and events in the everyday world. As James King mentions, twofold vision "condemns political and religious repression."[36] "And twofold Always" suggests that Blake's normal waking state involves such penetrating intellectual analysis. Beer associates threefold vision with the "innocent pleasure given to those enjoying the pleasures of marriage and domesticity" and identifies this state as Beulah. But as *Milton* makes clear, Beulah is more properly the realm of the unconscious, a way station between Eternity and Ulro. Dreamers and visionaries may briefly achieve threefold vision (Beulah). Fourfold vision, says Beer, is "at once absolute in its certainty and essentially unseizable for the purposes of immediate visual representation." But as the verses in Blake's letter to Butts make clear, one may touch upon fourfold vision, however fleetingly. King clarifies that fourfold vision means the capability of glimpsing Eternity. Or as Grimes mentions, "Fourfold vision is vision which engages all four regions of psyche and cosmos. It is redeemed vision capable of seeing the divine city."[37] It should by now be obvious that Geoffrey Keynes's explanation of the four types of vision as material, intellectual, emotional, and spiritual errs by reducing threefold vision to an emotional state what is a matter of the unconscious.[38] Figure 9.2 sums up the interpretation of the stages of vision as I will refer to them.

Given *Milton*'s opposition to materialism and the poem's visionary nature, its composition participates largely in twofold and threefold vision. Twin illustrations support this conclusion by distinguishing between Blake's physical condition and his dead brother Robert's spiritual state. In the first, a star (Milton) enters Blake's left foot (materiality), while in the other the star enters Robert's right foot (spirituality). As in Jung's comment on Blake's "Jacob's dream," stairs signify spiritual ascent. There are steps to the side of each figure: three in "William," four

Single vision	Twofold vision	Threefold vision	Fourfold vision
Materialistic perception of the physical world via the five senses and scientific perception (the world of Eiseley)	Intellectual/moral reflection on physical reality (for example, the social commentary in Blake's *Songs*)	Access to the unconscious through dream, imagination, or vision (Jung's visionary mode)	Access to the spirit world through psychic functioning (the realm explored by Monroe and accessed by Blake)

Figure 9.2 Blake's four types of vision.

in "Robert," because, in King's words, "Robert has entered the world of fourfold vision, whereas his brother lives in the fallen world of Generation which permits him only momentary glimpses of Beulah." King also states that

> the artist, who is a visionary dreamer, briefly enters Beulah in order to be refreshed and to communicate its essence to fellow mortals; [but] in rare moments, mortals see into the world of Eden—closely allied to Jerusalem—and thus have a glimpse of eternity.[39]

The evidence in the biographies and in Blake's letters, however, suggests greater participation in fourfold vision on Blake's part. In other words, these materials show that Blake, as an artist, had more than a connection to the unconscious. As a psychic, he also had access to residents of the spirit world and they to him. If his creative work was a product of the entire fourfold spectrum of vision, then threefold vision was for him a more everyday state than some have acknowledged; and he must have been able to touch fourfold vision in much the same way as he is often thought to have touched the threefold.

First, a clarification of terms seems in order. "Mystic" and "psychic" are roughly synonymous, though there are significant differences for my study. According to the *OED*, a mystic is "any person who seeks by contemplation and self-surrender to obtain union with or absorption into God, or who believes in the spiritual apprehension of truths which are beyond the intellect; a person who has or seeks mystical experiences."[40] "Psychic" implies a broader spectrum of functioning than the mystic achieves: "A person who is regarded as particularly susceptible to supernatural or paranormal influence; a medium; a clairvoyant."[41] Both mystics and psychics see visions, but "psychic" encompasses many other gifts of the spirit, some of which have been touched on in previous chapters. Mysticism and psychic functioning can both be intra- and extra-psychic, but psychics have the greater connection to the spirit world. Both mystic and psychic can passively receive, but the psychic can also actively participate. Most importantly, the mystic's vision is primarily threefold, the psychic's primarily fourfold. With these differences in mind, let us have a fuller look at the previous criticism.

There is disagreement over the presence of fourfold vision in Blake's life and work. Frye devotes a "General Note" to Blake's mysticism, concluding that "if mysticism means primarily the vision of the prodigious and unthinkable metamorphosis of the human mind . . . then Blake is one of the mystics." The point is merely that Blake is interested in human psychology, not that he has a threefold mystical connection to the unconscious, and certainly not that he has a fourfold psychic connection to the spirit world. On the matter of mysticism, Denis Saurat more generously states that "Blake's desire drew him into mysticism, towards visionary reality, separating him from his fellow-men, because Milton's reason bade him try to mend this world; and Blake's desire attempted to create another." Saurat's remark suggests a combination of twofold vision's moral imperatives within human community and threefold vision's access to the unconscious. Even more inclusively, Witcutt believes that "the dream-country [threefold vision] was as real to Blake as the land of waking life." And G. E. Bentley frankly acknowledges evidence that points toward some degree of fourfold or spiritual vision: "All his life Blake communed with spirits, and this communion was his greatest joy"; "the spirits spoke to him when he was engaged on all his poems and drawings."[42]

Of course, other theories point to Blake's vision as either two- or threefold. Raine is the most conservative in describing a twofold vision:

> Blake's fiery vision has nothing to do with extra-sensory perception. The vision of which he speaks is the ability to see the real nature of the things that are before our eyes, of the people we know and meet here and now in this world, of all creation, of one another and of ourselves. It is not some other world, but this world that is not as the materialists suppose.[43]

No doubt her belief that Blake's work is derivative accounts to some extent for her reluctance to credit him with a higher type of vision. Beer seems to be somewhat more generous than Raine in crediting Blake with "developing an original form of self-hypnosis, which enabled him to meditate between his subconscious and his writing powers."[44] But earlier Beer states that Blake merely "enjoyed the power of eidetic vision, a condition in which human perception projects images so powerfully that the perceiver cannot easily tell the difference between them and images in the physical world." In Jungian terms, Beer's remark means that Blake is a "primitive," one who projects the contents of his unconscious mind onto reality and cannot tell the difference between the two. For example, Beer believes that the youthful Blake's reading of "Bunyan's accounts of 'the Shining Ones'" may have led to his famous vision of angels in a tree. Later Beer does admit "that perception is not bounded by the organs devoted to it," but his skepticism provides the more lasting impression.[45] Therefore, we are left to wonder if Blake's vision was primarily threefold or fourfold: did he mostly delve down into the collective unconscious, or could he frequently see into the spirit world? The biographies and letters provide a great deal of evidence that suggests the latter.

Here is Bentley's summary of Blake's earliest experiences:

> From his earliest childhood Blake saw visions. When he was four years old, God put his head to the window and set the child screaming, and once "his mother beat him for running in & saying that he saw the Prophet Ezekiel under a Tree in the Fields." Later, when he was eight or ten, one day as he was walking on Peckham Rye, near Dulwich Hill in the Surry countryside not far from his grandfather's residence in Rotherhithe . . . he saw "a tree filled with angels, bright angelic wings bespangling every bough like stars". When he told this story at home, it was "only through his mother's intercession . . . [*that he escaped*] a thrashing from his honest father, for telling a lie."

Later, Bentley cites Samuel Palmer's statement to confirm that Blake was in fact beaten by his father as punishment for his visions:

> When very young Blake used to go out for walks in the country & would frequently come home & describe the angels he had seen in the trees— His father was so angry at first with his accounts at first [*sic*] that he treated them as falsehoods & severely whipped him several times[.]

Fortunately, as George Richmond recalls, Blake found a more sympathetic audience than his reluctant mother and his harsh father:

> Blake spoke most tenderly of an old nurse[.] 'Twas to her he related his first vision—when a lad out walking at harvest time he saw some reapers on the fields & amongst them angels[;] he came home & told his friends but all of them laughed at him excepting this old nurse, who believed what he told her—He always spoke of her with great affection.[46]

Since Blake is wide awake when he experiences these visions, a threefold connection to the unconscious seems unlikely to account for "God" or the angels. The young fellow must actually be seeing spiritual beings in a fourfold way, and his experiences with his father and the old nurse may have particular significance for a reading of *Milton* as psychological allegory. Although it is Palamabron who is traditionally considered the Blake-figure in the poem, the brutal father and the sympathetic old nurse suggest a possible identification between Blake and the character Milton, as well as the root of Blake's disapproval of natural religion and his awareness that the male psyche needs a feminine complement. In a biographical context, the wrestling match reflects Blake's resentment at being punished by his father for having visionary experiences. The match thus includes a degree of wish fulfillment, for Milton remakes Urizen in ways that Blake himself could not remake his conservative father. To further the analogy, the uniting of Milton and Ololon reflects the mature Blake's affirmation of the feminine in the higher vision that the old nurse validates.

More directly relevant to the poem are the comments that Blake makes on the appearance of Milton's spirit. Ackroyd includes Blake's recollection that "Milton lov'd me in childhood & shew'd me his face."[47] The quotation is from "To My Dearest Friend, John Flaxman, these lines," in Blake's letter of September 12, 1800: "Angels stand round my Spirit in Heaven, the blessed of Heaven are my friends upon Earth. / . . . Now my lot in the Heavens is this, Milton lov'd me in childhood & shew'd me his face."[48] Ackroyd dismisses the statement's fourfold flavor by suggesting "that Milton's inspired example first visited him when young. The seventeenth-century poet was in any case 'in the air' of the period. "[49] In its full context, however, Blake's remark about his childhood strengthens the case for a fourfold interpretation. Not only is the young Blake fond of Milton's poetry; but Milton evidently shows his face in a more literal way, as also seems to be the case later in Blake's life. Saurat quotes Crabb Robinson's recollection of Blake's statement on the matter:

> I have seen him as a youth and as an old man with a long, flowing beard. He came lately as an old man—he said he came to ask a favour of me. He said he had committed an error in his *Paradise Lost*, which he wanted me to correct, in a poem or a picture. But I declined. I said I had my own duties to perform. . . . He wished me to expose the falsehood of his doctrine taught in the *Paradise Lost*, that sexual intercourse arose out of the Fall. Now that cannot be, for no good can spring out of evil.[50]

The unbelievable part is not that Blake would see an apparition but that the spectral Milton would misremember the scene in his own poem where Adam and Eve make love before the fall.[51] Milton's emphasis on chastity well into his adult years was a point of contention with Blake; but the strange inaccuracy belies Blake's more fundamental concern with Milton's religion, emphasis on reason and the classics, and impact on eighteenth-century English thought.

Another fascinating instance of fourfold vision occurred as the young Blake was sitting in an abbey. Desiree Hirst tells the story:

> They [visionary experiences] were repeated during his time in the Abbey when he was sometimes actually locked in the great church after hours and once suddenly saw it "fill with a great procession of monks and priests, choristers and censer-bearers, and his entranced ear heard the chant of plain-song and chorale, while the vaulted roof trembled to the sound of organ music". This kind of time traveling proved not unusual in Blake's life.[52]

Hirst's suggestion that Blake was seeing an actual service taking place in the past resonates with a similar phenomenon in *Milton.* Grimes believes that "the assimilation of Milton and then Los to Blake himself is recognition that a figure from the past, a poetic character, and a man of the present are not sealed off from one another in visionary perception." That is a reasonable statement, but Grimes then issues a caveat against "jumping to the fallacious conclusion that imaginative time is reversible or that sequence is being denied. Blake is not attempting to wreck the fabric of chronology."[53] Blake is not denying that time seems linear to the human mind; however, he *is* attempting to enact in *Milton* the idea that one moment contains all moments—that all time is simultaneous. The clock ticks on Earth, time becomes relative as one journeys into the unconscious, but God sees all times as one. Clearly, both the vision in the abbey and the uniting of Milton with Blake suggest that a psychic capable of three- and fourfold vision can veer from the flight path of time's arrow. Hirst's conclusion, however, is not the only possibility. There are at least two other ways to interpret the young Blake's visionary lock-in, and both strengthen the sense of four fold vision. He could have perceived the psychic imprint of years' worth of services, or he may have witnessed in real time a service taking place in the astral version of the abbey.

Like the biographies, the letters support the view that Blake achieved a fourfold vision, one that was both fully conscious and extrapsychic. In fact, the letters provide an overview not just of Blake's visionary experiences but also of his cosmology and belief system, with special emphasis on the three years at Felpham and the composition of *Milton*. Blake's fourfold vision continued and was part of his daily life during the three years when he and his wife stayed in Felpham. First and foremost, Blake is convinced of the reality of the spirit world. On September 21, 1800, he considers Flaxman to be his "Friend & companion from Eternity" and mentions "our ancient days before this Earth appear'd in its vegetated mortality to my mortal vegetated eyes."[54] The statement resonates nicely with *Jerusalem*, plate 77: "Imagination [is] the real & eternal World of which this Vegetable Universe is but a faint shadow, & in which we shall live in our Eternal or Imaginative Bodies, when these Vegetable Mortal bodies are no more" (E 231). So there are physical and spiritual worlds, as well as physical and spiritual bodies; and death is a transition out of the physical world/body into a spiritual dimension. Blake's personal experience of seeing spirits gave him great confidence in the afterlife, as his consolatory letter to Hayley attests on May 6, 1800:

> I am very sorry for your immense loss [the death of Hayley's son, Thomas Alphonso Hayley, four days earlier], which is a repetition of what all feel in this valley of misery & happiness mixed. . . . I know that our deceased friends are more really with us than when they were apparent to our mortal part. Thirteen years ago I lost a brother [Robert, his youngest brother, who had died in February 1787] & with his spirit I converse daily & hourly in the Spirit & See him in my remembrance in the regions of my Imagination. I hear his advice & even now write from his Dictate. Forgive me for Expressing to you my Enthusiasm which I wish all to partake of Since it is to me a Source of Immortal Joy: even in this world by it I am the companion of Angels. May you continue to be so more & more & to be more & more perswaded that every Mortal loss is an Immortal Gain. The Ruins of Time builds Mansions in Eternity.[55]

Whereas Blake is capable of glimpses into the spirit world as the previous letter suggests, it is not until his own death that a full and permanent fourfold vision takes hold. George Richmond records the event in a letter to Samuel Palmer on August 15, 1827:

> Lest you should not have heard of the Death of Mr Blake I have Written this to inform you—He died on Sunday night [12 August] at 6 Oclock in a most glorious manner. He said He was going to that Country he had all

> His life wished to see & expressed Himself Happy, hoping for Salvation through Jesus Christ—Just before he died His Countenance became fair. His eyes Brighten'd and He burst out into Singing of the things he saw in Heaven. In truth He Died like a Saint as a person who was standing by Him Observed.[56]

In between pre-existence and death, Blake retains a psychic connection to spirit, which furthers his poetry and visual art. His mention of writing from his brother's dictation suggests that he receives nonphysical assistance in his work. Bentley quotes him as stating, "'My Angel Artist in the skies[,] / Thou mayst inspire & control / a Failing Brother's Hand & eyes / or temper his eccentric Soul.'"[57] Blake receives aid, but the "Angel Artist" may be either an actual angel, a spirit like Robert, or Blake's own pre-birth spirit; for as he tells Flaxman on September 21, 1800,

> I am more famed in Heaven for my works than I could well concieve. In my Brain are studies & Chambers fill'd with books & pictures of old, which I wrote & painted in ages of Eternity before my mortal life; & those works are the delight & Study of Archangels.[58]

In general, "the Spiritual World" and "Visions of Eternity," are a source of his creative work, as he states in his letter to Trusler on August 23, 1799.[59] *Milton*, Blake suggests in his July 6, 1803 letter to Butts, has such a source. The poem is

> a Sublime Allegory, which is now perfectly completed into a Grand Poem. I may praise it, since I dare not pretend to be any other than the Secretary; the Authors are in Eternity. I consider it as the Grandest Poem that this World Contains. Allegory address'd to the Intellectual powers, while it is altogether hidden from the Corporeal Understanding, is My Definition of the Most Sublime Poetry.[60]

The statement is not unlike Jesus's intent in his parables, Jung's notion that a text reveals its meaning over time, or Loren Eiseley's idea of the "concealed essay, in which personal anecdote was allowed gently to bring under observation thoughts of a more purely scientific nature."[61] The motif of dictation comes up as well in an earlier letter to Trusler on August 16, 1799:

> But I hope that none of my Designs will be destitute of Infinite Particulars which will present themselves to the Contemplator. And tho' I call them Mine, I know that they are not Mine, being of the same opinion with Milton when he says That the Muse visits his Slumbers & awakes & governs his Song when Morn purples the East, & being also in the predicament of that prophet who says: I cannot go beyond the command of the Lord, to speak good or bad.[62]

His friends' comments support the conclusion that Blake is reporting straightforwardly on his composition process. In his August 26, 1799 letter to George Cumberland, he quotes Trusler:

> *Your Fancy*, from what I have seen of it, & I have seen variety at Mr Cumberland's, seems to be in the other world or the World of Spirits, which accords not with my Intentions, which, whilst living in This World, Wish to follow *the Nature of it*.[63]

In the same vein, R. H. Cromek writes the following to Blake in May of 1807:

> I *have imposed on myself* yet more grossly in believing you to be one altogether abstracted from this world, holding converse with the world of spirits! simple, unoffending, a combination of the *serpent* and the *dove*. I really blush when I reflect how I have been cheated in this respect.[64]

If Blake did not have psychic ability to touch fourfold vision and to direct his psychic perceptions into art, it is unlikely that he would have elicited Cromek's envy. When Blake claims, "I converse with my friends in Eternity, See Visions, Dream Dreams & prophecy & speak Parables unobserv'd & at liberty from the Doubts of other Mortals," as he writes to Butts on April 25, 1803, he means it literally.[65]

Felpham certainly appears to have facilitated Blake's visionary experiences, as he indicates to Flaxman on September 21, 1800, at the beginning of the Blakes' stay there.

> Felpham is a sweet place for Study, because it is more Spiritual than London. Heaven opens here on all sides her golden Gates; her windows are not obstructed by vapours; voices of Celestial inhabitants are more distinctly heard, & their forms more distinctly seen, & my Cottage is also a Shadow of their houses.[66]

To Butts he writes on October 2, 1800, "Receive from me a return of verses, such as Felpham produces by me, tho' not such as she produces by her eldest Son [Hayley]." These verses include the lines "My Eyes did Expand / Into regions of air / . . . Into regions of fire," as well as "My eyes more & more / Like a Sea without shore / Continue Expanding."[67] It appears that Felpham is conducive to opening "the doors of perception" (E 39)—to spiritual experience and the writing of poetry. Nearing the end of his time by the sea, Blake comments on the composition of *Milton* in his letter to Butts on April 25, 1803.

> But none can know the Spiritual Acts of my three years' Slumber on the banks of the Ocean, unless he has seen them in the spirit, or unless he should read My long Poem descriptive of those Acts; for I have in these three years composed an immense number of verses on One Grand

> Theme, Similar to Homer's Iliad or Milton's Paradise Lost, the Persons & Machinery intirely new to the Inhabitants of Earth (some of the Persons Excepted). I have written this Poem from immediate Dictation, twelve or sometimes twenty or thirty lines at a time, without Premeditation & even against my Will; the Time it has taken in writing was thus render'd Non Existent, & an immense Poem Exists which seems to be the Labour of a long Life, all produc'd without Labour or Study. I mention this to shew you what I think the Grand Reason of my being brought down here.[68]

In a Jungian context, the setting "on the banks of the Ocean" suggests that Blake's poem participates in the visionary mode of composition, which taps into the oceanic collective unconscious. Indeed, the sea is Jung's key image for the deep unconscious, as demonstrated in chapter 3. Yet Blake insists that *Milton*'s composition is not psychological but spiritual, that he touched the fourfold realm of pure spirit and managed to transcribe what he witnessed and experienced onto paper. Blake receives "immediate Dictation . . . without Premeditation," and "twelve or sometimes twenty or thirty lines at a time" come to him in what *Milton* calls "a pulsation of the artery" (E 126), the moment of artistic inspiration. Blake's long poem is more *received* than created. Obviously, the language echoes the poet Milton's assistance from his

> Celestial Patroness, who deignes
> Her nightly visitation unimplor'd,
> And dictates to me slumbring, or inspires
> Easie my unpremeditated Verse.[69]

That the resulting poem, a new kind of psycho-spiritual epic, is the "Grand Reason" or purpose for spending three years in Felpham implies that the unborn spirit who became William Blake may have planned his life's experiences in ways that he is not allowed to remember but can recognize in retrospect. Blake came "down here" not only to Felpham from London but also to Earth from Eternity.

If there were only one account of Blake's psychic experience, it would probably be a metaphor for a conventional composition process. But repeated references to "dictation," angelic visitations, visionary experience, and the corroboration of friends constitute a preponderance of evidence that Blake was capable of regular fourfold vision. Whereas other critics will grant that he has a fairly penetrating threefold vision into the collective unconscious, it seems obvious that he also has an extensive fourfold vision of the spirit world that transcends the ability to access archetypal images from the collective unconscious. He is not just a visionary poet but also a *psychic* poet. If *Milton* is the product of significant high-level vision, it stands to reason that it may include a cosmology that is compatible with conclusions about psi in previous chapters—conclusions that follow from the unity of all things via the One Mind. It is to this possibility that we now turn.

Ways of seeing in *Milton*

Near the end of book 2, Blake leaves no doubt in the reader's mind that he is against deism/natural religion/materialism. Before the union of Milton and Ololon, these lines appear: "this Newtonian Phantasm / This Voltaire & Rousseau: this Hume & Gibbon & Bolingbroke / This Natural Religion! this impossible absurdity" (E 141). Here is a summary of Howard's interpretation of the passage: Bacon (science); Locke (empiricism); Newton (mathematical laws); Gibbon ("sneering skepticism"); Bolingbroke, Voltaire, and Rousseau (natural religion). All of these figures represent "delusions spawned by the selfhood to control man in society"; Blake is against the "rationalism in materialism" that they represent.[70] Part of the purpose of Milton's return to Earth, then, is to underscore the insufficiency of such single vision and to correct errors in the realm of twofold vision. The latter is accomplished partly through Jungian individuation played out on a cosmic scale—Milton integrates his shadow and anima by curbing his ego/persona in favor of compensatory balance. But the poem is not merely intellectual, moral, and psychological; it is also quantum and metaphysical. As a direct reflection of the fourfold nature of its author's vision, *Milton* it is the kind of poem created by an author who has cleansed the doors of his perception and is capable of seeing the universe in a grain of sand. As a result, many of the poem's statements about the mind and the cosmos are in sync with insights from this book's introduction on the convergence of Jungian thought and the new physics.

The problem of perception. Blake states in plate 36 that his purpose in writing "all these Visions" is "to display Natures cruel holiness: the deceits of Natural Religion" (E 137), which convince persons to believe that only sensory data are true. In single vision, the senses become the outer boundary of perception:

> The Eye of Man [is] a little narrow orb closd up & dark
> Scarcely beholding the great light conversing with the Void
> The Ear, a little shell in small volutions shutting out
> All melodies & comprehending only Discord and Harmony.
> (E 99)

Paradoxically, the senses' purpose is to *restrict* perception and all but prohibit vision: "These [are] the Visions of Eternity / But we see only as it were the hem of their garments / When with our vegetable eyes we view these wond'rous Visions" (E 123). Other passages point to the way the single vision of the senses curbs or entirely blocks human potential "now [that] the Starry Heavens are fled from the mighty limbs of Albion" (E 100):

> Every thing in Eternity shines by its own Internal light: but thou
> Darkenest every Internal light with the arrows of thy quiver
> Bound up in the horns of Jealousy to a deadly fading Moon,
> And Ocalython [Rintrah's Emanation] binds the Sun into a Jealous Globe

> That every thing is fixd Opake without Internal light
> So Los lamented over Satan, who triumphant divided the Nations.
> (E 104)

The word "divided" suggests division not only among nations but also within the psyche. As the poet laments a bit earlier on the same page, "The Separation was terrible." As well, the passage prefigures Blake's statement in plate 13 about the "Two Limits: first of Opacity, then of Contraction[;] / Opacity was named Satan, contraction was named Adam" (E 107). Contraction refers to the way in which the physical senses close off the higher types of vision. The results include single vision within the limitations of the physical senses and the shortcomings of natural religion. Bloom's equation of the two in the phrase "materiality or opaqueness" obscures the relationship that Blake intends.[71] Contraction (materiality, bodily life, Adam) limits vision to sensory data (opacity), and then the emphasis on reason over Imagination leads to error (Satan, natural religion). Even Blake himself feels the effects of contraction: "O how can I with my gross tongue that cleaveth to the dust, / Tell of the Four-fold Man, in starry numbers fitly orderd / Or how can I with my cold hand of clay!" (E 114). Yet, in multiple ways, *Milton* describes exactly that: a fourfold understanding of reality. We have already seen, in the previous section, that Blake-as-artist touches on fourfold vision in his composition of the poem; now the task is to chart the implications of fourfold vision for its content.

Space-time and the infinite. "Los is by mortals nam'd time[;] Enitharmon is nam'd space," Blake states in plate 24 (E121). That the character Los represents time, and his Emanation Enitharmon space, suggests that time and space are not really separate or that they are, as physicists would say, "relative." The following passage on space-time contrasts the limits of the senses and of scientific investigation with the higher reality that the visionary understands.

> As to that false appearance which appears to the reasoner,
> As of a Globe rolling thro Voidness, it is a delusion of Ulro
> The Microscope knows not of this nor the Telescope. they alter
> The ratio of the Spectators Organs but leave Objects untouched
> For every Space larger than a red Globule of Mans blood
> Is visionary: and is created by the Hammer of Los
> And every Space smaller than a Globule of man's blood. opens
> Into Eternity of which this vegetable Earth is but a shadow:
> The red Globule is the unwearied Sun by Los created
> To measure Time and Space to mortal Men.
> (E 127)

Instruments enable a scientist to make small things appear larger, but this alteration in the "ratio of the Spectators Organs" does not allow one to see an object's essential nature. The truth that scientific method obscures is that even the smallest imaginable unit—"every Space smaller than a Globule of man's blood"—contains the whole of creation, as hologram theory asserts. Paananen rightly notes that "infinity awaits us in either direction—as every twentieth-century scientist knows."[72] The passage thus resonates with the imperative in "Auguries of Innocence" that we must attempt

> To see a World in a Grain of Sand
> And a Heaven in a Wild Flower
> Hold Infinity in the palm of your hand
> And Eternity in an hour[.]
>
> (E 490)

In the following passage from *Milton*, there is a connection between these lines from "Auguries" and *The Marriage of Heaven and Hell*'s proverb about perception: "If the doors of perception were cleansed every thing would appear to man as it is: infinite" (E 39).

> Seest thou the little winged fly, smaller than a grain of sand?
> It has a heart like three; a brain open to heaven & hell,
> Withinside wondrous & expansive; its gates are not clos'd,
> I hope thine are not; hence it clothes itself in rich array;
> Hence thou art cloth'd with human beauty O thou mortal man.
> Seek not thy heavenly father then beyond the skies:
> There Chaos dwells & ancient Night & Og & Anak old:
> For every human heart has gates of brass & bars of adamant,
> Which few dare unbar because dread Og & Anak guard the gates
> Terrific! and each mortal brain is walld and moated round
> Within; and Og & Anak watch here; here is the Seat
> Of Satan in its Webs; for in brain and heart and loins
> Gates open behind Satans Seat to the City of Golgonooza
> Which is the spiritual fourfold London, in the loins of Albion[.]
>
> (E 114)

Here the fly stands in for the grain of sand, and the "doors of perception" that need cleansing have become closed gates. The tiny fly's openness to infinity ("heaven & hell") contrasts with the human heart and brain, which are confined by gates, walls, and moats, and are guarded by Satan's henchmen, the giants Og & Anak. Contraction and opacity thus limit our vision; but if we open the gates, we will see "the City of Golgonooza," Blake's holy city of art, not merely the hem of the garment but the "rich array." Whereas Satan promotes limited vision, heart and brain are capable of higher vision because they are already infinite, like the fly and the grain of sand. Nor should we seek God "beyond the skies" (perhaps a veiled allusion to the telescope) because "All deities reside in the human breast" (E 38). To go *out there*, we must explore *in here* because the whole universe is folded within us.

After entering Blake's soul, Los makes the following statement that furthers the argument about time:

> I am that Shadowy Prophet who Six Thousand Years ago
> Fell from my station in the Eternal bosom. Six Thousand Years
> Are finished. I return! both Time & Space obey my will.
> I in Six Thousand Years walk up and down: for not one Moment
> Of Time is Lost, nor one Event of Space unpermanent.
> But all remain: every fabric of Six Thousand Years
> Remains permanent: tho' on the Earth where Satan
> Fell, and was cut off all things vanish & are seen no more
> They vanish not from me & mine, we guard them first & last
> The generations of men run on in the tide of Time
> But leave their destind lineaments permanent for ever & ever.
>
> (E 117)

As previously noted, human beings perceive time as an arrow; but its true circular nature means that the past is always available. In keeping with that geometrical metaphor, the passage states that all times are simultaneous and that nothing is ever lost to the mind's eye: "for not one Moment / Of time is Lost, nor one Event of Space unpermanent / But all remain." Los is expressing the basic premise of remote viewing, which is that all information is eternally present and can be accessed by a mind that slips the bonds of contraction and opacity.

The provenance of art. Just as the events of *Milton*, though described in linear fashion, are actually simultaneous (witness, for example, the multiple times Milton enters Blake's left foot), so also poetic inspiration takes place instantaneously:

> Every Time less than a pulsation of the artery
> Is equal in its period & value to Six Thousand Years
> For in this Period the Poets Work is Done: and all the Great
> Events of Time start forth & are concievd in such a Period
> Within a Moment: a Pulsation of the Artery.
>
> (E 127)

According to this passage, there is no difference between a momentary pulsation of an artery and six thousand years: they are one and the same; one moment contains all moments. Therein the Sons of Los create by "Giving to airy nothing a name and a habitation / Delightful! with bounds to the Infinite putting off the Indefinite / Into most holy forms of Thought: (such is the power of inspiration)" (E 125). Blake echoes Shakespeare's statement on artistic creation, which is cast ironically as Duke Theseus's negative description of the poet: the Duke's critique is actually Shakespeare's apology for poetry. (Blake could have accomplished something similar by allowing Gibbon skeptical remarks that actually support the

Imagination.) The allusion to Shakespeare affirms Blake's sense that *Milton* was dictated to him by authors in the spirit world. Art comes from beyond the physical world, and it takes at least three fold vision to bring it into physical reality. Here is the excerpt from *A Midsummer Night's Dream*:

> And as imagination bodies forth
> The forms of things unknown, the poet's pen
> Turns them to shapes and gives to airy nothing
> A local habitation and a name.
> (5.1.14–17)[73]

The key word is "forms," which parallels Jung's archetypes. Blake and Shakespeare are describing the visionary mode of artistic production in which art comes from the collective unconscious and enters the poet's psyche in a moment of passive inspiration. Jung believes that "something suprapersonal . . . transcends our understanding to the same degree that the author's consciousness was in abeyance during the process of creation" (*CW* 15, 116–75). This process—aided by the imagination—is threefold vision; a more direct sense of dictation from a specific spirit (Robert, for example) is fourfold. *Milton* suggests that art is the product of both types; and in each case the moment of inspiration transcends linear time.

We are multiple bodies. Opening the heart and the brain to perceive the infinite is possible because we have within us different bodies—etheric, emotional, mental, causal—and *Milton* touches on a number of them.[74] Blake's description of Milton's descent in plate 15

> Like as a Polypus [Latin, octopus] that vegetates beneath the deep!
> They saw his Shadow vegetated underneath the Couch
> Of death: for when he entered into his Shadow: Himself:
> His real and immortal Self: was as appeard to those
> Who dwell in immortality, as One sleeping on a couch
> Of gold
> (E 109)

describes the descent of the Spectre—the part that needs reforging—into a physical body, while Milton's "real and immortal Self" remains in Eternity. Although what descends is hard to fit into a metaphysical box, it seems clear that what remains in eternity is the causal body or soul and that what descends participates in the emotions and intellect.

The poem's astral dynamics become clearer in plate 26 (E 123–24), the most metaphysical section in the entire work. Here are the things that the "vegetable eyes" cannot perceive. First, souls travel back and forth between Eternity and the Earth. There are "Two Gates thro which all Souls descend," each like a two-way street: "The Souls descending to the Body, wail on the right hand / Of Los; &

those deliverd from the Body, on the left hand." Souls come and go between Eternity and the Earth. Sometimes, though, the Spectre blocks efficient transit:

> Souls incessant wail, being piteous Passions & Desires
> With neither lineament nor form but like to watry clouds
> The Passions & Desires descend upon the hungry winds
> For such alone Sleepers remain meer passion & appetite.

Here disembodied souls are totally consumed by their unchecked desires, like those in Dante's second circle or Monroe's "flesh pile." Blake then notes that "as the Spectres choose their affinities / So they are born on Earth, & every Class is determinate / But not by Natural but by Spiritual power alone." In other words, souls choose their bodies and life situations depending on what their individuation requires. A final statement—"And every Natural Effect has a Spiritual Cause, and Not / A Natural: for a Natural Cause only seems, it is a Delusion / Of Ulro: & a ratio of the perishing Vegetable Memory"—suggests at least that earthly events signify something beyond themselves. If perception is cleansed, then consciousness registers the needs of the unconscious and the imperatives of the spirit. Human life is a matter of spiritual purpose. (The passage probably does not refer to the causal body, but "Spiritual Cause" resonates tantalizingly.)

From eternity to Earth. A bit like the souls that transit through Gates, Milton descends through a trans-dimensional vortex.

> The nature of infinity is this: That every thing has its
> Own Vortex; and when once a traveler thro Eternity.
> Has passd that Vortex, he percieves it roll backward behind
> His path, into a globe itself infolding; like a sun:
> Or like a moon, or like a universe of starry majesty,
> While he keeps onwards in his wondrous journey on the earth
> Or like a human form, a friend with whom he livd benevolent.
> As the eye of man views both the east & west encompassing
> Its vortex; and the north & south, with all their starry host;
> Also the rising sun & setting moon he views surrounding
> His corn-fields and his valleys of five hundred acres square
> Thus is the earth one infinite plane, and not as apparent
> To the weak traveler confin'd beneath the moony shade.
> Thus is the heaven a vortex passd already, and the earth
> A vortex not yet pass'd by the traveler thro' Eternity.
>
> (E 109)

The vortex is the vehicle for Milton's Spectre's return to "the Sea of Time & Space" (E 110). Frye calls it "a spiral or cone of existence," describing it as reverse perspective, with the apex of the cone of vision pointing away from us.

> Blake says that everything in eternity has what he calls a "vortex" (perhaps rather a vortex-ring), a spiral or cone of existence. When we focus both eyes on one object, say a book, we create an angle of vision opening into our minds with the apex pointing away from us. The book therefore has a vortex of existence opening into its mental reality within our minds. When Milton descends from eternity to time, he finds that he has to pass through the apex of his cone of eternal vision, which is like trying to see a book from the book's point of view; the Lockian-conception of the real book as outside the mind on which the vision of the fallen world is based. This turns him inside out, and from his new perspective the cone rolls back and away from him in the form of a globe. That is why we are surrounded with a universe of remote globes, and are unable to see that the earth is "one infinite plane." But in eternity the perceiving mind or body is omnipresent, and hence these globes in eternity are inside that body.[75]

These remarks are at least as difficult to understand as the lines Frye seeks to explicate, but one aspect seems out of sync with Blake's metaphysics. The task of higher vision is not to connect the mind and some object like a book but for the mind to see the object's connection to infinity. Milton's descent enacts the way in which a cleansed perception can open to the infinite through even a miniscule object like a grain of sand. The vortex's two functions—as metaphor for perception and as transport for Milton from Eternity to Earth—come together in Mark Lussier's belief that *Milton* is compatible with quantum theory. Arguing that Blake's vortex is a black hole, the critic asserts perceptual cleansing:

> one reading of the vortex passage leads inward into perceptual events in generation designed to open up onto eternity, extending from consciousness to cosmos. However, the poem is equally concerned with the passage from eternity, a passage into time and space as "eternal consciousness" becomes embodied.[76]

This analysis of Blake's vortex is exactly right.

Fourfold vision. I have been arguing that Blake's vision regularly extends beyond the collective unconscious into the realm of pure spirit and that *Milton*'s composition and content reflect the poet's fourfold vision. A psychic like Blake has access to all levels of vision, even if he cannot fully dwell in the afterlife until the moment of his transition. A final passage from plate 35 confirms the idea that fourfold vision is more widely achievable than previously assumed, and it does so by a surprising reversal: *Immortals* share a degree of perceptual limitation and the need for annihilation.

> So spake Ololon in reminiscence astonishd, but they [Daughters of Beulah]

> Could not behold Golgonooza without passing the Polypus
> A wondrous journey not passable by Immortal feet, & none
> But the Divine Savior can pass it without annihilation.
> For Golgoonoza cannot be seen till having passd the Polypus
> It is viewed on all sides round by a Four-fold Vision
> Or till you become Mortal & Vegetable in Sexuality
> Then you behold its mighty Spires & Domes of ivory & gold.
>
> (E 135)

Fourfold vision is required to "behold Golgonooza," the holy city of art; but one must first pass the Polypus: "for every Man born is joined / Within into One mighty Polypus, and this Polypus is Orc," or in Damon's words, "the hatred men bear each other" (E 127).[77] The polypus is fallen humanity, "society in a fallen state."[78] So passing the Polypus represents a soul's immersion in "the Sea of Time and Space"—a trip through the vortex to become human. Unless one is Jesus, imaginative vision requires either annihilation—individuation, the integration of ego/persona (negation)—or sexual activity on the part of those who would achieve fourfold vision. Beer states that "the fourfold vision of the artist can give him a sight of the heavenly city," and he agrees that it can be "glimpsed—if only momentarily—in sexual activity."[79] Sexual activity fires the imagination, as Golgonooza's masculine Spires and feminine Domes imply. What, then, is required to achieve fourfold vision? The passage suggests an answer: becoming fully human through complementary processes—individuation and sexual activity. Although the artist is more likely to achieve such vision than an ordinary person, the potential for all four types of vision is part of our human makeup. Ultimately, Blake's purpose is not to sequester fourfold or even threefold vision in the province of the artist but to suggest that the process of individuation, such as the self-annihilation that Milton undertakes, can lead the nation to a higher state of vision because everyone participates in the One Mind.

Notes

1 Northrop Frye, *Fearful Symmetry: A Study of William Blake* (Boston, MA: Beacon, 1947); and Harold Bloom, *Blake's Apocalypse: A Study in Poetic Argument* (Garden City, NY: Doubleday, 1963).

2 Frye, *Fearful Symmetry*, 345.

3 Kathleen Raine, *Blake and the New Age* (London, UK: George Allen & Unwin, 1979), n.p. The quotation appears in the Foreword.

4 Laurence Binyon, *The Drawings and Engravings of William Blake*, ed. C. Geoffrey Holme (London, UK: Studio, 1922). Binyon includes only three illustrations from *Milton*: the first depicts a pi-shaped stone structure and includes text from plate 6 ("the Hammer of Los"); the second includes text from plate 36 ("Ololon step'd into the Polypus") and shows Blake's cottage at Felpham; the third shows a male figure lying unconscious on a rock, with a female figure embracing him (Albion and Jerusalem and/or Milton and Ololon).

5 *MDR*, 195–96.

6 Milton Oswin Percival, *William Blake's Circle of Destiny* (New York: Octagon, 1938).

7 The earliest study is W. P. Witcutt's *Blake: A Psychological Study* (1946; repr., Port Washington, NY: Kennikat, 1966). John Howard says much that resonates meaningfully with Jungian psychology in *Blake's* Milton*: A Study in the Selfhood* (Cranbury, NJ: Associated University Presses, 1976). Kathleen Raine frequently draws connections to Jung in *Blake and the New Age*, but she is more directly Jungian in "C. G. Jung: A Debt Acknowledged," in *Jungian Literary Criticism*, ed. Richard P. Sugg (Evanston, IL: Northwestern University Press, 1992), 167–76. Finally, Harold F. Brooks's three essays are also directly Jungian: "Blake and Jung: Blake's Myth of the Four Zoas and Jung's Picture of the Psyche," *The Aligarh Critical Miscellany* 1, no. 1 (1988): 47–74; "Blake and Jung II: The Fall into Disintegration," *The Aligarh Critical Miscellany* 2, no. 2 (1989): 158–74; and "Blake and Jung III: Reintegration," *The Aligarh Critical Miscellany* 5, no. 1 (1992): 41–89. Brooks's first article is sometimes referred to as "Blake and Jung I."

8 Raine, *Blake and the New Age*, 8–9, 13, and 16. Blake's time at "Pars' drawing-school"; his apprenticeship to an engraver; and his study of art, architecture, mythology, the Bible, Gnosticsm, alchemy, and Caballa (the last three shared with Jung) may account for a good number of Blake's "visions." She also credits Swedenborg for Blake's idea that God or the Infinite lies within us.

9 Brooks, "Blake and Jung II," 160.

10 Brooks, "Blake and Jung III," 67–68.

11 Witcutt, *Blake*, 24–25 and 40. The lines of verse appear in Blake's letter to Thomas Butts of November 22, 1802. See Geoffrey Keynes, ed., *The Letters of William Blake* (New York: Macmillan, 1956), 77.

12 Wittcut, *Blake*, 18.

13 S. Foster Damon, *A Blake Dictionary: The Ideas and Symbols of William Blake*, rev. ed. (Hanover, NH: University Press of New England, 1988), 42.

14 Jack Lindsay, *William Blake: His Life and Work* (New York: George Braziller, 1979), 181.

15 Of course, Blake indulges in some black-and-white thinking here. Milton obviously took major inspiration from the Bible, not just the classics, as Blake surely knew. He would later create illustrations for "On the Morning of Christ's Nativity" and *Paradise Lost*. In the former poem, Milton even banishes the classical gods.

16 William Wordsworth, "The World Is Too Much with Us," in *English Romantic Writers*, ed. David Perkins, 2nd ed. (Fort Worth, TX: Harcourt, 1995), 341.

17 Peter Ackroyd, *Blake* (New York: Knopf, 1996), 311.

18 Harold Bloom, *The Visionary Company: A Reading of English Romantic Poetry*, rev. ed. (Ithaca, NY: Cornell University Press, 1971), 101; Denis Saurat, *Blake and Milton* (New York: Russell, 1965), 109; Bloom, *Blake's Apocalypse*, 325; and Damon, *A Blake Dictionary*, 309.

19 Keynes, *Letters*, 85.

20 Ibid., 89.

21 Bloom, *Blake's Apocalypse*, 309.

22 Frye, *Fearful Symmetry*, 333.

23 Bloom, *Blake's Apocalypse*, 312. Bloom considers Satan to be "error incarnate," the "history of religion," and worldly status (*Blake's Apocalypse*, 320 and 354; and *Visionary Company*, 100). Critics also consider Satan in the following terms. For Frye, Satan represents "the consolidation of error," "moral virtue," "passive conformity," "the spirit of inertia," "established religion, philosophies, and social conditions," the commandments, and worldly prosperity (*Fearful Symmetry*, 333). Victor N. Paananen considers him to be "Newton's Pantocrator" or the materialist's limiting view of the universe (*William Blake* [Boston: Twayne, 1977], 121). Mona Wilson holds that Satan is "Reason as Error" (*The Life of William Blake*, ed. Geoffrey Keynes, new ed. [New York: Oxford University Press, 1971], 200). For a helpful reading of Elect, Reprobate, and Redeemed, see Eric G. Wilson, *My Business Is to Create: Blake's Infinite Writing*

(Iowa City: University of Iowa Press, 2011), 40–41. Perhaps Blake took some inspiration in establishing Palamabron as the harrower from an everyday sight at Felpham. He notes in his letter to Butts on September 23, 1800 that "a roller & two harrows lie before my window" (Keynes, *Letters*, 53).

24 Bloom, *Blake's Apocalypse*, 311.
25 Lindsay, *William Blake*, 179.
26 Bloom states:

> The Spectre in Milton is everything that impeded his lifelong quest to achieve a societal and artistic form that would unify man in the image of God. The Spectre is therefore every impulse towards dualism, which must include the impulse that shaped the God and Satan of *Paradise Lost* as antithetical beings, and then assigned so much of human energy and desire to Satan.
>
> (*Blake's Apocalypse*, 309)

27 Ronald L. Grimes, *The Divine Imagination: William Blake's Major Prophetic Visions*, ATLA Monograph Series No. 1 (Metuchen, NJ: Scarecrow Press and the American Library Association, 1972), 29.
28 Keynes, *Letters*, 155.
29 For a similar recognition of error, see W. B. Yeats's "The Lake Isle of Innisfree," where the speaker says, "I will arise and go now" (*Selected Poems and Two Plays of William Butler Yeats*, ed. M. L. Rosenthal [New York: Macmillan, 1962], 12–13).
30 For left vs. right, see, for example, Grimes, *The Divine Imagination*, 24; and M. Wilson, *The Life of William Blake*, 194. Damon perhaps overstates a bit in suggesting that left signifies Urizen (*A Blake Dictionary*, 349).
31 Bloom, *Blake's Apocalypse*, 329.
32 Ibid. 329; and Paananen, *William Blake*, 125.
33 My reading of the left foot/sandal episode is supported by Bloom, *Blake's Apocalypse*, 331; Frye, *Fearful Symmetry*, 338; Paananen, *William Blake*, 126; and Joseph Anthony Wittreich, Jr., *Angel of Apocalypse: Blake's Idea of Milton* (Madison: University of Wisconsin Press, 1975), 250.
34 Damon, *Blake Dictionary*, 385.
35 Keynes, *Letters*, 79; and John Beer, *William Blake: A Literary Life* (New York: Palgrave Macmillan, 2007), 126.
36 James King, *William Blake: His Life* (New York: St. Martin's, 1991), 167–68.
37 Grimes, *The Divine Imagination*, 26.
38 Keynes, *Letters*, 77.
39 King, *William Blake*, 172 and 167–68.
40 *OED*, s.v. "Mystic," def. 2.
41 Ibid., s.v. "Psychic," def. B.1.a.
42 Frye, *Fearful Symmetry*, 432; Saurat, *Blake and Milton*, 137; Witcutt, *Blake*, 106–7; G. E. Bentley, Jr., *The Stranger from Paradise: A Biography of William Blake* (New Haven, CT: Yale University Press, 2001), 100 and 166.
43 Raine, *Blake and the New Age*, 25. On page 26, she rightly quotes Blake's letter to Trussler of August 23, 1799, which elegantly supports her point: "This World Is a World of imagination & Vision"; therefore, "to the eyes of the Man of Imagination, Nature is Imagination itself. As a man is, So he Sees. . . . To Me This World is all One continued Vision of Fancy or Imagination" (Keynes, *Letters*, 35–36).
44 Beer, *William Blake*, 140.
45 Ibid., 5, 10, and 26–27. A parallel experience occurs at Felpham. Bentley notes that while there Blake saw "'trees & fields full of Fairy elves'" and quotes his statement about seeing a fairy funeral (*The Stranger*, 218). Seeing fairies may illuminate Blake's mention of Gnomes in *Milton*.

46 Bentley, *The Stranger*, 19–20 and 494. The italicized insertion appears in the text.
47 Ackroyd, *Blake*, 311.
48 Keynes, *Letters*, 47.
49 Ackroyd, *Blake*, 311.
50 Saurat, *Blake and Milton*, 99.
51 John Milton, *Paradise Lost*, in *The Riverside Milton*, ed. Roy Flannagan (Boston, MA: Houghton Mifflin, 1998), 4.690–774. Lines 742–43 demonstrate the point unmistakably: "nor *Eve* the Rites / Mysterious of connubial Love refus'd."
52 Desiree Hirst, "What Did Blake Believe? A Study of William Blake's Religion," *The Aligarh Critical Miscellany* 1, no. 1 (1988): 76. Hirst cites Alexander Gilchrist's biography but does not provide full bibliographic information. I assume that she means *The Life of William Blake with Selections from His Poems and Other Writings*, new and enl. ed. edited by Alexander Gilchrist (1880; New York: Phaeton, 1969), 7. She also cites Thomas W. Malkin's *A Father's Memories of His Child* (London, UK: n.p, 1806), 422.
53 Ronald L. Grimes, "Time and Space in Blake's Major Prophecies," in *Blake's Sublime Allegory: Essays on* The Four Zoas, Milton, Jerusalem, ed. Stuart Curran and Joseph Anthony Wittreich, Jr. (Madison: University of Wisconsin Press, 1973), 61.
54 Keynes, *Letters*, 51.
55 Ibid., 43.
56 Ibid., 206.
57 Bentley, *The Stranger*, 226.
58 Keynes, *Letters*, 51.
59 Ibid., 34.
60 Ibid., 88.
61 Loren Eiseley, *All the Strange Hours: The Excavation of a Life* (New York: Scribner's, 1975), 182.
62 Ibid., 33. See Milton, *Paradise Lost*, 7.29–30.
63 Ibid., 37–38.
64 Ibid., 161.
65 Ibid., 84.
66 Ibid., 50–51.
67 Ibid., 57.
68 Ibid., 85.
69 Milton, *Paradise Lost*, 9.21–24.
70 Howard, *Blake's* Milton, 19–20.
71 Bloom, *Blake's Apocalypse*, 348.
72 Paananen, *William Blake*, 128.
73 I comment at length on Theseus's statement in *A Jungian Study of Shakespeare: The Visionary Mode* (New York: Palgrave Macmillan, 2009), 23–31.
74 I have used Steven Lumiere, "Energy Reality," accessed on May 16, 2012, http://www.energyreality.com/index.htm#tour. Terminology differs, but Lumiere's divisions are sufficient for our purposes here.
75 Frye, *Fearful Symmetry*, 350.
76 Mark Lussier, "Blake's Vortex: The Quantum Tunnel in Milton," *Nineteenth-century Contexts* 18, no. 3 (1994): 271–72.
77 Damon, *Blake Dictionary*, 308 and 332–33.
78 Lindsay, *William Blake*, 176.
79 Beer, *William Blake*, 49. See also Marsha Keith Schuchard, *William Blake's Sexual Path to Spiritual Vision* (Rochester, VT: Inner Traditions, 2008).

CONCLUSION

The main assumptions under consideration here are that everything is connected because of its participation in the One Mind—Jung's *unus mundus*, which encompasses all that is, including the collective unconscious—and that universal connectedness has implications for the future of literary criticism. Since Jung's psychological writings imbricate the scientific and the metaphysical, they provided a helpful starting point for my study, which has attempted to do the same in a literary context. Although nicely illustrating a traditional Jungian archetypal approach, Nathaniel Hawthorne's "Young Goodman Brown" reaches in subtle ways toward unity through the collective unconscious. The enemy of metaphysical unity, however, is scientific materialism, Loren Eiseley's impediment in "The Secret of Life." Both he and Jung are empiricists, but the weight of skepticism weighs more heavily on Eiseley. John Milton's transcendental monism has an affinity with Jung's own cosmology and provides a fitting contrast to materialism's dead ends. Both Milton and Jung affirm versions of the One Mind, whose implications are explored in chapters 3–7. Given the connectedness of all things, physical and nonphysical, as well as the proliferation of multiple worlds, a variety of phenomena arise and receive attention in connection with Jung's works: altered states, out-of-body experience, UFOs, synchronicity, and forms of psychic functioning (remote viewing and channeling). Robert Jordan's *The Wheel of Time* series and Blake's visionary epic *Milton* sum up much that is relevant to the One Mind, including a negative view of materialism, the space-time illusion, and a cosmology that spans the seen and the unseen. The final two chapters also contribute a new theory of fantasy literature based on amplification and psi and an upgrade of Blake's vision from generally threefold/visionary to generally fourfold/psychic.

Previous literary critics have successfully applied Jung's theory of the archetypes of the collective unconscious and other concepts or have demonstrated the relevance of his writings to different schools of critical theory. My previous book, *A Jungian Study of Shakespeare: The Visionary Mode*, employs a mixture of these approaches, but only its metaphysical analysis of Shakespeare's *A Midsummer Night's Dream* anticipates the present study's engagement with Jung's writings about mysticism, quantum physics, and the afterlife. In considering three realms (consciousness, the unconscious, and a transcendent realm), my analysis of *Dream* foreshadows the threefold cosmology presented here. The One Mind includes the physical world/personal unconscious, the quantum world/the collective unconscious, and the world of pure spirit. The implication of such inclusiveness is that the Self encompasses not only the archetypes of the collective unconscious but also a wider spectrum of experience. The Self now includes nonphysical beings, the higher self, one's own spiritual "bodies," and physical beings from other planetary systems. The One Mind has further implications for the provenance of art, the subject matter of literary criticism, theoretical approaches, and access to historical information previously thought to be unrecoverable. This study has expanded the range of Jung's writings considered relevant to literary criticism from those that support archetypal and theoretical readings to those that consider the scientific and the metaphysical. By using these texts as touchstones for the analyses in the preceding chapters, I have attempted an enhancement in the realm of literary criticism akin to Milton's use of the red clay of Succoth on Urizen in Blake's epic: a remolding of the old into the new.

In the remainder of this conclusion, I will shift the emphasis away from Jung in order to explore a final implication of the One Mind, the idea that there is no "Other." In the process, I will anticipate some possible trends in literary criticism that may unfold in the next few centuries. Since the One Mind is the key concept in an approach that may well characterize the future of literary study, it makes sense to speculate further on what that future might look like.

The speculation begins with two familiar concepts. The first is what Milton calls "one first matter," which is the primordial consciousness—Jung's pleroma or *unus mundus*—that unites all things and all beings.[1] This speculation, however, relates to a second concept, the Great Chain of Being, which depicts a hierarchy of creation, with God at the top, then angels, the saints, humans, nonhuman creatures, plants, rocks, and, at the very bottom, Satan.[2] This concept needs a modern scientific version of the monist makeover that it receives in *Paradise Lost*, book 5, where Rapael describes what critics call the "Scale of Nature," which I have renamed the Scale of *Being* because it encompasses both physical creation and the nonphysical realm. But given the unity of all things because of the "one first matter," or the low-grade primordial consciousness, the idea of hierarchy will undergo a transformation and leveling into a plane of connectedness, with difference no longer meaning separation or implying a qualitative hierarchy because separation in all its forms is an illusion. There is One Mind in the universe, and all things participate in it in the same way that a part of a hologram contains the whole image. Given that assumption, the all-inclusive One Mind will bridge the perceived gaps between human beings and their foreign brethren, the natural world, intelligent life from other planetary systems, and even beings in the nonphysical world. Thus the One Mind's challenge to separation in all of its forms has heady implications for the future of literary criticism.

I begin with one of my old friends, an essay entitled "'Indians': Textualism, Morality, and the Problem of History," in which Jane Tompkins tiptoes around, and perhaps unknowingly reflects, the problem of separation.[3] As Tompkins, a professor of American literature, pored over secondary and then primary historical texts in order to enhance her understanding of the interaction between Native Americans and Europeans in colonial America, she noticed that people who had looked at the same thing had come up with vastly different interpretations. Seeing is perspectival, which means subject to an individual person's biases; and the particular nature of bias depends heavily on one's historical/cultural situation. In this *presentist* view of history, our own subjectivity is the lens through which we view historical events. The author might well have pushed one step further, as Patricia Nelson Limerick does, to suggest that when we study history we are in a sense making history by seeing it through the lens of our own point of view.[4] In any case, Tompkins's essay emphasizes a perspectival and presentist approach to history. While she overcomes her relativistic despair by realizing that she does have *some* facts to go on, her study of various texts has awakened her to moral problems that persist in the present day; it is just that the tools of postmodern literary criticism leave her unable to act. "The moral problem that confronts me now," she writes, "is not that I can never have any facts to go on, but that the work I do is not directed toward solving the kinds of problems that studying the history of European-Indian relations has awakened me to."[5] Implicit in her confession is an assumed separation: her inability to act resides partly in the notion that the needy are the Other. That is, she duplicates the "problem of history" that she writes about because historical texts are as perspectival and slippery as are present-day native American social issues. Consequently, how she views the past is projected onto her present and stymies her future. How can she help those who are separate, even if she wants to, when the tools at her disposal are based on an assumed separation and designed to unpack perspectives rather than to take concrete action? As she reaffirms the poststructuralist angst that she claims to have partly overcome, the essay ends on a somber note.

Approaches to literature further Tompkins's point that historical writing reflects the cultural moment. Numerous types of literary criticism—for example, psychoanalytic criticism, feminist criticism, postcolonial theory, and ecocriticism—respond to their respective historical/cultural situations. Psychoanalytic criticism responds to the "discovery" of the unconscious mind. Feminist theory responds to the women's movement. Postcolonial theory responds to increased cultural sensitivity to the plight of oppressed peoples in underdeveloped parts of the world. Ecocriticism acknowledges that human agency imperils the Earth. Also, "metaphysical criticism"—the subject of this book—responds to Jungian psychology and to developments in physics and parapsychology. These five widely varied approaches to literature arise from and reinforce their respective historical/cultural moments. But in order to understand what literary criticism may look like, say, in the year 2300, we need to transcend a *presentist* view of literary texts and embrace a *futurist* approach that attempts to predict the situation of human culture several centuries in advance.

To begin with, present-day human beings generally still assume that we are apart from, and superior to, external nature, which is the Other. If one follows Father Thomas Berry, the genesis of this split was the Bubonic Plague in the thirteenth century, when the human response to nature bifurcated into religion and science, the latter being the root, Berry believes, of the current environmental crisis.[6] As we look toward the future, advances in Artificial Intelligence (AI) may result in our assumption that we are even more separate and more superior because there will be a new layer beneath us on the Scale of Being. More than being merely co-creators with God, we will, in a sense, *be* gods if we can create machine souls, as computer scientist Maureen Caudill anticipates in stating that machines can develop a soul by becoming sufficiently complex, much as a brain becomes a mind. Machine souls, however, are "rudimentary" because they possess only "situational awareness" and "self-awareness." What makes them "incomplete and partial" is their inability to love. Caudill suggests that the first intelligent androids may emerge as early as 2015, along with wide-ranging ethical dilemmas.[7] If she is right (and developments such as Syri, the talking iPhone, suggest that she may well be), literary theory will have to include some kind of techno-criticism that reflects machine consciousness and our role in creating it. Given what we may create from silicon circuits, our estimation of ourselves, if not our actual position, may be subject to what Jung calls inflation, "an exaggerated sense of self-importance."[8] More likely, such inflation will be counterbalanced by clarification and redefinition of humans' place on the Scale of Being.

The clarification. We are quickly approaching a tipping point in the global environmental crisis when the ecosystem will rouse itself like Milton's "strong man after sleep" and shake off billions of people.[9] As J. Gary Sparks writes, "When, as subjects, we realize that we too can be objects, and when we know how that feels, we change. When we know matter as a subject, not just as an object, we are no longer the same."[10] The sudden shift of human status from acting subject to receiving object will necessitate a shift from the view of nature as the Other to the view that humans must share the planet harmoniously with all other living things. Three hundred years from now, with the Gaia Hypothesis having reached Dean Radin's fourth stage of acceptance (discussed in the introduction), humans will consider themselves part of a global biological system. Since we are what Peter Russell elegantly calls the "Global Brain" and therefore part of a planetary organism,[11] being above plants and animals on the Scale of Being will no longer imply that they exist solely for our own use; instead we will have to recognize our role as stewards and co-inhabitants of the ecosystem. We and nature will be One. Robert A. Monroe gives a glimpse of humans' future harmony with nature in *Far Journeys* when he visits a future beyond the year 3000. A greatly reduced human population now communicates nonverbally; there are no roads or ships or aircraft; and we no longer burn oil. Consequently, human beings have transformed themselves; and the Earth "*has been restored to its original ecological balance, the way it was before humans upset it so severely*" (emphasis in the original).[12]

As a result of this enhanced understanding of humans' intimate connection to nature, literature will reflect a more sustainable relationship with the external world; and literary criticism will emphasize the ecocriticism that we see today.[13] Criticism will continue to revisit texts that include the exploitation of nature and provide critique, much as feminist criticism revisits female characters in works by male writers. Ecocriticism will also reflect and promote a new and more holistic view of humans' relationship to nature, much as some critics today try to steer society away from war and destruction toward harmony and wholeness. From a Deep Ecological vantage point, then, critics will reevaluate texts from an enhanced tropological perspective. That is what is meant by *clarification* of our place in the Scale of Being: humans will understand that hierarchy does not mean separation, that nature is not the Other, that survival depends on seeing ourselves as partners in a worldwide biological system, and that reevaluation of literary expressions of our relationship to nature is necessary and beneficial. As in Tompkins's analysis, the historical moment will color the literary interpretation; but in the future, that perspective will be apocalyptic, an unveiling of our human situation as it really is—a plane of connectedness whose underpinning is the One Mind.

The redefinition. Our status in the hierarchy will be *redefined* when there is official recognition that the Earth—as Steven M. Greer emphasizes—is being visited by extraterrestrials who are many thousands to millions of years more technologically advanced than we are. Whatever one's evaluation of the present evidence may be, if and when it is possible to achieve official acknowledgement that such visitation is real, the news will come as a huge shock, particularly to those who espouse a religious belief system in which human beings are the only intelligent life in the universe. Not only will we be organisms sharing the planet with other organisms, as in the ecofriendly view just described, but we will also be just one of innumerable intelligent life forms in the universe. Some of them will have the technology to visit us, but we probably will not yet have the technology to visit them, unless Greer's claims about advancements based on retrieved ET technology turn out to be correct.[14] It is not that we will sink on the Scale of Being but that it will be redefined to include other intelligent species whose evolution is arguably more highly advanced than our own. Various implications and consequences arise from this shift. Our initial impression will be that we have suffered a debasement; but the official paradigm will eventually broaden from human experience alone to an awareness of intelligent life regardless of its provenance, and from participation in a global village to oneness with intelligent life everywhere in the universe. We will have not just the United Nations but also the Galactic Federation. There will be no Other on Earth or in the heavens. Humans will take their place in the cosmic community as equal participants with animals and ETs alike.

Of course, the illusion of separation will not die an easy death, as the following homology clarifies. Colonial discourse is to postcolonial literature as ET literature about humans is to human discourse about our encounters with Them. The present sense that human groups embody Otherness will yield to a sense of human solidarity, with Otherness being projected onto the ETs and humans occupying the subaltern position. What Mary Louise Pratt in “Arts of the Contact Zone” calls “autoethnography” (self-description that merges native and dominant idioms in order “to intervene in metropolitan modes of understanding,” which means to talk back), may characterize the relationship not between human groups but between us and our visitors from space. Thus the autoethnographic moment will not be limited to a racial, ethnic, or colonial group but will encompass what is quintessential to our species as over against extraterrestrial culture. Similarly, Pratt’s concept of “transculturation,” which means that a subordinate people adopts the discourse of the dominant group in order to collaborate with and even gain entry into that group, may come to characterize the way in which human beings orient themselves toward ET species.[15] When we start communicating with ETs, the result will be of interest to literary critics to the extent that writers resist or adopt a new idiom, methodology, or paradigm, In addition, if ETs are to humans as humans are to machines, perhaps machines will start communicating with us in much the same way that we will engage with the ETs.

Pratt’s concepts encapsulate some of the dynamics between human races that encounter each other for the first time, and something similar may occur between humans and extraterrestrial species. Autoethnography and transculturation characterize this “birthing period.” Texts about the clash between alien and human values may give rise to a new strain of ethical criticism.[16] There must be an enormous difference, for example, between human beings who view consciousness as individual and isolated, and a telepathic species for whom all thoughts and feelings participate in a shared awareness, or a species that has conscious access to its own version of the collective unconscious, the storehouse of racial memory. But over time, and perhaps by the year 2300, humans will gradually come to recognize and affirm their part in a cosmic collective, which implies conscious awareness of participation in the One Mind. Acknowledging this Oneness will obviate the notion of separation. We will know, at last, that there is no “Other”; and the result will be a universal peace that enables our species to reach beyond the confines of our own solar system to explore a universal plane of connectedness.

Finally, just as there will be no sense of separation between human groups or between humans as a whole and our extraterrestrial neighbors, there will also be no sense of separation between living persons and those who have migrated back to the realm of pure spirit. We will acknowledge, and both literature and literary criticism will reflect, the fact that we are spiritual beings having a physical experience. Whereas criticism in the twentieth century considered the unconscious mind, criticism in the twenty-fourth century will emphasize the One Mind as the reason for the continuity of consciousness between life and the afterlife. The result will be the sort of metaphysical criticism that appears in nascent form in this book, with emphasis perhaps on channeled text. Chapter 7 provides an example of Shakespearean sonnets channeled from the afterlife, and I predict that such collaboration between authors in the spirit and writers on earth will be electronic, as will communication with ETs (devices will interface with consciousness).

Monroe mentions "this Probability: in the year 2025, a boy in Locale I pushs [*sic*] a button on a device much like a portable radio. I perceive the Signal and turn my attention to him." There are already plenty of examples to bear out the truth of his prediction: "instrumental transcommunication" (ITC) enables contact with deceased persons via telephone, television, radio, fax machine, and computer.[17] Soon we will not have to rely on a remote viewer like Joe McMoneagle or a channeler like Mrs. Dowden. We will be able to "dial up" Aemilia Lanyer and ask if she is the female subject of Shakespeare's Sonnets. We ought to be able to "download" *Cardenio*, the bard's lost play, from the Akashic Record and to ask him questions the about the "lost years," his time in London, and the strange mention in his will of his "second-best bed." It is also possible that we will be treated to completely new Shakespearean plays, written in Eternity. This time, though, the interface will be ITC rather than the unconscious mind of a spirit medium.

The assumption that the human being is a nexus of mind, body, and spirit—that we *are* ghosts in machines—implies the necessity of a paradigm shift in mainstream psychology and the addition of a metaphysical "sense" to the traditional ways of viewing literature: literal, allegorical, tropological, and anagogical. Consider, for example, James Joyce's "Araby." A grown man recounts his younger self's embarrassing journey to a bazaar called Araby (literal). The language suggests that he is a knight on a quest or crusade (allegorical). The story provides moral lessons about the dangers of sentimentality, erotic love, and self-delusion, along with postcolonial allusions to Irish nationalism (tropological). Details like the apple tree and the tire pump lying like a snake in the grass have spiritual significance (anagogical). But the little boy's repetition of "'*Oh love! Oh love!*'" and the ensuing apparition of Mangan's sister necessitate a metaphysical sense of interpretation.[18] The girl does not literally appear in the room as a result of linguistic conjuration; but her likely appearance in the boy's imagination has implications for the role of the mind, as well as its connection to the One Mind, in human experience. In addition, if string theory correctly suggests that reality is made up of ten dimensions and if alternative realities do exist, then perhaps the boy's passionate mantra temporarily gives him a glimpse into another realm where Mangan's sister is genuinely present. It may be that "Araby" provides a momentary glimpse into what David Bohm calls the "multiverse."[19]

The possibility of such an interpretation arises from the unity and hence the accessibility of everything within the One Mind. And if there *is* One Mind in the universe, then there really is no such thing as the Other, for all is connected. In turn, the future of literary criticism will reflect the connectedness implicit in the quantum entanglement of space-time, matter, and thought, as well as the greater unity of all that is. The separation implicit in Milton's Scale of Being is illusory; but he is right about the "one first matter," which implies that all things and all persons are connected through a common origin and building block. As a result of these realizations, ethical criticism should eventually prove helpful in resolving the moral and epistemological quandary in which Tompkins finds herself, as well as global problems ranging from pollution to war. In short, what we do to "others" we do to ourselves because we are all related, not on a hierarchy that has qualitative implications but on a leveling plane of connectedness where beings recognize the precious nature of consciousness in all its diverse forms.

Notes

1 John Milton, *Paradise Lost*, in *The Riverside Milton*, ed. Roy Flannagan (Boston, MA: Houghton, 1998), 5.472.
2 See E. M. W. Tillyard, *The Elizabethan World Picture* (New York: Vintage, 1944), 25–82.
3 Jane Tompkins, "'Indians': Textualism, Morality, and the Problem of History," in *Ways of Reading: An Anthology for Writers*, ed. David Bartholomae and Anthony Petrosky, 4th ed. (Boston, MA: Bedford/St. Martin's, 1996), 618–34.
4 Patricia Nelson Limerick, "Empire of Innocence," in Bartholomae and Petrosky, *Ways of Reading*, 417–32.
5 Tompkins, "'Indians,'" 633.
6 Thomas Berry, *The Dream of the Earth* (San Francisco, CA: Sierra Club, 1988), 125.
7 Maureen Caudill, *Suddenly Psychic: A Skeptic's Journey* (Charlottesville, VA: Hampton Roads, 2006), 142 and 137.
8 Daryl Sharp, *C. G. Jung Lexicon: A Primer of Terms & Concepts* (Toronto, Canada: Inner City, 1991), 72.
9 Milton, *Areopagitica*, in Flannagan, *The Riverside Milton*, 1020.
10 J. Gary Sparks, *At the Heart of Matter: Synchronicity and Jung's Spiritual Testament* (Toronto, Canada: Inner City, 2007), 172.
11 Peter Russell, *The Global Brain: Speculations on the Evolutionary Leap to Planetary Consciousness* (Los Angeles, CA: Tarcher, 1982).
12 Robert A. Monroe, *Far Journeys* (New York: Doubleday, 1982), 206–15.
13 Ecocriticism has not been part of my project, but it is worth noting the good work that other Jungians have done in this area. Six texts stand out as a suitable starting place in Jungian ecostudies. First, Jung's own writings on the subject appear in *C. G. Jung on Nature, Technology & Modern Life*, ed. Meredith Sabini (Berkeley, CA: North Atlantic, 2008). Jerome S. Bernstein addresses the "environmental illness complex" in chapter 17 of *Living in the Borderland: The Evolution of Consciousness and the Challenge of Healing Trauma* (New York: Routledge, 2005), 204–22. Rinda West knits together ecology, analytical psychology, and literature in *Out of the Shadow: Ecopsychology, Story, and Encounters with the Land* (Charlottesville: University of Virginia Press, 2007). The most recent studies are Stephen J. Foster's *Risky Business: A Jungian View of Environmental Disasters and the Nature Archetype* (Toronto, Canada: Inner City, 2011); Bernie Neville's *The Life of Things: Therapy and the Soul of the World* (Ross-on-Wye, UK: PCCS Books, 2012); and Susan Rowland's *The Ecocritical Psyche: Literature, Evolutionary Complexity and Jung* (New York: Routledge, 2012).
14 Steven M. Greer, *Hidden Truth—Forbidden Knowledge* (Afton, VA: Crossing Point, 2006). References to ET technology appear throughout the text.
15 Mary Louise Pratt, "Arts of the Contact Zone," in Bartholomae and Petrosky, *Ways of Reading*, 531 and 533.
16 For a recent study of ethical criticism, see Siobhan Craft Brownson, "Ethical Criticism in the Classroom" *Peer English* 3 (2008): 105–17.
17 Monroe, *Journeys Out of the Body* (1971; New York: Doubleday, 1977), 274. One will discover much information on ITC by doing a search of the web. Here is one example:

> Ms. Laurie Monroe, who is the daughter of Mr. Robert Monroe, switched on a new computer which she recently bought and soon found a file dated the

> anniversary of [her] father's death. She opened the mail which said[,] "I'm fine. . . . Say hello to everyone." Mails have frequently arrived since then, sometimes with attached images or voices. It seems those mails are directly sent into memories [hard drives] because they could still arrive after the phone line was disconnected. Later, the institute built a new lab for several hundreds [*sic*] thousand dollars to devote to this phenomena [*sic*], ITC.
>
> ("History of ITC," accessed June 4, 2012, http://www.asahi-net.or.jp/~qr7s-tmym/ITC/History_E.htm#Monroe)

18 James Joyce, "Araby," in *The Riverside Anthology of Literature*, ed. Douglas Hung 3rd ed. (Boston, MA: Houghton, 1997), 29.

19 David Bohm, *On Creativity* (New York: Routledge, 1998), 114.

BIBLIOGRAPHY

Ackroyd, Peter. *Blake*. New York: Knopf, 1996.

Adams, Richard P. "Hawthorne's *Provincial Tales*." *The New England Quarterly* 30, no. 1 (1957): 39–57.

Adamson, J. H. "The Creation." In *Bright Essence: Studies in Milton's Theology*, edited by William Bridges Hunter, C. A. Patrides, and Jack H. Adamson, 81–102. Salt Lake City: University of Utah Press, 1971.

Aebi, Tania, with Bernadette Brennan. *Maiden Voyage*. New York: Simon and Schuster, 1989.

Allen, Percy. *Talks With Elizabethans: Revealing the Mystery of "William Shakespeare."* London, UK: Rider, 1947.

Angelucci, Orfeo M. *Nature of Infinite Entities*. San Diego, CA: Talk of the Times, 1952.

———. *The Secret of the Saucers*. Amherst, WI: Amherst, 1955.

———. *Son of the Sun*. Los Angeles, CA: DeVorss, 1959.

"Apocryphal or Deuterocanonical Books." *Christian Classics Ethereal Library*. http://www.ccel.org/.

Aquino, John. *Fantasy in Literature*. Washington, DC: National Education Association, 1997.

Attebery, Brian. *Strategies for Fantasy*. Bloomington: Indiana University Press, 1992.

"Atlantic Rowing History." *The Atlantic Rowing Race*. http://challengebus.co.uk/race/tarr/history/htm.

Attrill, Heather. "Lore, Myth, and Meaning—for Postmoderns: An Introduction to the Story World of Robert Jordan's *Wheel of Time* Sequence." *Australian Folklore: A Yearly Journal of Folklore Studies* 18 (2003): 37–76.

Augustine, Saint. *St. Augustine's Confessions*. Translated by William Watts. 2 vols. Cambridge, MA: Harvard University Press, 1961.

———. *The Literal Meaning of Genesis*. Translated by John Hammond Taylor, vol. 2. In *Ancient Christian Writers*, edited by Johannes Quasten et al., no. 42. New York: Newman, 1982.

Bateson, F. W. *Wordsworth: A Re-interpretation*. New York: Longmans, 1954.

Bevington, David, ed. *The Complete Works of Shakespeare*. 4th ed. New York: HarperCollins, 1992.

Beer, John. *William Blake: A Literary Life*. New York: Palgrave Macmillan, 2007.

————. *Wordsworth in Time*. Boston, MA: Faber, 1979.

Bentley, G. E., Jr. *The Stranger from Paradise: A Biography of William Blake*. New Haven, CT: Yale University Press, 2001.

Bernstein, Jerome S. *Living in the Borderland: The Evolution of Consciousness and the Challenge of Healing Trauma*. New York: Routledge, 2005.

Berry, Thomas. *The Dream of the Earth*. San Francisco, CA: Sierra Club, 1988.

Bevington, David. "A. L. Rowse's Dark Lady." In *Aemilia Lanyer: Gender, Genre, and the Canon*, edited by Marshall Grossman, 10–28. Lexington: University Press of Kentucky, 1998.

Binyon, Laurence. *The Drawings and Engravings of William Blake*. Edited by C. Geoffrey Holme. London, UK: Studio, 1922.

Blanford, Percy. *An Illustrated History of Small Boats: A History of Oared, Poled and Paddled Craft*. Buckinghamshire, UK: Spurbooks, 1974.

Bloom, Harold. *Blake's Apocalypse: A Study in Poetic Argument*. Garden City, NY: Doubleday, 1963.

———. *The Visionary Company: A Reading of English Romantic Poetry*. Rev. ed. Ithaca, NY: Cornell University Press, 1971.

Bohm, David. *On Creativity*, edited by Lee Nichol. New York: Routledge, 1998.

———. *Wholeness and the Implicate Order*. New York: Routledge, 1980.

———, and F. David Peat. *Science, Order, and Creativity*. 1987. 2nd ed. New York: Routledge, 2000.

Bolduc, David G. "Famous Small Boats." 2009. Accessed July 30, 2012. http://www.microcruising.com/famoussmallboats.htm.

Brewer, D. S. "*Wanderer*, Lines 50–57." *Modern Language Notes* 67, no. 6 (1952): 398–99.

Brooks, Harold, F. "Blake and Jung: Blake's Myth of the Four Zoas and Jung's Picture of the Psyche." *The Aligarh Critical Miscellany* 1, no. 1 (1988): 47–74.

———. "Blake and Jung II: The Fall into Disintegration." *The Aligarh Critical Miscellany* 2, no. 2 (1989): 158–74.

———. "Blake and Jung III: Reintegration." *The Aligarh Critical Miscellany* 5, no. 1 (1992): 41–89.

Browne, Sir Thomas. *Religio Medici*. In *The Broadview Anthology of Seventeenth-Century Verse & Prose*, edited by Alan Rudrum, Joseph Black, and Holly Faith Nelson, 465–88. Peterborough, Canada: Broadview, 2000.

Brownson, Siobhan Craft. "Ethical Criticism in the Classroom." *Peer English* 3 (2008): 105–17.

Buchanan, Lyn. *The Seventh Sense: The Secrets of Remote Viewing as Told by a "Psychic Spy" for the U.S. Military*. New York: Paraview Pocket, 2003.

Burton, Robert. *The Anatomy of Melancholy*. 3 vols. New York: Dutton, 1932.

Calder, D. G. "Setting and Mode in *The Seafarer* and *The Wanderer*." *Neuphilologische Mitteilungen* 72, no. 2 (1971): 264–75.

Callaghan, Dympna. *Shakespeare's Sonnets*. Malden, MA: Blackwell, 2007.

Campbell, Joseph. *The Hero with a Thousand Faces*. Princeton, NJ: Princeton University Press, 1985.

Campbell, Thomas. *My Big TOE: A Trilogy Unifying Philosophy, Physics, and Metaphysics*. 3 vols. United States: Lightning Strike, 2003.

Caudill, Maureen. *Suddenly Psychic: A Skeptic's Journey*. Charlottesville, VA: Hampton Roads, 2006.

Clemoes, Peter. "*Mens absentia cogitans* in *The Seafarer* and *The Wanderer*." In *Medieval Literature and Civilization: Studies in Memory of G. N. Garmonsway*, edited by D. A. Pearsall and R. A. Waldron, 62–77. London, UK: Athlone, 1969.

Colacurcio, Michael J. "Visible Sanctity and Specter Evidence: The Moral World of Hawthorne's 'Young Goodman Brown.'" In *Nathaniel Hawthorne's Tales*, edited by James McIntosh, 389–404. New York: Norton, 1987.

Conforti, Michael. *Field, Form, and Fate: Patterns in Mind, Nature, and Psyche*. Rev. ed. New Orleans, LA: Spring Journal, 2003.

Cook, Reginald. "The Forest of Goodman Brown's Night: A Reading of 'Young Goodman Brown.'" *The New England Quarterly* 43, no. 3 (1970): 473–81.

Crews, Frederick. *The Sins of the Fathers: Hawthorne's Psychological Themes*. New York: Oxford University Press, 1966.

Cross, J. E. "On the Genre of *The Wanderer*." *Neophilologus* 45 (1961): 63–75.

Curry, Walter Clyde. *Milton's Ontology, Cosmology, and Physics*. Lexington, KY: University of Kentucky Press, 1957.

———. "Milton's Scale of Nature." In *Stanford Studies in Language and Literature*, edited by Hardin Craig, 173–92. Stanford, CA: Stanford University Press, 1941.

Damon, S. Foster. *A Blake Dictionary: The Ideas and Symbols of William Blake*. Rev. ed. Hanover, NH: University Press of New England, 1988.

Dawson, Terrence. "Literary Criticism and Analytical Psychology." In *The Cambridge Companion to Jung*, edited by Polly Young-Eisendrath and Terrence Dawson, 269–98. 2nd ed. New York: Cambridge University Press, 2008.

Donnelly, Phillip J. "'Matter' versus Body: The Character of Milton's Monism." *Milton Quarterly* 33, no. 3 (1999): 79–85.

Douglas, Claire. "The Historical Context of Analytical Psychology." In *The Cambridge Companion to Jung*, edited by Polly Young-Eisendrath and Terence Dawson, 17–34. New York: Cambridge University Press, 1997.

Eagle Feather, Ken. *Travelling with Power: The Exploration and Development of Perception*. Charlottesville, VA: Hampton Roads, 1992.

Eiseley, Loren. *All the Strange Hours: The Excavation of a Life*. New York: Scribner's, 1975.

———. *The Firmament of Time*. New York: Atheneum, 1960.

———. *The Immense Journey*. New York: Random House, 1957.

———. *The Unexpected Universe*. New York: Harcourt, 1964.

Elliott, Ralph W. V. "The Wanderer's Conscience." *English Studies* 39, no. 5 (1958): 193–200.

Empson, William. *Seven Types Of Ambiguity*. London, UK: Chatto and Windus, 1956.

Erdman, David V. *The Complete Poetry and Prose of William Blake*. Rev. ed. Berkeley: University of California Press, 1982.

Evans, Andrew. *Thoughts, Tips, Techniques & Tactics For Singlehanded Sailing*. The Singlehanded Sailing Society. Accessed July 30, 2012. http://www.sfbaysss.org/tipsbook.

Fallon, Stephen M. *Milton among the Philosophers: Poetry and Materialism in Seventeenth-Century England*. Ithaca, NY: Cornell University Press, 1991.

Faulkner, William. "A Rose for Emily." In *The Riverside Anthology of Literature*, edited by Douglas Hunt, 3rd ed., 253–60. Boston, MA: Houghton, 1997.

Feinstein, Sandy. "Milton's Devilish Sublime." *Ben Jonson Journal: Literary Contexts in the Age of Elizabeth, James and Charles* 5 (1998): 149–66.

Felser, Joseph M. *The Myth of the Great Ending: Why We've Been Longing for the End of Days Since the Beginning of Time*. Charlottesville, VA: Hampton Roads, 2011.

Fike, Francis. "Correspondent Breeze: The Course of a Romantic Metaphor." *Renascence: Essays on Values in Literature* 32 (1979): 3–12.

Fike, Matthew A. *A Jungian Study of Shakespeare: The Visionary Mode*. New York: Palgrave Macmillan, 2009.

———. "*Light at Midnight* and the Art of Synchronicity." *Conversations in the Field* 1, no. 7 (2010): 1–8. http://thejungiansociety.org.

———. "The Literary Matrix of Loren Eiseley's 'The Secret of Life.'" *The CEA Critic* 72, no. 3 (2009): 17–36.

———. "Reiki and Jung: An Introduction." *Conversations in the Field* 1, no. 2 (2010): 1–10. http://thejungiansociety.org.

———. Review of Steven M. Greer's *Hidden Truth—Forbidden Knowledge* and *Contact: Countdown to Transformation: The CSETI Experience 1992–2009. TMI Focus* 32, no. 3–4 (Summer/Fall 2010): 10–13. http://www.monroeinstitute.org/resources/book-reviews/hidden-truth-forbidden-knowledge.

———. Review of Thomas Campbell's *My Big TOE: A Trilogy Unifying Philosophy, Physics, and Metaphysics*. *TMI Focus* 31, no. 3–4 (Summer/Fall 2009): 11–14. http://www.monroeinstitute.org/resources/book-reviews/my-big-toe.

———. "The Role of the Unconscious in the Writing Process." *Peer English: The Journal of New Critical Thinking* 1, no. 1 (2006): 45–55.

———. "Thinking Metaphysically: The Challenge to Fundamentalism in the Works of Robert A. Monroe." *Peer English: The Journal of New Critical Thinking* 3 (2008): 91–104.

———. "'The Wanderer' and the Psychology of Sailing." In *Reading the Sea: New Essays on Sea Literature*, edited by Kevin Alexander Boon, 77–99. New York: Fort Schuyler, 1999.

———. "We Are One Psyche: A Jungian Approach to Hawthorne's 'Young Goodman Brown.'" *Postscript* 27, no. 9 (2012): 1–20. www.pachome.org.

Fletcher, Anthony. *Gender, Sex, & Subordination in England, 1500–1800*. New Haven, CT: Yale University Press, 1995.

Fletcher, Harris Francis. *The Intellectual Development of John Milton*. Urbana: University of Illinois Press, 1961.

Foster, Stephen J. *Risky Business: A Jungian View of Environmental Disasters and the Nature Archetype*. Toronto, Canada: Inner City, 2011.

"Fractal." *Dictionary.com*.

Franz, Marie-Louise von. *On Divination and Synchronicity: The Psychology of Meaningful Chance*. Toronto, Canada: Inner City, 1980.

———. *Shadow and Evil in Fairy Tales*. Rev. ed. Boston, MA: Shambhala, 1995.

Freud, Sigmund. *The Standard Edition of the Complete Psychological Works*. Edited and translated by James Strachey. 24 vols. London, UK: Hogarth, 1966.

Frey, Leonard H. "Exile and Elegy in Anglo-Saxon Christian Epic Poetry." *Journal of English and Germanic Philology* 62, no. 2 (1963): 293–302.

Frye, Northrop. *Fearful Symmetry: A Study of William Blake*. Boston, MA: Beacon, 1947.

Galloway, Andrew. "Dream-Theory in *The Dream of the Rood* and *The Wanderer*." *The Review of English Studies* 45, no. 180 (1994): 475–85.

Gifford, Edwin and Joyce. "The sailing characteristics of Saxon ships as derived from half-scale working models with special reference to the Sutton Hoo ship." *The International Journal of Nautical Archaeology* 24, no. 2 (1995): 121–31.

Gilchrist, Alexander. *The Life of William Blake with Selections from His Poems and Other Writings*. 1880. New and enl. ed. New York: Phaeton, 1969.

Gordon, I. L. "Traditional Themes in *The Wanderer* and *The Seafarer*." *The Review of English Studies* N.S. 5, no. 17 (1954): 1–13.

Green, Charles. *Sutton Hoo: The Excavation of a Royal Burial-Ship*. London, UK: Merlin, 1963.

Greenblatt, Stephen. *Will in the World: How Shakespeare Became Shakespeare*. New York: Norton, 2004.

Greenfield, S. B. "*The Wanderer*: A Reconsideration of Theme and Structure." *Journal of English and Germanic Philology* 50 (1951): 451–65.

Greer, Steven M. *Contact: Countdown to Transformation—The CSETI Experience 1992–2009*. Crozet, VA: Crossing Point, 2009.

———. *Disclosure: Military and Government Witnesses Reveal the Greatest Secret in Modern History*. Crozet, VA: Crossing Point, 2001.

———. "The Disclosure Project." 2010. http://www.disclosureproject.org.

———. *Extraterrestrial Contact: The Evidence and Implications*. Crozet, VA: Crossing Point, 1999.

———. *Hidden Truth—Forbidden Knowledge*. Crozet, VA: Crossing Point, 2006. Print.

Grimes, Ronald L. *The Divine Imagination: William Blake's Major Prophetic Visions*. ATLA Monograph Series No. 1. Metuchen, NJ: Scarecrow Press and the American Library Association, 1972.

———. "Time and Space in Blake's Major Prophecies." In *Blake's Sublime Allegory: Essays on* The Four Zoas, Milton, Jerusalem, edited by Stuart Curran and Joseph Anthony Wittreich, Jr., 59–81. Madison: University of Wisconsin Press, 1973.

Guiley, Rosemary Ellen, ed. *Harper's Encyclopedia of Mystical & Paranormal Experience*. New York: HarperCollins, 1991.

Hait, Elizabeth A. "The Wanderer's Lingering Regret: A Study of Patterns of Imagery." *Neophilologus* 68, no. 2 (1984): 278–91.

Hannah, Barbara. *Jung: His Life and Work—A Biographical Memoir*. New York: Putnam's, 1976.

Harbus, Antonia. "Deceptive Dreams in *The Wanderer*." *Studies in Philology* 93, no. 2 (1996): 164–79.

Hardy, Thomas. "The Last Chrysanthemum." In *The Complete Poems of Thomas Hardy*, edited by James Gibson, 149. New York: Macmillan, 1976.

Harper Study Bible. Edited by Harold Lindsell. Grand Rapids, MI: Zondervan, 1971. Revised Standard Version.

Hart, D. Bentley. "Matter, Monism, and Narrative: An Essay on the Metaphysics of *Paradise Lost*." *Milton Quarterly* 30, no. 1 (1996): 16–27.

Hasenfratz, Robert. "*Wanderer*, lines 45–57 and the Birds of Diomede." *Journal of English and Germanic Philology* 92, no. 3 (1993): 309–24.

Hawthorne, Nathaniel. "Young Goodman Brown." In *Nathaniel Hawthorne's Tales*, edited by James McIntosh, 65–75. New York: Norton, 1987.

Hayles, N. Katherine. *The Cosmic Web: Scientific Field Models and Literary Strategies in the Twentieth Century*. Ithaca, NY: Cornell University Press, 1984.

Hayman, Ronald. *A Life of Jung*. New York: Norton, 1999.

Heaton, Peter. *The Singlehanders*. London, UK: Hastings House, 1976.

Hemingway, Ernest. *A Farewell to Arms*. 1929. New York: Scribner's, 1969.

Henderson, Richard. *Singlehanded Sailing: The Experiences and Techniques of the Lone Voyagers*. 2nd ed. Camden, ME: International Marine, 1988.

Hieatt, Constance B. *The Realism of Dream Visions: The Poetic Exploitation of the Dream-Experience in Chaucer and His Contemporaries*. The Hague: Mouton, 1967.

Hirst, Desiree. "What Did Blake Believe? A Study of William Blake's Religion." *The Aligarh Critical Miscellany* 1, no. 1 (1988): 75–88.

"History of ITC." Accessed June 4, 2012. http://www.asahi-net.or.jp/~qr7s-tmym/ITC/History_E.htm#Monroe.

Holt, Ted, and John Gilroy. *A Commentary on Wordsworth's* Prelude *Books I–V*. Boston, MA: Routledge, 1983.

Hotson, Leslie. *Mr W.H.* New York: Knopf, 1964.

Howard, John. *Blake's* Milton*: A Study in the Selfhood*. Cranbury, NJ: Associated University Presses, 1976.

Hoyle, Fred. *The Black Cloud*. New York: Harper, 1957.

Hubler, Edward. *Shakespeare's Sonnets and the Commentators*. New York: Basic, 1962.

Hunter, William B. *The Descent of Urania: Studies in Milton, 1946–1988*. Lewisburg, PA: Bucknell University Press, 1989.

Huppé, B. "The *Wanderer*: Theme and Structure." *Journal of English and Germanic Philology* 42 (1943): 516–38.

Irwin, W. R. *The Game of the Impossible: A Rhetoric of Fantasy*. Urbana, IL: University of Illinois Press, 1976.

Jacobi, Jolande, and R. F. C. Hull, eds. *C. G. Jung: Psychological Reflections; A New Anthology of His Writings 1905–1961*. Bollingen Series 31. Princeton, NJ: Princeton University Press, 1970.

Jaffé, Aniela. *Was C. G. Jung a Mystic? and Other Essays*. Einsiedeln, Switzerland: Daimon Verlag, 1989.

Jay, Martin. *Downcast Eyes: The Denigration of Vision in Twentieth-Century French Thought*. Berkeley: University of California Press, 1993.

Jayne, Edward. "Pray Tarry With Me Young Goodman Brown." *Literature and Psychology* 29 (1979): 100–13.

Jordan, Robert. *New Spring: The Novel*. New York: Tor Fantasy, 2004.

———. *The Wheel of Time*. 12 vols.; vols. 12 and 13 with Brandon Sanderson. New York: Tor Fantasy, 1990–2010.

———, and Teresa Patterson. *The World of Robert Jordan's* The Wheel of Time. New York: Tor Fantasy, 1997.

Joyce, James. "Araby." In *The Riverside Anthology of Literature*, edited by Douglas Hunt, 27–31. 3rd ed. Boston, MA: Houghton, 1997.

Jung, C. G. "Approaching the Unconscious." In *Man and His Symbols*, edited by C. G. Jung and Marie-Louise von Franz, 18–103. New York: Doubleday, 1964.

———. *The Collected Works of C. G. Jung*. Edited by Sir Herbert Read, Gerhard Adler, Michael Fordham, and William McGuire. Translated by R. F. C. Hull. 20 vols. Bollingen Series 20. 2nd ed. Princeton, NJ: Princeton University Press, 1953–79.

———. *Jung Speaking: Interviews and Encounters*. Edited by William McGuire and R. F. C. Hull. Bollingen Series 97. Princeton, NJ: Princeton University Press, 1997.

———. *Letters*. Edited by G. Adler and Aniela Jaffé, trans. R. F. C. Hull, 2 vols. Bollingen Series 95. Princeton, NJ: Princeton University Press, 1975.

———. *Memories, Dreams, Reflections*. Edited by Aniela Jaffé. Translated by Richard and Clara Winston. New York: Vintage, 1989.

———. *Psychological Types or The Psychology of Individuation*. Translated by H. Godwin Baynes. New York: Pantheon, 1962.

———. *Seven Sermons to the Dead.* In *The Gnostic Jung*, edited by Robert A. Segal, 182–93. Princeton, NJ: Princeton University Press, 1992.

———. *Zarathustra Seminar*. Edited by James Jarrett. Princeton, NJ: Princeton University Press, 1988.

———, and Wolfgang Pauli. *The Interpretation of Nature and the Psyche. Synchronicity: An Acausal Connecting Principle*. New York: Pantheon, 1955.

Kelly, Maurice. *This Great Argument: A Study of Milton's* De Doctrina Christiana *as a Gloss upon* Paradise Lost. Princeton, NJ: Princeton University Press, 1941.

Kennedy, Charles W., trans. *An Anthology of Old English Poetry*. New York: Oxford University Press, 1960.

Kerrigan, William. *The Sacred Complex: On the Psychogenesis of* Paradise Lost. Cambridge, MA: Harvard University Press, 1983.

Keyhoe, Donald E. *Flying Saucers from Outer Space*. New York: Holt, 1953.

Keynes, Geoffrey, ed. *The Letters of William Blake*. New York: Macmillan, 1956.

King, James. *William Blake: His Life*. New York: St. Martin's, 1991.

Knox-Johnston, Robin. *A World of My Own*. New York: Pocket, 1971.

Kruger, Steven F. *Dreaming in the Middle Ages*. Cambridge Studies in Medieval Literature, no. 14. New York: Cambridge University Press, 1992.

Lachman, Gary. *Jung the Mystic: The Esoteric Dimensions of Carl Jung's Life and Teachings*. New York: Penguin, 2010.

Lansdown, Richard. "Transitional Objects: The Spots of Time in *The Prelude* of 1799." *The Critical Review* 42 (2002): 14–34.

Laszlo, Ervin. *The Connectivity Hypothesis: Foundations of an Integral Science of Quantum, Cosmos, Life, and Consciousness*. Albany, NY: State University of New York Press, 2003.

Leslie, Desmond, and George Adamski. *Flying Saucers Have Landed.* New York: British Book Centre, 1953.

Leslie, Roy F, ed. *The Wanderer*. Manchester, UK: University of Manchester Press, 1966.

Lewalski, Barbara Kiefer. *The Life of John Milton: A Critical Biography*. Rev. ed. Malden, MA: Blackwell, 2000.

———. *Writing Women in Jacobean England.* Cambridge, MA: Harvard University Press, 1993.

Leva, Patricia. *Traveling the Interstate of Consciousness, a Driver's Instruction Manual: Using Hemi-Sync To Access States of Non-Ordinary Reality*. Longmont, CO: Q Central, 1997.

Lieb, Michael. "Milton and the Metaphysics of Form." *Studies in Philology* 71 (1974): 206–24.

Limerick, Patricia Nelson. "Empire of Innocence." In *Ways of Reading: An Anthology for Writers*, edited by David Bartholomae and Anthony Petrosky, 417–32. 4th ed. Boston, MA: Bedford/St. Martin's, 1996.

Lindenberger, Herbert. *On Wordsworth's* Prelude. Princeton, NJ: Princeton University Press, 1963.

Lindbergh, Charles. *The Spirit of St. Louis*. New York: Scribner's, 1953.

Lindsay, Jack. *William Blake: His Life and Work.* New York: George Braziller, 1979.

Lumiansky, R. M. "The Dramatic Structure of the Old English *Wanderer*." *Neophilologus* 34 (1950): 104–12.

Lumiere, Steven. "Energy Reality." Accessed May 16, 2012. http://www.energyreality.com/index.htm#tour.

Lussier, Mark. "Blake's Vortex: The Quantum Tunnel in Milton." *Nineteenth-century Contexts* 18, no. 3 (1994): 263–91.

Macrobius. *Commentary on the Dream of Scipio*. Translated by William Harris Stahl. Records of Civilization, Sources and Studies, no. 48. New York: Columbia University Press, 1952.

Malkin, Thomas W. *A Father's Memories of His Child*. London, UK: n.p., 1806.

Manry, Robert. *Tinkerbelle*. New York: Harper, 1966.

Mansfield, Victor. *Synchronicity, Science, and Soul-Making: Understanding Jungian Synchronicity through Physics, Buddhism, and Philosophy*. Chicago, IL: Open Court, 1995.

Marshall, Ian, and Danah Zohar. *Who's Afraid of Schrödinger's Cat? All the New Science Ideas You Need to Keep Up with the New Thinking*. New York: William Morrow, 1997.

Martin, Catherine Gimelli. "'Boundless the Deep': Milton, Pascal, and the Theology of Relative Space." *English Literary History* 63, no. 1 (1996): 45–78.

May, Edwin C. "The American Institutes for Research Review of the Department of Defense's Star Gate Program: A Commentary." http://anson.ucdavis.edu/~utts/may.html.

McDonald, Russ. *The Bedford Companion to Shakespeare: An Introduction with Documents*. 2nd ed. Boston, MA: Bedford/St. Martin's, 2001.

McIntosh, James, ed. *Nathaniel Hawthorne's Tales*. New York: Norton, 1987.

McMoneagle, Joseph. *Mind Trek: Exploring Consciousness, Time, and Space Through Remote Viewing*. Charlottesville, VA: Hampton Roads, 1997.

———. *The Stargate Chronicles: Memoirs of a Psychic Spy*. Charlottesville, VA: Hampton Roads, 2002.

Melville, Herman. *Moby Dick or the White Whale*. New York: Signet, 1961.

Men Who Stare at Goats. Directed by Grant Heslov. 2009. Beverly Hills, CA: Overture Films, 2010. DVD.

Midgley, Graham. "The Wanderer, Lines 49–55." *Review of English Studies* N.S. 10, no. 37 (1959): 53–54.

Miles, Margaret. "Vision: The Eye of the Body and the Eye of the Mind in Saint Augustine's *De trinitate* and *Confessions*." *The Journal of Religion* 63, no. 2 (1983): 125–42.

Milton, John. *Areopagitica*. In *The Riverside Milton*, edited by Roy Flannagan, 997–1024. Boston, MA: Houghton Mifflin, 1998.

———. *Complete Prose Works of John Milton*. Edited by Don M. Wolfe. 8 vols. New Haven, CT: Yale University Press, 1953–1982.

———. *Paradise Lost*. In *The Riverside Milton*, edited by Roy Flannagan, 296–710. Boston, MA: Houghton, 1998.

Moen, Bruce A. "Answers to Frequently Asked Questions." *Afterlife Knowledge*. Accessed July 30, 2012. http://www.afterlife-knowledge.com/answers.

———. *Exploring the Afterlife Series*. 4 vols. Charlottesville, VA: Hampton Roads, 1997–2001.

Monroe, Robert A. *Far Journeys*. New York: Doubleday, 1982.

———. *Journeys Out of the Body*. 1971. Updated ed. New York: Doubleday, 1977.

———. *Ultimate Journey*. New York: Doubleday, 1994.

Moores, D. J. "Young Goodman Brown's 'Evil Purpose': Hawthorne and the Jungian *Shadow*." *Journal of Evolutionary Psychology* 27, no. 3–4 (2005): 4–16.

Nänny, Max. "Chiasmus in Literature." *Word & Image* 4 (1988): 51–59.

Neville, Bernie. *The Life of Things: Therapy and the Soul of the World*. Ross-on-Wye, UK: PCCS, 2012.

Nicolson, Marjorie H. "The Spirit World of Milton and More." *Studies in Philology* 22, no. 4 (1925): 433–52.

Niebuhr, Reinhold. *The Self and the Dramas of History*. New York: Scribner's, 1955.

Norén, Karl-Johan. "The Rand-Mat-Perrin tripod." http://hem3.passagen.se/kjnoren/jordan/tripod.html.

"Orfeo M. Angelucci." *Archives*. http://www.archives.com.

"Orfeo M. Angelucci." *Wikipedia*. Accessed July 30, 2012. http://www.wikipedia.com.

Ostrowski, Witold. "The Fantastic and the Realistic in Literature: Suggestions on How To Define and Analyze Fantastic Fiction." *Zagadnienia Rodzajów Literackich* 9.1 (1966): 54–74.

Owen, W. J. B. "*Wanderer*, Lines 50–57." *Modern Language Notes* 65, no. 3 (1950): 161–65.

The Oxford English Dictionary. 2nd ed. 20 vols. Oxford, UK: Clarendon, 1989.

Paananen, Victor N. *William Blake*. Boston, MA: Twayne, 1977.

Papin, Liliane. "This Is Not a Universe: Metaphor, Language, and Representation." *PMLA* 107, no. 5 (1992): 1253–65.

Peat, F. David. *Synchronicity: The Bridge Between Matter and Mind*. New York: Bantam, 1987.

Percival, Milton Oswin. *William Blake's Circle of Destiny*. New York: Octagon, 1938.

Perkins, David, ed. *English Romantic Writers*. 2nd ed. Fort Worth, TX: Harcourt, 1995.

Post, Laurens van der. *Jung and the Story of Our Time*. New York: Vintage, 1975.

Pratt, Mary Louise. "Arts of the Contact Zone." In *Ways of Reading: An Anthology for Writers*, edited by David Bartholomae and Anthony Petrosky, 528–42. 4th ed. Boston, MA: Bedford/St. Martin's, 1996.

Predmore, Richard. "'Young Goodman Brown': Night Journey into the Forest." *Journal of Analytical Psychology* 22, no. 3 (1977): 250–57.

Puthoff, Harold E., and Russell Targ. "A Perceptual Channel for Information Transfer over Kilometer Distances: Historical Perspective and Recent Research. In *Mind at Large: Institute of Electrical and Electronic Engineers Symposia on the Nature of Extrasensory Perception*, edited by Charles T. Tart, Harold E. Puthoff, and Russell Targ, 13–76. New York: Praeger, 1979.

Rabkin, Eric S. *The Fantastic in Literature*. Princeton, NJ: Princeton University Press, 1976.

Radin, Dean. *The Conscious Universe: The Scientific Truth of Psychic Phenomena*. New York: HarperEdge, 1997.

———. *Entangled Minds: Extrasensory Experiences in a Quantum Reality*. New York: Paraview Pocket, 2006.

Raine, Kathleen. "C. G. Jung: A Debt Acknowledged." In *Jungian Literary Criticism*, edited by Richard P. Sugg, 167–76. Evanston, IL: Northwestern University Press, 1992.

———. *Blake and the New Age*. London, UK: George Allen & Unwin, 1979.

Ridgway, John, and Chay Blyth. *A Fighting Chance*. Philadelphia, PA: Lippincott, 1967.

"Robert Jordan: The Name Behind the Wheel." *Locus* 44, no. 3 (2000): 6–7 and 76.

Rohrberger, Mary. "A Psychoanalytic Reading of 'The Wanderer.'" *Cimarron Review* 1, no. 2 (1967): 70–74.

Rosenthal, M. L., ed. *Selected Poems and Two Plays of William Butler Yeats*. New York: Macmillan, 1962.

Rowland, Susan. *C. G. Jung and Literary Theory: The Challenge from Fiction*. New York: St. Martin's, 1999.

———. *C. G. Jung in the Humanities: Taking the Soul's Path*. New Orleans, LA: Spring Journal, 2010.

———. *The Ecocritical Psyche: Literature, Evolutionary Complexity and Jung*. New York: Routledge, 2012.

———. *Jung as Writer*. New York: Routledge, 2005.

Rowse, A. L. *Sex and Society in Shakespeare's Age: Simon Forman the Astrologer*. New York: Scribner's, 1974.

———. *Shakespeare's Sonnets: The Problems Solved*. 2nd ed. New York: Harper, 1964.

Rumble, Thomas C. "From *Eardstapa* to *Snottor on Mode*: The Structural Principle of 'The Wanderer.'" *Modern Language Quarterly* 19, no. 3 (1958): 225–30.

Russell, Peter. *The Global Brain: Speculations on the Evolutionary Leap to Planetary Consciousness*. Los Angeles, CA: Tarcher, 1982.

Russell, Ronald. *The Journey of Robert Monroe: From Out-of-Body Explorer to Consciousness Pioneer*. Charlottesville, VA: Hampton Roads, 2007.

Sabini, Meredith, ed. *C. G. Jung on Nature, Technology & Modern Life*. Berkeley, CA: North Atlantic, 2008.

Saurat, Denis. *Blake and Milton*. New York: Russell, 1965.

———. *Milton: Man and Thinker*. New York: Dial, 1925.

Schlain, Leonard. *Art & Physics: Parallel Visions in Space, Time & Light*. New York: HarperCollins, 1991.

Schnabel, Jim. *Remote Viewers: The Secret History of America's Psychic Spies*. New York: Dell, 1997.

Schoenbaum, S. "Loony and the Oxfordians." In *Shakespeare: An Anthology of Criticism*, edited by Russ McDonald, 4–13. Malden, MA: Blackwell, 2004.

———. "Shakespeare's Dark Lady: A Question of Identity." In *Shakespeare's Styles: Essays in Honour of Kenneth Muir*, edited by Philip Edwards, Inga-Stina Ewbank, and G. K. Hunter, 221–39. London, UK: Cambridge University Press, 1980.

Schrödinger, Erwin. *Mind and Matter*. Cambridge, UK: Cambridge University Press, 1959.

Schuchard, Marsha Keith. *William Blake's Sexual Path to Spiritual Vision*. Rochester, VT: Inner Traditions, 2008.

Schul, Bill, ed. *The Psychic Frontiers of Medicine*. New York: Ballantine, 1977.

Schultz, Howard, and Joy Schultz. "Metaphysics." In *A Milton Encyclopedia*, edited by William B. Hunter, Jr., John T. Shawcross, John M. Steadman, Purvis E. Boyette, and Leonard Nathanson, vol. 5, 114–30. Lewisburg, PA: Bucknell University Press, 1979.

Schwartz, Stephan A. *The Secret Vaults of Time: Psychic Archeology and the Quest for Man's Beginnings*. New York: Grosset, 1978.

Segal, Robert A. Introduction to *The Gnostic Jung*, edited by Robert A. Segal, 3–52. Princeton, NJ: Princeton University Press, 1992.

"Seth: The Spiritual Teacher that Launched the New Age." Accessed May 29, 2012. http://www.sethlearningcenter.org/.

Sethna, K. D. *"Two Loves" and "A Worthier Pen": The Enigmas of Shakespeare's Sonnets: An Identification through a New Approach*. New Delhi, India: Arnold-Heinemann, 1984.

Severin, Tim. *The Brendan Voyage*. New York: Avon, 1978.

Shakespeare, William. *The Complete Works of Shakespeare*. Edited by David Bevington. 4th ed. New York: HarperCollins, 1992.

Sharp, Daryl. *C. G. Jung Lexicon: A Primer of Terms & Concepts*. Toronto, Canada: Inner City, 1991.

Sheldrake, Rupert. *A New Science of Life: The Hypothesis of Formative Causation*. Los Angeles, CA: Tarcher, 1981.

Slocum, Joshua. *Sailing Alone Around the World*. 1900. New York: Dover, 1956.

Smith, Paul H. *Reading the Enemy's Mind: Inside Star Gate, America's Psychic Espionage Program*. New York: Tor, 2005.

Smithers, G. V. "The Meaning of *The Seafarer* and *The Wanderer*." *Medium Ævum* 26, no. 3 (1957): 137–53.

Sparks, J. Gary. *At the Heart of the Matter: Synchronicity and Jung's Spiritual Testament*. Toronto, Canada: Inner City, 2007.

Spenser, Edmund. *The Faerie Queene*. In *Edmund Spenser's Poetry*, edited by Hugh Maclean and Anne Lake Prescott, 1–499. 3rd ed. New York: Norton, 1993.

Stein, Murray. *Jung's Map of the Soul: An Introduction*. Chicago, IL: Open Court, 1998.

Storm, Howard. *My Descent into Death and the Message of Love Which Brought Me Back*. Great Barrington, MA: Clairview, 2000.

Suedfeld, Peter. *Restricted Environmental Stimulation: Research and Clinical Applications*. New York: Wiley, 1980.

———, and Jean L. Kristeller. "Stimulus Reduction as a Technique in Health Psychology." *Health Psychology* 1, no. 4 (1982): 335–57.

Sugg, Richard P. *Jungian Literary Criticism*. Evanston, IL: Northwestern University Press, 1992.

Stillinger, Jack, ed. *Selected Poems and Prefaces by William Wordsworth*. Boston, MA: Houghton, 1965.

Tacey, David. *Jung and the New Age*. Philadelphia, PA: Brunner-Routledge, 2001.

Talbot, Michael. *The Holographic Universe*. New York: HarperCollins, 1991.

Targ, Russell. *Limitless Mind: A Guide to Remote Viewing and Transformation of Consciousness*. Novato, CA: New World Library, 2004.

——, and Jane Katra. *Miracles of Mind: Exploring Nonlocal Consciousness and Spiritual Healing*. Novato, CA: New World Library, 1998.

———, and Harold E. Puthoff. *Mind-Reach: Scientists Look at Psychic Ability*. New York: Delacorte, 1977.

Tart, Charles T. *The End of Materialism: How Evidence of the Paranormal Is Bringing Science and Spirit Together*. Oakland, CA: New Harbinger, 2009.

———. *PSI: Scientific Studies of the Psychic Realm*. New York: Dutton, 1977.

Tennyson, Alfred. "Ulysses." In *Victorian Poetry and Prose*, edited by Lionell Trilling and Harold Bloom, 416–18. New York: Oxford University Press, 1973.

Tillyard, E. M. W. *The Elizabethan World Picture*. New York: Vintage, 1944.

Timmerman, John H. *Other Worlds: The Fantasy Genre*. Bowling Green, OH: Bowling Green University Press, 1983.

Todorov, Tzvetan. *The Fantastic: A Structural Approach to a Literary Genre*. Trans. Richard Howard. Cleveland, OH: Press of Case Western Reserve University, 1973.

Tomalin, Nicholas, and Ron Hall. *The Strange Last Voyage of Donald Crowhurst*. New York: Stein and Day, 1970.

Tompkins, Jane. "'Indians': Textualism, Morality, and the Problem of History." In *Ways of Reading: An Anthology for Writers*, edited by David Bartholomae and Anthony Petrosky, 618–34. 4th ed. Boston, MA: Bedford/St. Martin's, 1996.

Tritt, Michael. "'Young Goodman Brown' and the Psychology of Projection." *Studies in Short Fiction* 23, no. 1 (1986): 113–17.

Tucker, Susie I. "Return to *The Wanderer*." *Essays in Criticism* 8, no. 3 (1958): 229–37.

Tymn, Marshall B., Kenneth J. Zahorski, and Robert H. Boyer. *Fantasy Literature: A Core Collection and Reference Guide*. New York: Bowker, 1979.

Vickers, Brian. *Classical Rhetoric in English Poetry*. London, UK: Macmillan, 1970.

"The Wanderer." In *An Anthology of Old English Poetry*, translated by Charles W. Kennedy, 5–8. New York: Oxford University Press, 1960.

Wedd, Mary R. "Wordsworth's Stolen Boat." *The Wordsworth Circle* 11 (1980): 243–48.

Weiskel, Thomas. *The Romantic Sublime: Studies in the Structure and Psychology of Transcendence*. Baltimore, MD: The Johns Hopkins University Press, 1976.

West, Rinda. *Out of the Shadow: Ecopsychology, Story, and Encounters with the Land*. Charlottesville: University of Virginia Press, 2007.

Wilson, Eric G. *My Business Is to Create: Blake's Infinite Writing*. Iowa City: University of Iowa Press, 2011.

Wilson, John Dover. *An Introduction to the Sonnets of Shakespeare for the Use of Historians and Others*. New York: Cambridge University Press, 1964.

Wilson, Mona. *The Life of William Blake*. Ed. Geoffrey Keynes. New ed. New York: Oxford University Press, 1971.

Witcutt, W. P. *Blake: A Psychological Study*. 1946. Port Washington, NY: Kennikat Press, 1966.

Wittreich, Joseph Anthony, Jr. *Angel of Apocalypse: Blake's Idea of Milton*. Madison: University of Wisconsin Press, 1975.

Wolfe, Gary K. *Critical Terms for Science Fiction and Fantasy: A Glossary and Guide to Scholarship*. New York: Greenwood, 1986.

Wood, Theodore E. B. *The Word "Sublime" and Its Context 1650–1760*. The Hague: Mouton, 1972.

Woodhouse, A. S. P. "Notes on Milton's Views on the Creation: The Initial Phases." *Philological Quarterly* 28, no. 1 (1949): 211–36.

Woods, Suzanne. Introduction. In *The Poems of Aemilia Lanyer:* Salve Deus Rex Judaeorum, edited by Suzanne Woods, xv–xlii. New York: Oxford University Press, 1993.

Wordsworth, William. *The Prelude: Or, Growth of a Poet's Mind*. In *Selected Poems and Prefaces by William Wordsworth*, edited by Jack Stillinger, 193–365. Boston, MA: Houghton, 1965.

Wyndham, John. *The Midwich Cuckoos*. London, UK: Michael Joseph, 1957.

INDEX

Taylor & Francis

eBooks

FOR LIBRARIES

ORDER YOUR FREE 30 DAY INSTITUTIONAL TRIAL TODAY!

Over 23,000 eBook titles in the Humanities, Social Sciences, STM and Law from some of the world's leading imprints.

Choose from a range of subject packages or create your own!

Benefits for you

- Free MARC records
- COUNTER-compliant usage statistics
- Flexible purchase and pricing options

Benefits for your user

- Off-site, anytime access via Athens or referring URL
- Print or copy pages or chapters
- Full content search
- Bookmark, highlight and annotate text
- Access to thousands of pages of quality research at the click of a button

For more information, pricing enquiries or to order a free trial, contact your local online sales team.

UK and Rest of World: **online.sales@tandf.co.uk**

US, Canada and Latin America:
e-reference@taylorandfrancis.com

www.ebooksubscriptions.com

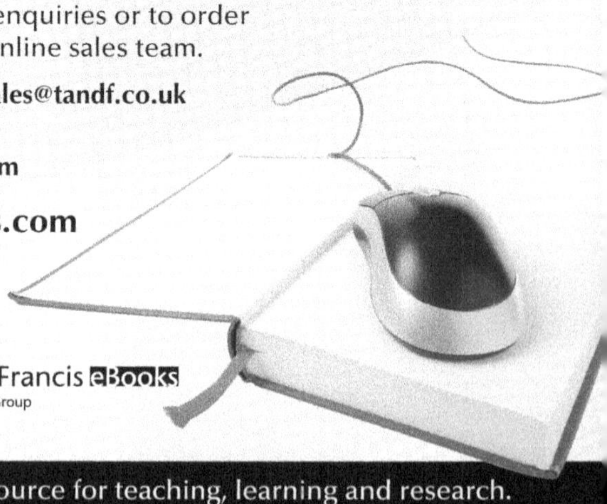

ALPSP Award for BEST eBOOK PUBLISHER 2009 Finalist

Taylor & Francis eBooks
Taylor & Francis Group

A flexible and dynamic resource for teaching, learning and research.

For Product Safety Concerns and Information please contact our EU
representative GPSR@taylorandfrancis.com
Taylor & Francis Verlag GmbH, Kaufingerstraße 24, 80331 München, Germany

www.ingramcontent.com/pod-product-compliance
Ingram Content Group UK Ltd.
Pitfield, Milton Keynes, MK11 3LW, UK
UKHW011001180926
475701UK00004B/506
* 9 7 8 0 4 1 5 7 1 1 8 8 3 *